Divided by Terror

Divided by Terror

American Patriotism after 9/11

∙∙∙

JOHN BODNAR

The University of North Carolina Press Chapel Hill

This book was published with the assistance of the William R. Kenan Jr. Fund of the University of North Carolina Press.

Set in Charis by Westchester Publishing Services

Library of Congress Cataloging-in-Publication Data
Names: Bodnar, John E., 1944- author.
Title: Divided by terror : American patriotism after 9/11 / John Bodnar.
Description: Chapel Hill : University of North Carolina Press, [2021] |
    Includes bibliographical references and index.
Identifiers: LCCN 2020044271 | ISBN 9781469662619 (cloth) |
    ISBN 9781469679303 (pbk) | ISBN 9781469662626 (ebook)
Subjects: LCSH: September 11 Terrorist Attacks, 2001—Social aspects. |
    Patriotism—United States—History—21st century. | War on Terrorism,
    2001–2009. | War and society—United States.
Classification: LCC HV6432.7 .B625 2021 | DDC 973.931—dc23
LC record available at https://lccn.loc.gov/2020044271

Cover illustration: Army Honor Guardsmen during a dignified transfer
of a fallen soldier, Dover Air Force Base, Delaware, July 8, 2009.
U.S. Department of Defense, http://www.defense.gov/observe
/photo-gallery/igphoto/2001154180. The appearance of U.S. Department
of Defense (DoD) visual information does not imply or
constitute DoD endorsement.

For

John, Ian, Francesca, and Sophie

Contents

Illustrations

Divided by Terror

Introduction

The Patriots' Debate

. . . .

As the Twin Towers smoldered and family and friends desperately sought news of loved ones on the morning of September 11, 2001, millions of American citizens rallied to the flag in a patriotic wave that swept the nation. Many vowed to unleash a reign of terror on those responsible for the carnage and destruction. Yet, countless other Americans were reluctant to use the 9/11 assaults as a basis for a worldwide war and recoiled from its implications, choosing instead to bear witness to the death and suffering it brought. Both sides of this divide identified as loyal, patriotic Americans doing what they felt best honored their country and the citizens it lost that day. This dispute, fundamentally about the meaning of patriotism, its ideals, and how to exercise it especially when the nation is threatened, is not new. It has informed politics, citizenship, and America's sense of inclusion and exclusion for centuries, perhaps most dramatically during wartime. But in the dawn of the twenty-first century, with a legacy of heroic wars followed by the quagmire that was Vietnam, the 9/11 attacks forced Americans to reckon with the bloodshed in their backyard that took them by complete surprise. Emotions ran amok as people attempted to make sense of the assaults and ensure that they never happened again. *Divided by Terror* provides a lens into this unsettled time and the turbulent debate over patriotism that ensued from the shock of 9/11. Traumatized and angry, the Americans profiled in this book articulated their feelings in countless ways, including patriotic rhetoric, personal memoirs, mourning practices, commemorative memorials, angry reprisals, online postings, works of art, and film. Visions of a military victory over global terrorism competed for attention with serious doubts over the nation's rush to battle. Ultimately the book argues that at the beginning of a new century Americans became more divided than united over a war on terror and even over the idea of patriotism itself.

Of course, political leaders were never far from the patriots' debate: harnessing, manipulating, and vying for the allegiance of their constituents. George W. Bush recognized that al-Qaeda, the terrorist group that launched the spectacular attack on the nation, was a dangerous adversary. Fueled by a deep sense of hatred over the presence of American forces in Muslim lands such as Saudi Arabia and a visceral hatred of Jews and American support for Israel, the Islamist terror organization caused Bush to realize not only that the nation might be in danger of more assaults but that its influence in the oil-rich Middle East was in jeopardy. He immediately declared a global war. To Bush and his vice president, Dick Cheney, the United States now entered a conflict of cataclysmic proportions in which the threat to the nation and its hegemony in the Middle East was so profound that aggressive tactics had to be implemented at once. In short order the administration began a hunt for enemies by capturing terrorist suspects, launched military attacks abroad, and empowered federal law enforcement agencies to round up immigrants in the homeland.

For Bush and many Americans, war was the only strategy to pursue in light of 9/11: crush the enemy and also remind would-be enemies that American military force reigned supreme and existed to ensure the supremacy of the nation, its ideals, and its people. Not everyone agreed with the president, however, with critics questioning his very terminology, arguing that "terrorism" was too elusive a term to serve as a descriptor of a war. The point was that since terrorism could erupt at any time or in any place in the future, a battle against it would lead to a "forever war" with no end in sight. Barack Obama actually dropped the designation of the conflict as a war against terrorism in 2009 when he said we were not fighting a "tactic" but specific networks of enemies who sought to harm America. In time, Bush's forceful moves would provoke a much more powerful response, however, than a contest over nomenclature or wartime objectives. His global war would actually precipitate a massive domestic quarrel grounded not only in political issues but in deeply personal matters and private emotions that have yet to be fully captured or understood. Millions of citizens would tap their patriotic instincts to support the idea of a war against evil in the world, but many equally patriotic Americans would question vehemently the premise that a War on Terror was even justified. Ultimately the conflict would become a fight not simply over naming rights or threats to the nation but over how the encounter with terrorism should be understood.[1]

Patriotism was central to this intense discussion because it offered a framework in which people could imagine their relationship to the nation to which they belonged and that was now under attack. In 2002 President Bush even declared that September 11th would henceforth be known as Patriot Day, a time in which the "heroic sacrifices" of first responders and the nation's soldiers would be commemorated in order to inspire others. Patriotic myths and rituals have always been important during episodes of state-sponsored violence because of the cognitive power they possess to help shape feelings and beliefs. They can rally populations to a cause and transform the horrors of warfare into mythical tales of valor and heroism. The language of patriotism can serve as a cleansing agent capable of wiping away or justifying, at least on the surface, the cruel realities of death, trauma, sorrow, and, less understood, the utter sense of confusion over what is taking place. Patriotic symbols and narratives have the ability to turn tales of vengeance into love stories and family tragedies into chronicles of exemplary service, renovations necessary to retain allegiances in difficult times.

Yet, patriotism is a layered concept that attempts to weave together dissimilar strands of thoughts and feelings. Patriotism must expand its ethic of love to embrace not only political relationships but human connections as well. Love of country as an abstract thought must be interlaced with bonds of affection for particular people a citizen knows, neighbors or even brothers-in-arms that serve in the same battle group, and even strangers. As much as patriotism reveres love, it can also foster fear and hatred for those the nation seeks to vanquish or marginalize. And, importantly, it needs to justify why its celebration of loving relationships can lead to so much pain and sorrow. Inevitably patriotism faces the extremely difficult task of tempering or even erasing the effects of traumatic ruptures war brings to people's lives. It is never a given that the connection between the love one feels for a nation and the love one feels for other people can be sustained when the former leads to the obliteration or disfigurement of beloved friends or relatives. Thus, parents (often called "Gold Star" Mothers or Fathers) who confront the remains of a son or daughter killed in battle may or may not be willing to wave the flag. The merger of private and public affection, a necessary fusion in any patriotic ideal, is never guaranteed.

Because patriotism's rhetorical project is so ambitious, it takes many forms, and this book focuses on the two that are most prominent as well as the most divisive: war-based and empathic patriotism. To delineate between these two, I borrow liberally from the political scientist Steven Johnston, who has probed the multifaceted nature of patriotic feeling and lamented the extent to which a war-based sense of loyalty, promoted by Bush, swept across America after 9/11. According to Johnston, war-based patriotism undercuts patriotism's ethic of love by nurturing hatred and aggression or reducing its focus to militarism and a highly forceful version of nationalism. Johnston felt this version of loyalty was duplicitous because it concealed "the damage that it does through professions of love," although that is certainly part of how its cultural appeal can serve a nation's war effort. He also regretted that its popularity seemed to be contingent on destroying others, sanctifying death, and ultimately erasing a "tragic sensibility" from the experience of war itself.

Johnston preferred a more human-centered version of patriotism, "patriotism at its best" rather than "patriotism at its worst," that sought to confront mythical versions of war with "painful truths." He does not use the term "empathy" in his formulation, but he makes it clear that he would like to see citizen loyalty embrace a sense of mutualism more than one rooted in belligerence. His hope was that a more direct acceptance of the tragedy war brings rather than a celebration of myth would provoke a wave of sympathy grounded in the realization that military clashes led not to grand victories but human suffering. Optimistically Johnston and others have suggested that such an awareness might provoke a deeper reflection over how, going forward, things could be made better for the living. Johnston hypothesized that democratic societies might see in the memory of mass violence a need to confront their cruel ways, "atone for their sins," and address their failings. His favored brand of patriotic thought would cause citizens to improve their nation and its social relations rather than "eternalize" the virtue of sacrifice or glorify death. Johnston makes the good argument that democracies cannot ultimately come to terms with their many failures—bad wars, intolerance, inequality—if they do not temper the impulse to glorify the aggression they engender and replenish the emotions of a "war-based" version of national identity, sentiments that inherently dismiss the value of human needs and connections in favor of pride, power, and chauvinism.[2]

The tug of war between a patriotism that is empathic, willing to recognize the torment it can bring and acknowledge the pain of others, and one that is war based or redemptive and reluctant to come to terms with the suffering it might provoke merits attention because it speaks to the ongoing problem of deciding just what the character of American national identity should be. *Divided by Terror* is especially concerned with this issue and the quandary citizens faced during the War on Terror, as they did in earlier wars, over the terms of endearment they invoked to declare their loyalty. It is not a comprehensive account of the war's politics, battle strategies, or leaders. It has more to say about Bush than Barack Obama—in part because it focuses on the first decade of the struggle. Its goal is to examine the realm of sentiments and thoughts that circulated among the citizenry after 9/11 as they sought to embrace a patriotism that would sustain them (and their country) in the wake of the catastrophe of the terror assaults and for-ever after. Would they resort to a liberal, critical version of patriotism aimed at pointing out national flaws in order to correct them, or would they opt for a conservative notion that their homeland was a splendid, morally righteous nation beyond reproach? After 9/11 there were plenty of examples of Ameri-cans responding honorably to the needs and concerns of other citizens. The selfless actions of first responders was a vivid example. Citizens also drew on genuine feelings of sympathy and empathy by organizing programs such as "Operation Support Our Troops—America," which sent care packages to those who served. Soldiers performed heroic acts to protect their comrades in distant battlefields, deeds that reaffirmed ideals of a virtuous American tem-perament. There were also thousands of citizens who called for harsh repri-sals against enemies and even the expulsion of immigrants from the land they loved and that had taken them in. In a number of striking instances, ar-dent patriots even castigated fellow citizens who mourned the loss of loved ones, an act designed to deny the reality of anguish many endured and their pleas that the nation become more caring and less aggressive.

A spread-eagle type of national identity hell-bent on the exercise of mil-itary power and xenophobia has long been central to the goals of a right-wing patriotism. This political dream, frequently energized by a fear of foreigners or racial minorities, enjoyed a rebirth in many European coun-tries near the end of the twentieth century and in the United States in the years after 9/11. After the attacks it served as a rationale for fostering a more militarized version of American loyalty, suspending the civil rights of Muslims in America, launching increased surveillance of American citi-zens as authorized in the Patriot Act of 2001, and even resorting to the torture of suspected enemies. Its polar opposite has been and continues to be a more liberal or civic form of empathic patriotism attuned to an ideal that all men and women be granted dignity and equal rights. Contingent upon the core emotion of empathy, this version of Americanism celebrates the ability to see in others what we see in ourselves. It is more inclined to mourn the dead or injured rather than simply to name them heroes. War-based and empathic patriotisms need not be mutually exclusive. People do not simply opt to reside in one camp or another and can harbor conflicting strains of these attitudes. One can lament the human damage of war and still honor those who carry out the fight or endorse the suspension of civil rights. A brutal war can be fought for the purpose of making the world safe for democracy and ensuring essential human freedoms. In reality, how-ever, these polestars of national identity have not mixed well; war-based patriots have often worked to make empathic sentiments a taboo subject and vice versa.

In the immediate aftermath of 9/11, war-based patriotism commanded a higher ground than its empathic cousin, and this sounded a few early warning bells. Philosopher Martha Nussbaum worried that the outpouring of patriotic ardor and belligerent nationalism she saw in America at the time would actually restrain our capacity to feel compassion for others. She was troubled in this moment that an ethos of American supremacy or "the humiliation of the other" would prevail. Sympathy for other people was indispensable to Nussbaum's hope for an interconnected and less nationalistic world. She assumed if people were open to the distress of strangers they would see an image of themselves as potential victims and be less indifferent to the suffering of those they did not know.

Divided by Terror argues not only that Nussbaum's fears were justified, however, but that a grassroots rebuke of this war-based version of Americanism emerged in many cultural forms—popular, vernacular, official, and more—sparking a fierce dispute that would polarize the nation itself. War-based patriots often exalted over the triumphs in the War on Terror without considering the damages the war brought. Some of these individuals, having turned their back on the need to continue the struggle for democracy, denied basic legal rights to fellow citizens or newcomers to the nation itself. Yet, in what amounted to a widespread resistance movement, many Americans were simply unwilling to embrace a patriotism enmeshed in militarism, consumed with the pursuit of enemies and indifferent to the evidence of trauma all around them. Witnesses to pain and death insisted that empathy toward victims rather than glorification of violence was a more authentic way to approach the War on Terror and the patriotism that should underscore it; they insisted that the memory of dreadful losses and ghastly killings not be reworked into a patriotic culture infused with words and symbols that were didactic, detached, and inspirational. They rejected the thought that military victory was central to the official narrative of America's response to the attacks and suffering could somehow be redemptive. It was not that these empathic patriots were weak. Rather, they perceived in the brutal experiences of wartime the need to reinvigorate efforts to ensure that an ethic of caring and justice would not perish from national life.[3]

George W. Bush recognized immediately after 9/11 that the very character of the nation itself was at stake in the quest for a righteous, heroic frame on the war. In his speech during a National Day of Prayer and Remembrance three days after the terrorists' assaults, he made it clear that the War on Terror would involve more than a defense of the homeland. Its ultimate goal was not only to defeat the nation's enemies but to "rid the world of evil." The world created by God, the president proclaimed, was of "moral design" and eternally one of "goodness, remembrance, and love." In his interpretation of God's plan, and the heritage of the homeland he was defending, "grief and tragedy and hatred" are only temporary. He believed that by unleashing the power of the American military he could restore a world filled with God's kindness and love that terrorists had damaged. For him battle would allow Americans to recognize their true virtuous nature or, in his words, "introduce us to ourselves." He explained to the nation's citizenry that "we have seen our national character in eloquent acts of sacrifice" such as the heroic efforts to save victims at Ground Zero in New York and the long lines that citizens formed to donate blood. "The world has seen our fellow Americans are generous, kind, resourceful and brave," he asserted.[4]

By casting America's fight against terrorism within such a virtuous light, Bush went beyond a simple declaration that the nation would strike back and bring death and destruction to its enemies. Indeed, his speech was designed to blunt the acknowledgment of such a reality. Instead, he chose to tap into a mythical narrative, or what many have called America's "civil religion," that had been invoked many times before. This creed inextricably tied the nation's military actions to the will of God, a tenet that aimed to forestall a full appraisal of the horror and terror that was to follow. Abraham Lincoln did as much when he argued that the slaughter of the Civil War could also be redeemed. For the Civil War president, however, redemption was contingent on rededication to the democratic ideal of a government of the people, by the people, and for the people—patriotism at its best—and not simply a reaffirmation of God's plan for the nation.[5]

Bush's wish to cast the war into the traditional patriotic framework of a noble cause, however, ran into a problem that he and his supporters may not have fully anticipated. While the War on Terror was conceived in a new century, the legacy of the preceding one saw historic highs like World War II or the civil rights movement weighed down by record lows: racial violence, gender abuse, genocide, and the grim realities of the war in Vietnam. In the recent past the status of the victim in American culture and society had gained a degree of currency it previously lacked; the reality of anguish was now more widely acknowledged and discussed. Consequently the ability of a sovereign power like the United States to hide the effects of mass trauma behind a banner of militant nationalism was no longer as powerful as it once was.

Some have argued that the pervasiveness of so many traumatic images in our times has actually led to a certain degree of indifference or "numbness" to human suffering, an "empathy fatigue." This argument underestimates, however, the active agency of war-based patriots to suppress or rework traumatic episodes into alternative versions of the truth. Certainly political leaders and many citizens felt the need to fold the reality of trauma, which by definition is impossible to comprehend, into soothing myths and inspirational tales in order to sustain positive renditions of a nation's character. Neoliberals like Bush were also keen to put the critical perspectives on war derived from Vietnam to rest. *Divided by Terror* makes it clear, however, that war-based patriots, never assuming that citizens would be insensitive to evidence of suffering, worked tirelessly to suppress its expression. Even more strikingly a massive wave of voices fought this repression and insisted that they found the War on Terror confusing, more distressing than noble, and an unwanted rupture in their personal lives. No wonder so many of the cultural projects that reworked the war focused more on the damage Americans were capable of causing than on the terrorists themselves. As the war moved outward around the globe, the patriots' debate turned inward to contemplate just who we were as a people.[6]

Relations between patriots became frayed because the empathic version of patriotism with its sensitivity to distress now threatened to do more than simply expose the bitter realities of the War on Terror. Its inclination toward a deeper reflection on the war and national identity had the potential to instigate what political scientist Simon Stowe has called "remedial actions," measures designed to use a legacy of suffering to make things better in the future. Lincoln's call for greater justice and democracy was remedial, as was the United Nations' Universal Declaration of Human Rights in 1948 after the horrors of World War II. Both strove to build a better world by acknowledging the trauma and bloodshed of the past and affirming that they should not be repeated.

Central to the mission of turning the memory of violence into a quest for social improvement rather than simply a celebration of victory or valor was the ability of individuals and societies to mourn and grieve. Historian Dominick LaCapra noted this need to "engage" the reality of grievous losses at various sites of mourning, including commemorations, rituals, novels, and films. By working through tragic memories rather than erasing them, he asserted that societies would have a chance to craft a future better than the past. This book argues that war-based patriots were aware of the possibility that public mourning might lead to questions of accountability or a push for democratic reforms like the need to respect religious differences or grant rights to those they felt did not deserve them. Thus, they worked assiduously to discredit many who grieved or opposed the War on Terror by resorting to the use of "ideological lures" designed to make American violence righteous.[7]

This debate between a war-based and an empathic patriotism, ultimately a contest between sustaining grand patriotic myths and acknowledging the shocking realities of violent conflicts, was not new. It emerged in the political and cultural climate of previous wars Americans have fought. At the center of this argument was a quest for a suitable culture of loyalty that would encourage the relinquishing of individual rights and personal ties to the authority of the nation-state and its call for sacrifice and death. Citizens had to grapple with questions about why they had to fight, why their sacrifices were noble, and what sort of legacy would be inscribed in the collective memory of the nation itself once the battles had ended.

Scholars essentially agree that much of the patriotic culture so prevalent in modern America today was initially forged in response to the Civil War. Prior to the outbreak of these hostilities, Americans tended to be wary of maintaining large standing armies. In the 1860s, however, the divided nation and its leaders were suddenly faced with the task not only of assembling large armies but organizing thoughts and practices designed to instill feelings of devotion to the nation itself and the battle at hand. In the face of unprecedented levels of carnage, citizens responded by creating ceremonies and rhetoric that sanctified the idea of dying for one's country, praised the heroism of those who fought and died, and composed an ardent defense of a militaristic version of patriotism that would prove to be a powerful script to deploy when justifying wars and raising armies for decades to come.

As historian Melinda Lawson has demonstrated, this was not an easy task. Prior to 1861 loyalty in America was grounded mostly in personal and local ties. The popular view of the nation was as an entity that guaranteed citizens their rights but did not routinely expect them to surrender their lives or kill in its name. Lawson demonstrated how this new version of patriotism was promoted extensively in the North during the Civil War through a host of grassroots activities such as fairs, parades, and even art exhibits that fostered support for the troops and raised money to care for those who were wounded. Patriotism itself at this time often rose to the level of piety; eulogists began to invoke the idea of noble sacrifice to console the bereaved in a way that rivaled biblical teachings.[8]

The logic of a war-based patriotism that fostered a high regard for warrior valor and sacrifice became dominant in the public memory of the Civil

War after it ended. In his pathbreaking examination of the war's commemoration, historian David Blight reveals how celebrations of male bravery and saving the Union became so powerful that they obscured from public view the essential fact that the war had also been a fight for racial justice and an event that brought trauma and pain to thousands of families. Although the link between sacrifice and the struggle for democracy received less attention in the commemoration of veterans and their battlefield deeds among the larger public, Blight traces the emergence of an alternative strand of patriotism forged by African Americans rooted in a collective memory of the struggle that was focused on their attainment of freedom. Emancipation Day, January 1, became a major celebration in the black community even as the war still raged. It continued to enjoy substantial support for decades after 1865 even though former slaves still faced hostility and violence in America including the threats of lynching, poverty, and segregation.[9] Indeed, Emancipation Day celebrations might be considered one of the first manifestations of empathic patriotism in America.

This veneration of veterans, which represented the beginnings of a trend to inscribe soldier sacrifice into the idea of national identity, not only was vast but over time came to include former Confederate fighters who had supported the quest to preserve the harsh system of slavery. Stretching the limits of patriotic mythmaking, old fighters from the North and the South eventually found common ground that privileged battlefield heroism over a shared democratic vision of emancipation, celebrated at events such as the huge veteran encampment on the fiftieth anniversary of the Battle of Gettysburg in 1913. The gathering at the Pennsylvania site ensured that male valor, a central tenet of war-based patriotism, dictated the tenor of the public remembrance of this pivotal battle. Most Union veterans held as an "article of faith" that they had earned an enormous level of gratitude for saving the Union. Meanwhile, former Confederate soldiers told themselves they had fought bravely for "independence" and failed only because their opponents had superior resources. Already in the South the defense of a slave society had taken a mythical turn with the dedication of grand monuments to heroic Confederate generals such as Robert E. Lee and Stonewall Jackson. Virtue and victory were certainly the main themes at the Gettysburg celebration, while democratic chants and traumatic memories were mostly pushed to the side. The significance of Lincoln's famous speech at the same site in 1863 and his call to turn tragedy into democracy receded over time. So did the strenuous pleas of Frederick Douglass, a former slave and staunch abolitionist who, for years after the war, in Memorial Day orations and eulogies for Lincoln, kept reminding his audiences that the human sacrifice of the war should be remembered not as a shining example of soldier courage but a mighty struggle for emancipation and "universal suffrage."[10]

World War I mostly served to reinforce the war-based patriotic culture that rose to prominence after the Civil War. Historical scholarship has affirmed that America's involvement in this global conflict significantly expanded the power of the state over the rights of its citizens and the ability of the government to shape the meaning of the war itself. No official act enhanced the trend to expand state authority more than the Selective Service Act of 1917, a measure that brought 2.8 million men into the armed services whether they wanted to be or not. Two million men also volunteered for national service, and legislation was approved that punished anyone deemed guilty of obstructing the draft or even articulating an antiwar position. A Committee of Public Instruction was created by the Wilson administration to censor news reports about the war and promote an uncritical version of patriotism. Wilson went so far as to institute the wearing of gold-star arm bands by women in mourning in an attempt to moderate their tendency to dress only in black, a practice that he felt did not impart any sense of nobility to the act of dying for one's country.[11]

The war-based patriotism of the era again supported illiberal sentiments as it did in the previous century when it blocked a full embrace of the legacy of emancipation. Activists in the labor movement, many of whom were immigrants, were attacked and some were arrested in a time marked by what historian Christopher Capozzola has called a "hysteric patriotism." A radical labor union such as the Industrial Workers of the World with many foreign-born members was essentially destroyed by the government.[12] A high point in the crusade to establish this more bellicose and less empathic variant of patriotism was the dedication of the Tomb of the Unknown Soldier at Arlington National Cemetery in 1921. Arlington, as scholar Micki McElya has demonstrated, had been established after the Civil War as a sacred site designed to bring a greater sense of honor to those who died for the nation. The tomb itself, with its simple, classical design, concealed the body parts of an unidentified American soldier who fell in France. At the interment, President Warren Harding invoked a myth of American innocence by remarking that the dead soldier went into battle "with no hatred for any people in the world but hating the war and the purpose of war for conquest."[13]

While there were similarities in the patriotic culture that followed both the Civil War and World War I, there were important differences as well.

Empathic patriots, wary of the celebration of death and willing to expose to a greater extent the harsh realities of the fight, now commanded a greater public voice. Literary scholar Steven Trout has shown how the dedication of the Tomb of the Unknown Soldier also provoked a good deal of cynical commentary such as John Dos Passos's poem "The Body of an American." The noted author bitterly criticized the interment of the unidentified soldier at Arlington for covering up the true horror of the man's death and its attempt to turn tragedy into honor. Trout notes the rise of an empathic patriotism in popular and high culture during and after the war, finding it in a range of mediums ranging from art by African American and white veterans that failed to ratify a heroic view of the war and works of literature produced by Dos Passos and Ernest Hemingway that were filled with critical commentary. Trout is able to conclude that America was unable to produce a master narrative or "stable body of collective memory" regarding World War I, which made more space available for the conflicting styles of patriotism, unlike the Civil War.[14]

Tensions evident in the patriotic culture of World War II mirrored the experience of World War I. The government again expanded its authority to enforce patriotic action by drafting millions of individuals into the armed forces and established a propaganda office, this time called the Office of War Information, to spread and encourage sentiments and demonstrations of democracy and justice. President Franklin Roosevelt himself made a special effort to enshrine this world struggle within a framework of democratic reforms with his articulation of the Four Freedoms and declarations such as the Atlantic Charter in 1941. The charter, promising men and women everywhere that they could live out their lives "in freedom from fear and want," helped to rally people throughout the world to the allied cause and justify the carnage to come. In the 1940s the great effort to defeat fascism was called a "people's war," a sign that patriotism could be embedded in more than the love of country and could also be rooted in remedial promises for fairness and a better life.[15]

In the postwar era the tide of democratic promises that circulated during the wartime culture encountered a strong challenge from war-based patriots intent upon promoting militarism and conservative values more than liberal ones. In the early years of the Cold War, patriotic celebrations took on more of a martial and even religious quality. Armed Forces Day was initiated in 1950 to celebrate the nation's military prowess, and national holidays and sporting events began to include demonstrations of weaponry such as plane flyovers. Early Cold War patriotism included a healthy dose of devotion to authority that challenged empathic patriotism, which still sought to make good on wartime promises that sacrifice would lead to a more just and fair society. By the 1990s Americans almost never referred to World War II as a "people's war" and were more likely to call it a "good war" fought by an exceptionally patriotic generation. Celebrations of the loyalty and dedication of this "greatest generation" became almost mythic the more commemorations of the Four Freedoms and Roosevelt himself faded into a distant memory. In Tom Brokaw's best-selling book on this highly loyal demographic, patriotic citizens claimed that the war was a character-building experience that offered them valuable life-lessons such as dedication and hard work. No trace of the incredible level of trauma and sorrow coming from the struggle remained in this popular version of World War II. A similar flight from trauma was evident in the aesthetics of the World War II memorial dedicated in the nation's capital in 2004.[16]

This noble and triumphant view of World War II, so prevalent in the contemporary era, stood in stark contrast to the wave of remembrances that swept the United States just after the war ended. In the late 1940s the bodies and body parts of dead Americans were rounded up from all over the globe, and many were brought home to be reinterred in somber ceremonies of mourning in local communities. Best sellers written by veterans of the war offered a generally critical view of the war's carnage and even the nature of American fighters who seemed to demonstrate a penchant for violence and human destruction. These points were at the heart of Norman Mailer's famous war novel, *The Naked and the Dead* (1948). Mailer, a veteran of the Pacific campaign, felt the democratic promises of wartime would not be realized because, as he saw it, the men who fought for America were inherently authoritarian and bloodthirsty.[17]

It was the war in Vietnam, however, that offered the greatest challenge to the goal of war-based patriots to recast the nation's wars in terms of honor and muffle themes of mourning and sorrow. Obviously the highly contentious politics over Vietnam left a critical remembrance that was hard to dismiss after the troops were withdrawn from Southeast Asia. Scholarship on the cultural impact of the war has certainly recognized the powerful ability of the conflict to resist efforts to mythologize its legacy. Historian Christian Appy's study of the war and its relationship to national identity makes it clear that the war in Vietnam shattered what he called a central tenet of American decency: the belief that American power constituted a distinctive force for good in the world. Appy notes, however, that while the war brought home in a forceful way a lesson of human suffering, it also ignited a determined attempt by the "political right" to rebuild "American power, prestige, and patriotism" and move national politics in a "rightward dimension." While he recognizes that American leaders were reluctant to use military force abroad for a time after Vietnam, he concluded that the 9/11 attacks "decisively destroyed the cautionary lessons of Vietnam" and pushed leaders such as George W. Bush into an aggressive global war on terror. Enabled by presidential policy and the impact of a sudden attack, war-based patriotism was poised to thrive again.[18]

Yet just as war-based patriotism never became the only patriotism in America and faced a counternarrative from empathic patriots during and after earlier wars, the debate gathered even more steam after Vietnam, which bled into 9/11. Much serious discussion over the impact of Vietnam on America's patriotic culture has centered on the impact of the Vietnam Veterans Memorial that was dedicated in Washington in 1982. Its powerful disclosure of suffering and death via the listing of the names of all the war dead stands in stark contrast to national memorials such as the Tomb of the Unknown Soldier and the national World War II Memorial, which are absent the names of the fallen. (Names of the dead from earlier wars were sometimes placed on memorial structures but were generally local in nature.) By listing the names of the dead, the Wall acknowledged the trauma that war-based patriots sought to hide when memorializing earlier wars. When the Wall opened to the public, thousands of empathic visitors brought personal items such as photos and letters and placed them near the names of those they loved and missed. Historian Kristin Ann Hass, who has studied this public reaction, has persuasively argued that the "gifts Americans brought to the Wall" were part of a large-scale negotiation about patriotism and nationalism. For her, Vietnam "disrupted the expectation that dead soldiers can be retired to a stoic, martyred memory of heroism."[19]

With long-established patriotic motifs weakened by the weight of revelations of massive death and suffering, traditionalists steeped in a more heroic view of warfare began to look for ways to restore faith in the use of American military power in the world. In his extensive study of the creation of the Vietnam Veterans Memorial, Patrick Hagopian has highlighted the ascendance of a narrative of national healing as a means to reach a common ground between the ardent doves and hawks who fought over Vietnam. A "discourse of healing" allowed people to discuss the planned memorial without revisiting contentious issues of the war's validity and its failure to result in an American victory. According to Hagopian even the administration of Ronald Reagan, a president who felt Vietnam was a noble undertaking, eventually supported the memorial and the idea of healing despite the fact that many conservatives railed against its nonheroic aesthetics. Reagan and his advisers concluded that the frank admission of death and loss could actually "draw the sting out of memories of Vietnam" and help unite the nation even if it was in terms of sorrow rather than victory.[20]

War-based patriots were not about to let a therapeutic rendition of the war stand alone. In 1984 a statue of three surviving infantrymen was placed near "the Wall" with the survivors of the war looking back at their fallen comrades. An American flag was also added to the site and the words "God Bless America" were inscribed on the veterans' memorial itself in an effort to restore a shred of a traditional patriotism. Eight years later a statue recognizing the contributions of women to the war effort was added to the memorial grounds. Unlike the 1984 memorial, the Vietnam Women's Memorial still did not leave the suffering behind, as one of the female figures appeared as a nurse holding a wounded soldier in her arms. Hagopian also documented the many memorials to Vietnam that were dedicated throughout the United States. He found that most presented the names of the local dead and made the point that Americans were somehow "victims" in this bloody struggle and not belligerent "agents of violence" that wreaked havoc in a foreign land.[21]

The War on Terror that began in earnest after 9/11 was more than a knee-jerk response by leaders like George Bush and Dick Cheney to a sudden attack. It was also an intentional action shaped by long-standing beliefs that Americans could again be seen as devoted patriots and not "agents of violence." War-based patriotism had been challenged in varying degrees after all major wars beginning with the Civil War but was ready for a resurrection when the terrorist planes hit the Twin Towers. The tragic aspects of warfare would again be minimized. Calls to limit the human damage would be cast aside. *Divided by Terror* will suggest that powerful currents of antidemocratic behavior would be unleashed in the form of a hostile and aggressive campaign against immigrants and others in the homeland in a fashion similar to the era of World War I. In some ways the War on Terror was unique in that its original rationale was actually grounded less in democratic promises than the major wars that preceded it.[22]

The leaders who led America into the war were not unaware that soldiers suffer and that critical perspectives over the use of American military power were widespread in the aftermath of Vietnam. They had chosen to forget or revise those lessons, however, and were confident that the use of the nation's destructive power in Afghanistan and Iraq would be fully justified by powerful traditions of American patriotism and virtue. For them myth trumped reality, and faith eclipsed trauma. George W. Bush, for instance, clearly saw 9/11 as another version of Pearl Harbor, a perspective that would help frame his use of force in a highly righteous and noble way. Bush and his supporters wanted security, revenge, and to some extent to establish American power in international affairs. They may have assumed that the public would follow in lockstep given the patriotic outburst that followed 9/11, but *Divided by Terror* demonstrates that nothing could have been further from the truth. No one knows what the memory of the yet-unfinished struggle against terrorism will be in the time to come or even when the war will end. Before all the memorials are dedicated and the books written, however, it is already clear that the search for an appropriate patriotic frame on the global contest has been highly disputed, filled with skirmishes over how one can best declare one's loyalty, and resistant to traditional mythologies that have come to stamp similar cultural battles in the past.

1   First Responses

. . . .

A War on Terror was only one of myriad responses to the spectacular assault on the United States. While many citizens certainly reacted with a militant patriotic fervor and called for a decisive military defeat of distant enemies, others were bewildered by the events of 9/11 and overwhelmed by uncertainty and confusion. The sense of security they felt in their everyday lives was shattered by the dramatic impact of the destruction that took place at Ground Zero, the Pentagon, and Shanksville, Pennsylvania. News coverage was continuous, air transportation was suspended for days, and rumors of more assaults were rampant. Conspiracy theorists charged that the government actually allowed the attacks in order to secure a rationale to launch a global war. Some falsely claimed that Israel was behind the attacks in order to foster a war against its enemies and that no Jews died at Ground Zero, having been warned in advance to stay away from work on the fateful day. To the extent that there was something like a national psyche, it was clearly traumatized. People lost their bearings and felt suspended in a twilight zone saturated with conflicting sensations of fear, sorrow, insecurity, and anger. Everyday routines that guided daily life were knocked off balance. Concerns of what the next day would bring were exacerbated. Interviewed in late September 2001, First Lady Laura Bush recalled how "apprehensive" she felt staying in the White House in those days. "There was just so much uncertainty associated with everything that happened," she said. "I worried . . . that there would be some sort of strike back immediately. I think that was the scary part." She readily admitted that she was "nervous" and "anxious."[1]

The first lady was not alone. National surveys reported that nearly one-half of all Americans experienced symptoms of posttraumatic stress after the attacks. An even greater proportion expressed fears of additional attacks similar to Laura Bush's, a dread that contributed to widespread feelings of vulnerability. Pharmacists reported a spike in demand for antianxiety medicines. Psychologists have argued that such disruptions in feelings and attitudes also prompted a widespread quest to discover the "meaning" of the shocking event, a process that apparently helped to calm the anxiety as well. They explained that terrorism tends "to shatter people's beliefs in a benevolent and predictable world" and thus intensifies a renewed quest to reestablish not only a sense of security but stable meanings that can wipe away clouds of doubt.[2]

In an atmosphere of confusion and vulnerability, a traditional war-based patriotism steeped in ideals of heroic warriors and military prowess was an important way in which many Americans sought to restore a sense of security and normalcy. National devotion served as an antidote to fear and doubt in the immediate aftermath of the attacks, although the dread and uncertainty remained. Patriotism's implicit call for expressions of loyalty to the nation and its institutions helped to unite the populace and, at least on the surface, transform the pandemonium of the times into a wave of purposeful action.

Citizens demonstrated their allegiance by displaying national symbols like the flag or even tattooing national emblems like the American eagle on parts of their body. Bloomingdale's department store in New York began selling a replica of the flag made from Waterford Crystal, calling it the "Emblem of the Land that We Love." The store proclaimed that such souvenirs "reminded us now more than ever of freedom, tolerance, and bravery." An advertising executive forced to drive from Las Vegas to New York after air flights had been suspended was so struck by the outpouring of patriotic signs that he saw on his trip that he had his company create an advertising campaign for the Miller Brewing Company that included slogans such as "America the Beautiful" and "Go U.S.A." The sale of American flags and other similar items rose dramatically, with many stores reporting that they had difficulty keeping their shelves stocked. A rare exception to this occurred in a general store run by Mennonites in Lancaster County, Pennsylvania, whose pacifist owners actually decided not to stock their shelves with flags, explaining that flag waving would only encourage "jingoistic attitudes and actions." They may have had a point, but the local populace, at least at this time, was not amenable to Mennonite and Amish beliefs about nonviolence steeped in the teachings of Jesus and criticized the proprietors for being "anti-American." Soon the owners found shelf space for this popular national emblem. Rallying around the flag and similar American icons promised to temper the huge wave of insecurity that swept over the land; patriotism like religion and other traditional values offered steadiness in stormy seas and a promise that normalcy would be restored.[3]

Mixed Emotions

Flag-waving may have alleviated some concerns, but it did not obliterate widespread confusion and apprehension. The many communications citizens sent to the Library of Congress in the fall of 2001 in response to a request for people to send a record of their personal reactions to 9/11 vividly illustrates the mayhem the attacks brought. A series of emails a man sent to a friend describes rapidly shifting emotions: annoyance, shock, anger, pity, and fear. In his first note he reported that there was "another explosion at the WTC. . . . Goddamnit I have to go to a meeting now. . . . Mother Fuck. The South Tower is now down." He then sent a second message saying that "the president is in the air. . . . The south tower collapsed. . . . Liberation of Palestine is claiming responsibility. Sears Tower is being evacuated." In subsequent emails he told his friend that "bodies were falling from the buildings. . . . Somebody will fucking pay for this. . . . I feel very sorry for these people. . . . There has been an explosion on capitol hill. . . . Seven planes have been hijacked. . . . Bush is a wimp. . . . I am going to my igloo in Antarctica." His thoughts were swarming. He was not even close to a point of having a clear and reasoned interpretation of what he had just witnessed.

Others near Ground Zero at the time were no closer to grasping what happened than the emailer. A businessman from Arizona in New York for a meeting was standing in the lobby of the Hilton Hotel across from the towers when he noticed papers floating to the ground outside. His first thought was that there might be a ticker-tape parade in the city. When he saw smoke coming from one of the towers, he called several colleagues that he was about to meet to make them aware of the strange scene unfolding before him.

The visitor reported that he was suddenly startled to see "four large objects falling from the buildings." He soon realized they were human bodies that "blew apart like if you dropped fruit off a rooftop and they left large red stains." He noticed "the torso of one person skitter in one direction and while the legs went in another." "This all happened in a second or two," the stunned spectator recalled. When he realized that he was watching people fall to their deaths, he tried to look away from the falling objects, thinking that that would be a "less horrible" option. He concluded that to continue to gaze at the point of impact he would have to be "a sick bastard" living in a "morbid society." Returning to his hotel room he saw more falling bodies but tried not to stare. "They floated by my window like leaves in the wind," he mused, "I saw at least fifty people go by."

Repulsed by the horror and gripped by fear, this stranger in the city soon joined large crowds heading uptown away from the site of danger. When the towers fell, he realized "tons of people were dead." Adding to his sense of revulsion and confusion was the fact that all he could think about was returning to his hotel to retrieve his luggage. Later as he watched television reports of death tolls, he became infuriated because they were unable to convey the stark viciousness of splattered bodies that he had witnessed. He wondered what it must have been like for people inside the towers fleeing down stairways and feeling the intensity of the burning inferno inside. He was also put off by news coverage that obsessed about death counts. In his mind there was something "sick and twisted" in this fixation on matters that might better be "left unspoken." Ultimately the response of this startled visitor was one of repugnance and distaste over witnessing the brutal end of fellow human beings.[4]

Laura Barti also witnessed the horror of Ground Zero. While working on the fifty-ninth floor of the North Tower, she felt the building actually "shake and sway." Instantly she headed for the stairs, passing firemen on the way up whom she later realized were probably killed when the structure fell to the ground. Her first thoughts as she fled, however, were more practical: "The air is cleaner as we go lower"; "Spirits are good, breathing is good"; "Finding little things to laugh at keeps us from freaking out." Once on the ground, she headed for the Hilton Hotel, where she felt the vibration from the collapse of the second tower. Soon she too joined the march uptown, where she joked with a friend whose shoe had broken that they both would have worn more sensible footwear if they knew there was going to be a "bombing."

Later, reflecting on her getaway, Barti was not laughing but experiencing something close to a religious experience. She did not frame the day as an attack upon a nation or even upon political freedom but an event that, in her view, was part of a divine plan. For her the goals of the terrorists were not as important as "God's plan for me." In her mind she was able to find a way out of the tower before it collapsed because of heavenly intervention. She was actually saddened by the prospect of a war because it might bring harm to people she cared about, although she acknowledged that the cost of freedom could be high. Her ambivalence toward a military response to the attacks was not matched by her faith. She insisted that everyone now needed to seek "the Lord's guidance."[5]

One did not have to be at the site of the attacks to experience confusion, fear, and other strong but contradictory emotions. Cynthia Fukami, a professor of management at the University of Denver, decided to collect the "evolving thoughts and emotions" of faculty and students in management courses from throughout the nation to the dramatic attacks. Most instructors made it clear that students were basically stunned by what they saw. Ann Mooney at Stevens Institute of Technology in New Jersey reported that many of her students actually saw the buildings collapse and were so distraught they simply began to roam the campus. Not far away at Fordham University, two instructors indicated that "the emotional weight of the sadness and the terror were like a mantle difficult to lift for several days." Mooney felt that the tragedy had such an impact on daily life that students needed to be free to find their own way to cope with all that had happened.

At Bloomsburg University in Pennsylvania, students were asked to write down their thoughts and feelings about 9/11. Many viewed the assault as "the end of the world," and a few saw 9/11 as the start of World War III. Other classes reported that students and teachers began talking about what had happened in order to try to make sense of it. Some teachers felt that in exchanging opinions and feelings of the day, people achieved a level of comfort at a moment that seemed frightening. In a class at Illinois State University, students decided to sell T-shirts and send proceeds to a relief fund for victims. Their instructor also saw value in this exercise because it offered students training in "decision making techniques" and "establishing purchase orders via the internet." At Texas Tech a professor concluded that the horrific affair had actually caused her students to show more compassion toward others."[6]

At West Georgia College, students similarly exhibited a range of reactions, but they seemed to coalesce around the theme of shock, loss, and fear. "Although my life is not affected as deeply as some," an undergraduate said, "I worry about the terrorists' next move and am concerned for the safety of my uncle who is a pilot in Atlanta." Another student claimed he experienced anger at first, but his feelings soon changed to "sadness" over the thought of so many children watching their parents going to work on September 11th and never seeing them come home. A fellow student was also upset by the realization that many families who lost loved ones would endure suffering and now "only wanted to be around people I loved and let them know I loved them."[7]

In Iowa, a location far removed from Ground Zero, residents also grappled with the stunning news of what had happened on 9/11. Janet Freeman heard about the plane crashes the morning of 9/11 on her radio as she sat in her home in Iowa City. Seeing the two towers crumple on television prompted her to clean her house as a way to settle her emotions. She began scrubbing the stove, cleaning her oven, and washing floors. It was three o'clock in the afternoon before she realized that she was still wearing her pajamas and that her hands were covered in dirt. Another Iowa City resident, Jessica Kardon, felt nauseated after seeing the calamity and felt like vomiting. She kept searching for small tasks to tackle as the day passed. When her son asked her if they had lost any relatives in the carnage of the day, she told him that they had not but she felt as if they had. At the public library in Iowa City, Maureen Delaney felt "great shock and sadness." She was duly impressed by the "bravery of the rescue workers" but could not shake feeling depressed over the realization that so many had to die. In writing a poem on 9/11, she could only think about "people noise, explosions, screaming."[8]

In Fort Dodge, Peter Rouderbush, who taught in the town's high school, felt "stunned, shocked and upset." Personally he said he also felt "abused." Rouderbush claimed there were no good reasons for the attacks and felt it was imperative for students to discuss them and why they occurred in the first place. Other Iowa residents claimed for a time they thought the entire image at Ground Zero was simply the results of "special effects" on television. Lorna Truck of Des Moines felt "extreme sadness for all those who lost their lives" and actually kept hoping it was not really true. She recalled being profoundly aware of all the lives that were lost and regretted that many bodies would never be found."[9]

It was not unusual for citizens who actually thought the attacks could lead to war to express hope that such an event could be avoided because so many blameless people would be harmed. One California resident insisted that "we show our humanitarian side to the people of Afghanistan" rather than launch an attack against them. A few citizens noted that there were other ways to resolve issues "besides bombing and killing innocent people." A person who said he hated "all the 'hawk' rhetoric and the 'wanted dead or alive' mentality" felt that in war the "collateral damage was always too great. "Enough Death!" Others insisted that if there was to be any sort of violent reprisal, it should be limited to finding and killing Osama bin Laden and not be expanded into a wider attack upon Afghanistan.[10]

In Knoxville, Tennessee, a group of local citizens installed a temporary memorial ten days after the 9/11 planes crashed to honor those who died. Called a "Wall of Unity," the structure was placed near a shopping center with the aim of fostering an "environment of unity, healing, and brotherhood." Residents were encouraged to post their own "words, remembrances, and icons of encouragement" during a two-month period from September to November 2001. Notes on the wall show that Americans were anything but united in their responses to the attacks, and instead reveal the sweeping range of thought that pervaded the public mind in the aftermath of 9/11 that included religious faith, compassion, patriotic vengeance, and hopes for peace:

"Always keep the faith and God will see you through"
"Jesus is with us"
"They have darkened our hearts but we will see the lights once again. May God bless."
"For all the parents who lost children in the terrorist attacks. Jesus will be here for you."
"Jesus loves you, this I know."
"May those who are strong stand up for what they believe in and let them stand strong. We cannot be broken by acts of hatred but brought together."
"Divided We Fall. United We Stand."
"All Races. All Colors. All Religions. All Americans. Together we unite and pray. God bless us all."
"Love your nation. Love your neighbors. Keep hope alive and wish for the best."
"Sometimes the price of peace for our children is ourselves going to war."
"We will kill you."
"Run Osama Run."
"Fellow veterans again let us lead the way in prayer, in patriotism, in performance and in perseverance."
"Such a cowardly attack on innocent people and now more innocence will have to be shed for the nation to regain her freedom and safety."
"Hate and violence are not the answer. I hope you find peace."
"For those who lost their loved ones. I wish peace and healing."
"No More War."
"I hate war. I love America."[11]

United We Stand

War-based patriotism was often characterized by an aggressive stance and strong desire for revenge on the perpetrators of the attacks. Cultural critic

William Bennett wrote that in the days after 9/11 "across the nation a patriotic ardor burned bright" as Americans discovered their sense of being "one people." For him this attitude represented a welcome change after the turmoil of the Vietnam era and the cultural wars that had pitted staunch defenders of a romantic view of America against some of its native-born protesters. Bennett argued that the present was a moment of "moral clarity" steeped in unquestioned love of country and a desire to carry the flag into battle. He felt that now Americans unanimously held a "righteous anger and resolve and a firm belief that America was a country worth fighting for."[12]

Evidence of citizen unity and bellicosity could be found everywhere. In a letter to the editor of the *Indianapolis Star* just after the attacks, an Indiana woman wrote that the only thing the terrorists accomplished by their actions was to "sow the seeds of their own destruction." William Stanley of suburban Carmel wrote to the same paper saying that "today, Americans speak with one voice. We must declare all out war against terrorism. We expect the president to hunt down those responsible. We want them destroyed. This is war and we must protect ourselves." David Osborne from Noblesville insisted that Americans "hunt down the culprits." Osborne drew parallels between the attacks and World War II and suggested that if citizens stand together, this would make for their "finest hour." In Dallas, Texas, Ken Goldberg, the operator of a shooting range, attracted customers by putting up images of Osama bin Laden as a target. Goldberg, who admitted to carrying a big .45-caliber Winchester Magnum pistol himself during these stressful times, came up with his idea for a target because he felt "we all need that fantasy of striking back." Phil Beckwith, a retired truck driver from Wyoming, placed an advertisement in his local newspaper calling for the "killing" of "Arab people." He felt their bodies should then be placed in pigskin and buried so that they would never be able to enter heaven. A man in Ogden, Illinois, claimed that if he could get his hands on bin Laden, he would "skin him alive and pour salt on the wounds." Fox News Network told its news anchors that they might inject personal pro-war outlooks into their reporting. Geraldo Rivera, a Fox correspondent based in Afghanistan at the time, made it clear that if the chance presented itself, he would consider killing bin Laden himself.[13]

A burst of patriotic unity was also noticeable in African American neighborhoods. Brian Gilmore, a resident of Washington, D.C., who saw a huge cloud of smoke rising from the Pentagon on his way to work on 9/11, recalled that many residents in his part of town were visibly "distraught" by images of falling towers in New York and readily backed calls for revenge. Hearing phrases like "Bomb them" and "Kill them" from people who lived nearby, Gilmore was truly surprised to hear blacks on talk radio in the nation's capital calling for deportations and the "profiling" of Arab Americans for the good of the nation. The attacks caused Cheryl Pinsette Brown and her spouse to put a flag in front of their home in Georgia because they felt America needed to be defended. She acknowledged the historic maltreatment of blacks but drew inspiration from her family's proud record of military service that had been firmly established by her father and brother. Dwonna Goldstone, a black professor in Tennessee, watched the events of 9/11 unfold with her interracial class. She recalled that she immediately felt "more patriotic" and sang along with others, "God Bless America." Goldstone even wrote a letter to National Public Radio expressing a "new sense of pride" in what it meant to be an American. Tony Morgan, working at a Brooklyn hospital, explained that he had not always been proud of what America had done to black people but was now moved by scenes of the devastation at Ground Zero and wanted to help others in any way he could.

A number of prominent African American leaders were also quick to call upon their brethren to rally behind the flag. The Reverend Al Sharpton insisted that on 9/11 his personal agenda became a "platform for all America." He felt deeply that the people killed in the terrorist attacks died because they were Americans and not because of any particular race or creed. While doing a radio show a few weeks after 9/11, he told a caller who claimed that there seemed to be few flags flying in black neighborhoods that African Americans had a long record of fighting for America during its many wars despite the reality of racism and would be willing to do so again. Kweisi Mfume, president of the National Association of the Advancement of Colored People, also encouraged blacks to put aside their many grievances, for this was "a time for all Americans to stand united." While civil rights leader Jesse Jackson certainly supported a patriotic response to 9/11, he revealed a more empathic sense of patriotism when he expressed reluctance to back the idea of another war. To Jackson the proper response to the terrorist threat was not a military crusade that would harm innocent people but a greater investment in religious faith and prayer. In the aftermath of the attacks, he urged people to donate blood wherever they could "regardless if one was white, black, Arab, Jew, gay or straight." For him the people of America were of "one blood."

Certainly not all African Americans were ready to fall into a patriotic line and rally behind the flag. Haunted by the sordid history of racial oppression in America, some African Americans were among the first to raise reservations about the revival of a war-based patriotism that had failed to deliver social justice to them as a reward for past sacrifices. Singer Alicia Keys told an interviewer, "I see lies in the flag." The writer Alice Walker argued that the fear cast by bin Laden over America had already been a lived reality for many American citizens. A group of black firefighters in Florida refused to ride on their fire engine while it flew an American flag. John Wideman wrote in *Harper's Magazine* that he could not support George Bush's call for a Global War on Terrorism because of his memories of racist treatment while growing up in Pittsburgh. Wideman felt that the president's invocations of war and patriotism simply obscured the harsh realities of "underclass African-Americans living below the poverty line" and "young people of color wasting away in prison." He also questioned attempts to proclaim America as an innocent actor on the global stage when it had a long history of perpetrating misdeeds as well. In a survey conducted at a "public university in the Midwest," students who said their racial identity was more important to them than their American identity were less likely to engage in "symbolic acts of patriotism." One female respondent in the study said she had never felt particularly patriotic because of her "extensive knowledge of black history in the United States." And the African American poet Amiri Baraka caused a stir when he published "Somebody Blew Up America," with verses that eschewed patriotic rhetoric in favor of those that summoned up memories of slavery and the homegrown terrorist organization named the "Klan."[14]

Pollsters picked up, however, on the substantial public preference for a fight. In a survey taken just after the assaults, some 85 percent of the respondents claimed they supported a military response. The poll showed that many citizens who had not been strong supporters of President George W. Bush were now willing to back him in some plan of attack. One woman told the pollsters that she didn't like the idea of American lives being lost but "we just can't sit here and let them continue to do it because they will probably do it again." Joy Hess, a library clerk in Medford, Oregon, said that she had a son in the military and that she recognized the cost of revenge but "there is no other way to get across that we mean business."[15]

"United We Stand" became a rallying cry for many Americans after the attacks, promising stability, community, and potency when so many felt vulnerable and unsure. The slogan soon appeared on billboards, T-shirts, and even a stamp with the postal service explaining that it stood for America's core values of freedom, liberty, and justice. The motto was an old one with a martial heritage—it had been dispatched during the Civil War and

World War II as a rallying cry for unanimity in the face of threats to the nation itself. People now performed this sense of unity with prayer vigils, the lighting of candles, and recitations of the Pledge of Allegiance. Individuals waited in line to donate blood nearly everywhere. In one week the Red Cross raised more than $128 million in donations. Students in Columbia, South Carolina, raised a half-million dollars to buy a new fire truck for the City of New York to replace one lost in the attacks. In Plymouth, Indiana, a teacher insisted that the "Pledge of Allegiance" now held "greater meaning" than it did before 9/11. A student in her class remarked that reciting it made him feel like he was in a "safe environment." And another classmate claimed that the pledge made her feel "happy" and "like we are one country—together." Looking back in 2011, a reporter in Massachusetts recalled that the "country cried" after 9/11 but it was evident that a "sense of community extended from Portland, Oregon to Portland, Maine." The Gallup organization discovered that in the period from 2002 to 2004 the number of citizens describing themselves as "extremely proud to be an American" reached a peak of around 70 percent. In January of 2001 only 55 percent indicated the same level of loyalty. By 2016 the figure had slipped down again to 54 percent. Gallup and other polling organizations attributed the rise directly to what they felt was an "elevated sense of patriotism" emanating from the events of 9/11.[16]

Charlton Heston, in his role as president of the National Rifle Association (NRA), applauded this visible surge of patriotic display. He proclaimed in the *American Rifleman* that "our national spirit has been lifted by the flags fluttering from automobiles, the pro-American window decals, the displays of patriotism that adorn our doorways, our businesses, and our athletic events." To this noted actor, "rejuvenated nationalistic emotions" had even helped to foster greater harmony between the races and between liberals and conservatives. Heston wrote approvingly of the fact that American bombs would darken the skies over Taliban and al-Qaeda strongholds and urged all Americans to support the military and wave the flag during these trying times. In fact, the NRA not only supported retaliation but reworked the legacy of 9/11 into another argument of why Americans needed to be armed. The association's executive vice president, Wayne LaPierre, mounted a strong effort on behalf of those who now argued that pilots needed to carry handguns. He wrote that "American history would not have been forever stained with the horror of September 11 and thousands of innocent people would still be alive" if the pilots had been carrying such weapons. To him the right to bear arms was "our original 'homeland security'" and a "moral imperative."[17]

Heston's unambivalent linking of the flag, war, and patriotism was increasingly echoed by citizens in the days and weeks following the attacks, as demonstrated by responses to the Library of Congress's call to Americans for documentation of their reaction to 9/11. In an email he wrote to friends who subsequently forwarded his message to others, Aaron Brune noted that while "our dawn was grayed by ash, flames filled our horizon . . . [and] freedom in America was transformed into a "sickening mass of twisted steel," he drew strength from displays of courage and compassion he saw all around him. He even suggested that there was an ingrained commitment to valor in America and a real love of "Old Glory." Brune was certain that such traits would see the nation through this rough patch as they had in the past. Patriotism would triumph over nervousness and fright.

Brune's faith in the power of the nation was rooted in his family's history as well as his view of the past. He and his wife had both served in the military because as children they had learned the values of "honor, courage, and compassion." He also affirmed that the couple believed in "superheroes (moral and otherwise) . . . and in white-hatted lawmen." "We take our hats off, cover our hearts and salute when Old Glory is raised and retired." He concluded his epistle by insisting that Americans would protect their freedom and warned potential enemies that "America is coming."

Recipients of Brune's missive generally endorsed his romantic sense of patriotism and righteousness. One recipient, who claimed she hailed from "small town USA," praised Brune by stating that "without men like you who will stand up for their country what kind of country will we have? What kind of home would you have to come home to?" Although this writer was a "mother and wife," she insisted that she would fight alongside Brune and made it clear she would pray for him, his kin, and "our country." She also hoped that he would have the strength and courage to carry on "without allowing it to harden your heart."

Another correspondent marveled at how well Brune articulated a "mixture of feelings that America feels today." She noted that "each of us is from a different position in life, age, ethnicity and yet anger boils inside of us." She was sure that when Brune looked into the eyes of his children he imagined nothing but the safety and warmth that "an American family can give." She now presumed that the warmth he had felt for his family had cooled into a "very cold anger. We all hold that anger now. . . . Today I would put on a uniform and march off to war against our attackers."[18]

John Kotzian also shared Brune's willingness to fight. Within minutes after the first tower fell, Kotzian sent an electronic message declaring that he could not believe "this shit" and calling for "death to the perpetrators." He felt the last time the United States was dragged into such a conflict it ended with Hiroshima. "May God forgive us all," he cried, "but we need to find bin Laden and kill him." When he saw the second tower fall, he said it was time to "do some major thumping." He admitted that he had never been so scared in his life but consoled himself with the thought that the war to be fought would at least not be waged in the homeland but abroad. In his mind, if Afghanistan did not hand over bin Laden it should be destroyed within a week. Another man noted in his response to the Library of Congress that the assault on America would surely mean war and that people he loved might be involved. He supported such a conflict, however, and only hoped "George Jr. can live up to his father's reputation . . . and kick some ass now."[19]

The Library of Congress's collection of post-attack responses contains many echoes of Kotzian's case for war. Peter Rouderbush of Fort Dodge, Iowa, felt George Bush was correct in gaining the support of other nations to plan an attack to rid the world of terrorism. Rouderbush did have reservations over the carnage that a war would produce, but he was sure the United States would prevail. Another Iowan said America should hunt down the terrorists "like animals and execute them on television." A radio talk show host in the state advocated bombing Afghanistan "back to the Stone Age." A college student who had always considered himself a "peaceful person" now wanted to fight. He insisted that the attacks had helped him understand the patriotism his parents had always displayed which he felt had come from their memory of Pearl Harbor. He liked very much the slogan "United We Stand" and said now he was more willing to fight than ever. And another resident "craved the destruction of those that did this."[20]

Heroic self-sacrifice, a corollary of a war-based patriotism, was also celebrated at the time by many citizens who expressed their admiration for the passengers who attempted to retake Flight 93 before it crashed in Pennsylvania. Many of the emails at the Library of Congress were directed to the families of those who died as a way of offering consolation. But they also tended to ratify the logic of patriotic sacrifice. A missive sent to the children of Todd Beamer, one of the leaders of the passenger revolt on the plane, told his offspring that their father was a hero "in the most true and ultimate way." The writer felt that someone they cared about who worked at the Capitol Building in Washington may have been saved by the actions of Beamer and his colleagues and asserted that we will all pass on someday but "not all as heroes."

Another letter addressed to the families of the four men who led the passenger revolt on the plane, Beamer, Jeremy Glick, Thomas Burnett, and Mark Bingham, expressed the feeling that their loved ones were special individuals who gave their lives for a noble purpose. "They are true American heroes who will be in the hearts of every American. Their sacrifices will be remembered always, as I am sure you will always remember their amazing spirit and the love they had for you." In another note a woman expressed amazement that these "four American heroes" could muster the strength and conviction to protect America from attack."[21]

Beata Suranyi, a soldier assigned to a detail at the Pentagon to look for bodies and human remains, was impressed by the dedication of Red Cross personnel and the "small army of chaplains" offering counseling services to survivors in the aftermath of the crash at the site. Suranyi also reported that she witnessed not only a considerable amount of grief at the Pentagon but much anger as well. Many people told her that it was imperative to keep terrorists out of the country and backed ideas for tightening America's borders. She also drew a sense of optimism from the turmoil because she saw so many people attempting to help others or wearing patriotic symbols on their clothing. She was particularly moved by the applause her own unit received as they left the rubble after a trying day of looking for body parts. To her it felt like everyone was "a fellow American." For Suranyi the soldier, however, patriotic sensations of unity did not necessarily translate into a call for war; the gruesomeness of uncovering human remains had moderated such an impulse. She claimed if ordered to fight she would do so but "was not champing at the bit for payback."[22]

The Commander in Chief

George W. Bush did not share Suranyi's reservations. Backed by public opinion polls, the president declared for war soon after 9/11. Bush commented that his first visit to Ground Zero had definitely reinforced his love for America as he quickly took steps to initiate military action. Unfettered by the sense of doubt and puzzlement that plagued many of his fellow citizens, the president injected a dose of patriotic certainty into the highly unstable stew of emotions that coursed through the nation at the time. A USA/CNN/Gallup Poll in the fall of 2001 on whether the United States should mount a military response to the attacks showed 86 percent favored such retaliation against Afghanistan. Only 62 percent of those asked favored a long-term war against terrorism, a discrepancy that suggested some hesitancy toward the idea of a prolonged conflict that constituted more than simply payback against al-Qaeda. Some 31 percent argued that the nation's response should be limited to punishing specific terrorists. Such polls, however, seldom probed the complexity of individual feelings. Single questions did not capture the more intricate nature of moods and views evident in information collected in a more open-ended fashion by institutions. Polls are shaped by the questions asked; most of the material in collections like those at the Library of Congress were simply volunteered without any specific prompts. Thus, the president's decision to go to war was not lacking in public approbation, but it clearly represented an oversimplification of what many of his co-nationals actually felt and thought.[23]

It was also clear that important mainstream news outlets in the United States fell in line rather quickly with the views of Bush's war-based patriotism. In the immediate aftermath of 9/11, major television networks focused almost entirely on the terrorist assault. Key television news anchors such as Tom Brokaw and Dan Rather put aside any effort at objective news analysis over what the nation might do next to embrace with passion the idea that America would "fight back." Both of these veteran reporters quoted Bush directly in fueling the call for war. Brokaw promised viewers that "freedom would be defended." Rather drew from the president the point that "we will find and punish those responsible for these cowardly events" and famously declared in an interview that he was ready to "line up" if the president called him. *Time* quickly issued a special edition with color photos of the damage done on 9/11, calling it a "Day of Infamy," a direct reference to the attack on Pearl Harbor in 1941 that launched another war. The same issue also included an essay that made the case for Americans tapping into their sense of "rage" rather than pondering carefully what next steps they might take and embarking on an orgy of retribution that would "exterminate men like Osama bin Laden and those who conspire with them in evil mischief." Some news outlets did suggest that the 9/11 assaults should be seen as a crime requiring the arrest of individual perpetrators more than an act that called for a vast military campaign. In one study of this debate, scholars found that those driven by vengeance were more intent on launching a war; people arguing for criminal arrest were more resistant to military action because they worried over the killing of civilians.[24]

As Bush formulated his post-attack policy, he moved quickly to wipe away strains of compassion and misgivings over perpetrating more violence that existed in the population. First, he encouraged citizens to go about daily tasks such as shopping in the hope few would dwell on the bitter realities to come. His rhetorical strategy was to cast the war as a moral drama in which an impeccably righteous nation had been harmed by evil forces in the world and was now justified in punishing enemies by any means it saw fit. The process of witnessing, contemplating the causes and effects of all of the grief and sorrow that many felt and a key tenet of an empathic patriotism, was suspended in favor of a belligerent form of allegiance meant to encase the emotional anarchy 9/11 triggered. Reservations about horrors to come and the possible slaughter of more innocents would be articulated but contained within a message and mission intent upon eliminating doubt and bewilderment. Such was the metaphorical power of war and its attendant belief in heroic sacrifice that acts normally considered repugnant would now be labeled as praiseworthy.

This need for a war appeared to be very much a part of the president's initial response to 9/11. Bob Woodward, who was able to interview the president and his chief associates, noted that as early as 9:30 A.M. on the morning of the plane attacks, Bush told his vice president, Dick Cheney, that "we are at war." Shortly thereafter he remarked to his staff that "somebody is going to pay for this." His national security advisor, Condoleezza Rice, later recalled being struck by the "clarity" the president showed in the first days after 9/11 regarding the necessity for an extensive campaign against al-Qaeda. The chief executive even told King Abdullah of Jordan weeks after the attack that there was a certain level of "bloodlust" in America and that while it would not drive our reaction, "pretty soon we have to start displaying scalps." She felt 9/11 had "transformed" him into a wartime president and his staff into a "war council." Bush also felt that a war was necessary to keep Americans focused on the fight against terrorism as they retreated back into the routine of daily life. When the secretary of defense, Donald Rumsfeld, felt his office shake after a plane hit the Pentagon, he too saw war on the horizon and felt that "our building became a battleground."

Scholars like Raymond Haberski have argued that Bush operated within a tradition of American civil religion that intuitively sanctioned the use of mass violence as an extension of a divine plan. Integral to this way of thinking was the idea that the nation and the soldiers who carried out its brutal plans were operating on a moral plane that exonerated them from any charge of wickedness. For Haberski and many others who have examined American civil religion, the nation's sponsorship of cruelty was not simply legitimated by the will of the people but actually "validated by a higher power," a belief that exempted the United States from any degree of accountability for the damage it might inflict. Bush's moral sense was reinforced in his first cabinet meeting after 9/11. The president called upon his secretary of defense, Rumsfeld, to offer a prayer. The secretary quickly responded with an invocation that reminded all of the unique relationship he felt that existed between a divine being and the American people. He proclaimed that it was a "faithful God" that had given the American people the "birthrights of life and liberty" that they must now defend.[25]

Bush laid out his framework of righteousness, his antidote for witnessing and confusion, in a series of speeches in the months after September 11th. On the day of the terror assaults, he highlighted the basic goodness of the American people. The president observed that the horror of the attacks revealed not only "the very worst of human nature" but the selflessness of the nation's citizens who "responded with the best of America" with daring rescues and care for strangers and neighbors. He also assured citizens that "our military is powerful and is prepared" and that the first priorities would be to help the injured and prevent any further attacks. Announcing his intention to launch a divinely inspired military response, Bush promised that America and its allies would stand together "to win a war against terrorism." He followed with a citation from Psalm 23: "Even though I walk through the valley of the shadow of death, I fear no evil, for You are with me."

Three days later at a National Day of Prayer and Remembrance held at the National Cathedral, Bush merged moral clarity and patriotic unity to address the considerable uncertainty over assaults. He declared that those assembled that day had come before God to pray for the missing and the dead. Admitting that Americans are still grieving and cannot yet answer all questions associated with 9/11 because "they do not yet have the distance of history," the chief executive inferred that reprisals need not wait for further clarification. "Our responsibility to history is already clear: to answer these attacks and rid the world of evil," he declared in illuminating the path forward. He felt a war had already been waged against America but that "this peaceful nation" can be "fierce" when "stirred to anger." Expanding on his moralizing agenda and mythical conception of a virtuous American character, the commander in chief now proclaimed that America's "true colors" had been revealed in "eloquent acts of sacrifice" in the cauldron of adversity where rescue workers toiled past exhaustion and thousands volunteered to serve in any way they could. Turning again to the tenets of religious faith, Bush emphasized the power of prayer and how Americans everywhere were invoking appeals to God in search of reassurance and consolation after the rupture of terrorism. The president then offered a prayer of his own asking for the "resolve" that would be needed to fight the war to come and divine "guidance" in determining the actions the nation would take.[26]

Bush further refined his moral stance on terrorism in his State of the Union speech in January 2002. He affirmed that the nation was at war but the state of the union had never been stronger. He marveled at the fact that in the four months since the "hour of shock" citizens had begun to rebuild New York and the Pentagon, rallied a "great coalition" for war, rid the world of thousands of terrorists, destroyed Afghanistan's terrorist training centers, saved people from starvation, and freed a country from oppression. He was able to proclaim that on the night of his speech Afghanistan and America were actually partners in fighting the terror campaign and even giving women greater rights and opportunities in that distant nation, a belated nod to the idea of remediation. The War on Terror had now become not only an exercise in self-defense and revenge but a struggle to spread democracy throughout the world.

Bush not only touted achievements since 9/11 but put forward a broader vision for fighting the war beyond Afghanistan. He called attention to a need to confront regimes like Iran, Iraq, and North Korea that sponsored terrorism and possibly had weapons of mass destruction that could bring harm to America again. The president made it clear that he would not allow "the world's most dangerous regimes" to threaten the nation with ominous weapons. Repeating his point that war can bring out the best in America as a nation as he felt it did on 9/11 and minimizing its potential for trauma and grief, he expressed the conviction that Americans were embracing "a new ethic and a new creed": "Let's Roll," a reference to a phrase used by passengers on United Flight 93 before attacking terrorists who had hijacked their plane. He felt he detected the same fighting spirit in the sacrifice of soldiers, the fierce brotherhood of firefighters, and the bravery of ordinary citizens. "We have glimpsed a new culture of responsibility," he insisted. For the president, tragedy had only intensified the selflessness of citizens and "brought us closer to God." Excursions into violence were again seen as redemptive.[27]

Of course, Bush was not only interested in crafting a coherent rhetoric that avoided the emotional roller coaster many had ridden since 9/11 and justified the use of force. He was also part of an effort to revive notions of American military might in the decades after Vietnam and diminish traces of trauma and regret from the failed effort in Southeast Asia. Andrew Bacevich has argued persuasively that by the later stages of the twentieth century, Americans of various backgrounds had become "enthralled" with military power, high-tech weaponry, and "the soldiers that use them." Bacevich suggested that the combination of sophisticated weaponry and patriotic soldiers had come to define the American character, a formula that blended easily with a deep faith in God's will. This was to be sure an idealistic way to frame violent acts that were at their very core sordid and regrettable no matter who perpetrated them. Bacevich, like others, stressed the evangelical flavor of Bush's conception of a War on Terror as a fight to rid the world of evil. He noted how after 9/11 evangelicals like Reverend Billy Graham rallied to Bush's call to arms and his Manichaean view of the world.[28]

Bush's memoirs offered further proof of how his religious fervor and anger drove his thought process in September 2001. He presented himself to readers as a born-again Christian who surmounted problems with heavy drinking that threatened to harm his health and his family life. In search of solutions, he arranged a personal meeting with Billy Graham at which the renowned evangelist showed the future chief executive the value of intense Bible reading and how he could come to see his actions on earth as an extension of God's will.[29] And Bush made it clear that he was outraged by 9/11. "My blood was boiling. We were going to find out who did this and kick their ass." As many other Americans did, he compared the assault to the Japanese bombing of Pearl Harbor. He was also impressed with the heroism of the passengers on United Flight 93. As he prepared to address the nation on the catastrophe, he recalled that he drew strength from his faith and from American history, citing Abraham Lincoln's "moral clarity and resolve" in what he called a clash between freedom and tyranny that could only be solved by victory in war.[30]

In explaining his first major move of a new war, the decision to go into Afghanistan, Bush again drew on his ethical outlook and his noble view of America. He acknowledged that his decision would lead to the loss of American lives and bring sorrows, but was convinced that those willing to fight were more than ready to make the necessary sacrifices. Early in the war he had decided to write letters to family members of Americans lost on the battlefield to honor their devotion and express the gratitude of the nation. He told one widow whose husband died in Afghanistan that he knew her "heart aches" but that her partner had died in a "fight against evil" and for a "noble cause—freedom." At the end of a speech he gave in late October 2001, he quoted from a letter he had received from a child whose father was in the military. "As much as I don't want my dad to fight, I am willing to give him to you," the youngster wrote. Later in the book he related another story of how the widow of Air Force sergeant John Chapman handed him a note that said that "John did his job, now you do yours."[31]

Bush's blend of Manichaeism and patriotism was rhetorically smart. As David Keen has suggested, it brought a form of "magical thinking" to a public that was not totally clear as to what was happening and, as patriotic oratory intends, both justified and minimized the suffering that had just occurred and that was to come to both Americans and those they attacked. Interestingly, Bush's remarks after 9/11 not only invoked references to religion and loyalty but often referred to historic images from the Old West. Shortly after the terrorist assaults, Bush referred several times to the fact that he wanted a form of frontier justice in pursuit of terrorists and invoked a memory from his boyhood of seeing posters that called for the capture of outlaws "dead or alive," a trope that could sanction the vanquishing of enemies by any means possible. In another talk just after 9/11 he indicated the "noose is narrowing" around those responsible for the attacks. Frontier myths about vigilante justice made sense to Bush because they suggested that the pursuit of suspects would not need to be impeded by any set of laws or legal procedures.[32]

Afghanistan

Only six days after 9/11 Bush signed off on a plan to go to war in Afghanistan and allow the Central Intelligence Agency (CIA) to conduct covert operations in that country with permission to kill or detain members of al-Qaeda anywhere in the world. On October 7, 2001, less than one month after al-Qaeda flew planes into the World Trade Center, Bush announced in a televised address that American forces were now on the offensive in Afghanistan in an attack labeled Operation Enduring Freedom.[33]

Almost immediately after Bush declared war, currents of uncertainty and a widespread aversion to killing innocent civilians rippled through the population, pointing to the rise of a wave of empathic patriotism that, while modest, clearly expressed opposition to the bombings in Afghanistan. Several thousand people attended a peace rally in Union Square in New York singing antiwar songs and carrying candles and a banner announcing their hostility to the president's decisions as they were announced.

A small group of about fifty protesters stood nearby, calling the adversaries of war "traitors" and claiming they were being supported by Taliban propaganda. Yet, a former Vietnam vet addressed the antiwar rally and insisted that he did not want to see Americans die because of a "militaristic cowboy" or be dragged into a long land conflict in Asia. Reuben Schafer, who lost a grandson in the Twin Towers, told the rally that an attack on Afghanistan did not make him feel any better. In fact, he said it made him feel worse because the government was using the memory of his grandson's death to cause suffering for other people in other lands.[34]

The *New York Times* received a host of letters at the beginning of the War on Terror reflecting doubt about what Bush was doing. Philip Sedlak of Arlington,Virginia, wrote that it was appropriate to capture the leadership of al-Qaeda for their criminal acts and that this would be a greater deterrent against terrorism in the future than a war that would transform terrorists into martyrs. Mary Ellen McNish, an official with the American Friends Service Committee, argued that "our history teaches that bloodshed only leads to more bloodshed" and demanded that the bombing stop. "Our grief is not a cry for retaliation," she asserted. For her terrorism must be stopped at its root cause and not be fed the "seeds of vengeance." A writer from New Jersey felt the president "was unduly bellicose, morally simplistic, and socially insensitive." Another war protester challenged the administration's idea of moral clarity. "The notion that we are crusaders on behalf of God and can carry out God's will is wrongheaded in our multicultural, democratic state."[35]

On the other side of the rising debate about patriotism, Bush's defenders hailed their leader and his decision. A Chicago resident compared the president's speech of September 20th to a joint session of Congress, an address that praised the heroics of the passengers on Flight 93, to Franklin Roosevelt's "Day of Infamy Speech" in 1941. He felt it would promote the same type of unity America experienced after Pearl Harbor. The writer recalled that his father had always reminded him of how fortunate we were in America to have so much freedom and that we need to be ready to pay any price to defend it if we are to leave our children a "safe world." Another admirer of the chief executive felt strongly that Bush had prepared the nation for a "messy conflict that could drag on for decades" in a war in which "we will never know when the last bomb had been planted." And a citizen from Florida compared Bush's September 20th speech to the rhetoric of Winston Churchill in World War II and hoped it would now galvanize America to support the military crusade ahead.[36]

Belligerent loyalists continued to be confronted by empathizers setting a path for a divided legacy of responses to 9/11 for years to come. Some of the most ardent hostility to Bush's plan to attack Afghanistan came from individuals who lost loved ones on 9/11. Rita Lazar, whose brother was killed in the North Tower when he remained behind to help a wheelchair-bound friend, heard the president actually refer to her sibling's selflessness in his speech at the National Cathedral. She was moved to write a letter to the *New York Times* expressing the hope that the nation was not so deeply hurt that it would "unleash forces we will not have the power to call back" in "my brother's name and mine." Lazar would have preferred that the United States use the attacks as an opportunity to launch initiatives to make the world a safer place by working through international organizations or making multilateral treaties. David Potorti, whose brother was also killed in the North Tower, expressed regret over hearing too many talk-radio programs calling upon America to bomb "them." Potorti recalled that his mother grieved so much from the news of her son's death that she did not want anyone else to feel the pain she did. He argued that the United States should seek justice but not necessarily look to punish other people. Darrill Bodley, a music professor whose daughter, Deora, died on Flight 93, told a reporter at a memorial service for the young woman that "we must not retaliate in kind as if our cause allows us to." He was concerned that the United States would mimic the ideology of the terrorists by unleashing violence because it thought that God was on its side.[37]

Phyllis and Orlando Rodriguez, like many others who lost loved ones on 9/11, also framed their views of post-9/11 politics in terms of their anguish. When they realized that the death of their son Greg and others at Ground Zero would soon be used as a rationale for starting a war in Afghanistan, they became upset. They did not want others to experience the misery they felt. Just three days after the 9/11 attacks, the couple circulated an email on the Internet titled "Not in Our Son's Name." They wrote about sharing their grief with their son's wife and friends, neighbors, and colleagues who worked with him. Instead of seeking revenge, however, they insisted in their Internet transmission that they wanted no revenge and no more suffering and dying perpetrated "in our son's name."[38]

The couple also wrote a letter directly to the president. They let him know their son was one of the victims at Ground Zero and that they had read about his request for congressional resolutions giving him "undefined power" to respond to the terror attacks. "Your response to this attack does not make us feel better," they exclaimed, "it makes us feel worse." These empathic patriots made it clear that they strenuously objected to the government taking actions that would cause suffering to parents in other lands in the name of their son. They told the chief executive that this was not the time for America to act as a bully and urged him in the strongest possible terms to develop peaceful solutions to terrorism, "solutions that do not sink us to the inhuman level of terrorists."[39]

Years later the Rodriguezes participated in the making of a documentary about their experience and the impact it had on their lives over time. Told from the perspective of distraught parents, the narrative opens with a recounting of Greg's death. He apparently had called his mother on 9/11 to tell her there was a fire at the World Trade Center but that he was fine. He asked her to relay that news to his wife. A period of profound mourning followed the loss of their son. For a time the couple became so numb that they stopped giving interviews because they brought waves of grief; it simply became too hard to speak of the tragedy at all. Two months after 9/11 on the occasion of Greg's birthday, Phyllis could not stop crying at all. Her daughter came to comfort her, but Orlando said they were a family that still had to figure out how to deal with the loss they endured. Phyllis was so upset by seeing the constant replays of the planes hitting the towers that she stopped watching television entirely for a time.

In 2006 Phyllis revealed that she felt an empathetic twinge for the mother of Zacarias Moussaoui, a French citizen put on trial for conspiring to plot the 9/11 attacks. Her response was not based on the facts of the trial but her perception of how mothers felt when their sons suffered. She was especially moved by the sight of Moussaoui's mother crying when she saw her son put into chains. Phyllis felt the man was also a victim, in this case, of "Islamists" who manipulated him and even a "scapegoat" of the Bush administration. Eventually Phyllis arranged to meet with Moussaoui's mother and the film depicts them embracing and developing a close relationship. The American woman insisted that they "were linked though suffering and sadness."[40]

Some went further than simply expressing their own thoughts and took more direct action to defend their empathic point of view. In November 2001, September 11 Families for Peaceful Tomorrows was formed by people like Potorti who had lost loved ones in the terrorist attacks. Convinced that war was not the answer and critical of Bush's decisions, they felt strongly that a War on Terror would not eliminate the root causes of terrorism, which they felt were social and economic difficulties that generated hatred and extremism. They also felt strongly that it would be preferable for the nation to look for more "life-giving" responses to the attack rather than simply give in to the emotions of fear and anger. Potorti explained that when searching for a name for their group, they came across Martin Luther King's 1967 speech on the Vietnam War, "Beyond Vietnam: A Time to Break Silence," in which the civil rights leader asserted that "wars are poor chisels for carving out peaceful tomorrows. One day we must come to see that peace is not merely a distant goal that we seek but a means by which we arrive at that goal."

In 2002 a delegation from Peaceful Tomorrows went to Afghanistan and visited the homes of some families directly harmed by American bombs. These war protesters wanted to raise awareness of the killing of innocent civilians from the American bombing in contrast to the vast public attention directed toward American victims on 9/11. During a ten-day visit, delegates met children whose domiciles were destroyed, who were not able to sleep due to nightmares, and who stopped talking completely. In hospitals they saw the effects of "cluster bombs" in the form of missing limbs and dead children. Witnessing the grim realities of war, Bodley, for one, came to feel that he had been "naive" before the American bombing began and had actually prayed there would be no civilian casualties. After visiting Afghanistan he came to the conclusion that there should never be wars again. By the end of their tour many participants issued critical appraisals of American media outlets that had referred to the bombing as "bloodless" and a "flawless use of sophisticated weapons." These citizens had seen with their own eyes how American bombs had "severely affected" common people in Afghanistan and brought them pain and distress.[41]

Predictably, questioning presidential war policies in the immediate aftermath of 9/11 was bound to stir controversy, and emails sent to the offices of Peaceful Tomorrows make the point clearly. One irate person wrote, "Congratulations on being the 'Jane Fondas for the Millennium,' and I mean that in the worst possible connotation. Your position is deplorable and your actions are disgusting. You have no education regarding war and the need for defending our country," the critic opined. One critic expressed condolences to members of the group for the loss of their loved ones but castigated their "liberal, victim position" as "pathetic." This writer insisted that members of the organization should have their citizenship revoked and be "jetted out of the country." Others told them they were ignorant of history and cited World War II as an example of how violence could solve problems. Often their compassion was attacked: "Refusing to fight and utterly capitulating to an enemy isn't 'compassionate' it's cowardly." Another writer charged Peaceful Tomorrows with "exploiting their dead relatives by forcing their anti-war agenda on people who can no longer speak for themselves." And an angry critic called members of the peace group "rich, chicken shit morons" who are "killing this country" by refusing to advocate a forceful response to terrorism.[42]

One month after the visit by Peaceful Tomorrows, Global Exchange, an international human rights group, organized another trip to Afghanistan in February 2002 to document the killing of innocent civilians. Global Exchange's team traveled to ten Afghan provinces and was able to chronicle some 824 Afghan civilian deaths at the time, although any count they made would not have been entirely accurate. Upon their return the group posted online photos and stories about some of the victims they had met. One narrative told of Amina, an eight-year-old girl in Kunduz province, who was in her kitchen preparing tea when her home came crashing down on her entire family. The child managed to climb out of the rubble and ran to her uncle's home for help. When her uncle and other relatives returned they found mostly body parts with the exception of Amina's father, who survived. Her mother and seven other children were killed as was her father's brother and his family, a total of sixteen family members in all. Amina told the visiting Americans that in addition to frequent headaches she "thinks of her mother all the time." Her father, "a humble cobbler," insisted that the Americans should help them because "they bombed our houses and killed our children."

In Qalaye Niazi, a village in Pakita province, a resident told the delegation that his relations were participating in a joyous wedding celebration for his brother when American planes attacked their village. The reporter, Janat, survived because he had temporarily left the village to run an errand. When he returned he said he saw blood and pieces of flesh everywhere. "I still don't know how many members of my family died on that day," he related. He searched the area for a week but claimed he was still unable to identify many of the corpses. "You would never believe there was a beautiful groom and bride here," he lamented; "you would think that such a day never existed." Estimates of the actual body count in the village differed widely. Some local observers claimed thirty-two people were killed. A United Nations observer said fifty-two residents were slaughtered, including twenty-five children. One report went as high as 107. A report in *The Guardian* in 2002 indicated that although the "US central command" claimed no collateral damage in the raid, there was plenty of evidence of civilian deaths that included not only human remains but "bloodied children's shoes and skirts, bloodied school books, the scalp of a woman with braided hair, butter toffees in red wrappers, and wedding decorations." The Pentagon said it had information that there were senior Taliban and al-Qaida officials at the site, but local villagers disputed that claim.[43]

Other peace organizations tried to rework the idea of patriotism itself as they looked for ways to stop the Bush administration's rush to war. Conservatives who backed Bush generally condemned the actions of groups who advocated pacifism or sympathy for those harmed by American actions as "anti-American." But ardent patriots who were also opponents of the war believed that their cause could be justified within another American tradition that was strongly compassionate. Their goal was to reorganize feelings in such a way that they would not be seen as antimilitary but primarily as citizens working within a humanitarian tradition. In the fall of 2001 the Women's International League for Peace and Freedom contended that the people of the world were watching closely to see what the United States would do after the terrorist attacks. The group appealed for leaders to demonstrate a resolve to maintain traditions of democracy and respect for all people and "break the cycle of violence and retribution." In response to the launching of the bombing in Afghanistan a number of peace groups, often referencing the antiwar movements against the Vietnam War, pleaded for a "higher form of patriotism" that would oppose war and brutality and the tendency to praise such actions. Other organizations such as the American Friends Service Committee, the Fellowship of Reconciliation, and Pax Christi also took up the charge to reorient patriotism from the pursuit of violence to the quest for improved human relations. These groups did not deny that the United States had a "just cause" for war after the horror of 9/11 but felt in Afghanistan it was waging its fight in an unjust manner that led to the killing of the guiltless.[44]

Pax Christi, a Catholic peace organization, sent a letter to Bush in November 2001 that articulated its reasons for resisting the assault on Afghanistan. It argued that bombing raids and ground attacks, especially the use of cluster bombs that killed indiscriminately, had made an already existing humanitarian disaster in which millions of Afghan people were struggling to survive in deteriorating weather conditions much worse. The peace group claimed that war only begets more war and suffering; it also affirmed that such violence would not stop terrorist activities that were, in their view, spawned by despair and exclusion. "We cannot use God's name to justify the recourse to violence," the letter stated; "priority must be given to non-violent means." Pax Christi also mounted a critique of globalization, which it blamed for contributing to a rising disparity in wealth between rich and poor nations that provokes feelings of anger and frustration. In their newsletter the organization chastised American bombing runs for making it more difficult to get relief aid to struggling people and appeared exasperated by the fact that Bush had declared that the nation was not at war with the Afghan people when the reality of the attacks had created a "humanitarian crisis" there.[45]

In February of 2002 the U.S. Catholic Bishops issued a pastoral letter titled "Living with Faith and Honor after September 11th," which called for a review of the government's response to terrorism and condemned "indiscriminate attacks on innocent people" in cities like Kabul and Kandahar. The prelates stressed that, like other Americans, they certainly shared the sense of "loss and pain, anger and fear, and shock and determination" that resulted from 9/11. The bishops also expressed their admiration for the "selflessness" of the firefighters, police, and other brave individuals who gave their lives to save others. They acknowledged that the "dreadful deeds" of 9/11 certainly could not go unanswered, but they urged "restraint" and greater attention to the root causes of terrorist activity which they felt, along with others, were poverty and injustice. Finally, they made a plea that now seemed necessary in a world divided between good citizens and "evil doers" and asserted that "every life is precious whether a person works at the World Trade Center or lives in Afghanistan."

These prelates also placed a special responsibility on American leaders charged with leading the nation's course of action in troubled times. They offered prayer and consolation for all Americans who were risking their lives in Afghanistan and for those who suffered in the homeland as well. Yet, they felt "national leaders" bear a "moral burden" to explore as many nonviolent responses to the situation as possible. "Even if the cause is just," the bishops wrote, "the grave moral obligation to respect the principles of non-combatant immunity and proportionality remain in force and must govern our nation's political and military decisions." They understood that military force could be directed at those who employ terrorism but "not at the Afghan people."[46]

Few public leaders seemed to heed the prelate's call and publicly question the administration's Afghanistan policy, but Barbara Lee, who represented Oakland, California, in Congress, expressed grave reservations over the move to a global war. Lee was the only member of Congress to vote against a joint resolution that authorized the president to take military action against "nations, organizations, or persons" that were determined to be linked to the September 11th attacks or gave refuge to terrorists who might perpetrate future attacks. Lee worried that the bill actually constituted a "blank check" that would allow the president and his successors to attack any country or enemy for an unspecified period of time; on a personal level she also made it clear that she simply did not trust Bush.

Not surprisingly, Lee's position provoked support from empathic patriots and derision from war-based loyalists. One backer of the congresswoman wrote that she feared American forces will ignore their moral compass and go in search of an enemy that may prove very elusive and that "more innocent people in Afghanistan, Iraq, and Pakistan will fall victim." Another supporter argued that the United States would become like the terrorists themselves if it bombed Kabul and killed people oppressed by the Taliban dictatorship who had no part in the decision to harbor terrorists' operations in that country. Others told Lee that the administration had to take a more cautious approach to fighting terrorism rather than starting a war against "unknown adversaries at unknown costs." "In these days of grief there seems to be a madness afoot," one citizen wrote, "and far too many people have been swept up by their anger and have lost touch with the their basic faculties of judgment." Many agreed with Lee that the president should not be handed a blank check and that a more "measured response" was warranted.

Lee's critics rejected her expressions of caution and felt the circumstances warranted extreme measures. Her opponents argued that the nation had no choice but to enter a warlike state and that this member of Congress did not understand the severity of the threat the nation faced. One letter writer, who identified as a "peaceful person" who abhorred gun violence, was certain that the United States had to do all that it could to protect its children from harm. One of Lee's constituents declared that it was time to "take the sword and slay that plague of a peaceful society." The congresswoman's African American heritage also evoked racist remarks. One writer asked her if she would have been more supportive of war if more blacks had been killed on 9/11. Another called her an "American dog—a black mutt" and told her to find another country to live in.[47]

Pearl Harbor

It was common for many Americans, including the president, to compare the 9/11 attacks to Pearl Harbor, a response that implicitly endorsed any decision to enter a global war again. The similarities with the attack in Hawaii and much of the World War II narrative were striking. The nation was shocked by the surprise bombings in 1941 that led to a war that resulted in the killing of unprecedented numbers of innocent civilians and military personnel. Both the spot where the Twin Towers fell and the one where the first atomic bomb exploded were now referred to as Ground Zero. George Bush went so far as to dub 9/11 the "Pearl Harbor of the twenty-first century." On the sixtieth anniversary of Pearl Harbor in December 2001, he asserted that 9/11 would now stand alongside Pearl Harbor as a moment "when our way of life again was brutally and suddenly attacked." Public opinion polls showed considerable support for the decision of both Bush and Franklin Roosevelt to respond militarily, but there was one significant difference between the two presidents' rhetorical responses to war. Bush talked about the need to meet threats to the nation but stressed that any form of retaliation would not require a significant amount of sacrifice on the part of citizens and urged Americans to continue to enjoy their everyday lives. Roosevelt made it clear that citizens would be faced with immense challenges as an entire nation mobilized for war and was unflinching about the grim realities citizens would face. For Roosevelt the painful realities of warfare could not be concealed.[48]

While the idea of war was already a significant part of the public consciousness to a much greater extent before Pearl Harbor than it was prior to 9/11, both attacks generated a good deal of anger and cravings for retaliation— cornerstones of a war-based patriotism. The 1941 interviews conducted by the Library of Congress with ordinary citizens make this abundantly clear. A World War I veteran told interviewers that he fought in 1917 for democracy but now wanted to fight "with hate in my heart." He said he now looked forward to killing the Japanese and claimed that if he came across one who was wounded he would pass that person by. His patriotic fervor was so heated, he insisted that he would kill his own father if he opposed America and even advocated chasing "every damn skunk—German, Russian, the Japanese" now in the United States back to where they came from. A respondent in Madison, Wisconsin, asserted that "the Japs or any other enemy with whom they may be aligned will find us a determined, united people ready to fight to the finish, their finish." Another man in Burlington, North Carolina, now dreamed of a day when "Tokyo would be set afire . . . a fire like nobody ever heard tell of. . . . I don't care if they burn."[49]

A small sample of African American voices in the 1941 interviews suggested that blacks responded by affirming their loyalty to the United States as well. Interviewed in a billiard hall in the nation's capital, one man noted that he had fought for America in the past and would do so again. "There's never been in the annals of American history a black man being a traitor," he asserted. He noted that white people like Benedict Arnold "have always been traitors." A bricklayer felt that now that the country was at war everyone regardless of race should be patriotic and support the president. Regarding Japan, he expressed the hope that America would "wipe her off the face of the earth." The Reverend W. J. Faulkner, a black minister, argued that the races had been divided too long at home and that he hoped now all people in the country would unite into an "invincible army of patriots who will work for the triumph of Christian democracy and brotherhood throughout the world."[50]

The fact that America and its president moved directly from the 9/11 attacks into a War on Terror should not obscure the reality that not all Americans stood united behind the decision to go to war. A sense of revenge was natural under the circumstances, and long-standing ideals of a war-based patriotism stood ready to justify any battles to come. In the fall of 2001, many citizens and their leaders found reassurance in traditional symbols of American patriotism like the flag. Yet for many others such emblems failed to eradicate their confusion or assuage their concerns over the prospect of more violence. Many citizens and peace organizations pointed out that while America had a right to defend itself, it could not presume it had free hand to shoot and kill at its own discretion. Human welfare still mattered to citizens whose loyalty was centered as much on a concern for others as it was on a desire to remain safe from attacks. The battles over what it meant to be a loyal American, revived in the immediate aftermath of the attacks and then in reaction to sending the military to Afghanistan, escalated and expanded in a variety of venues and formats as citizens pondered how to commemorate 9/11 and memorialize its victims.

· ·

The terrorist attacks of September 11, 2001, produced countless memorial projects in the United States, and many incorporated the names of the dead into their design. Earlier commemorative styles like the Tomb of the Unknown Soldier dedicated in 1921 tended to downplay the tragic fate of the singular person and staked "their commemorative claim" on the nobility and moral grandeur of the soldier's sacrifice for the welfare of the nation. This changed with the erection of the Vietnam Veterans Memorial in 1982. Scholars like Kirk Savage note that the Vietnam memorial was not intended to restore a time-honored faith in the nation and its future after years of killing and dying, but was instead meant to be therapeutic and "heal a collective psychological injury" caused by the reality of American suffering and the contentious politics of the era. This was, at base, empathic patriotism put into practice. At the memorial, often called "the wall," visitors were invited to reflect upon the tragic consequences of the war rather than be told a heroic tale about the American expedition in Southeast Asia or, for that matter, receive a reaffirming message about America's virtue. In privileging a design driven by empathic rather than war-based patriotism, the Vietnam Veterans Memorial sparked a fierce dispute over the nature of loyalty that would be a harbinger of what would come during the War on Terror.[1]

In suggesting that the public memorialization of war has become more attuned to registering the grim realities of combat and human suffering, scholars have inferred that it has become less mythical. Bearing witness to the fate of the individual and to the blood Americans shed has clearly undermined older efforts to transform human pain into some grand artistic form. Roland Barthes has famously noted how myth depoliticizes our perspectives and certainly our historical imaginations, simplifying the complex realities and contentious interests that mark political life in the past and in the present. Memorial projects inevitably become embroiled in this fundamental project to renovate the legacy of suffering and death by inventing ways to mourn losses and, for that matter, to decide just who the objects of our grief shall be. Consider for a moment the legendary version of America's role in World War II. It is a narrative centered on the impeccable virtue of the generation that fought the conflict more than on the pain and cynicism many felt in the 1940s over the death of loved ones or the way they were treated in the military. This is not to say that a patriotic version has no basis in truth; it is more the case that a long political struggle to make sense of World War II and commemorate it has largely ended with the triumph of a narrative that is highly mythical and less therapeutic than the one inscribed on the Vietnam wall. A war-based patriotism has come to overshadow one that is more empathic. In fact, it is fair to say that in the time that Americans considered memorializing 9/11, they lived not only under the spell of the Vietnam Veterans Memorial but under the cultural legacy of American virtue that was enshrined by the celebration of "the Good War" in the 1990s and the elation of winning the recently completed Cold War. This meant that although the impulse to recall the victimization associated with 9/11 was powerful, the need to restore hope in the power of the nation to create both heroic citizens and beneficial futures remained an influential goal.

This tension between the conflicting needs to recall human tragedy and elevate it to a higher plane or even forget it completely was most blatantly evident at Ground Zero in New York. At this central site of remembrance regarding the War on Terror, the names of individuals killed on 9/11 are prominently displayed. Indeed, the rules of the competition that led to the final memorial design for the site required individual recognition of those who died in New York (including six who died in a 1993 attack at the World Trade Center), at the Pentagon, and in Shanksville, Pennsylvania. Yet in surrounding the final display of names with the sounds and views of rushing water, a tree-lined plaza, and towering skyscrapers, this site of remembrance also appropriated personal loss in order to serve larger social and political needs. When journalist Maureen Dowd saw the submissions of the finalists for the memorial at Ground Zero in 2003, she lamented that they "prettified" the horror of 9/11 and failed to capture the real grief and anger that Americans felt. Today, at Ground Zero, her initial thoughts have been realized.[2]

Actually the permanent memorials that have already been built to the victims of 9/11 in places such as Lower Manhattan, the Pentagon, and Shanksville do not constitute a first response to the problem of how the attacks and the carnage they brought should be remembered. Such a reaction was seen long before anything of permanence could be erected in the spontaneous memorials that sprouted up at various sites throughout the nation. In the time before dead individuals could be honored and appropriated for public purposes, private citizens mounted a wide range of images, objects, and messages in all sorts of places. These makeshift remembrances appeared in fields, on fences, alongside fire stations, and on street corners. They revealed that the first commemorative impulse was a knee-jerk response to trauma and rupture and the confusion they brought. Complex negotiations between powerful political interests that sought to replace or at least temper feelings generated by a sudden sense of shock and alarm came later. Indeed, it would not be a stretch to argue that the permanent memorials that have appeared in many locations since 2001 represent an attempt to discipline the wild assortment of painful emotions that popped up at impromptu sites and bring about a remembrance of 9/11 that was more orderly and useful in efforts to downplay the violence of the War on Terror itself.[3]

Spontaneous commemorative actions are essentially acts of resistance. They emanate from attitudes in which people suddenly feel unstrapped from traditional ideas of authority and key relationships in their lives. They express spirits that are not always part of romantic myths such as the nobility of dying for one's country, although it is possible for them to endorse such ideals as well. Untethered, people feel free to express themselves in any way they see fit. Essentially these first-stage acts of remembrance are driven mostly by the fractures violence brings to everyday life. George Bush's decision to embark upon a global war on terror was a coherent political strategy; New York City's final plan to redevelop Ground Zero around concepts of commercial development was another. But the people who pasted a photo of a missing loved one on a wall after the 9/11 attacks or attached a baseball cap to a fence in a field near Shanksville after Flight 93 crashed were not so sure of what had just happened, how best to commemorate the past, or whether a war was even necessary. Their sense of remembrance was not "strategic" or focused on images and messages that offered a degree of consolation or restored faith in the nation and its ability to administer a better future for all. Rather, they were trying to come to terms with the distress they felt or "learning to live with loss." Their remembrance was unsettled and often focused on the question of how the dead could be remembered rather than on acts that hastened their erasure from public memory or plans for how they could be put in the service of larger national objectives.[4]

New York City

The earliest commemorations of the terrorist attacks on September 11, 2001, in New York were initiated by men and women who had just witnessed the devastation and now frantically sought some clue as to the whereabouts of those they held near and dear. Moods of private anguish dominated public expressions of remembrance. Posters attached to walls throughout the city were dramatic examples of this response. These flyers were partially a reaction to rumors that many of the workers at the Twin Towers were injured and lying unidentified in the city's hospitals. That is why many were placed on walls near medical facilities. Regrettably, those rumors were later discredited by the knowledge that few survived the collapse of the buildings. Posters did not frame the missing in mythical or heroic terms, although many saw first responders as heroes. Mostly they offered basic information on those who disappeared—name, age, height, place of work—along with a photograph. They encased the tragedy in terms of personal loss or an extreme sense of dread people felt over not knowing the fate of those they cared for deeply. At their most fundamental level, they understood 9/11 not as an attack on America but as a stunning end to loving relationships that defined their private lives.

Evidence of personal heartache and mourning were widespread in the city in the aftermath of such a catastrophic event. Candles burned everywhere. Jordan Schuster, a student at New York University, spontaneously decided to tape large panels of butcher paper on the pavement near Union Square where people could "write messages of grief, outrage, and remembrance." At a handball court in the Inwood section of Manhattan, a shrine was created to honor Brian Monaghan, a local carpenter who died in the collapsed buildings. The *New York Times* began a series of short pieces called "Portraits of Grief" that offered brief biographies of the missing and the dead with reporters identifying their subjects from the posters hanging around town and then followed up with calls to their families. Mostly these vignettes recorded basic details of a person's life with glimpses into matters of family, work, and leisure. There was, to be sure, a touch of the heroic in some stories. One notice told of Andrew Desperito, a fireman, who in his "final hours" escorted a woman to safety from the North Tower, and another noted that John D'Allara, a policeman, never hesitated to save people or even animals from harm. Even more powerful was the way the stories sometimes exposed the private realm of suffering and pain such as the reality of children losing parents who loved them. One woman recounted how she had given her firefighter/spouse a kiss before he left for work on 9/11 and told him to be careful. Another man explained how he could no longer drive over the Verrazano-Narrows Bridge because it forced him to look in the direction of Ground Zero where his wife had perished. The popularity of these stories, certainly innovative forms of obituaries, demonstrated an empathic dimension to public mourning that was possible in a culture less constrained by the forces of tradition and myth.[5]

People tapped the inner recesses of their hearts and souls to perform thousands of impulsive commemorative acts. In the first year after the tragedy many traveled to lower Manhattan to erect improvised memorials that reflected an array of opinions and feelings over how the attacks and the victims should be understood and remembered. Banners, signs, flowers, teddy bears, baseball hats, photos of the dead, and a host of religious symbols such as votive candles, crosses, and angels were placed by fire stations or buildings in Lower Manhattan. Paul Johnson has described what he calls an "altar" erected several blocks from Ground Zero that consisted of a wooden cross with a red, white, and blue banner below it containing the words "God Bless America" and silhouettes of the Towers. A large plastic angel was placed under each tower. At this site a Christian nativity scene, a Hindu image of Ganesha, and a Yankee baseball cap could also be seen. Johnson noted the religious nature of many of these objects but also made the astute observation that this more popular form of American religious belief lacked the coherent political agenda that Americans had used for decades to justify major military campaigns and impart to them the approval of God. President Bush had done as much to launch the battle against terrorism. At Ground Zero the deployment of popular religious icons demonstrated a more diffuse cultural response that invoked narratives and beliefs people held about death. Ordinary people turned to religious faith simply as a healing aid to endure traumatic times and not as a justification for a war.[6]

Seth Low, who interviewed schoolchildren about their reaction to 9/11, astutely argued that in the aftermath of the attacks people turned to "less regimented" sites like Union Square or even a handball court and to unconventional suggestions for commemorating the event. Four months after the attacks, many students told Low that they were ready to move on from what had happened. Some called for building a new Yankee Stadium and higher buildings than the ones that were lost to show that the attacks had only made New York stronger. One student wanted to build five buildings in a circle at the site that would be connected by colored rings with a memorial of some kind in the center. A few students wanted a piece of the original tower put into any memorial to show that New York was moving on and was not just going to create a cemetery to remember what happened. Another young student suggested that "two hollow towers open to tourists with glass elevators and a memorial at the bottom" be created at the site.[7]

One religious symbol that attracted considerable attention was a cross formed from steel beams that had fallen in the collapse of the towers. During the operation to clear debris and search for human remains at Ground Zero, Frank Silecchia, a worker at the site, discovered the structure and took it as a sign that God had not abandoned citizens like him in the aftermath of such terrible evil. A few days after his discovery, Silecchia saw a Franciscan priest, Father Brian Jordan, blessing human remains at the site and asked him if he wanted to see "God's house." The cleric too was moved by the sight of the cross standing amid the rubble and soon persuaded city officials to put the religious symbol on a concrete pedestal where he could offer services. Jordan quickly became known as the "chaplain of the hard hats." Whenever work crews felt the need for a blessing or a prayer, Father Jordan fulfilled it. He even tended to the needs of relatives of the many victims who visited the site. Pete Dutro, a tattoo artist who went to offer his services free to visitors at Ground Zero, later said that most people asked that the image of the cross be inscribed on their bodies, more than the national flag or the names of victims. They told him repeatedly that they wanted a tattoo so that they would never forget the events of 9/11.

Today the cross sits underground inside the 9/11 Memorial and Museum at Ground Zero. Museum text explains that workers engaged in the cleanup "struggled to come to terms with the horrific circumstances" in which they worked. They were particularly intent on making sense of the reality of human remains all around them and the reality of "utter destruction." The cross, for these workers, became a source of "comfort" and "solace." Locating the symbol in the museum, however, proved to be a difficult process. Joshua Chadajo, executive director of the Coalition for Jewish Concerns, argued that it had no place in a national museum because it did not represent the religious beliefs of a number of the victims. He asserted as well that had the steel beams somehow ended up in the shape of the Star of David, it would not have attained such public significance. A court case brought by a group called American Atheists actually tried to stop the museum from exhibiting the cross, but a federal appeals court rejected their claim, affirming that it was historical in nature and did not intentionally discriminate against anyone.[8]

The proliferation of private sentiments did not necessarily mean that traditional patriotic myths were cast aside. On the contrary, threads of traditional patriotic feeling and imagery were deployed everywhere after 9/11, a sign of how thoroughly they had been incorporated into the body and soul of so many citizens. A war-based patriotism was not simply challenged in this public response as much as it was forced to share cultural space with a variety of other sentiments and thoughts. American flags were widely displayed with some surveys suggesting between 74 percent and 82 percent of Americans affixed the flag to the outside of their home. Todd Gitlin, a former student radical and antiwar protester from the 1960s, now felt the need to hang a flag from his window in New York. Gitlin remarked that he took inspiration from the actions of the passengers on Flight 93 that most likely saved numerous lives in Washington, D.C. At "United We Stand" rallies in various cities and towns, people dressed in red, white, and blue and marched alongside firefighters and police officers. The slogan also appeared on official license plates in several states. Radio stations played both songs of patriotism and consolation such as Lee Greenwood's recording of "God Bless the U.S.A." and Simon and Garfunkel's "Bridge over Troubled Waters." At Ground Zero itself, a symbolic flag-raising, echoing the iconic image of a similar flag-raising on Iwo Jima in 1945, captured enormous public attention. In the immediate aftermath of the fall of the Twin Towers, a news photo of three New York firefighters hoisting the flag amid the smoking ruins projected an image of loyalty and strength in a society filled with emotional turmoil.[9]

Ground Zero

Ground Zero was a mess after the collapse of the Twin Towers. Twisted steel, broken glass, and human remains littered the space and created a gigantic pile of rubble. This sense of utter destruction and chaos drove not only impulsive commemorative acts but a larger effort toward a "strategic remembrance" suited to meet the needs of powerful political interests in the present. The grassroots effort to come to terms with the horror of what had just happened was soon joined by leading city officials who wanted to move away from the harsh reality of a traumatic event and the anarchy of feelings that circulated in the city. Even as crews went about the massive cleanup and family members trekked to the ruins in hopes of finding some evidence of what had happened to a cherished friend or relative, public officials began to articulate their own commemorative views. Ed Koch, a former mayor, advocated constructing replicas of the buildings that were lost. Workers at the cleanup site were apparently split on Koch's suggestion; some agreed with it and others favored the creation of a memorial park. Rudolph Giuliani, the mayor of the city in 2001, had a plan of his own. Moved by feelings of distress and anguish at the time, Giuliani argued that the space should become a "magnificent memorial" whose design "comes from the heart." He meant that the pain felt by the victims' families had to be recognized in some way at the site that had become "the final resting place of their loved ones." He also argued that any commemoration had to contain an appropriate sense of national history, for he saw this location as "hallowed ground" like Normandy or Gettysburg. In his mind, and in the minds of many, traumatic losses needed to be respected but also attached to some traditional ideal of combative heroism and loyalty. Looking down into the vast pit left after debris was carted from the pile of ruins, the New York mayor remarked that site gave him not only a feeling of sorrow but "a tremendous feeling of patriotism."[10]

In 2001 the governor of New York, George Pataki, established the Lower Manhattan Development Corporation (LMDC) to organize efforts to re-build on the site of the fallen towers. It was at this point that a mélange of private and even patriotic emotions would be forced to accommodate elites striving to restore the city's image as a commercial center. Neither Pataki nor Giuliani was ready to cede the space to the idea some families of vic-tims held that it should simply recall and honor the dead. The unvarnished exposure of raw grief and emotion was simply too threatening to elites and patriotic interests. Pataki like Giuliani was looking to find a way to add elements of historical significance and national virtue to the site. Along with many others, the governor also feared a migration of business activity from the city if moneymaking space was not rebuilt quickly; he was keen to reclaim the skyline and restore the current of commerce that had been disrupted. This multiplicity of goals led to a process by which the LMDC held two competitions, one for an overall design of the site itself and an-other specifically focused on the creation of a memorial. The winning blue-print for the entire sixteen-acre site was crafted by Daniel Libeskind, an architect working in Berlin, who had immigrated to New York as a child and expressed the classic immigrant reverence for the nation as a re-nowned land of opportunity and freedom. Libeskind's original plan proved popular, in part because it sought to blend several goals including the de-sire for the recovery of commercial space, the invocation of patriotic imag-ery, and the need to recognize the tremendous loss of life.[11]

Called "Memory Foundations," Libeskind's site plan included a sky-scraper topped by a spire that would eventually reach the historically sig-nificant height of 1,776 feet. The building itself contained design features intended to evoke the image of the nearby Statue of Liberty, a structure he called a "global symbol of optimism." Enterprise and patriotism were to be joined by a museum that would wrap around the sacred footprints of the Twin Towers. For Libeskind the footprints of the towers would best be left as open pits inviting visitors to gaze down at bedrock that had supported them. The object of their gaze, however, in Libeskind's mind, would not be the rock layers themselves but a giant slurry or retaining wall that had been built to hold back the waters of the Hudson River. The slurry wall was significant because it had been one of the few structures of any kind to survive the crushing collapse of the towers or what the architect called "unimaginable trauma." He felt the wall symbolized the durability of American democracy itself. Architectural critic Philip Noble has argued that although a specific competition for a memorial at the site was yet to take place, the slurry walls represented Libeskind's concept of what such a memorial should be. The renowned architect also included a special feature called the "Wedge of Light" which was essentially a triangular-shaped plaza in front of a transit center to be constructed at the location. The idea was to have sunlight flood the plaza each year on September 11th in such a way that the rays of the morning sun would strike the floor of this public space at the precise points they would have illuminated it on 9/11/01.[12]

The rationale Libeskind offered for his overall concept revealed a great deal about the process of memorialization in general and issues central to the reworking of Ground Zero in particular. Although he clearly accepted the popular feeling in New York that the skyline had to be reclaimed in some manner and that commercial activity needed to be reactivated, he enveloped his overall plan with the rhetoric of patriotic memory that had long been a powerful influence in shaping public remembrance in America. The contemporary Americanization of the Holocaust that included stories of American soldiers helping to liberate some of the "death camps" and the opening of the United States Holocaust Memorial Museum in the nation's capital actually helped to shape the rationale Libeskind offered for his design. He stressed the fact that his parents were Holocaust survivors who eventually cast their lot with America by emigrating to New York in 1959. As a young boy he said he recalled his first sight of the Statue of Liberty and claimed he had never forgot how it symbolized freedom. "If you are an immigrant kid it is the most incredible sight," he wrote. Libeskind also made it clear that his deep connection to the persecution of European Jews had sensitized him to many of the issues relevant at Ground Zero. "Because of who I am I have thought a lot about matters like trauma and history," he affirmed. He believed his work in Berlin had also made him sensitive to the problem of deciding how much the signs of a painful past could be preserved in public and how much they could actually be erased. Consequently his site plan included not only an acknowledgment of 1776, the year the Declaration of Independence was proclaimed, but an unadorned look at the extent of destruction by showing all that remained of the towers was bedrock and the slurry wall.

Perspectives on Ground Zero could never be the sole preserve of influential officials or imaginative architects, however. And patriotic rhetoric could not always placate the feelings of all family members who lost loved ones at the site. Many (but not all) relatives of the dead saw Ground Zero not as a site for commercial development but as a graveyard and a sacred spot that still contained the traces of those they loved. People who lost loved ones were intent to see that nothing done at Ground Zero would obliterate the legacy of loss that occurred there and its harsh consequences for them. Organizations such as the 9–11 Widow's and Victim's Family Association, for instance, worked to see that "financial or political interests" did not dominate the final decisions on the remaking of Ground Zero. The fact that the remains of 1,113 individuals of the 2,752 who were killed were never found continued to cast a pall over any discussion of how the city could redevelop the site. In recognition of the impact of mass death, Mayor Giuliani set up a procedure that allowed relatives of the dead to receive an urn containing dust from the rubble at Ground Zero. The LMDC did organize a Families Advisory Council consisting of relatives of the victims who were intent on seeing that a memorial at the site would convey honor and reverence for the dead, an idea that was actually hotly contested at times by one member of the LMDC board who wanted to ensure that any memorial space did not dominate commercial uses of the area. Tensions between advocates of the sacred and the secular did not go away, but when the LMDC initiated its specific competition for a memorial, only one representative of the grieving families ended up on the jury. This did not stop members of the September 11 Families Association, however, from trying to influence the final selection; Lee Ielpi, a retired New York City fireman who had searched Ground Zero for signs of his son's remains, and other members of the association lobbied to see that at least the footprints of the original Twin Towers, a distinct reminder of loss, were left untouched and preserved.[13]

The depth of feelings of many family groups was evident in their determined opposition to a proposal to build an International Freedom Center in one corner of the sixteen-acre Ground Zero site. The idea was to build a museum that included not only exhibits pertaining to the 9/11 attacks but displays that recounted the horrors of previous incidents of hatred and intolerance such as the oppression of Native Americans and the treatment of slaves in the United States and the unfortunate consequences they brought. The idea for the museum came largely from Tom Bernstein, a New York City developer and former business partner of President George W. Bush. Another Bush associate, Roland Betts, actually ended up on the board of the LMDC. Bernstein and others saw the ideal of freedom as one that stood opposed to the intolerant outlooks that drove terrorism in the first place and felt it deserved a special place in any commemoration of the attacks.

History lessons, no matter how valuable and relevant, were still seen by some family members as an intrusion into space that was considered sacred. There were also concerns that the implications of showing horrifying events from the American past such as slavery would unnecessarily tarnish the highly virtuous view of America at a time when it was at war in Afghanistan and Iraq. Public opposition to the center spiked with the publication of an article by Debra Burlingame in the *Wall Street Journal* on June 7, 2005. Burlingame, whose brother was the captain of the American Airlines flight that crashed into the Pentagon on 9/11, attacked the Freedom Center as "inappropriate and unpatriotic." Motivated to become a "witness for my brother," she had helped found 9/11 Families for a Safe and Strong America, a group that not only mourned lost loved ones but also supported the agenda of the war-based patriotism of the Bush administration. Burlingame was incensed by almost any effort to memorialize the site in a way that would diminish the aggressive patriotic feelings of 2001 when people carried "hand-painted signs of national unity" and "faded flags" and told stories of "unbearable heartache and unimaginable courage." She was particularly furious at the prospect that visitors to the site might be subjected to a "slanted history lesson" or a didactic lecture on the meaning of freedom instead of a respectful tribute to our "individual and collective loss." In her mind people would visit the site primarily because they saw what had happened on 9/11 and because they wanted to be at the place where "heroes died." Joining her feelings of sorrow to a spirit of patriotic revenge, she complained that dispensing stories of past genocides and exploitation "over the ashes of Ground Zero is like creating a Museum of Tolerance over the sunken graves of the USS Arizona."

Burlingame was also contemptuous of some of the individuals who were pushing the idea of the center in the first place. Basically she felt that they did not deserve to receive federal subsidies such a project might bring because they had been outspoken critics of Bush's policies. Thus, she chastised Bernstein for making "inflammatory claims of a deliberate torture policy at Guantanamo Bay" and felt such accusations impeded America's war to vanquish terrorism and foster freedom in the world. She also noted that Bernstein was a human rights activist—apparently an unforgivable transgression—who had filed a lawsuit against Donald Rumsfeld, the secretary of defense, on behalf of detainees in Iraq and Afghanistan. Eric Foner, whom she labeled a "radical-left history professor," also came under fire for attacking what he felt was the "apocalyptic rhetoric" of the Bush White House. Michael Posner, another human rights activist, was chastised for leading an international effort to "Stop Torture Now." The controversy over the center led by some family members and the impact of Burlingame's essay finally caused New York governor George Pataki to remove the Freedom Center from Ground Zero planning completely.[14]

Although Libeskind had won the competition for the Ground Zero master plan, a second competition was held in order to select the memorial itself. Michael Arad and Peter Walker submitted the winning design, named "Reflecting Absence." Their basic idea was to preserve the sense of devastation and loss that took place at Ground Zero by leaving the footprints of the towers visible. Arad's and Walker's footprints, however, no longer offered somber visions of rocks and a huge retaining wall but more pleasing vistas of massive pools with water continuously cascading down their sides. Arad felt that the pools represented "voids" that would also foster a deep sense of "contemplation" of lives that were lost at the spot. His original idea also called for ramps that would allow visitors to descend to the bottom of the pools where they could peer through the falling water and ponder the emptiness that had been left by the collapse of the Twin Towers. In essence this concept obliterated Libeskind's hopes for a more rustic memorial design centered on the slurry walls and exposed bedrock that still stood strong after everything else had been reduced to debris. As most of the literature on this topic makes clear, however, commercial interests driving the execution of a plan for Ground Zero worked assiduously to alter much of what Libeskind and Arad and Walker had crafted. Because of security concerns for the structure and the desires of architectural rivals, Libeskind's Freedom Tower was never built in its original form; "Reflecting Absence" was also altered in time. Walkways to the bottom of the pools were taken out. The empty spaces he had imagined at ground level that surrounded the pools were eventually filled with trees meant to serve as symbols of rebirth.[15]

Controversies over what to do with the footprints and the representation of human death consumed a great deal of attention among those charged with selecting a final memorial design. Maya Lin, who designed the Vietnam Veterans Memorial, and James Young, a scholar who served on the German commission to select a Holocaust memorial in Berlin, now served on the jury to select the 9/11 memorial. They felt strongly that any memorial at Ground Zero should not only remember lives lost but suggest the possibilities of renewal as well—"remembrance and reconstruction." Young has argued that he felt Ground Zero accomplished this goal by re-membering 9/11 as much more than a "permanent breech in our lives." Thus, the devastation conveyed by the footprints in "Reflecting Absence" was essential in his view but ultimately had to be tempered by the sooth-ing effects of falling water and the impact of surrounding trees meant to suggest regeneration. Obviously the existence of a new skyscraper also conveys a sense of moving on. It was this way of thinking that caused ju-rists like Lin and Young to take a more critical view of one of the designs that competed against "Reflecting Absence." In a plan titled "Passages of Light: Memorial Cloud," visitors' eyes would be drawn downward to the names of the dead imprinted in a radiating circle of light on the floor and upward to a large "crystalline cloud" or canopy. Jurists tended to feel that the spectacular architectural effect of the canopy would detract too much from idea of loss itself which the footprints suggested and the legacy of death and destruction that needed to remain at the site.[16]

Some critics like Marita Sturken have insightfully suggested that a balance between commemoration and commerce was never achieved at Ground Zero. For her the "fetishizing of the footprints of the two towers" was not about achieving harmony between remembering and moving for-ward but represented a "modernist" attempt to push away the reality of death and destruction into a more abstract realm. "Footprints" for her rep-resented a replacement of the truth of the rubble and, perhaps, body parts themselves. She noted that even figures of first responders do not dot this landscape (something that has evoked criticism from New York firemen and policemen) and the Slurry Wall can only be seen in an underground museum in a much more antiseptic environment. Sturken's point was that modern American culture was inclined to "step back" from the harsh reali-ties of trauma and, thus, not as willing to register the pain of human loss as it might be. For her people waving "small flags as a sign of our patriotism" or buying souvenirs at sites of mass death like Ground Zero falsely reassured the public that as a society we could "contain and control" the devastating impact of violence and trauma in our lives. Today Ground Zero demonstrates this with trees, waterfalls, soaring buildings, a transit center, and a mu-seum that helps to organize knowledge of what took place. Author Paul

Goldberger has observed that Ground Zero was never going to achieve the "grandeur, clarity and purity" of the Washington Monument. In part, of course, this was due to the conflict of interests that met in New York to decide what to do with this space. But to the extent that it is able to hide the unpleasantness of the past, Ground Zero does share some similarities to the obelisk in our nation's capital.[17]

There is no mention of the terrorist attacks on the plaza at Ground Zero. The details of the tragedy that befell New York on 9/11 can only be found underground at the National September 11 Memorial Museum which opened in 2014 and which is located near the footprints and Liberty Tower. The names of the dead from the towers, first responders, and victims from the plane crashes and those who worked at the Pentagon are engraved on bronze parapets at the waterfalls, but visitors do not learn directly why they died. The idea for a museum began to take shape in 2006 partly in response to the failure of the Freedom Center to attract sufficient support. According to Urban Anthropologist Elizabeth Greenspan, members of the LMDC began working with consultants to expand upon Arad's idea of an "interpretive center" and formulated a plan for a facility that would not only educate people about what took place in 2001 but honor the victims as well. Greenspan correctly pointed out that the museum became the antithesis of the Freedom Center, for it devoted most of its exhibits to the day of the attack; efforts to consider the larger significance of what 9/11 might have meant or steps that could be taken to improve America's relations with potential adversaries were eschewed.

This is not surprising, because eleven of the museum's board members were relatives of the victims, including Debra Burlingame. The "big politics" of the time—the rise of al-Qaeda, the onset of wars in Afghanistan and Iraq—receive scant attention. There are brief references to Guantánamo on a time line of events near the Slurry Wall and a photo of Osama bin Laden recruiting adherents, but all of this could easily be missed. Visitors can also watch a short feature on those who perpetrated the attacks. In 2015, outside the main flow of visitation off to the side of the main lobby, an orientation film was shown called *Facing Crisis: America under Attack*. In this presentation political leaders like George Bush, Condoleezza Rice, and George Pataki recall their reactions to the attacks. The president says that he "became a wartime president" on 9/11. Overall, however, there is very little about that war or even patriotism in the collection of exhibits that follow.

The emphasis in the museum is on the victims of the attacks, and artifacts and objects that evoke images and stories from the tragic day. Many are poignant, such as wallets and wedding rings from Ground Zero as well as huge steel tridents from the structure of the towers that are prominently displayed upon entering the facility. Todd Beamer's watch, which he wore during the heroic attempt to reclaim Fight 93, is exhibited as well as a damaged fire truck that reminds visitors of the heroic attempts of many first responders. The two-ton crossbeam that served as a religious icon during the cleanup now sits in the museum, in the words of *New York Times* reporter Patricia Cohen, as a "hunk of iron" offering evidence of a crime. Text accompanying the cross note how cleanup workers struggled to come to terms with the reality of utter destruction and body parts. Yet, any display of human remains themselves proved to be too much of an affront to relatives and others involved with the museum planning. Some remains are actually entombed in a repository behind the Slurry Wall. Visitation to this sacred place is not allowed to the general public and is restricted to next of kin, who can enter a space called the "Reflection Room." Color photographs of each victim are displayed in another room for general viewing in a manner that prompted one reviewer to see the entire display as a reaffirmation of American innocence. Another reminder of death, photos of trapped individuals jumping from the burning tower, has been placed in an alcove off the main path of visitor traffic where one is instructed to choose whether to observe these gruesome scenes or not.

Photographic evidence of people jumping to their deaths from the burning towers actually evoked a good deal of disapproval immediately after they were published in September 2001. Many newspapers that published the images did so only once because they received scathing criticisms from readers. Certainly many found such a direct exposure to tragedy discomforting. Yet, the photos were also seen as unnecessary intrusions into private space, whether it was an individual's last moment before dying or a family's horror that did not need to be made public. A reader protested to the *Chicago Tribune* that a "man's last moments on Earth" should not be "exploited all over the Country." The writer reminded all that the dying person was "someone's brother, husband, neighbor, and co-worker." And families who lost loved ones at Ground Zero were also upset by the suggestion the photos made it appear that their relatives had elected to jump to their death rather than do all they could to the very end to get back to their familial home.[18]

Private Ground

Memoirs involving the tragedy at Ground Zero represent another form of commemoration. Although they reflect some of the forces that shaped larger public debates over how to remember the tragedy at Ground Zero, they are much more about personal loss and rupture. This was certainly true of the stories told by Lauren Manning and Marian Fontana, grief-stricken women who endured the pain of 9/11. They narrated their traumatic experiences in terms of family disasters in which relationships were shattered and, where possible, individuals struggled to restore some sort of personal stability. The prominent affairs of the city and the nation that were bent upon restoring commerce, creating inspiring public art, or proclaiming patriotism and the need for war entered their stories only in a minor way. Collective needs meant considerably less to these survivors who continued to bear witness to horrendous setbacks in their lives.

Lauren Manning worked for Cantor Fitzgerald, a financial services company that lost some 650 employees who worked just above the impact zone in One World Trade Center on September 11th. She managed to escape the horror of the upper levels of the tower but not before she was so badly burned that she needed to be put into an induced coma to survive. Her remembrance of a near-death experience is primarily a story of the arduous struggle she endured to restore something of the life she had before 9/11. She credits the devotion and care rendered by her husband with helping her to survive a "journey through a harsh and unforgiving landscape of pain" and the desire she was able to muster to see her son again. There are distinct touches of patriotism in her tale. She recalls her father taking her to visit the Civil War battlefield at Gettysburg as a child. Her dad made it clear to the family that this was a site that commemorated American "valor and sacrifice" and the "bravery of young soldiers who had fought and died in these fields." She is even able to recall her father's words almost verbatim. He told his offspring that the "Union soldiers were willing to give their lives for what they believed in and this country was saved right there." In recalling her own passage from pain to love, she now thought about Lincoln's Gettysburg Address and the necessity of sacrifice, which she felt reflected "what it means to accept the honor of being an American." She even offers support for an American war of revenge, something that was not really a part of the Ground Zero commemorations. While she was in the hospital, her spouse told her of the attacks the United States had launched in retaliation for 9/11 and of soldiers who had heard her story and sent her messages that they were fighting in her "honor."[19]

Manning seeks to commemorate a personal struggle. She informs her readers that her brush with death and her encounter with suffering altered some of her perspectives on life, especially her drive to succeed at work. She now claimed she came to appreciate to a greater extent the really "worthwhile" things such as the people she loved and life's "smaller pleasures." For her the experience of recovery ultimately "was a voyage back to those I loved."[20]

Marian Fontana, who lived in the Park Slope section of Brooklyn, watched the towers crash on television and immediately sensed that her husband, Dave, a New York firefighter, was dead. Her story is more heavily based in the trauma she experienced and the gloom that engulfed her than Manning's tale of recovery. She conveys in great detail a transitional period of her life when nothing was certain and reality was positioned somewhere between life and death, between sorrow and hope. She inhabited the type of liminal space that public commemoration normally seeks to obliterate. "I am stunned by the depth of my sadness," she wrote; "it seems to reach into my body as a cancer. Suddenly nauseated, I run into the bathroom and hang over the toilet, my stomach churning and lurching like a dryer full of heavy clothes." As she wanders through her neighborhood, everything seems "alien and strange" to her. Nothing is as it usually is. Flags are mounted everywhere, newsstands are covered with photos of the burning towers, and a large crowed has gathered in front of her husband's fire station which is illuminated by hundreds of tall vigil candles with photos of missing firemen pasted to the station wall.[21]

Back in her home, she fashioned a small makeshift memorial to Dave consisting of an Irish flag—a salute to a heritage he treasured—candles, rosary beads, and a black-and-white photo of the couple smiling in their backyard. She still retained hope that he may be found, but such expectations slip away as she sits near the fire station and listens to stories of searchers finding body parts and skin hanging from jagged steel at Ground Zero. More than Manning, Fontana keenly observes the political world that emerges around Ground Zero and how it relates to the unstable state of trauma and grief in which she finds herself. Confined to a realm of mourning, she clearly does not share the elements of a war-based patriotism and the sense of revenge that Manning seems to support. She was particularly angered when city officials announced a plan to close Dave's fire station which lost twelve of the twenty-seven men stationed there. To her this structure not only was a site that was important to her husband and their neighborhood but had served as "a place of refuge for me in my grief," a spot where she could talk to others who suffered like she did. Soon Fontana joined a large rally that was able to keep open this highly personal site of remembrance.[22]

The grieving widow was particularly critical of political leaders who she felt were devoid of empathetic impulses and failed to share her deep sense of remorse. Worse yet, she felt they were appropriating personal tragedies like hers for larger ends. She was unsettled by a speech given by the wife of the governor of New York at the funeral of a firefighter that noted the heroism and bravery of American troops fighting in Afghanistan. For Fontana the politics of the war had no place at ceremonies dedicated to private grieving and mourning. She hated the fact that politicians always seemed to show up at funeral services and make speeches so they could make a "hasty exit" before the more "difficult parts of the mass begin" and painful eulogies were offered. For her eulogies really mattered, for they were the "ultimate testament of love" that those who cared for the deceased could keep and remember. When Rudolph Giuliani called her and expressed a desire to talk at Dave's funeral, she told him she did not want politicians in attendance. She explained that her husband really did not like politicians, who are now portrayed as intruders into a private realm of love and sorrow, and that she wanted only speakers who knew her dead spouse personally.[23]

In the tribute Fontana offered at her spouse's funeral held in a Catholic church in October of 2001 she made it quite clear how she saw the attacks at Ground Zero. These were not assaults on America or even on the commerce and power of New York but actions that destroyed her family and someone she loved. "I never imagined losing Dave. He seemed impossible to bring down, as solid, strong and indomitable as the towers seemed to be," she told those assembled to bid him farewell. She also regretted his lost future, the fact that he would be denied opportunities to father more children, travel, surf, and even extinguish more fires. "Dave was an amazing person" who loved rugby, Ireland, the ocean, and a "cold pint of Guinness." She then turned to her young son and told him to keep his father in his heart, for "love is the only thing that lasts forever."[24]

Fontana also had an opportunity to express her views to the LMDC, since she was appointed to its Family Advisory Council. From her perspective, she saw Governor Pataki as the "voice of Oz" working behind the scenes to ensure that redevelopment interest predominated in the reconstruction of the memory site. "I find it hard to reconcile my personal loss with the big politics of all this," she wrote. Marian Fontana had witnessed the "resiliency of the human spirit" and saw people from across the nation and world mobilize in unprecedented displays of unity and strength. But gradually she concluded that this tide was "shifting and the events of September 11 were becoming a powerful political pawn to rebuild and even start wars." An invitation to the White House and President Bush's State of the Union address in 2002 had already contributed to such suspicions. As she sat in the balcony listening to the president address the nation, she said she came to feel like a "hypocrite." She saw in the president's rhetoric and war policies an exploitation of her husband's death. At one point she simply decided not to stand and applaud with others during the talk, a decision that caused many sitting nearby to "flash her dirty looks . . . as if I'm chewing the Bible during church."[25]

Mourning in the Suburbs

Many of the victims of Ground Zero, of course, did not live in Manhattan but commuted to the island from nearby boroughs and suburbs. The farther away a town was from New York City, the harder it was for powerful politicians and officials to mitigate the legacy of the death and violence. Staten Island was one of those unfortunate locations where many commuters and dedicated firemen and police officers lived. Some 274 residents of the borough never returned home after 9/11. Reports of victims from the island became so numerous that at one time the city council began naming streets in their honor. It also turned out to be the site of the Fresh Kills landfill where much of the rubble and human remains from Ground Zero were deposited. Barges that normally carried trash now ran day and night from lower Manhattan to the west shore of the island with some 650 tons of debris per load. At this gruesome location FBI agents and city police sorted through all the material looking for evidence of the crime that was committed, personal belongings, and body parts that may have been missed at Ground Zero. Workers at the site and federal agents often spoke of their labor at the landfill as a "sacred duty" and "God's work." When DNA evidence allowed for the identification of human remains, workers put the victims' photos on walls of nearby sheds.[26]

Wendy Pellegrino, an island resident who had once worked at the World Trade Center, could not sleep the night of the terrorist attacks. She remembered it as the "worst day of my life" and felt a deep sense of "fear and panic." Afraid that there would be more attacks on America and acutely aware that many firemen, in particular, had died, she went to her garage and made a sign that proclaimed "God Bless Our Heroes" and drove it into the ground in a triangular traffic island in the middle of an intersection near her home. She also started tying red, white, and blue ribbons around trees. Soon other citizens followed suit, adding personal objects as they had elsewhere such as candles, flowers, photos of the missing, and pictures of dead firemen and even statues of angels. Pellegrino felt the angels were appropriate because she was convinced that they guided her project. Soon the small plot of ground that came to be known as "Angel's Circle" was inundated with photos of the dead, votive candles, and more angel-like figures as private emotions infiltrated public space. It eventually became a permanent site of mourning where people gathered to remember loved ones and where the names of the Staten Island dead would be read aloud for years to come. In 2014 Pellegrino attended a ceremony of remembrance at the location and read a poem in honor of a mother who lost her son at Ground Zero and who would routinely visit the memorial in order to feel closer to her lost child. The poem, titled "A Mother's True Price" (written by Timothy Letts), in tone and content refused to alleviate painful memories and tearful episodes, key aspirations of a war-based patriotism. The composition spoke of how a grieving mother is plagued with pain and grief "every second" of her life.[27]

In Westchester County, New York, residents were also shocked by the attacks and lamented the loss of friends and relatives. Rob Astorino recalled how people hugged and cried after 9/11. "We remembered the good times and we mourned the emptying of joy from our lives at countless funerals." A memorial project led by the Westchester Family Victims and Survivors Group heavily focused its activities on the remembrance of county residents who were killed. One hundred and nine steel rods, one for each local casualty, rose upward and came together eighty feet in the air in the form of a spire. The memorial was named The Rising, after the title of a Bruce Springsteen song that blended themes of sadness and hope as it reflected on 9/11. In his lyrics Springsteen wrote of a sky of "blackness and sorrow" but also one of "love." At the base of each rod, relatives were given an opportunity to have a message engraved to a departed loved one. Most were essentially personal. For instance, a note dedicated to Alex Ciccone noted that he was a "loving husband, son, dad, brother. To the world you were one person but to us you were the world." Some critics later observed that the memorials in the suburbs reflected a somewhat "idealized notion of family life" with their many references to children's soccer games and Little League parades. In part this was the intent of Frederic Schwartz, the architect, who felt the design would invite families and visitors to look back in memory at those who were lost and forward and upward together toward the sky as the individual strands came together in one spire. But the memorial was also a reflection of just how difficult it was for commemorative actions to stamp out traces of personal sorrow and familial loss.[28]

Middletown, New Jersey, was another suburb hit hard by the violence in lower Manhattan. Thirty-seven commuters from the town lost their lives in the collapse of the Twin Towers. Town residents reacted to this sudden breach in their lives by frantically looking for any news of loved ones or pouring into local churches to pray as bells tolled throughout the day of September 11th. Startled citizens filled the Adoration Chapel of St. Mary all through the night and could be seen "praying, moaning, and rocking" and "crying hysterically. On the second night after the attacks, local resident Kevin Casey went to Ground Zero searching for some sign that his wife might still be alive. He recalled that he was not ready for the "total obliteration of hope."[29]

Confirmation of death only made matters worse for those whose loved ones did not return. Sherry McHeffy recalled having coffee when she heard the news that the planes hit the towers where her son worked. The medical examiner refused to let her see the young man's body because of the nature of his injuries. She was haunted by the examiner's words that he was "crushed but intact" and continually wondered if he had almost made it out. The news hurt even more because her husband had just left her nine months earlier. Another woman sank into a "dark mood" not only because her spouse was killed but because there were no remains to bury. It is no wonder that for many in Middletown, Ground Zero seemed not like a place in need of commemoration or a rationale for war but simply a "giant amphitheater of death."[30]

Gail Sheehy, who directly observed the response of Middletown's residents to the devastating effects of the attacks, was able to document the affective states of survivors forced to deal with trauma in their lives in the months after 9/11. Many explained how they felt "emotionally numb, ill tempered, anxious, jumpy and constantly on alert." Some who endured grievous losses felt like "zombies" on some days and "bounced off the walls in hyperactivity" on others. As is often the case when experiencing post-traumatic stress, people relived the horror of the past through nightmares and sudden flashbacks. Even smells or sounds that reminded them of 9/11 might activate an unwelcome return of images like the televised picture of towers falling, chest pains, or even a terrible sense of dread.[31]

Middletown resident Kristen Breitweiser not only learned that her spouse, Ron, died at Ground Zero but eventually was horrified by the news that all that was left of him was a hand with a wedding ring on it. Like others who were shocked by the unfolding of events on that day, she did not see the fall of the towers so much as an assault upon America but as an event that shattered the loving relationship she had with her husband and young daughter. Ron had actually called her on the morning of 9/11 to tell her that he was all right but that the North Tower was in flames and people were jumping to their death. She actually turned on her television in time to see his tower burst into flames. Soon she was crying hysterically on the phone with friends and unable to fully process what had just happened. A week after the towers fell, Breitweiser composed a letter to her daughter that revealed her traumatized state. She wrote: "I have an aching pit in my stomach. Is it because I haven't eaten in two days? Is it because I am on Xanax and an antibiotic or is it because I am so scared and so deeply and profoundly wounded?"[32]

The memorial Middletown created for its missing citizens was essentially therapeutic and lacked some of the commemorative aspirations at Ground Zero that sought to efface a sense of tragedy. Instead, a remembrance of sorrow and profound loss haunted the community's remembrance. Located near the commuter station from which many of the fallen had last departed and where their cars sat unclaimed after the towers fell, a memorial garden was dedicated in a formal ceremony on September 11, 2003. Developed by a local committee that included several family members, the commemorative site featured a tranquil setting with landscaping, a walking path, and a separate memorial stone as a "lasting tribute" for each victim. John Corzine, a New Jersey senator, spoke at the dedication ceremonies and noted that Ground Zero may be in New York, "but there's an emotional ground zero" in New Jersey for the hundreds of families from the state who suffered losses. Former governor Christine Todd Whitman also spoke and stayed on the message of that day, which was more about recalling the lingering effects of a tragedy than moving on from them or putting their legacy to political uses. "Here in Middletown," she said, "September 11th has a meaning all its own." In this moment it was less about an attack upon the nation by evildoers in the world and more about "a day ordinary people left their homes for their regular jobs from the station next door. . . . September 11th tore apart families and shattered dreams. It produced the raw ache of personal loss and the empty feeling of helplessness."[33]

Inscriptions on the individual memorials replicated Whitman's invocation of anguish and private loss. John Pooher's memorial recalled a "cherished husband, son, brother, friend" who gave to others "love and laughter" and who would be "forever missed and never forgotten." Felicia Hamilton was remembered simply as a "woman with a gentle soul" whose "heart was open to those she loved. She was our best friend. Our confidant. Our mother." Robert Emmett Parks was described as a "devoted, loving man with an infectious laugh." Those who loved him wrote that he would be "forever in the hearts of the lives he touched." And Jane Beatty was missed by those who knew her and who regretted there had been "no time to say goodbye. You were gone before we knew it."

New Jersey also built an official state memorial to the 746 residents from the state who died on 9/11. The names of the dead are inscribed on twin brushed stainless steel walls that face one another. Anyone standing in the middle of the walls and looking toward New York can see a clear view of lower Manhattan and the space where the Twin Towers once stood. The New Jersey site is surrounded by groves of dogwood trees that are meant to signify strength and renewal with their annual springtime bloom. Two small sections of steel beams from Ground Zero stand at the west entrance to the memorial itself. The idea is that while the skyline of the city across the river will change, the memorial will be permanent, a constant reminder of emptiness so many felt. The memorial itself was titled Empty Sky, again drawing upon a Springsteen song focused upon all that was lost with only a hint of revenge: "I woke up this morning, I could barely breathe, Just an empty impression, in the bed where you used to be. I want a kiss from your lips. I want an eye for an eye. I woke up this morning to an empty sky."

The memorial's quest to ensure that feelings of heartbreak remain and its stress on the individuals who died are consistent with the nature of commemoration in the suburbs surrounding Ground Zero. Kevin Coyne noticed this pattern and referred to the outer rings of memorials as a "necklace of grief." In the case of the state memorial for New Jersey, the aesthetics of the memorial were shaped to a considerable extent by the fact that many relatives of the victims played key roles in the commemorative process. Rick Cahill, who lost a son when the towers fell, was chair of the New Jersey 9/11 Memorial Foundation. He actually saw the North Tower fall from a distance and realized at once his eldest son, Scott, was on the 104th floor. In an interview in 2006 he indicated that he still prefers to honor his son at the New Jersey site and not at Ground Zero. "It was the local community that came out and supported my families during those weeks," he explained. One woman who attended the anniversary event told a reporter that she came to "bear witness" to her dead husband and indicated she still found his loss very painful: "It's like a hole in your heart that's just there forever."[34]

Shanksville

United Airlines Flight 93 was the only one of the four planes hijacked on September 11th that did not reach its intended goal. It crashed in a field in a rural section of western Pennsylvania near the town of Shanksville when the plane's passengers tried to retake control of the aircraft from the hijackers. Although the precise target of the terrorists was not known, it was widely believed to be either the White House or the Capitol Building, since the plane was on a direct path toward Washington, D.C. Many immediately labeled the passengers brave and true patriots for trying to stave off an attack on the nation's capital. Vice President Dick Cheney would later remark that "an act of heroism" brought down Flight 93. Within six months of the crash federal legislation was introduced to create a new national memorial honoring the passengers and crew. The bill authorizing the memorial proclaimed that the passengers had acted courageously to thwart an attack on Washington and made it clear that a memorial at Shanksville was justified, in part, to "honor" them.[35]

The link between the deaths at Shanksville and patriotic honor remained strong in the years after the crash as visitors arrived to gaze at the site and officials and family members considered various proposals for a permanent memorial. Inevitably the project provoked disagreements that had characterized commemorative planning at other locations. Yet, Shanksville was not New York City and was not subject to the complex theater that resulted from the clash of high-profile political leaders, powerful businessmen, architects, family members, and various members of the public. There was no urge to restore a skyline or commercial activity in Shanksville. In fact, there was substantial sentiment to preserve the tranquil nature of this bucolic location in southwestern Pennsylvania, a point that in the end helped make the memorial site appear more like a cemetery. And the casting of the passengers as valiant actors allowed the Shanksville memorial to sustain its links to a traditional patriotic mythology to a greater extent than was possible amid the range of interests that had to be accommodated at Ground Zero.

At the ground breaking for the permanent memorial in 2009, speakers referred to the passengers as basically warriors serving in the early stages of a new war. Secretary of the Interior Ken Salazar affirmed that the memorial would forever honor the passengers on Flight 93 who "fought and were victorious over the forces of evil." The governor of Pennsylvania, Ed Rendell, noted how the passengers stopped the terrorists from using their plane "as a weapon" against the nation's capital and made it clear the living could never repay their "courage."[36]

The horrific crash at Shanksville left almost no trace of the plane or the forty passengers and four terrorists. Wallace Miller, a local coroner who investigated the crash site, recalled that the destruction was so complete that it was almost impossible to see any form of human remains or aircraft parts. The absence of ruined buildings and piles of rubble, however, did not deter tourists from visiting the grounds on which the disaster took place, which was actually a relatively short drive from the heavily traveled Pennsylvania Turnpike. Visitors not only viewed what little was left of the plane but soon began to invest the site with a variety of meanings that sprang from feelings and thoughts that coursed through their hearts and minds. This mix of popular responses to the crash is apparent from a reading of cards and messages that travelers began leaving at the site soon after 9/11 and systematically collected by the National Park Service.[37]

Most tourists who recorded their thoughts at Shanksville saw the site of the crash as hallowed ground. The passengers were viewed as traditional patriotic heroes who were bravely defending their country. And in the logic of a war-based patriotism, the nation they served was a highly virtuous one blessed by God. Alexander Riley and other scholars have gone so far as to suggest that the story of Flight 93 was heavily imbued from the beginning with the "reverential cultural myths of God and country." In this particular version of what had happened at Shanksville and what had happened to the nation, many citizens also expressed the view that in this time of turmoil and danger God could be counted on to help protect America and those who had given their lives for its well-being.[38] Consider a selection of these heartfelt declarations from 2003 and 2004:

I don't have the words to express my feelings. Thank you for your ultimate sacrifice, for your total unselfishness and generosity. I will never forget your deeds in the skies and your earthy gifts to all of us. May Jesus and Mary comfort you, your families and give you the reward you have earned.

God meant for all those people to be on the flight because he knew they had the courage and the heart to do what needed to be done. And if they hadn't been there to stop the terrorist's plans they might have succeeded in their evil plot. They did God's will, thinking of others before themselves. So rejoice because right now they are with the Lord. God bless all who sacrificed themselves so others may live.

You were the first heroes of the 21st century. Thank you once again for being true Americans.[39]

As Americans learned more about the details of the nation's military retaliation in Afghanistan and Iraq, the single-minded focus on heroism and virtue apparent at Shanksville was expanded to justify the War on Terror. A number of visitors now included the militant words "Let's Roll" in their responses, an expression articulated by Todd Beamer, one of the passengers who led the assault on the plane's cockpit in an effort to regain control of the flight. A war veteran just back from overseas traveled to Shanksville and wrote that as he looked over the Pennsylvania landscape and saw the site of the crash, he never felt prouder to be an American. "Nineteen and one-half years ago I chose to become an American soldier. The people of flight 93 had no time to make such a choice in their destination," he wrote, "and because of these people many lives were saved. God bless the people of America and God Bless the United States military." Another soldier just returned from Afghanistan was more blunt. He argued that the "heroes" of Flight 93 gave others the courage to fight and suggested that the nation "nuke" the terrorists and "let God sort them out." And a "proud mom" noted the tragic death of her son who was killed fighting in Fallujah in Iraq but now took solace in her belief that he was "fighting for our freedom here in America."[40]

Not everyone, of course, joined the call for a patriotic war of revenge. A visitor from Philadelphia wrote shortly after the crash that he sincerely hoped the site would not be used to justify wars in the Middle East and the exercise of prejudice against Islam. This particular person felt there was already too much "pro–Iraq war sentiment" in the United States despite the fact that Iraq had "absolutely nothing to do with these attacks." Another tourist noted the natural beauty of the Shanksville landscape and found it "incomprehensible that nearly five years ago death came screaming from the sky." This person conveyed the hope that the spirit of the dead passengers would be used for the "achievement of peace and understanding" so in the future airline passengers would not have to face the prospect of being hijacked. "I pray for this country," this writer said, "to have the kind of leadership to foster understanding." In a card posted to a bulletin board at the site in 2010, a tourist responded to a statement made by another visitor who wanted to "nuke" the nation's enemies and insisted that Shanksville be a place to recall honor but not hate and anger.[41]

Before the creation of a permanent memorial at Shanksville, tourists created a commemorative edifice of their own. Shortly after the crash, visitors to the field in Pennsylvania began attaching decals of all sorts, patches from military units, baseball caps, and an assortment of photographs to a fence. One woman left a United Airlines flight attendant uniform and another person placed a uniform of the Shanksville Volunteer Fire Department at the site. A member of a special forces unit left a brick taken from a Taliban compound in Afghanistan. Someone left a large Christian cross. On guardrails around the grounds, people pasted patriotic bumper stickers and even scrawled vows of revenge. Like improvised memorials everywhere, the thematic tone of this commemoration was more prone to reflect private sentiments of loss than mythical notions that turned tragedy into redemption.[42]

Mirroring commemoration on Staten Island, one prominent feature of the spontaneous memorialization at Shanksville was the appearance of small figures of angels, painted in red, white, and blue stripes that contained the name of each American who died on Flight 93. At Shanksville these figures appeared to serve as religious symbols that reinforced the virtuous view of the heroic passengers who were seen in this context as saviors sent by God. They helped sanctify the war they ostensibly fought. To recast the heroes of Flight 93 as angels was to ensure that their brave deeds had earned them a special place not only in the nation's collective memory but in a spiritual world where they would be rewarded by heavenly authority. Notations on a number of visitor cards also brought angels into the discussion. Visitors from Indiana expressed the hope that "angels" would "stay and protect" the dead because of the "wonderful tribute you gave our country." Another visitor called the dead passengers "angels above who made the supreme sacrifice." Others commented that they thought some representation of angels should always be placed at the crash site. At the very least, angels reflected a popular way of reworking the rhetoric of patriotism and religion and the connection many felt existed between the two.[43]

By 2003 the National Park Service had already started planning for a memorial at Shanksville. Federal legislation called for the creation of a "dignified memorial landscape that was quiet in reverence yet powerful in form." The goal was to transform what was a "common field" into "a field of honor forever." Legislation authorized the formation of a Flight 93 advisory commission, a federally appointed body charged with evaluating design proposals and making final recommendation for a memorial to the secretary of the interior. The commission was to work on the project in conjunction with a host of "partners" that included "Families of Flight 93," National Park Service officials, and a diverse group of citizens from the region and the nation called the "Flight 93 Memorial Task Force." Guidelines for an architectural competition instructed competitors to incorporate key themes in their plans such as honoring the "heroism, courage and enduring sacrifice" of the passengers in order to inspire hope among the living. Instructions also asked that a message that would be "timeless in its power and conviction" and venerate "this hallowed ground as the final resting place of 40 heroes" be crafted. This formal effort to encase the trauma of the flight within patriotic frames, noticeably tempering some of the religious attitudes of many, moved forward as people continued to visit, write on cards, and deposit objects. Ironically, several tourists did note that the best memorial would be one that left the temporary memorial in place. Several said they were deeply moved by the variety of personal items they saw. "Leave the memorial as it is," one person wrote; "a formal memorial is not what I want to see. I was more touched by what people wrote and left." Another commentator claimed that the "temporary memorial is by far the most emotional place I have ever visited."

As the National Park Service approached the time when formal designs for a memorial would be required, it began to ask visitors to record not only their reactions upon seeing the site but their specific suggestions for what a permanent memorial might look like. Again, it was clear that despite the power of the makeshift commemoration, a large majority of the public agreed that the site be formally commemorated in ways that diminished the harsh reality of death and invoked aesthetics that were highly formal, patriotic, and sacred. Consider the following suggestions for a memorial.

"Just as Gettysburg is a national memorial in southeastern Pennsylvania so is Shanksville a national battlefield in the war on terrorism in southwestern Pennsylvania. The crash site should be preserved and dedicated to the crew members and passengers who sacrificed their own lives so many other lives could be saved as the flight would have created a disaster in our nation's capital."

"Like most Americans I am in awe of the heroes and courage shown by the passengers prior to the crash. I remember rumors swirling at the time about a fourth plane heading for the White House or the Capitol building. . . . It sent chills up my spine later that day when I heard that Dick Cheney remarked that the nation had probably just witnessed a true act of heroism. . . . I am not sure I could have risen to the occasion. As heartbreaking as the crash was for the nation, it was also such a strong symbol of our very best traits . . . of the American spirit: the willingness to fight back against evil and risk one's life to protect one another."

"The flight 93 memorial will mark the spot where Americans gave their lives defeating a sudden and vicious enemy. They had very little time to act and there was very little they could do and yet these men and women fought so bravely and heroically denying the enemy yet another victory that tragic day. This kind of courage and self sacrifice cannot be overlooked or forgotten. Our nation was born out of these virtues and by these virtues she has been preserved."

"Here is an idea for the Memorial—'Flight 93 Field of Angels.'" Have a panoramic view of the field made of material to last a lifetime. Marble, bronze etc. In the field would be silhouettes of angels hovering in a relaxed state. The names of all passengers who died in the crash would be noted to depict the Angelistic action that these people did to protect others that fateful day of Sep. 11, 2001. Above in the sky would be Jesus with his arms open wide and smiling rays of light down upon his Heroic Angels. Title the monument 'The Flight 93 of Angels' or Guardian Angels. Since it was an act of guarding others."[44]

From the start of the planning process environmental concerns also loomed large in the conceptualization of how Flight 93 might be commemorated, a result of the rural setting in which the plane went down. Although the landscape of the region is visually stunning with a series of ridges, valleys and "spectacular vistas," the site had been scarred by strip mining and acid runoff from mines that had contaminated the region's surface and groundwater. Much of the vegetation in the immediate area of the memorial site was not even native to the area, having been planted simply to restore the landscape after mining operations ceased. It was not surprising that the final plan to develop the site, therefore, involved not only the idea of a memorial structure but a vision for the surrounding countryside as well. The management plan for the site specifically called for the "healing of the landscape," in part through the planting of more trees and the development of a wildflower meadow. One stated goal was not only to "nourish our souls" or restore hope after death (as many commemorative projects are prone to do) but to "heal the land." The environmental makeover was very much imagined as part of an aesthetic that would enhance the sense that the land here was "sacred ground where human remains were entombed in the earth." Any suggestion that the environmental and political trauma of the past should be recalled in vivid terms or analyzed was destroyed.[45]

The competition for the memorial site was opened to both design professionals and the general public. This was felt to be the most inclusive and democratic way to proceed. The result was a huge pool of over 1,000 design suggestions. Two ideas quickly attracted much public comment. "Disturbed Harmony" was a plan that featured a 2.5-mile-long "Bravery Wall" made of stone that would guide visitors to the site of the crash and provide a time line for the events of 9/11. "The Crescents of Embrace" consisted of a long, curved walkway with forty red maple trees offering shade on a ridge line leading to an observation platform that provided a view of the sacred ground where the plane crashed. It also called for a tower near the gateway to the site with forty silver wind chimes. At the end of the walk visitors could also view a white marble wall with the names of the passengers and crew who died.[46]

Before the final choice was made, public comment on the final designs was again solicited from visitors. A large majority of the opinions they left tended to favor the idea that the memorial blend with the surrounding landscape. This point partially explained why "Disturbed Harmony" and "Crescent of Embrace" found so much favor with visitors. They offered "simplistic beauty" and strayed away from introducing man-made structures into the rural fields. "Crescent" did ignite a brief controversy when a number of commentators in the press thought the aesthetics of an arc or crescent would reference a prominent symbol of Islam. One reporter argued that the sight of an arc of red maple trees each fall would be a source of joy for al-Qaeda. Thomas Burnett, whose son died in the crash, warned his fellow jurors that they would become a "laughing stock" if they approved the design. Eventually the issue passed when minor revisions were made to the design by adding more trees in a way that transformed the arc into a circle.

A woman from Johnstown, Pennsylvania, who was fond of "Disturbed Harmony" felt it spoke more clearly of the victims with its use of the names of the dead and birthdates engraved on stones. She felt this served better as a "permanent marker of their resting place" and "connected the oneness of the spirit in the life and death of these people as true Americans." Another visitor preferred "Crescent of Embrace," however, because the use of trees and vegetation made it appear "life-affirming" and less intrusive upon the "sacred ground." Nancy Mangum, the stepmother of one of the crash victims, Deora Bodley, liked "Crescent of Embrace" best because it seemed "comforting" and allowed visitors and relatives to "experience the loveliness of the site as well as the remembered loved ones." Mangum's sister also liked this plan because it allowed her to visualize herself visiting in all four seasons but especially in September when "the beauty of the area harmonizes with the honoring of the victims." And an anonymous tourist favored the crescent plan because "it combines the history, personal remembrance, and a sense of hope . . . and elicits comfort."[47]

"Crescent of Embrace," with its centerpiece of a white marble wall at the end of a long walkway upon which the names of the passengers and crew were inscribed, won the competition. Human remains were buried at the actual spot of the crash, which is set apart from the wall and (like the remains from Ground Zero) not open to public visitation. For all the talk about heroes and angels that permeated discussions of the site, this wall, in the opinion of a number of critics, was clearly "minimalist" in its design and reminded many of Maya Lin's design for the Vietnam Veterans Memorial in Washington, D.C. It is true Shanksville's wall was white instead of black, but in the end it resisted the calls of many citizens and even family members to make the structure more heroic and to depict the passengers in more remarkable and, for that matter, religious terms. Its focus was on the dead. Some had suggested a memorial that portrayed the actual revolt of the passengers against the terrorists. Those who wanted to recall this early battle in the War on Terror in more heroic and patriotic terms, however, could take some satisfaction from President George W. Bush's speech at the dedication of the memorial in 2011. In his remarks the former chief executive offered a litany of patriotic acts that took place on 9/11. He remarked that one of the lessons of the day was that "evil is real and so is courage." He praised the firefighters and police officers who "charged up the stairs into the flames" at Ground Zero. He recalled how service members and civilians pulled friends and strangers from the rubble at the Pentagon. And then he turned his attention to the "extraordinary story that we commemorate here." He remembered that many passengers called loved ones before they mounted an assault that now constituted, in the words of the president, "one of the most courageous acts in American history." He felt their deeds left a legacy of "bravery and selflessness that will always inspire America."[48]

The Widows' Debate

In looking at the personal recollections of women who lost spouses in the crash in Pennsylvania, it is clear that tropes of patriotic heroism could be welcomed at times by those who grieved but fiercely resisted as well, a sign of how deeply the patriots' debate infiltrated the level of daily life. This tension is evident in memoirs authored by two women who were widowed by the passengers' assault on the terrorists; public rhetoric about heroism and the aesthetics of tranquility do not disclose the full range of feelings and outlooks these women experienced after the death of men so central in their lives. Lyz Glick wrote about the death of her husband, Jeremy, in order that her young daughter would have an impression of the father she would never know. Glick reasoned that when her child was old enough to read, Glick wanted her to understand that her father was more than a legendary figure who staved off a terrorist attack on the nation's capital. He was also a real person who loved his family deeply. Her story is particularly poignant because Jeremy was able to have a phone conversation with her from the doomed plane before it hit the ground; she knew he was probably not going to get out of the situation he was in alive.[49]

Glick recounts her own deep sense of loss, of course, but also explains how she was drawn into a very public role as one of the family members of the Flight 93 victims. Suddenly, in addition to her personal grieving, she was invited to take organized trips to the site near Shanksville and attend meetings at the White House to meet President George Bush. Like Marian Fontana, who attempted to limit the intrusion of public politics into her suddenly ruptured world, Glick was reluctant to cast her private misfortune into a patriotic framework. Gifts and mementos sent to her home by strangers from all over the country transformed the sun-room of her house into what amounted to another makeshift memorial with Bibles, T-shirts, and all kinds of objects. Two Vietnam veterans sent their Purple Hearts, a sign of how many saw the actions of the passengers as prime examples of selfless devotion to the nation. Yet, Glick rejected various reinterpretations of her husband's actions. "Jeremy didn't sign up to fight terrorism," she wrote; "his act was an act of love, not war. He did what he did because he wanted so very badly to come home to his wife and baby daughter." On another occasion when a group of relatives met President Bush, she again recoiled at his assertion that the Shanksville victims were really heroes. When Bush mentioned her husband, Jeremy, by name in his remarks, she recalled that she felt not pride but only pain that seemed like a "stab in the ribs" because it was another reminder that he was gone. At the White House that day, she said she felt much more comfortable discussing children with other widows and not talking about Flight 93 at all.[50]

Eventually Glick grew tired of the public role thrust upon her and the patriotic frames placed upon Jeremy's memory. She did not want the actions of her spouse to be forgotten but also did not want to become simply an "official 9/11 hero widow." And she never did accept the point made by Bush and Cheney that the passengers acted to save the White House or some other national landmark. Realizing that the vice president had already authorized Air Force jets to shoot down Flight 93 if it continued toward the nation's capital, she rejected assertions that her husband and his partners had saved anything in Washington, D.C., because it was already ably defended. During the media coverage of the first anniversary of the 9/11 attacks, she was upset to see references to the words "Let's Roll," the command issued by passenger Todd Beamer as he, Jeremy, and others charged the cockpit door on Flight 93. She felt that the first anniversary of the event was not a time to recount valor but to "mourn introspectively." In a moment of rebuke of official celebrations, Glick wrote that she felt it was more appropriate to find "a piece of you that needs work and work on it."[51]

Rather than take comfort in public tributes, Glick, as a witness to the war, made it clear that her husband's death brought her not honor but only unhappiness and a sense of deep sorrow over the shattering of her family life. She began to experience episodes of uncontrollable crying and started to seek help from a private therapist. Eventually she joined a "9/11 survivors therapy group" where she encountered people who had also lost loved ones in the fall of the World Trade Center. It was in these assemblages that she came to realize not that her husband was a hero but that there were others like her who had endured the horror of losing a loved one; human connections and the stories of others who shared her grief became vitally important. Eventually she became enamored with psychics and sought to learn what news she could get from "the dimension into which my husband had vanished." Near the end of her narrative, Glick related how she and Jeremy had always been fans of Kurt Vonnegut, the World War II veteran whose literature always recalled "the good war" in less than flattering terms. They were particularly taken with his notion of a "nation of two." Vonnegut had used this concept to suggest that when two people were in love they made up so much of each other's reality that it was as if they were the "sole citizens of their own country." To her this affectionate bond was the real history of her life and her loss, for it led to the birth of their daughter. At its core her story about Flight 93 was not a tale of patriotic valor but one of love lost.[52]

Lisa Beamer was another woman whose life was blown apart when her husband, Todd, died in the crash of Flight 93. Left with two young sons and an unborn child, Beamer, as she tells her story, turned to God in her darkest hours and felt that He responded by providing her with a "sense of peace and a confidence that the children and I were going to be okay." Living a good "Christian life" had always been important to her and Todd, an aspiration she attributed to the fact that they both had been raised in families that put a high value on religious faith and personal integrity. When they moved to New Jersey years before, one of the first things she and Todd did was to search for a church that appeared welcoming and made the "teachings of the Bible" relevant in their lives. In fact, most of the friendships they formed revolved around their religious community.[53]

Beamer's narrative, in fact, illustrated not only the power of religious devotion in helping people cope with crushing setbacks but the compelling attractiveness of patriotic dogma to make clear why at times citizens had to fight and die. "Independence, patriotism, freedom, and the American way of life were not trite clichés tossed around lightly in our family," she wrote; "they were highly valued treasures." She told of a relative who had served and died in World War II and how the American flag was proudly displayed at her home during holidays. She even expressed satisfaction in knowing that Todd had been aboard a plane that crashed without hitting Washington and causing further death and "calamity in our country." And she made it clear that she very much approved of the way Americans had celebrated the heroic actions of firefighters and police officers for their willingness to face danger in order to help save others on 9/11. In this regard she was moved to quote from John 15:13: "Greater love hath no man than this, that he lay down his life for his friends." She was more than gratified to see the vast public honor heaped upon the passengers of Flight 93 and references to their act as gallant sacrifice.[54]

Todd's father shared her patriotic perspective on his son's death. Driving back from California to New Jersey just after 9/11, he was reminded of "how vast and beautiful our nation is and how much our freedom and way of life are worth fighting for." At Todd's memorial service he told the audience that we all "serve the one and true God" and that Todd and his "newfound freedom fighters" certainly performed a moral deed in thwarting plans of the terrorists to bring more ruin to the nation. He too took comfort in knowing that the passengers had prevented possible attacks on the White House or the Capitol and claimed he knew with certainty that the hijackers did not have the name of Jesus on their lips in their final moments.[55]

Beamer shared Glick's observation that her husband was driven to attempt a takeover of the plane because he wanted to see his family again. In a visit to Shanksville she expressed appreciation for the condolences she received from local citizens and noted they were also proud to be associated with the "flight of heroes who had prevented further destruction of our country." Her book made it clear that she was in full agreement with the vast outpouring of national pride that had overtaken the tragic events of 9/11. When she attended the president's State of the Union speech in 2002 along with Liz Glick, she relished the fact that the president praised the passengers of Flight 93 for their courage and sacrifice and singled out Todd as "an exceptional man." She did feel that God had the power to prevent such atrocities from happening, but accepted them and their devastating consequences because of the faith she held in potent religious and nationalistic canons. She even felt that people of faith like her actually seemed to be less mournful and "fearful" of the future because they had "hope in the Lord" and knew they would see their loved ones again. Beamer expressed some sympathy for those who could not share her deep convictions and offered a promise that Jesus could really be the "answer to all of their life problems."[56]

The Pentagon

A memorial to the memory of 184 individuals who were killed on 9/11 when American Airlines Flight 77 struck the Pentagon was dedicated in 2008. The design of the Pentagon Memorial centered on the idea of individual loss as each victim is recalled in the form of a cantilevered bench made of stainless steel. A pool of water sits beneath each bench which is lit at night to create a soft glow throughout the site that sits adjacent to the huge government building itself. Each bench or "memorial unit" also contains the name of a victim, but the placement of the units as one enters the site is from the age of the youngest to the age of the oldest victim, a range from ages three to seventy-one. Visitors first see a granite line on the ground that indicates the time and date of the attack: "September 11, 2001 9:37 A.M." Tourists are then asked to take a more empathic turn and consider not only the death of innocents but something personal about them—their ages. At the entrance to the site an Age Wall indicates the ascending ages of the dead from a young child to an older man. No symbolic feature dominates the site such as a wall of names, although the entire memorial sits in the shadow of symbols central to the idea of a war-based patriotism, the Pentagon and Arlington National Cemetery.

As elsewhere, before an official memorial was created, an improvised memorial appeared near the Pentagon shortly after the attack. Citizens again expressed a multitude of emotions with teddy bears, flowers, miniature American flags, poems, and photos of the dead. Some people posted photos of model airplanes and fighter jets. Schoolchildren wrote messages calling for peace. Eventually a more patriotic stamp was put on many of the human remains from the catastrophe when some of them were buried at Arlington National Cemetery. In 2002 Secretary of Defense Donald Rumsfeld presided over the burial of a single casket with full military honors containing identified and unidentified remains from the Pentagon attack in ground already sanctified by the presence of the remains of American soldiers. The nephew of a woman whose remains were never found in the Pentagon rubble did express reservations at the time of the burial at Arlington over how the Bush administration was treating the deaths of people like his aunt. He felt these victims were being used to support calls for an invasion of Iraq, something he found difficult to accept.[57]

Family members of the victims soon began to push for a more coherent remembrance of the event and of the dead at the Pentagon. Jim Laychak, whose younger brother worked at the Pentagon and was killed in the attack, took much of the responsibility for soliciting corporate donations. Laychak and a few associates set up a Pentagon Memorial Fund and enlisted the help of a professional fundraiser. He also consulted with Pentagon officials about how the dead might be memorialized in the immediate aftermath of the crash as investigators still combed the rubble for body parts. Kathy Dillaber, who had been working in the Pentagon on 9/11 and who had lost a sister and many friends when the structure was hit, also helped raise funds through community theater projects in nearby Alexandria. In 2002 Congress authorized the Pentagon to build a memorial and the U.S. Army Corps of Engineers announced a worldwide design competition. The agency formed a group of the victims' family members to guide them on the project. Several locations were considered as a possible commemorative site, but family members insisted that the side of the building where the plane hit be chosen as the memorial site. The jury that made the final selection consisted of a mix of design professionals, landscape architects, and two former secretaries of defense, Melvin Laird and Harold Brown. Laychak and Wendy Chamberlin, who lost a father and a stepmother in the attack, represented the interests of the "Victims Family Steering Committee" on the selection panel. Laird and Brown originally wanted some military symbolism in the memorial design, but they came to realize that many of the dead were civilians and that grieving relatives of the dead who wanted a plan that allowed for "healing and reverie" had a compelling argument.

There was little didacticism in the final design suggestions. One idea called "Pentagon New Day Memorial" called for the erection of huge slabs of glass upon which visitors could draw or write messages in dew that would evaporate only to be replaced by new messages each day. Another called "American Elysium" featured a below-ground plaza with a long table and a bench for each casualty. Julie Beckman and Keith Kaseman, a married couple from Philadelphia who submitted the winning proposal containing a bench for each victim, said they were intent not on winning but on coming to terms with the grief they personally felt. Beckman actually saw flames engulf the South Tower in New York on 9/11. And they wanted to ensure that "dignity and respect" were conveyed for each person who was killed. It was also important for them that the commemorative site be seen as a place that invited contemplation more than moralizing. The memorial today certainly achieves the goal of its designers and meets the wishes expressed at the beginning of the design competition by officials that the commemorative location be a "peaceful intimate place" with "no flames, no bodies." Contemplation is possible, but the full force of trauma has again been substantially dulled.[58]

Living Memorials

Across the nation people also participated in a variety of commemorative endeavors that revealed the vast scope of sentiment that resided in the larger culture and the problem of coming to terms with the death and trauma the attacks brought. Out of a desire to recognize the devastation and interpret it as well, Congress asked the U.S. Department of Agriculture's Forest Service to launch an initiative called the Living Memorial Project (LMP). The idea was for the government agency to partner with local initiatives to use nature as a healing device. "Nature has been known to help heal the spirit and to reconstruct ourselves to live," promotional literature proclaimed. Officials believed that in the aftermath of 9/11 many people would seek solace in nature by walking through a neighborhood park, sitting in a garden, or looking out along a water's edge. Issuing cost-share grants, the Forest Service sought to support projects that would "invoke the resonating power of trees to bring people together and create lasting, living memorials to the victims of terrorism, their families, and communities and the nation."[59]

The landscape projects, carried out mostly in the northeastern part of the United States, were extensive and frequently blended natural features with man-made ones. They ranged from simple tree plantings to the creation of new parks. In Connecticut a living memorial was constructed on the shores of Long Island Sound that consisted of trees and shrubs planted among sand dunes and a "low lying memorial stone" as "a tribute to the individuals who lost lives filled with goals, hopes and plans for the future." Adding to the significance of this site was the fact that people standing there on 9/11 had been able to see plumes of smoke rising from Ground Zero on the horizon. Many in Connecticut expressed the idea that a location near the sea would inspire feelings that were "eternal." At Joel Barlow High School in Redding, Connecticut, two stone posts were installed on the grounds and a nature laboratory established in woods nearby which were seen as a "quiet place" capable of fostering "contemplation and peace." A graduate of the school, Peter Hanson, was killed along with his wife and daughter when American Airlines Flight 175 slammed into the South Tower. Hanson's father saw the plane hit the tower and later testified at the death penalty trial of Zacarias Moussaoui that the terrorists "took away our dreams. They took away our future."[60]

Local commemorative efforts were also abundant throughout the country and continued to mix patriotism with a number of other tropes. The common denominator in these remembrances was not a unified theme but a forceful attempt to obliterate the legacy of horror and human pain the 9/11 attacks brought. In San Ramon, California, a park dedicated to "honor" those who died included not only a grove of trees but a dog park, a children's play area, picnic areas, bocce courts, and a huge rock honoring all who died "with special recognition to Tom Burnett." Burnett, a passenger on Flight 93 who helped lead the charge against the terrorists in the cockpit, was a former resident of the city. Burnett was also honored in another landscape project at his alma mater, Pepperdine University, in what was called a "Heroes Garden." The memorial lauded him and the other passengers of Flight 93 for "sacrificing their lives to overcome terrorists intent on destroying American lives and landmarks in our nation's capital." Its organizers felt the location would serve essentially as a place of "private reflection." Indianapolis dedicated a memorial to 9/11, initiated by a local firefighter who helped in search and rescue at Ground Zero, in 2010. The site consisted of two 11,000-pound steel beams from the Twin Towers and two six-foot-high black granite walls that were placed near the beams with inscriptions recalling the horrific events in New York, Washington, D.C., and Shanksville.

Perched atop one of the beams is a bronze, life-sized sculpture of an American bald eagle with wings outstretched gazing east toward New York City. The citizens of Hilliard, Ohio, built the First Responders Park Memorial that included beams of steel from the World Trade Center that were "escorted to Ohio by police officers and firefighters." Granite walls were also built in the park upon which the names of all the dead from 9/11 were listed. In Tiffin, Ohio, a 9/11 commemoration also relied on landscapes with the creation of the "All Patriots Memorial Park." A steel beam from New York was placed upon a pentagon-shaped piece of granite. A Callery pear tree was also planted at the site to replicate a similar tree that managed to survive the devastation at Ground Zero.

At the George W. Bush Presidential Library and Museum in Dallas, dedicated in 2013, two twisted steel beams from Ground Zero were also erected. They served as a centerpiece for a display on 9/11 that used words and media displays to celebrate the strong leadership offered by the forty-third president after the attacks and the patriotism and generosity of the American people. At the Bush library 9/11 is memorialized as the start of a just war in which the Americans went forward "to defend freedom and all that's good in the world." The failure to find weapons of mass destruction is acknowledged, but visitors are also told that Saddam Hussein did have the capacity to produce them and may have been on the verge of doing so. The bullhorn the president used in his first visit to Ground Zero is also exhibited along with a media clip in which he used the instrument to tell workers chanting "USA, USA" that the people who knocked over the towers "will soon hear from us." The ubiquity of steel beams from Ground Zero placed in many locations throughout the United States confirms what Jonathan Hyman discovered when he photographed vernacular artwork people executed in the immediate aftermath of the attacks. In his travels he found a significant emphasis on the World Trade towers as a subject of murals, displays, and even tattoos. Hyman suggested that the towers, at least in this period, surpassed the importance of Uncle Sam or the Statue of Liberty as national icons.[61]

In their study of community-based memorials dedicated to 9/11, aside from the official structures erected in New York, Shanksville, and Washington, Erika Svendsen and Lindsay Campbell also found an eclectic mix of ideas throughout the country. The practice of naming the dead was surely prevalent. Many were also designed to create spaces that would "encourage reflection and healing." Patriotism as a theme seemed less apparent to Svendsen and Campbell, although it was widespread. To a considerable extent the authors of the survey found that many of these local projects sought to create a sense of "community cohesion" and invoked the concept that citizens were "stewards of green space." This is the reason so many integrated landscape elements like gardens, forests, and parks into their commemorative undertakings. The dead and sometimes the nation needed to be honored but not at the expense of the needs of the living to heal and to anesthetize the past by replacing its horrors with the tranquility of nature.[62]

The shadow of Vietnam had a powerful influence on the aesthetics of public commemoration around the time of 9/11 and arguably set the stage for expressions of empathic patriotism in memorials to the attacks. The impulse to mourn and grieve was widely inscribed particularly in makeshift memorials and in the practice of listing the names of the dead, actions flowing from a willingness to at least register the scope of human feelings over the tragedy rather than conceal them. Yet the therapeutic intent of that legacy and its insistence that painful realities of war and violence not be erased was not sufficient to stem efforts to soften the traumatic blow of 9/11 and the war it initiated by invoking ideas of patriotic virtue, environmental tranquility, religious faith, and even commercial rebirth. This mix of feelings and emotions was not simply driven by leaders. Clearly in the enormity of public opinion, citizens were divided over which patriotic sentiments should be used to remember the tragedy of these times, as they were over whether to start a war in the first place. This variety was not only a sign of a vast cultural debate over how to view the new war but an inclination that the turn to embrace trauma after Vietnam was powerful but far from decisive in shaping both wartime attitudes and an emerging collective memory in the aftermath of 9/11. The U.S. invasion of Iraq in 2003 would only heighten this tension between war-based and empathic patriots.

3 Unmasking Suffering and Iraq

The combative patriotism that drove the Bush administration to invade Iraq in 2003, ironically, triggered a powerful pushback. It is well known that over time public support for the assault on Saddam Hussein's regime began to erode, but we have already seen that powerful antiwar arguments were made when the United States attacked Afghanistan. In time this wave of dissent, at least in the United States, grew even larger. The failure to find weapons of mass destruction in Iraq was obviously a factor, but so was the news of trauma and grief that the war brought to Americans in their homes via newspapers, television, and returning veterans. Such disclosures carried a tide of information that weakened the hold a war-based patriotism had on the American psyche. An outburst of affective statements and stories describing the distress and pain the war brought to American families began to challenge the hope of war-based patriots not only to vanquish enemies but to conceal the damage they caused. Loyal citizens from various backgrounds, from Gold Star Mothers to religious leaders and prominent politicians, recoiled from war when reports brought information not about hidden weaponry but about human suffering; some began to mourn and grieve in public. Americans never fully capitulated to the voices of sorrow and sympathy, however. Ardent defenders of the president and the inherent virtue of the nation and its military often rose to disenfranchise expressions of grief and assault the credibility of those who chose at all costs to bear witness to the swelling load of tragic losses.

Preemptive War

George Bush saw the terrorist attacks of 2001 not only as grounds for military action but as an unexpected opportunity as well. In speaking with author Bob Woodward in the months after the attacks on America, the president expressed the idea that he actually had "big goals" that were about much more than striking back at al-Qaeda, the terrorist organization responsible for crashing the planes on 9/11. Rather, Bush divulged that he imagined "remaking the world" in ways that would actually end human distress. In the summer of 2002 he told an audience of Veterans of Foreign Wars that the times brought not only dangers but opportunities such as the eradication of poverty in the Middle East.[1]

High-minded sentiments, however, were not on the president's mind when he thought about Iraq. Although that nation was not part of the 9/11 assault on America, the president told his national security advisor as early as September 17, 2001, that he believed "Iraq was involved." He remarked that he was not prepared to strike them, however, until he had sufficient evidence. A week later the president called Donald Rumsfeld into the Oval Office and asked him to review plans the United States currently had regarding a military strike against Iraq and its dictator, Saddam Hussein. David Frum, a former speech writer for the president, recalled that he was asked in the fall of 2001 to formulate a justification for a war against Iraq for Bush's State of the Union address in January 2002. Vice President Dick Cheney, thinking about the immediate aftermath of 9/11, wrote in his memoirs that he remembered that the Central Intelligence Agency had "solid evidence" at the time of the presence of al-Qaeda members in Iraq. By the summer of 2002 the president offered hints of what was on his mind when he told an audience at West Point about his idea for a preemptive war that would come to be known as the "Bush Doctrine." The president reasoned that the Cold War policy of containment, long a pillar of American foreign policy in stopping the spread of communism, was no longer viable. Bush declared that in the face of "unbalanced dictators with weapons of mass destruction" America could no longer wait to react to another terrorist attack. The "war on terror will not be won on the defensive," the commander in chief warned.[2]

Bush and Cheney had been deeply suspicious of Hussein since the 1991 Gulf War, which had been led by Bush's father. In that encounter American forces drove Saddam Hussein out of Kuwait, an oil-rich nation he had just invaded. American fighter jets continued to fly over Iraq after the end of hostilities to impose a no-fly zone over its territory, and UN inspectors searched the ground for suspected weapons of mass destruction. The current president was also keenly aware that Hussein had tried to assassinate his father when he visited Kuwait in 1993. It was not completely surprising that Bush and Cheney suspected Hussein may have had some involvement with 9/11. Woodward offered plenty of evidence that Cheney and Rumsfeld were, in fact, keen on toppling the dictator well before September 2001. They were upset that Hussein continued to fire at American jets charged with the task of preserving the no-fly zone. And both men had been active in a neoliberal think tank known as the Project for a New American Century that was formed in 1997 to promote American global leadership and free market capitalism wherever it wanted after the end of the Cold War. Influential members of the group, including foreign policy insiders such as Paul Wolfowitz, who became Rumsfeld's deputy secretary of defense, and Richard Perle, had long been keen on toppling Hussein and establishing American hegemony in the Middle East. The group even wrote President Bill Clinton, warning him about the danger the Iraqi dictator represented to oil resources in the Middle East and his potential to use weapons of mass destruction.[3]

Richard Clarke, who served as national coordinator for security and counterterrorism for both Bill Clinton and George W. Bush, was convinced that Bush was intent on regime change in Iraq from the moment he entered the White House. Clarke told the president that the 9/11 attacks were orchestrated by al-Qaeda, a terrorist group centered in Afghanistan, but found that there was a powerful current of opinion in Bush's inner circle, especially in the minds of Rumsfeld and Wolfowitz, that the entire operation was too sophisticated to be pulled off by the terrorist group and that it must have had some sponsorship from a state like Iraq. Clarke wrote that three days after 9/11 Rumsfeld was talking out loud about going after Iraq and its dictator. And Cheney seemed "hell-bent" on attacking Iraq as if "nothing else mattered." Clarke did recall that Secretary of State Colin Powell called for caution in regard to moving against Hussein because such an action might have unfortunate consequences. Cheney also rejected suggestions from former national security advisor Brent Scowcroft that Iraq could be contained even if it had dangerous weapons. To the vice president, the post-9/11 era constituted a new world order where caution was not feasible.[4]

America invaded Iraq in March of 2003 with military support from allies such as Australia, Poland, and the United Kingdom. The goal of the offensive, which was dubbed "Operation Iraqi Freedom," a term that reflected the moralizing aspirations of war-based patriots, was to depose Saddam Hussein and his Ba'athist government, find and remove weapons of mass destruction which Bush felt could be used against America, and bring freedom to the Iraqi people. At the start of the campaign, popular opinion generally backed this first implementation of the Bush Doctrine. A CBS News poll indicated that some 63 percent of Americans supported the invasion, although the same amount hoped the president might find a diplomatic solution to the issue. Polling from the Pew Research Center showed that 71 percent of those responding felt the administration was making the "right decision" and only 22 percent considered it "wrong." A USA Today/ CNN/Gallup poll asked people if they favored invading Iraq with American ground troops to overthrow the dictator; 58 percent said they did.[5]

Cable news channels also offered strong support for the preemptive strike on Iraq with rhetoric that has been described as "hyperpatriotic" and filled with aggressive passions and intolerance toward dissent. The Fox News Channel and, to a lesser extent, MSNBC abandoned any degree of impartiality when it came to reporting on the war and became ardent supporters of the Bush Doctrine. Reporters began to refer to American soldiers as "our troops" in contrast to their adversaries in battle, who were labeled "terror goons." Fox News became the most watched source for cable news in the spring of 2003, although it had already begun to assert its supremacy with an aggressive patriotic tone in the immediate aftermath of 9/11. As American forces entered Iraq, MSNBC started displaying a portrait of President Bush in its main studio along with photos of men and women serving in the field. The network quickly cancelled the *Phil Donahue Show*, which it had just launched a few months earlier, because the host had become an outspoken critic of Bush's preemptive war doctrine. Even country radio stations joined the push to support the attack on Iraq. When the popular singing group the Dixie Chicks told an audience in London that they were ashamed of Bush for ordering the war and they were worried over the violence it would bring, many country stations stopped playing their records; listeners called them "unpatriotic."[6]

Pushback for Peace

In time the invasion of Iraq proved controversial for many reasons. In addition to not finding the dangerous weapons that the Bush administration feared might someday be used against America, the entire enterprise proved to be an expensive venture, costing some $1.5 trillion. This financial burden created a debt load that would be passed to future generations and was made worse by the fact that the administration enacted tax cuts at the same time. To a certain extent the public was insulated from much of the human cost of the war because the military was made up of volunteers, mostly from the working class, and not drawn from a draft that would have pulled soldiers from a wider spectrum of the population. The fact that the greatest sacrifices of the war were confined to a rather small portion of the populace, however, did not mean that calls for peace or assertions of rage over the killing and dying on all sides did not resonate with many citizens. Indeed, despite the opinion polls, which tended to offer narrow responses to very specific questions, Americans held an incredibly wide array of emotions and attitudes about Iraq and serious reservations about what their nation was doing right from the beginning.[7]

The American response to the War on Terror was partly framed within a larger contest that was already brewing before 2001 between neoliberals intent on expanding American power in the world and liberal activists wary of the use of such influence. Progressive activists had been mounting opposition to the exercise of both American corporate and military power on a global basis, which they saw as not only imperialistic but detrimental to the human rights of people in various locations. Some of their reservations were already manifested in a mild way at the start of the bombing of Afghanistan, but the move into Iraq only magnified such resistance. Neoliberals valued military might and the power of the free market; they were less responsive to human pain emanating from armed strikes or rising tides of inequality.

In 1999 many of these dissenters had initiated powerful demonstrations against the growing power of the World Trade Organization (WTO) over the world economy as it met in Seattle. Farmers from India and South America, union activists from the United States, and countless others converged to challenge WTO policies and confront police in the streets. Protesters were upset that rulings by the WTO seemed to favor corporate interests over those defending environmental and labor rights. In what became known as the "Battle of Seattle," street violence not only raised awareness of the impact of neoconservative economic policies of leading industrial nations like the United States but conveyed a sense that America's relationship with the rest of the world was exploitive and reflective of "corporate greed." To critics it was telling that the WTO had refused to link the protection of human rights and workers' rights to participation in the global economic system and actually forbade any form of discrimination against traded goods regardless of whether they were produced by processes that abused workers or the environment or not. Already skeptical of the ways American influence was exercised in the world, it did not take much of a leap for these activists to see a projected War on Terror as another effort by neoconservatives in the United States to use American power to bring human and environmental destruction to other parts of the globe and gain greater control over oil reserves. In such a scenario a war-based patriotism stood ready to insulate national leaders from passionate calls for a more democratic world.[8]

United for Peace and Justice (UFPJ) was one of the most powerful progressive voices that attempted to mobilize opposition to Bush's preemptive war. The organization was formed in October 2002, as concerns over Bush's plan to bomb Afghanistan fostered a merger of hundreds of liberal organizations. UFPJ's growth was particularly inspired by the life and death of Minnesota senator Paul Wellstone, who was killed in a plane crash as the group was being put together in Washington, D.C. Wellstone had been a staunch opponent of the 2002 congressional resolution authorizing the use of force against Iraq. He realized that there was considerable public opinion supporting Bush but felt it was "soft" and that he could still win reelection by staying true to his progressive policies. In fact, his opposition to the resolution and his antiwar views had attracted the attention of Bush and Cheney, who became directly involved in selecting a candidate to run against him as he sought a third term.[9]

Most of the activists in UFPJ agreed with the premise that the Bush administration's drive into Iraq was about more than fighting terrorism and involved an imperialistic grab for Middle Eastern oil. Human rights defenders also worried out loud that an invasion would bring harm to many innocent civilians in Iraq. Founding organizations of the UFPJ included the American Friends Committee, Black Voices for Peace, the National Council of Churches, the National Organization of Women, and September 11th Families for Peaceful Tomorrows. UFPJ made a dramatic impact on the debate over whether to go into Iraq when it helped to organize a massive international protest called "The World Says No to War." On February 15, 2003—on the eve of the invasion—millions of people around the world joined in the largest transnational antiwar protests in human history to try to stop the impending conflict. Chanting slogans like "No War in Iraq," "Not in My Name," and "No Blood for Oil," protesters raised their voices in cities around the world. In London crowds reached an estimated 500,000 and challenged Prime Minister Tony Blair's staunch support for the American president. German officials estimated the size of the crowd near the Brandenburg Gate at over 200,000.

Expressions at the rallies made it clear just how diverse the interests that were melding in opposition to Bush's actions were. In Chicago a group called the "Antiwar Marching Band" sought to counter "hate with joy." Wearing skeleton suits topped with "Uncle Sam paper hats," these musicians and their followers tooted kazoos and banged plastic buckets and aluminum pans to the tune of traditional patriotic melodies like "You're a Grand Old Flag." These protesters reasoned that by acting and dressing in a rather ridiculous manner they could mimic the blamelessness of innocent people everywhere, some of whom were being killed in Iraq. Many speakers at the

Chicago gathering also stressed the need for multicultural cooperation in America's foreign policy, raised awareness of the fact that Muslims were already being harmed in the United States in the aftermath of 9/11, and chanted "No Blood for Oil." When a "medic" took to warn the crowd against hypothermia and watch for anyone who seemed to be confused, a voice in the crowd yelled that it was the president who was really confused.[10]

Variety marked not only the messages and styles of protesters but their social backgrounds as well. The demonstrations were not simply assemblies of college students, as was sometimes case for many Vietnam War protests, but were composed of a broad cross section of demographic groups.[11] Most people who marched, while not students, were college educated. In the United States, from a sample of 5,000, protesters were more likely to be women (63 percent) than men and tended to be middle aged (ages forty-five to sixty-four) rather than young adults who ranged in age from twenty-five to forty-four. Only 8 percent of the American marchers said they were motivated simply by an adherence to pacifistic beliefs. Most were pulled into action by an outright rejection of the rationales the Bush administrations used to defend their decision. A large contingent, about one-fifth, indicated that they took to the streets because they felt the need to make a civic contribution to their society, a sign of the link between their sense of empathic loyalty and a concern for the welfare of others. British respondents, also living in a nation headed for a war in Iraq, mirrored the sentiments of the Americans. They tended not to be pacifists but mostly disagreed with the rationales given for the war. Pacifism did, however, play a more important role in the motivations of protesters in Germany (26 percent), Italy (50 percent) and Spain (34 percent).[12]

American Catholic bishops, like protesters in the streets, also took a strong stand on the issue of a global war on terror, another sign that opinion polls at the time failed to register the full depth and range of public attitudes on the preemptive war. On November 1, 2001 the bishops issued a major statement on a military response titled "Living with Faith and Hope after September 11" which stressed the need to treat terrorism as a crime and not an act of war, a definition that flew in the face of the response to the attacks by the Bush administration. While not advocating military interventions against any government, including Afghanistan, the prelates admitted that the United States had a "just cause" for a limited military response to defend itself against al-Qaeda and the Taliban. The clerics urged, however, that after 9/11 the United States had to define security broadly to address not only the need for possible military response but fundamental problems that could lead to the rise of terrorism in the first place such as poverty or intolerance. The bishops were clearly concerned that the nation might embark upon what they termed a "counterproductive overreaction" that was overly reliant on military force and succumb to the temptation to trade freedom for security. The idea of an "overreaction" was in fact central to explaining why the bishops, the Vatican, and church leaders around the world supported protests against an invasion of Iraq.[13]

Catholic, Episcopal, and Lutheran officials joined forces with one another to express their concerns, arranging meetings with Condoleezza Rice, Bush's national security advisor, on two separate occasions in 2001 to press their points. Admitting that the matter of Iraq was a difficult one, they made it clear that the idea of a preemptive war worried them most of all. They admitted that it was possible to respond preemptively to an attack that appeared imminent but refused to dismiss their long-standing beliefs that war needed to be based on a "just cause" and pursued only as a "last resort." In a statement dated November 13, 2002, they declared that lacking clear and adequate evidence of an imminent attack of a "grave nature," a war against Iraq "in light of current public information" would not meet the strict requirements of Catholic teaching for overriding the strong presumption they held against the use of military force. They also expressed concern that such a war would bring further hardship to the "long-suffering civilian population of Iraq."[14]

September 11th Families for Peaceful Tomorrows, an antiwar group formed by individuals who lost loved ones in the 9/11 attacks and that had already opposed the bombing of Afghanistan, also joined the Iraq coalition. Disheartened that a war had been launched in the names of their fallen relatives, Peaceful Tomorrows was quick to express its lack of support for another American military operation in response to the terrorist assault. In 2002 Derrill Bodley, whose daughter was killed in the crash at Shanksville, spoke for the organization when he wrote a statement titled "A Father's Plea for Peace." Bodley had actually met the president at a ceremony at the Pennsylvania crash site and had urged him at the time to listen to world leaders who warned against going down the path to war. In his statement Bodley invoked the idea of a compassionate American identity and insisted that as human beings Americans needed to produce the materials of peace and not war. "Shall we rain down bombs upon the people of Iraq?" he asked. "Shall we continue the death, destruction, and disease that has already been heaped upon Iraq?"

In January 2003, Peaceful Tomorrows sent its own delegation of empathic patriots to Iraq prior to the American invasion just as they had visited Afghanistan the year before. Members visited ordinary Iraqis in their homes and frequently discussed their mutual sense of grief over the loss of those near and dear. Such discussions were very much in line with the group's desire "to acknowledge our fellowship with all people affected by violence and war, recognizing that the resulting deaths are overwhelmingly civilian." Kristin Olsen, a member of the delegation to Iraq, described one such meeting in Basra with the family of Jamil Fedah, who was killed by an errant American bomb in the no-fly zone in December 2002. Olsen recalled meeting the mother of the dead man who sat draped in her black abaya flanked by several female relatives. As Olsen took her hand, the two women began to cry. Olsen told her over and over, "I am sorry. I am sorry."

It was not surprising that many members of Peaceful Tomorrows joined the large protests against an Iraq invasion in New York in 2003. Some members of the group truly resented Bush's reference to earlier demonstrations as simply "focus groups" on his foreign policy. In their estimation he seemed to show no respect for the "opinions of mankind." Peaceful Tomorrows made it clear in an official release that its members felt the planned invasion would be "illegal, immoral, and unjustified." Members claimed they knew what it felt like to suffer trauma and heartache and that they wanted to spare other "innocent families" the same pain. While they resolutely condemned the brutality of Saddam Hussein, they firmly believed that his bad behavior did not justify the fact that the government of the United States would bring more destruction to that nation.

Despite their noble intentions, Peaceful Tomorrows evoked considerable criticism for its visit to Iraq from belligerent patriots. One citizen wrote to Peaceful Tomorrows claiming that its members should be ashamed to call themselves Americans. The writer argued that Afghanistan was no longer living under an oppressive regime that had promoted terrorist activities as a result of the American attacks on that country. For this person a similar war on Iraq would bring about the realization of the hope that both families in the United States and "innocent families" in Iraq would be able to breathe a sigh of relief that governments like the Taliban and Ba'ath Party in Iraq would no longer be capable of providing the means to terrorize and murder innocent people. Another opponent emailed the group to say, "You make me sick." This individual argued that by not supporting a war against Iraq, the group was simply supporting a "bloodthirsty" dictator and only called for peace because its members were a bunch of "over aged hippy losers who burnt themselves out in the 1960s." Finally, a writer from Omaha told the peace activists that by visiting Iraq they were simply retracing the "unpatriotic" steps that actress-turned-war-protester Jane Fonda had taken in the 1960s by visiting Vietnam and insulting Americans who have fought and died for this country over the years.[15]

Larry Syverson and John Warner

Larry Syverson had not lost someone dear to him on 9/11, but he feared for the safety of his two sons who were serving in the military. Syverson began his own protest against the attack on Iraq in March 2003 by standing on the sidewalk in front of the federal courthouse in Richmond, Virginia. For five years he occupied this spot carrying a sign that read "Iraq oil is not worth my sons' blood." At home Syverson and his wife kept a vigil waiting for their sons to return by lighting candles in their dining room window and wrapping yellow ribbons around a pine tree in their front yard. Eventually the men would return home safely, although at one time or another both suffered from the harsh effects of post-traumatic stress disorder (PTSD). One was temporarily put on suicide watch in an army hospital and another endured a period of homelessness.[16]

The public nature of Syverson's personal grievance attracted considerable attention. Passing motorists would often honk their horns in a show of support, something that buoyed his spirits. Occasionally sympathizers would stand with him in a show of solidarity. And many elected to write him emails or letters. Michael Tucker, a filmmaker who had been to Iraq, wrote to say that if people at home knew what "these kids are going through physically and emotionally, they would demand Bush resign." Tucker noted how American soldiers frequently could not tell friend from foe in Iraq and stressed how many had joined the service simply to save for college but are now coming home "either dead or wounded." Tucker shared one of Syverson's beliefs that Iraq had nothing to do with 9/11; he particularly appreciated the fact that the Virginia father was willing to publicly proclaim his views when so many were "scared to speak up." Another sympathizer wrote to say that she was praying for the safe return for Syverson's sons. Having found the wait for her own son to come home as the "most wrenching experience of my life," she was now troubled by the realization that "a good deal of blood would still be spilled until the battle was finished." "Our days ahead look bleak," she feared. Another backer told the worried father that he could not "imagine the pain and worry you go through every day and night." This man's son had served in the navy in the Middle East and argued that the men who made the decision to go to war have never known the heartbreak of watching their buddy die or lose his arms and legs. A woman named Janis Mooradian told the Richmond dissident, "My heart is with you."[17]

Although Syverson made it clear to reporters that he supported the troops while critiquing the war, a stance that gave evidence of a compassionate patriotism, he still encountered a considerable degree of hostility from pro-war voices. As he stood on the sidewalk, hecklers frequently yelled to say that he should be ashamed of himself; many called him "unpatriotic," an ironic charge, since all four of his sons eventually served in the armed forces. A critic actually told him that he wished one of his sons would be killed in order to punish him for his dissent, so strong was the desire of some war-based patriots to silence the public expression of pain. One night someone threw eggs at his house; during a noontime protest a truck swerved so close to him that he was sure it was done intentionally. A man named Steve Gallimore wrote to Syverson to state his support for the invasion by arguing that Saddam Hussein himself might have been a "weapon of mass destruction in human form." Gallimore asked the worried parent, "How are you going to explain your position to families of those killed in Iraq, not all of whom oppose the war. . . . Do you mean to tell me they are maligned for a lost and erroneous cause?" And a woman named Kate Foster, calling herself a "patriot," let Syverson know she was grateful for the service his sons rendered but felt their father was a "coward who has no concept of what it takes to defeat the evil we now face since September 11th. . . . You frighten me because you are a direct threat to my freedom and security."[18]

Syverson also wrote to Virginia's two senators asking them to endorse his position that the president had knowingly used false data to invade Iraq. Both refused to accede to his wishes. John Warner responded by saying that he was "enormously proud" of George Bush and "our military" for ending the oppression of Saddam Hussein's regime. He argued that the Iraqi people were now enjoying freedom that had been denied them for decades. Warner noted that he served on the Senate Select Committee on Intelligence, where he saw no evidence that the administration engaged in any effort to distort information on Iraq, although he was "saddened" by "coalition casualties." Warner's Senate colleague, George Allen, claimed that he supported the president "for his resolve to protect the American people." Allen also expressed his appreciation for the sacrifice made by citizens who lost loved ones in Iraq for "our greater security." He insisted that America was now a "safer nation thanks to these heroes and their patriotic families."[19]

Warner's staunch support for Bush and the incursion into Iraq, a stance reinforced by the fact that he helped introduce the Iraq war resolution into the Senate in October 2002, actually flew in the face of most of the opinions on the matter he received from constituents in his home state. Letters to the senator like those from Syverson were overwhelmingly critical of Bush and his preemptive move. In time Warner would moderate this support, perhaps moved by the letters that came to him as well as the fact that the invasion degenerated into endless rounds of killing rather than any liberation for Iraq. By 2007 he opposed a Bush administration request for more American troops and actually called for some drawdown of troop levels in Iraq.[20]

Despite revealing some clear support for Bush's policies, the vast majority of Virginians who wrote Warner condemned the move into Iraq. A Bush backer did tell Warner that "it was the duty of the American people" to stand by the president. Another told the senator that he was proud of him for his "unwavering support of our country, our President, and our military personnel at this pivotal time in U.S. history." A pro-war citizen sent Warner a copy of a letter he had sent to Bush that thanked the president "for being a gifted leader—strong of heart and of great resolve." And another patriot wrote Bush and copied Warner indicating that a "few of our boys killed here and maimed there was a small price to pay to make our country safer."[21]

Opponents of what Bush was doing and Warner was supporting, however, were inclined to raise humanitarian concerns and convey moral outrage over the Iraq invasion. At times they made it crystal clear that these feelings were grounded in their sense of patriotism and the standards they wanted their nation to uphold. The intrusion into Iraq, in the opinion of one Virginian, "was morally wrong and totally out of character with the values of our nation. . . . Spraying the pockets of terrorism with our military might is not only ineffective it is also inhumane to the civilians whom we end up terrorizing." Another citizen asked Warner, would he be justified in shooting his neighbor just because he possessed guns and was a threat to his safety? This individual could not accept the fact that the United States had the right to "smite a nation, kill their babies and other innocents just because we feel it is threat to our country." One letter urged Warner to use his influence in Washington to check the "bloodlust" of the Bush administration. This constituent claimed, "Every day I pray for peace . . . a future where human life is priceless and differences co-exist . . . where war is no longer an option and we are truly free." Finally an American patriot told the senator that he grieved "for the murders of unarmed civilians and the deaths of soldiers in President Bush's outlaw aggression.[22]

The Dissent of Robert Byrd

In October 2002, Congress approved a resolution for the use of military force against Iraq. Overall support for the legislation was strong, although it tended to follow party lines. Some 60 percent of Democrats in the House and 42 percent in the Senate opposed the measure. Two senators who opposed it, Dick Durbin of Illinois and Kent Conrad of North Dakota, both felt that Iraq was not connected to 9/11 in any way. Their senate colleague _ Robert C. Byrd of West Virginia joined their dissent, fearing that a move into Iraq could lead to another Vietnam. Byrd also regretted the support he had rendered for the Gulf of Tonkin resolution in 1964. He remarked that the sight of visitors to the Vietnam Veterans Memorial in Washington still left him mournful. Byrd also felt the Bush administration appeared to be "hell-bent" on war and unwilling to listen to any alternatives.[23]

In March 2003, as American forces prepared to enter Iraq, Byrd made a memorable patriotic speech on the Senate floor. After watching the lead-up to the invasion, the senator exclaimed that he now carried a "heavy, heavy heart" and "wept" for his country. He insisted that the actions of the Bush administration to jump-start another military intervention had undermined respect for the United States throughout the world and it was no longer viewed as a "benevolent peacekeeper." "Our friends mistrust us, our word is disputed and our intentions are questioned," he affirmed. To the senator America's relationships with other nations were no longer based on reason because we were more intent on demanding obedience and threatening recriminations. Instead of isolating Saddam Hussein, Byrd felt America had only isolated itself with its proclamation of "a new doctrine of preemption which is understood by few and feared by many." He warned the president that because he had asserted the right to turn our firepower on any corner of the globe in its battle against terrorists the world had become a more dangerous place. "This administration has directed all of the anger, fear and grief which emerged from the ashes of the twin towers and twisted metal of the Pentagon toward a tangible villain, one we can see and attack. And villain he is. But he is the wrong villain. And this is the wrong war."[24]

Not unexpectedly Byrd's stance provoked a considerable response in the heated atmosphere of 2003. Letters and messages to his office again exposed the wide range of public opinion not only over Iraq but over the larger war on terror and the matter of loyalty to the nation. To a considerable extent missives endorsing his position also revealed the extent to which humanitarian concerns weighed heavily upon the minds of many Americans. Compassionate patriots worried not only about the harm that would come to American troops but the damage and injury Americans would bring to guiltless Iraqis as well. A constituent from Frankford, West Virginia, told Byrd that he could not understand why the president was so eager to enter a war with a "weak nation" in which "a lot of innocent people in Iraq will be killed and many of our men and women in our military." This person found the entire situation depressing and thanked Byrd for having the "courage to speak out against the foolish Bush policies." Another state resident urged the senator to rally his colleagues "to put an end to this administration's arrogant warmongering hysteria before there is any loss of American and 'allied' lives." He also felt the money spent on the invasion would be better used to improve "health services" to American citizens or shoring up social security. "Please continue to fight the battle for us common people whose voices are never heard." Another West Virginian pleaded with the senator to bring home American troops immediately. He argued that we cannot solve terrorism through increased violence against Iraqis; such action "can only lead to an increased cycle of violence such as exists in Israel and Palestine." This individual urged Byrd to see if Iraq could be given back to the Iraqis and if the money spent on the war could be diverted "to meet human needs." A Gold Star constituent told the senator that he was haunted by a photo he saw of a father asking the president if the war was worth it after losing his only son in the conflict. This writer felt that the president should be impeached. One West Virginian revealed that he was deeply troubled by the "humanitarian catastrophe" in Iraq and hoped that Congress could find a way to ensure that compassionate assistance be given to the Iraqi people."[25]

Many West Virginians also demonstrated a deep regard for the welfare of others—patriotism at its best—when they condemned the war's financial costs. These citizens tended to invoke the old contradiction between guns and butter and resented the fact that money spent on war could be better spent to meet pressing social needs. One of Byrd's constituents argued that it would be better to get "military people" out of Iraq and spend billions of dollars the war absorbed on investments at home. This writer, noting the closing of glass factories near Clarksburg, argued that "our people are losing jobs by the thousands and are factories are closing down." A resident of Morgantown loved Byrd's comment that Congress is not an ATM machine and felt the government should stop throwing good money after bad while "putting young men and women in harm's way."[26]

Some members of the public were troubled not so much because the financial costs might drain resources from social programs but because such expenditures opened the door for greed. A man from Huntington wrote Byrd insisting the troops be withdrawn because "the war was a fraud putting money into the pockets of big oil." This concerned citizen believed that Vice President Dick Cheney "got millions from Halliburton" and was now continuing to enrich himself at the expense of American troops. His reference was to a large corporation for which Cheney worked before the war and now had lucrative contracts to assist the war effort. A fellow West Virginian made a similar point, arguing that the war was only making "Bush's friends rich with military contracts and tax cuts." "This is a disgrace to the men and women serving our country," he charged; "America will not be free as long as the Bush administration gets its way."[27]

It was also clear that some of the state's citizens simply did not like the overall direction of Bush's policies. These West Virginians did not mince words when referring to the forty-third present. "He is taking our society down the wrong path and we and our children will be paying for years from now," one woman wrote. A former Vietnam vet felt that Bush had gone "too far to the right with the Patriot Act, [John]Ashcroft, and the Fox News Channel and hysteria and paranoia over terrorism." Another critic of the president wondered how America can be seen as liberating Iraq "when we have bombed the crap out of them." From Bluefield a woman wrote that the "actions of our president have caused me to have a heavy heart" and that she felt Bush was only "warmongering" to enhance his reelection bid in 2004. "Where did this man ever get the idea that he had the right to order an attack on a largely, defenseless nation like Iraq?" asked another Byrd devotee.[28]

The president certainly had his supporters, and they were not averse to sending their thoughts to the West Virginia senator as well. Several told Byrd that Bush had displayed fortitude with his plan of attack. Another inhabitant defended the president by arguing that "he has the balls to stand up and do what is right" and warned Byrd that he had better support the troops that were sent overseas. A man from Clarksburg admonished the senator to "get on board" with Bush and charged that Saddam Hussein had promoted terrorism throughout the world, "given thousands of dollars to the families of terrorists who were willing to kill themselves to take the lives of Jews in Israel and praised them for their sacrifice," and murdered his own people. To this constituent, Bush was a "great president who looks to God for guidance for all the decisions he has to make concerning our great nation. . . . It is time for our nation's leaders to start backing our president and military" and kneeling and praying for "God's guidance." A writer from West Union, West Virginia, who served in Vietnam declared that Bush made him proud to be an American and called upon the senator to withdraw his objections to the war.[29]

In his standard response, Byrd stressed that his opposition to the war did not mean he stopped supporting the troops. He did question the administration when it applied for more funds for the Iraq campaign and for paying contractors because the president had originally promised that such costs would be paid for from oil revenues generated from the takeover of Iraq. Byrd insisted over and over that he stood "foursquare behind our military" and supported all funding levels necessary to keep the troops safe." His loyalty, in other words, was more human centered than state centered. Because the members of the public were being asked to sacrifice their sons and daughters, the senator felt the Bush administration still had to do more than it had in explaining why it sought to expand the War on Terror into Iraq.[30]

The Death of Iraqis

Many Americans extended the sensitivity Byrd showed for American suffering to the agony experienced by people we fought as well. Activists like Marla Ruzicka, for instance, helped considerably in raising public awareness of damage the United States inflicted on others. As a young girl in the San Francisco area, Ruzicka had become a zealous defender of Native American rights and an ardent advocate of environmentalism. News of the murders of Arabs and Muslims in America as acts of revenge in the aftermath of 9/11, however, soon pushed her humanitarian instincts in a different direction. On her own she began to meet with residents of the large Afghan settlement in Fremont, California, not far from where she lived. It was here that she heard first-person accounts of refugees fleeing Afghanistan in the wake of U.S. bombings in the fall of 2002 and even debates among Afghans themselves over the relative merits of the American attack on their homeland. It was not long before Ruzicka was off to this foreign land to see the devastation for herself, listen to tales of families destroyed in remote villages, and visit the wounded in hospital wards. Back in California she began to work with groups intent upon raising funds to help families in Afghanistan harmed by American bombs.[31]

When members of September 11th Families for Peaceful Tomorrows visited Afghanistan in 2002, it was Ruzicka who helped arrange for the delegation to meet with Afghan families injured by the American aggression. Soon she began the systematic collection of as much specific information as she could find on the precise locations where the bombs hit, the names of the injured and the dead, and rough estimates of the damages to homes and property. In "tattered notebooks" she created the first "Afghan Civilian Casualty Survey," a direct act of protest to leaders and civilians who hoped to screen the consequences of the war from public view or remain indifferent to them. Rita Lazar, one of the key figures in Peaceful Tomorrows whose brother had died in the collapse of the World Trade Center, even helped Ruzicka bring some Afghan families to the U.S. Embassy in Kabul to make the case that they be compensated in some form. Eventually Ruzicka's tireless efforts to expose the plight of innocent Afghans harmed by Americans captured the attention of Senator Patrick Leahy of Vermont, who initiated successful efforts to get the government to offer modest payments to some of the victims for home repairs. On one occasion she even tried to shove some of her data into the hands of Donald Rumsfeld as he was getting into a car.[32]

Inevitably Ruzicka's empathetic instincts drove her to Iraq. She actually entered Hillah in 2003 just after U.S. rockets had wounded a number of children and adults. The young woman visited a local hospital where some of the injured had gone seeking medical aid, and she walked the grounds of the town looking for unexploded cluster bombs so she could alert civilians to their location and inform marines who had the ability to defuse them. Wearing an abaya, or robe—a dress often worn by Muslim women—she would move among the people of Iraq offering them her condolences and telling them that she was "so sorry we invaded your country. I'm so sorry we killed your people." As in Afghanistan, she also recruited some local students to help her compile a survey of Iraqis who were killed or wounded. Ruzicka was aware that American military policy called for the minimizing of civilian casualties, but she hated the term "collateral damage," which tended to obscure the harsh reality of human suffering that troubled her so much. She felt that whether one was for or against the war, under no circumstances should guiltless individuals be harmed. If they were, she insisted that the United States must help them "reconstruct their lives." Again, with the help of Senator Leahy, she was able to get Congress to offer some modest compensation to Iraqis which were administered at the discretion of military commanders in Iraq often to suppress the substantial anger that had emerged toward Americans who were serving there.[33]

Marla Ruzicka's death from a car bombing in Iraq in 2005 was an utter tragedy that drew attention from the press throughout the United States. Sarah Holewinski, writing in the *Washington Post*, felt that Ruzicka's efforts in eventually securing modest congressional funding for injured families in Afghanistan and Iraq should be "enshrined" in our war policies if we are to be "just a little bit better" as a nation. Holewinski noted, however, that the payments Americans did make fell far short of what was needed and that insurgents opposing the American presence often killed Iraqis who accepted them. Holewinski reminded her readers, and the Pentagon, that the airstrikes continued to hit areas populated by civilians and reiterated Ruzicka's belief that all human lives were sacred whether they were brave Americans serving in the war or guiltless families living amid the horrors of what Iraq became. Another report in the *Philadelphia Inquirer* called Marla "a one-woman human-rights dynamo who was able to focus attention on a subject many tended to ignore." "Civilian casualties are the inconvenient stain on the story of Iraq liberation," the newspaper proclaimed.[34]

Some Americans learned of the devastating impact their invasion was having on Iraq's civilians by simply going online. A young Iraqi woman in her early twenties who went by the alias "Riverbend" began to blog on her personal website soon after the Americans arrived in 2003. Her career now interrupted by the occupation and her "social life blown," Riverbend began reporting on the war and what it was doing to her homeland. Naming her blog "Baghdad Burning," this Iraqi witness was soon corresponding with people throughout the world, including many in the United States. Not surprisingly this insider's view of the situation was highly critical of the American presence. On August 19, 2003 she reported on the death of a boy about ten years of age in Anbar Province, northwest of Baghdad. He died during a raid by American forces on his family's residence. Riverbend noted that "his family is devastated" and that Iraqis had become terrified of such raids on private dwellings. "You never know what will happen—who might be shot, who might react wrong—what exactly the wrong reaction might be," she declared. To her the raids really did not accomplish anything at all. They only served as a "constant reminder that we are under occupation, we are not independent . . . we are not liberated . . . we are not safe in our own homes," she lamented.

Riverbend also duly documented much of the reaction she received to her dispatches, especially from Americans. Predictably her readers offered her a range of rejoinders. Some thanked her for providing a unique perspective on the war and seemed interested in trying to understand what was going on. Other irate viewers of Fox News sent her angry retorts because of her unfavorable perspective on the American operation. "I get emails constantly reminding me of the tragedy of September 11 and telling me how the 'Arabs' brought all of this upon themselves," she wrote. Riverbend failed to understand why some Americans could not understand why Iraqis were "bitter" over all that had happened and why a few of them wanted to throw bombs at "some 19 year old soldier from Missouri."[35]

In a culture increasingly more responsive to the human tragedy of war than to the demonstration of military dominance, it was actually not uncommon to read news articles in the United States about the harm America was bringing to the people of Iraq during the first years of the occupation. In 2004 Eric Ringham wrote in the *Minneapolis Star Tribune* about the children killed by gunfire and car bombs in Iraq. Ringham admitted that it was difficult to gain a true count of civilian deaths but pointed out that it was rather easy to read horrific accounts of such tragedies on a number of various websites such as Iraqibodycount.com. He argued strongly that the public should not remain indifferent to such losses and, indeed, was responsible for them, for the public had started this "war of choice." Ringham also showed how the war had led to a general deterioration in health conditions throughout Iraq because the violence had forced many international aid agencies to flee. Their departure was particularly regrettable, he noted, because it led to an increase in the deaths of children.

In the same year the *Dayton Daily News* filed a request under the Freedom of Information Act to examine cases of violence in Iraq that resulted in claims for compensation from the United States. The journal examined 4,611 civil claims alleging abuse and misconduct by American military personnel and found that only about one in four resulted in some form of reimbursement. The newspaper was struck not only by the fact that few knew about this process but by how much the details in the claims illustrated the extent of civilian losses. The paper was astonished to learn of civilians riding in cars and being riddled with bullets and people killed at checkpoints simply because they did not understand directions given to them. It noted that about 78 percent of the claims were initiated after

President Bush had declared that major combat operations were over. More to the point, the article argued that this "collateral damage" was helping to turn the Iraqi population against the Americans, who had ostensibly come to liberate them, and that this fact was making it harder for the nation's troops to defend themselves because they were never sure who was angry at them and who was not. The paper's writers were also struck by the fact that appeals for damages from the death of children were often denied.[36]

A key catalyst in turning public attention to the harm American forces had brought to the blameless in Iraq was the publication of two peer-reviewed articles in *The Lancet*, a British medical journal. The essays looked at the number of "excess" deaths the occupation caused above what normally would have been expected. In 2004 the authors of the studies estimated that some 98,000 people had been killed due to what they termed military combat, a general rise of "lawlessness" and poor health conditions. A second study two years later moved the cumulative total to a staggering 654,966 deaths that were attributed not only to the actions of American forces and their allies but to the onset of a bitter civil war among factions in Iraq. *The Lancet*'s findings were controversial because they were higher than estimates from several other sources including the Iraqi Ministry of Health. Many were also aware that the 2004 *Lancet* report was released just before the American elections, and some dismissed their findings as an attempt to discredit Bush. Subsequent calculations have continued to vary greatly, and there is still no agreement on just how many people in Iraq lost their lives because of the violence unleashed by the American attack in 2003. For instance, Iraq Body Count (IBC), a British organization supported by private donations, calculated that some 24,865 civilians, 10 percent of whom were under the age of eighteen, were killed in the first two years of the war and some 90,000 to 97,000 innocent Iraqis lost their lives over the first four years. IBC's estimates of "total violent deaths" in Iraq between 2003 and 2013 when the death of combatants on all sides are added to civilian totals amounted to 184,512.

Nongovernmental organizations like IBC and the American Civil Liberties Union wanted to bring to the public a truer assessment of the human bloodshed to counter official actions to blot out the bitter realities of military action and, by inference, mythical justifications of such struggles. IBC proclaimed that its very reason for being was that "our common humanity demands the recording of war deaths," and felt strongly that such evidence was fundamental to holding a nation accountable for its actions, something war-based patriots were loath to do. It made it clear that the United

States and the United Kingdom must bear "particular responsibility" for the carnage. In 2007 the American Civil Liberties Union elaborated on the impact of the war on civilians by making public hundreds of claims for damages filed by citizens in Afghanistan and Iraq. It felt compelled to do so because in its view, the Department of Defense had made "unprecedented efforts to control and suppress information on the human costs of the war," including paying Iraqi journalists to compose positive reports on the effect the American military presence was having and banning photos of caskets bringing home the remains of American soldiers.[37]

Even before the *Lancet* publications, Dennis Kucinich, a congressman from Cleveland, had spoken out against the Iraq War and warned of human slaughter in Iraq. In his 2003 book, *A Prayer for America*, Kucinich charged that Bush's plans for preemptive war were rooted not so much in necessity but in visions of "grandeur" and empire. The Ohio politician argued that there was no credible evidence linking Iraq with 9/11 and that it would be better to approach matters of global security in a cooperative manner with allies. He especially worried that "unilateral action" would set the nation on a "bloodstained path" that would not only destroy infrastructure in Iraq but lives, families, and homes as American forces engaged in house to house combat." Finally, for this liberal Democrat, an unjustified war would drain resources and weaken moral commitments in the homeland that could better be used to help people in need. He pleaded that America should "abolish weapons of mass destruction at home" such as joblessness, poverty, and hunger.[38]

In December 2006, Kucinich and Ron Paul, a Republican and later Libertarian congressman from Texas, sponsored hearings on the *Lancet* publications and the matter of Iraqi casualties in general. For Kucinich the hearings were justified because the death toll of Iraqis appeared to be reaching unbearable numbers but were still often ignored by the American public. While precise numbers were elusive, Kucinich estimated that for every American death some 200 Iraqis perished. "Consider the massive psychological impact of 9/11 and the resulting deaths have had on our nation," he reasoned, and "imagine the impact we would feel as a nation if over a period of three years we had the loss of lives as a percentage of our population that Iraq has had."

By this time Kucinich was also troubled by a rising American death toll that hit his district hard. In 2005 twenty-three marine reservists headquartered in Brook Park, a suburb of Cleveland, were killed in Anbar Province. Kucinich told the press that "the community's heart was broken." Local

homes quickly displayed American flags to honor the fallen, but the town's mayor made it clear the populace was in "shock." Kevin Rush, a reserve officer in charge of informing families of their losses, said it was extremely difficult for him to keep his emotions in check as he performed his grisly duties. "You can't let it seep inside you and devastate you," he explained. "If you let it get to you you would never survive."[39]

The Suffering of John Murtha

John Murtha was not only a prominent congressman from Pennsylvania but a former marine colonel who had served his country in Vietnam with pride. Murtha had built a reputation in Washington as a staunch supporter of the military in general and benefits for veterans in particular. He was quick to back the congressional resolution authorizing the use of military force against Iraq in 2002, although he expressed doubts about the potential costs of the entire operation. Consequently many pundits and even constituents were surprised in late 2005 when Murtha called for an American pullout from Iraq. Few at the time realized that the congressman not only had come to question the way the Bush administration was handling the war but was particularly bothered by the revelations of the abuse of Iraqi prisoners at Abu Ghraib.

Even more fundamental to Murtha's decision, however, was his growing sense of despondency over the human toll the war was taking. Frequent visits to Walter Reed Medical Center in Washington had allowed him an intimate look at the devastating physical and emotional injuries American troops had received from their tours of duty. Gradually the Vietnam vet began to question the patriotic rhetoric that drove the war in the first place and the human consequences he saw in the nation's wounded warriors. He was especially troubled by the experience of an Iraqi veteran from his district, which was located in western Pennsylvania, Salvatore Ross. While clearing land mines near Baghdad, Ross had been horribly wounded and lost not only his eyesight but both legs below the knee. He spent nearly a month in a coma and endured over a dozen surgeries. The young man had joined the army with enthusiasm, feeling that it would offer him a sense of adventure. He recalled that he felt he was doing something "patriotic" and came to love the "bonding" that took place among the men with whom he served. Murtha had pinned a Purple Heart on Ross and kept tabs on him after he left the hospital and returned to his hometown of Dunbar. Subsequent news that Ross was unable to pay his bills, had been drinking heavily, and had tried to assault a police officer disturbed this patriotic congressman greatly and left him with a distinctly tragic view of the war. "Sam Ross had an impact on me," Murtha told a reporter; "I just felt we had gotten to a point where we were talking so much about winning the war . . . that we were forgetting about the results of the war on individuals like Sam." He had also come to grieve after watching families crying uncontrollably as they stood at the bedside of loved ones at Bethesda Naval Hospital. By the fall of 2005 Murtha's direct encounter with distress and sadness convinced him that the battle in Iraq was unwinnable, and he called for a withdrawal.[40]

Around the same time Murtha began to turn against the war, his colleague in Congress Walter Jones of North Carolina also announced that he favored a troop withdrawal because he, like Murtha, felt devastated by the torment the war had brought to many families in his district. For years after the American occupation began, Jones wrote letters of condolence to the families of dead American soldiers as an act of "penance" for his initial support for the war. His missives began with the words, "My heart aches as I write this letter for I realize you are suffering a great loss." This empathic patriot was moved to undertake such a project after he met the widow of a man who died in Iraq in 2003 and watched as his young son played with a toy during memorial services at Camp Lejeune, North Carolina, a marine base situated in his district. He was suddenly overcome by a sense of guilt. "I will never forget the mistake I made," he told reporters in 2017. "I bought into believing that President Bush didn't really want to go to war. That's how naive I was at the time." Jones also created his own war memorial by placing photos of dead marines who were killed in the war and who had been stationed at Camp Lejeune on the wall outside his congressional office.[41]

Murtha's turn against the war was actually part of a general swing in that direction throughout Pennsylvania. His district, a heavily working-class area centered around Johnstown, was showing signs of disaffection from the conflict. The overall trend was due in part to the deaths of many of the state's reservists. By 2005 Pennsylvania ranked third behind only Texas and California in the number of National Guardsmen who had been killed. States also had to pay those troops, and some now argued that such a financial responsibility was becoming an economic drain.[42]

Murtha's decision became a national news story, especially because he had been such a staunch supporter of the war at its inception and all things military. Letters sent to the congressman reinforced the fact that his rethinking of the war not only attracted considerable attention but managed to expose the growing divide that existed in the United States over the conflict. Many citizens from his district and from other parts of the nation shared his regret over the tragic costs of the war while war-based patriots condemned him and his willingness to let such costs serve as a deterrent to its pursuit. Supporters revealed that they concurred with the congressman's disaffection from a fundamental tenet of a belligerent patriotism, which was to minimize the true realities of military conflicts; his supporters demonstrated that a belief in moral sentiments and a willingness to acknowledge the suffering of others were sufficient reason to halt the bloodshed.

Consider the words of a war critic from Newton, Massachusetts, who wrote to Murtha just after he had made his call for withdrawal. This citizen told the congressman that he had been "heartbroken to read about the young men and women injured in Iraq" because of their "life changing" injuries. The man was also upset because it seemed to him that payments many veterans received from the Department of Veterans Affairs appeared to be insufficient to cover their medical expenses. To him the poor treatment of veterans by the government "made a mockery of our promise to young men and women who enlist to bravely defend our country. . . . It feels like the 1960s all over again." A woman from St. Louis told Murtha that she supported him because the lives of American soldiers, "the well-being of the citizens of Iraq," and "our moral conscience as citizens compels us to demand better of our leaders." The ethical tenor of many Murtha backers was also evident in a statement that expressed satisfaction that the congressman had elected to proclaim his resistance because "it gives me hope that someone is witnessing the futility of the war effort." A resident of State College, Pennsylvania, told of coming to resent the way the war ruptured families when watching a soldier depart for Iraq.[43]

Some of Murtha's correspondents based their hostility to the war more on the dissatisfaction with Bush's policies than on humanitarian concerns, although both viewpoints mingled in the minds of many. A member of Murtha's district from Carrolltown told Murtha that he was an "inspiration" to those who have been branded "unpatriotic" for opposing the president's decision. A war resister from Massachusetts concluded that the battle in Iraq was an "abomination in the eyes of decency and all that we stand for." He also dismissed criticism of Murtha as mere "partisan retaliation" which he attributed to the Bush administration and "its power brokers with no credibility, no morality, no sense of how deeply shameful their behavior appears to the rest of the world." A Bush detractor from Utah declared that Murtha was a patriot but "Bush, Cheney, and Rumsfeld are 'chicken-hawks' willing to send others to war but were nowhere to be found when the call came to them."[44]

Dissent is generally a difficult road to travel in wartime; traditional understandings of patriotism require that people support the troops, the commander in chief, and the goal of vanquishing enemies. As such, Murtha attracted a considerable degree of contempt and scorn. His adversaries tended to invoke the mythical language of the Bush administration to defend the war in Iraq and the entire contest against terrorism as a defense of freedom in the world. A critic of the congressman's decision insisted that "our mission is honorable and our cause is righteous and for that I am proud to be called an American." A citizen from New York State told Murtha that "our fanatical adversaries are prepared to fight a multi-generational war to annihilate freedom loving people." This man felt that a consistent message should be sent to the nation's enemies "that their hatred for freedom loving people and their lust for taking innocent lives will be met by men and women who value freedom so much that they are willing to fight and die to defend it now and for generations to come until the end of time."[45]

Past wars also served as reference points for Murtha's detractors, especially the memory of the "good war." A writer from Florida reminded Murtha that the "Marines at Tarawa did not cut and run and they were fighting an empire whose aim was to conquer only the whole of the South Pacific." A World War II vet who had served in the navy maintained that his patriotic fervor well exceeded Murtha's, since the congressman now wanted to retreat from the battle in Iraq. He also chastised him for his failure to support "our Commander in Chief" and felt his dissent bordered on treason.[46] And a Vietnam vet recalled the experience of holding a comrade-in-arms as he died and claimed that he still felt pain and "visceral hatred for those cowardly, duplicitous politicians who robbed my brothers and me of the victory that our sacrifice deserved." Other correspondents compared Murtha to Vietnam dissenters like Jane Fonda and John Kerry, arguing that such opposition will only "embolden the enemy."[47]

Murtha was also charged with dishonoring the troops that were still fighting in Iraq, a sign of the ongoing tension between empathy and honor that lay at the heart of the domestic war over patriotism. A constituent reasoned that proud soldiers had already given their lives in support of "our Commander in Chief." She felt that these men and women were in a foreign country far away from home because they believed they could protect America. This writer asked Murtha to think about "saluting our flag along with our soldiers and praying for those who have a flag draped across their coffin in order to keep you and your loved ones safe." Another resident of his district concluded that Murtha's decision was "cowardly" and damaging to the morale of the troops. This man could not believe that the congressman had forgotten the "core beliefs" of the "warrior ethos" which he felt were the ideas of "mission above politics," "Do not accept defeat," and "Never leave a fallen comrade." A woman from California believed Murtha had become "anti-American" because his stance would harm men and women still in Iraq.[48]

Gold Star Mothers

Like Murtha, Cindy Sheehan was deeply affected by the human devastation that resulted from the overthrow of Saddam Hussein. Never a supporter of the president's preemptive war, she was utterly devastated when she received the news that her son, Casey, had been killed in Iraq just a week after his arrival in 2004. The young soldier also opposed Bush's policy of preemption but decided to enlist out of a sense of duty to serve his country. The distraught mother collapsed on being informed of his death and wailed out loud, refusing to sleep for two days for fear that she would have to relive the moment when she awoke again. For months she was filled with "pain and emptiness." Her daughter later claimed that she could never forget "the sound of her mother screaming for her son." When friends tried to console the grieving woman and tell her that things would get better over time, she angrily replied that they were "full of shit." And she steadfastly refused to accept arguments that Casey died to keep America free and insisted that he died only "to feed and enrich the war machine."[49]

Unable to find comfort in traditional patriotic clichés, Sheehan turned her sorrow and remorse into an open challenge to the war and the policies of the Bush administration. Seven months after Casey's death, she wrote a letter to the president informing him that his "reckless and wanton foreign policies killed my son, my big boy, my hero . . . murdered my oldest child." In doing so she attracted not only sympathy and support from others who shared her opposition to the war but a considerable amount of hostility from defenders of the authority of Bush and those who held fast to the tenets of a war-based patriotism with its precepts of heroism and splendid deaths.

Sheehan's antiwar crusade reached a peak in August 2005, when she staked out a protest site near Bush's ranch in Crawford, Texas. She was determined to meet with the president to ask him to explain what "noble cause" justified her son's death. When Bush refused to do so, Sheehan and a small group of supporters quickly erected a series of white crosses at the site with paper bags attached carrying the names of the fallen soldiers from the conflict. Sheehan hoped that her defiance of pro-war forces and American foreign policy would eventually lead to an end to the war in Iraq. In an interview from the Texas site for the *Real Time with Bill Maher* television show, she repeated her insistence that the war was not about freedom and democracy but was a quest for oil riches. She wanted it ended so "our leaders" would stop "abusing our children." She also expressed fear for the "millions of people in harm's way in Iraq," and remorse over the fact that her son would never know the experience of having children and grandchildren. Maher asked her if she had ever considered going over Bush's head to "Cheney and Rumsfeld." Sheehan responded that she felt she had already gone over the president's head "to the American people."[50]

A number of members of Gold Star Families for Peace joined Sheehan at the Texas site, as public support for the war began to decline. The organization had been launched by women who had lost loved ones in Iraq like Sheehan; Celeste Zappala, whose son Sherwood Baker was the first Pennsylvania National Guardsman killed in action since World War II; and Lila Lipscomb of Flint, Michigan, whose son Michael Pederson lost his life in a helicopter crash. Some of the activists who created Gold Star Families for Peace had already bonded when they carried crosses the previous year from Arlington National Cemetery to the White House in a march they called the "Trail of Mourning."

Zappala had actually been an avowed pacifist before the war and had urged her son not to enlist. The young man felt he needed the financial aid the guard offered to help pay off college loans, however, and in the time before 9/11 thought it unlikely that the National Guard would ever be sent to war. Several years after his death, his distraught mother reflected on his funeral. She recalled the display of full military honors, flags blowing in the wind, and "rifles fired into the spring air." She also remembered that Sherwood had told his brother that if he were killed in the war he wanted a funeral service filled with the type of patriotic rituals he actually received so that his son would always think of him as a hero, a sign of how the debate over the nature of patriotism often played itself out within families. His mother recalled clergymen speaking a good deal at his service of pride derived from serving the nation. By the time she returned home from the affair, however, Zappala felt that she "could not bear any more patriotic songs and posthumous medals being presented to me."[51]

Zappala actually held an online discussion from the Crawford protest site. She explained that when her son was killed in Iraq, she promised herself that she would "speak the truth for him." For her the war was a disaster, "a betrayal of the nobility our military and of the democracy they are charged to protect." She told her audience that she had always tried to preach nonviolence to her children and felt strongly that Iraq was not a just war at all but one based on "great stretches of logic and fact." She also stressed that sorrowful women like her were not "pundits on the Sunday talk shows." "We are just ordinary people, mostly middle-aged women, who have lost their kids and know it was wrong."

One online reader queried her as to why more Gold Star Family members had not spoken up and suggested that many felt the sacrifices their loved ones made were considered justified. Zappala opined that there were many views on the behavior of brokenhearted families but she certainly felt that some had been reluctant to publicly comment on their feelings because they still had loved ones serving in the military and feared they might become targets of some form of retaliation. "Understand please that it is agony to have your beloved one away in danger. The phone ringing is a threat; the unexpected knock at the door is terrifying," she revealed. "So many remain silent with the prayer that their person will just come home whole. . . . Many families just live in silent fear."[52]

Not only mothers assembled at Crawford. Fathers like Carlos Arredondo, the father of a man who joined the army because of promises of a bonus and help with college tuition, joined the mourners in Texas. Arredondo, who never supported or understood the war, was so distressed over the loss of his son in Iraq that he went into a rage and set fire to a van when he learned of the boy's death. After a year of psychiatric counseling and listening to phone messages left by his offspring before he died, Carlos decided to commemorate his fallen soldier. He assembled mementos from his son's life and death, including an American flag the government sent him, Alex's military uniform, his dog tags, and a small wooden coffin to which he attached a photo of the dead man, and tied it all together into a "rolling car" that he could pull along in patriotic parades and peace demonstrations wherever he went. Arredondo insisted that what he was doing in towing his makeshift memorial through the streets was not only a commemorative act to honor his son but also an effort to articulate his rage and misery in public.

Many relatives and friends of soldiers made their way to Crawford to publicly proclaim their sorrow and relate what the war really felt like. Every day they took the stage at the encampment to read letters from men and women who had served their nation revealing a stark reality these activists called the "ground truth," a version of the war they felt was largely unknown among the public-at-large. For instance, Cloy Richards, a marine, talked about the pain of finding out he had killed innocent women and children when he was in Iraq and noted that his brother, who had also served, had been traumatized from having to pick up body parts of two of his comrades after a car bomb attack. Mike Mitchell also arrived at the encampment to honor his son who was killed in the same clash that took the life of Casey Sheehan. He told reporters that the loss of the young man had turned his life upside down. "It just kind of churns you up." Larry Syverson temporarily left his sidewalk protest in Richmond, Virginia, to also join forces with the Gold Star Mothers. In a report he wrote for the newsletter of the Richmond Peace Education Center, he said that Camp Casey was all about a grieving mother and a "callous president." He also noted how impressed he was with many of the people he met at the location, including a woman who had elected to go on a two-week bus tour to protest the war despite the fact that her boss warned that her job would not be waiting when she returned.[53]

As Sheehan's protest grew, the small town of Crawford, Texas, was flooded with not only Sheehan's supporters but her detractors. Bush backers trekked to Crawford waving flags and singing patriotic songs. A pro-Bush encampment called "Camp Reality" sprouted up behind the Yellow Rose Gift Shop in Crawford, a souvenir store that sold President Bush dolls, T-shirts, and coffee cups. On the night of August 15, 2005, a resident of Waco named Larry Northern attached a bar and chain to the back of his pickup truck and ran over rows of white crosses, each bearing the name of a dead American soldier, that had been erected at the Sheehan site as reminders of the human cost of the war.

In Sacramento, staunch supporters of the president and the troops had launched an organization called "Move America Forward" in 2004. The group took aim at the mobilization in Crawford and organized a large caravan titled "You Don't Speak for Me, Cindy." Attracting supporters from throughout the nation, the convoy arrived in Crawford in late August 2005, seeking to draw attention away from the antiwar contingent and stress the deep support for the missions American troops undertook. The caravan culminated in a rally at the local football stadium, where a diverse crowd that included Gold Star parents who were proud of the military service and sacrifices their loved ones had made in Iraq and Afghanistan chanted, "Cindy, Go Home." Deena Burnett, whose husband was one of the passengers on Flight

93, joined this gathering, insisting that the United States needed to do all that it could to ensure that the terror attacks of 9/11 were never repeated. Several parents of fallen soldiers removed the names of their loved ones from the crosses that had been erected by the Sheehan camp; John Wroblewski, whose son was killed in Iraq, traveled from New Jersey to declare that American forces needed to be allowed to finish the mission they started. At one point a crowd of Bush supporters hung a large American flag from a crane and shouted, "George Bush, George Bush." In a tense atmosphere a Sheehan faction countered with the words, "war criminal, war criminal."[54]

Letters to the editor of the Waco (Texas) *Tribune* echoed this support for the war and criticized Sheehan and other protesters. Donna Reyes of Hewitt, Texas, observed that she felt the protests at Crawford were tarnishing the reputation of the troops who fought and died. Reyes referred to the fact that her son was a member of the marine corps and that such men enlisted knowing that they might be sent into a battle zone. "They went through the most arduous training just so they could protect the rest of us. They have earned something these protestors will never know: pride, respect, sacrifice and courage. It doesn't require courage to sit by the side of the road holding signs."[55]

Thomas Heath, who was a consultant to American companies that wanted to do business in Iraq, posted a "guest column" in the *Tribune* noting that he had recently spent several hours at the Sheehan protest site and concluded that it was a "circus." He felt that the attention Sheehan commanded had obscured the real patriotism he believed existed among the citizens of central Texas, especially because the region contained the huge army base at Fort Hood. "We owe our veterans much more than publicizing people of whom a great number are nothing more than professional protestors" he asserted. He made it clear that he felt the fight in Iraq was necessary to prevent terrorists from attacking the homeland.[56]

A teacher from Waco, Mary Duffy, took a more supportive stance toward the public dissent at Crawford. In another op-ed piece in the Waco press, Duffy reported that she had taken time to visit the encampment, just a short drive from her home, and was impressed by the essentially peaceful nature of the protest. She also looked for the cross dedicated to a cousin who died in the war and was disappointed to see tire marks on it from the night it was run over by Northern's truck. She felt Sheehan raised a "great question" by her actions: "What did these people die for?" She was unsure there was a good answer but satisfied that the "first amendment was alive and well in

Crawford." For her, "dissent must not be squelched. Blind obedience is not patriotism."[57]

National conservative voices, staunch supporters of the war from the beginning and always reluctant to impose a strongly empathic perspective on military violence, also tended to heap scorn on Sheehan and disenfranchise her public expression of grief. Thus, a Fox News report referred to her as a "crackpot." Radio talk show host Rush Limbaugh declared that Sheehan's story consisted of nothing more than "forged documents. . . . There is nothing about it that is real." Right-wing bloggers raised questions about her sexual orientation. Fox News host Bill O'Reilly told his millions of viewers that he felt Sheehan's protest was being driven by more than the pain of losing a son. To O'Reilly she was simply being directed by "anti-war radicals" like documentary filmmaker Michael Moore and had been "hijacked by some very far left elements." When O'Reilly later appeared on David Letterman's late night television program, however, he was roundly criticized by the host. A sympathetic Letterman argued that if O'Reilly had never experienced the type of loss that Sheehan did, he had no right to dismiss the woman's views the way that he had. For Letterman the real critical focus in the controversy over Sheehan's dissent should not be directed toward the Gold Star Mother but the president who led the march into Iraq in the first place. And the *New York Times* offered a more accepting view of Sheehan as well when it referred to the Crawford protest as part of an "insurgency at home" that was beyond the control of the Bush administration. The newspaper declared that it was now time for a "somber acceptance of the war's costs."[58]

The dissent of Gold Star Mothers at Crawford certainly ratified the *Times'* plea for a sober assessment of not only the war in Iraq but the entire global effort to wage a battle against terrorism. The traditional image of motherhood itself had for a long time been intimately tied to romantic and heroic views of the nation and its battle campaigns. Mothers were expected to be not only good parents but model citizens, paragons of loyalty who lent a powerful thread of virtue to an imagined community of citizens whose military actions were beyond reproach. That is why many called Sheehan a "bad mother" despite the horrific blow she suffered. It was not only that she called out Bush, but she failed to meet an idealized standard of motherly and feminine virtue that was inextricably linked to the larger paradigm of a "good war" fought by honorable people. Cynthia Franklin and Laura Lyons have noted insightfully how in 2007 a conservative, pro-war coalition called Freedom's Watch launched an advertising campaign to support the Bush administration "surge" of sending more troops to Iraq. Led by Ari Fleischer, who had at one time served as Bush's press secretary, the idea was to market powerful sentiments aimed at undermining those who wanted to "cut and run" and discredit mourning itself. Franklin and Lyons noticed that many of the ads featured images of nuclear families and "nice white homes." And these ads did not hesitate to present women who lost children either on 9/11 or in Iraq as devotees of the value of patriotic sacrifice.[59]

Shortly after protesters broke camp at Crawford, Gold Star Families for Peace, joined by allies like Military Families Speak Out and Iraq Veterans against the War, continued their antiwar campaign by launching a "Bring Them Home Now Tour." The plan was to sponsor rallies in various parts of the country and come together for a climactic event in the nation's capital. At stops along the way Sheehan and other women spoke to audiences about the pain that war had brought them. In Columbia, South Carolina, a local Gold Star Mother named Elaine Johnson talked about what it felt like to have your "son sent back to you in a box and not be allowed to look at him because of how much damage was done." She was pained not only by his death but by the thought that she was not even sure he was in the coffin. Jean Prewitt, who lost a son in Iraq, also spoke at the rally. At one time she had supported her son's enlistment, but his death forced her to completely reevaluate her views. She came to believe that the war was "senseless" and that the president had become "unsympathetic" to the concerns of those who mourned their war dead. At the South Carolina rally she said that at least she had the opportunity to see her son before he was buried and kiss him goodbye. "I can't imagine how Elaine dealt with that not even being able to say goodbye to her baby." The next day at Raleigh, North Carolina, Prewitt became visibly upset when some in the audience shouted at Sheehan that her son would be ashamed of her for protesting the war. Prewitt found it totally "unacceptable" that people would treat mothers who lost sons in such a fashion and felt "that they have no idea of what we are going through." Tour member Stacy Bannerman spoke about being worn out by her need to be incessantly "weeping" for the war's victims. "I am tired of watching parents plant crosses for their dead children day after godforsaken day. I am tired of placing flowers on empty boots and baby shoes," she revealed. Bannerman made it clear that the dreariness of "bearing witness" to human suffering and unending news of death was becoming too much to bear. "It drains my spirit to meet the widow's eyes;

to watch the fathers falter, falling to their knees," she cried. "Christ that makes me weak."[60]

The tour ended at a massive rally at the National Mall in Washington, D.C., in late September 2005. Veterans of the Crawford encampment were joined by many other antiwar groups and prominent speakers like the Reverend Jesse Jackson and Ramsey Clark, a former attorney general of the United States. At the rally on the National Mall, Sheehan, addressing a crowd in excess of 100,000 people, charged that the country was being led by an "out-of-control, criminal government . . . that condones torture." Pointing her finger at Congress, she asked rhetorically, "How many more of other people's children are you willing to sacrifice for the lies?" "Shame on you," she told the public at large for giving the president the authority to invade Iraq. Speechmaking was followed by a march around the White House at which some 300 protesters were arrested, including Sheehan, for demonstrating without a permit. At the same time a considerably smaller group of war supporters countered the much larger antiwar assembly. Diane Ibbotson, whose son died in the same battle that Casey Sheehan did, made it clear to reporters that she was in Washington with a number of Gold Star Families who support the war and noted that Sheehan does not speak for all those who have lost loved ones in the conflict. She said she understood Sheehan's heartache but could not accept the fact that she had questioned the integrity of "our leader" and felt to do so questioned the character of "the United States armed forces."[61]

Veterans against the War

A number of veterans joined grieving parents to challenge the decision to go after Saddam Hussein. As raw emotions were unleashed, iconic symbols of a war-based patriotism, brave warriors and loyal mothers, were turned upside down. Disgruntled veterans had formed Iraq Veterans Against the War (IVAW) in the summer of 2004. Provoked by beliefs that the government had not told the truth about the existence of weapons of mass destruction and the reality that the troops sent there were "ill equipped," these activists were convinced that the American public did not have an accurate view of the war and the extent of the human damage that was done in their name. Electing to use nonviolent principles of protest, the IVAW staged "street theater" demonstrations in which protesters wore camouflage jackets and disrupted traffic in a number of cities. In March 2007, a "platoon" of IVAW members reenacted a mass roundup of Iraqi civilians by American troops at the gates of the White House and on the National Mall. "Troops" shouted at Iraqis to "shut the hell up or I'll blow you're freaking head off."[62]

A major event sponsored by the IVAW mimicked the activities of anti-war soldiers from the Vietnam War. In March 2008, the veterans' organization sponsored a program called "Winter Soldiers: Iraq and Afghanistan." The four-day gathering, held at the National Labor College in Silver Spring, Maryland, provided a forum in which disgruntled vets provided eyewitness testimony on the harsh realities of the war on terror. They spoke of the killing of innocent people, the torturing of prisoners, instances of refusing to treat injured Iraqis and Afghan civilians, and in a few cases, the taking of "trophy photos" of individuals killed by Americans. Their refusal to cover up the tragic consequences of the war and the idea to name their program "Winter Soldiers," of course, was shaped by the legacy of Vietnam vets who in 1971 attempted to expose what they felt were "war crimes" committed by the United States in Southeast Asia. One marine, John Michael Turner, described killing an Iraqi man in front of the man's family and friends in Ramadi. In explicit and dramatic language, Turner disclosed that his first shot, which hit the man in the neck, did not kill him. Then the man "started screaming and looked right into my eyes. . . . I took another shot and took him out." Turner remembered how the victim's family carted away the corpse and how his own company commander congratulated him for his efforts. Turner expressed disgust over the fact that his commander offered a four-day pass to any soldiers who got their first kill by stabbing someone to death.[63]

Another American soldier, Michael Totten, also regretted the mistreatment of Iraqis. Serving in Karbala in 2003 and 2004, Totten described an incident in which a young boy was struck by traffic when crossing a four-lane highway. Totten's first instinct was to render aid, but he was prevented from doing so by his sergeant major, an order that disturbed him a great deal. He was also troubled by the language American troops used in describing Iraqis. He could not understand why so many soldiers often demeaned Iraqis sometimes by calling them "Hajis," when they were supposed to be liberating them. "Don't touch the people of Iraq's left hand," some of his colleagues would often remark, because "they wipe their ass with it." Totten concluded by saying he was sorry for his actions and asking for forgiveness.[64]

Additional testimony reinforced the theme that many of the soldiers sympathized with Iraqis because of the unjustified brutality they faced from the United States. Jeffrey Smith, a member of a National Guard unit from Florida, recalled an incident in which a Humvee came into his base towing a pickup truck filled with dead Iraqis. Smith was completely repulsed when one of the soldiers picked up a decapitated head and yelled, "We really screwed up these guys, didn't we?" He saw another enlisted man celebrating in the back of the truck on top of another body. To Smith most of the victims seemed to be merely teenage boys and "not really insurgents." He too felt like apologizing. Another marine lamented the "horrible treatment" of detainees who were underfed and often kicked in the ankles so much they could not stand to use the bathroom. This soldier said he felt dishonored by such practices and what he called the "intentional dehumanization" of Iraqis.[65]

Even Iraqi civilians were encouraged to speak at the Winter Soldiers assembly. Huda Jabbar Mohammad Ali, a resident of Baghdad, traveled to Maryland to tell how her husband was killed by occupation forces. While riding in a car with relatives, he was shot for no apparent reason. She claimed that six other civilians were also killed in the same part of the city on that day in a similar manner. The grief-stricken widow went to see American officials in the "green zone," or the protected area for American troops, to file for compensation for her tragic losses but nothing ever came of her request. She was left to care for her five children by herself with very little income to support them. Another Iraqi woman, Zahara Abbas, reconstructed the events of a night of terror in her home. While she was sleeping, American soldiers suddenly entered her house. First, they shot at the walls, which terrified her entire family. Then they initiated a search for weapons that caused considerable damage to the residence. Zahara was particularly upset by the fact that the troops took her daughter's school books. She asked her son to tell them in English that the volumes were merely for the girl's study of French. But soldiers simply hit the boy over the head "so hard his neck almost broke." The family was left not only with a huge bill to repair their domicile but with nightmares of the raid. The distressed woman claimed that she could still hear the sound of her daughter screaming and crying.[66]

Iraq veterans also spoke out again when they were interviewed by oral historians who published their perspectives on the war. Charlie Anderson thought the 9/11 attacks served as a valid rationale for war when he arrived in Iraq. His actual tour of duty, however, caused him to alter his point of view. He began to sympathize with many Iraqis when he saw them hurt by American forces; after his tour of duty was finished he suffered from PTSD. He recalled one night in Sadr City when he began shooting his weapons because his comrades began shooting theirs. He had no idea what they were firing at. Soon he saw women and elderly men running; "it was pandemonium." The incident caused him to wonder how people might discuss the war in the future. "Twenty years from now are they going to be talking about the day Americans came and shot up their village?" he wondered. Demond Mullins was also affected deeply by the brutality the invasion brought to blameless citizens in Iraq. He had come to know some of the children in his sector and enjoyed giving them candy bars. One of his young acquaintances actually helped to save some Americans from harm when he was able to tell them about the location of a bomb under a bridge that could have killed them. When he witnessed a comrade kill another Iraqi youth, he was greatly disturbed. At the end of tour, Mullins's executive officer told him that he was now a man. The returning vet considered that statement for a long time but was unable to reconcile this profession of masculinity with the exercise of cruelty to others.[67]

Garett Reppenhagen was the first active-duty soldier to join the IVAW. He had volunteered for military service as a twenty-four-year-old father of three who felt he was not making enough economic headway while working three jobs to make ends meet. He had noticed blogs by IVAW members on the Internet while serving in Iraq. Reppenhagen was also deeply troubled by seeing Iraqis who appeared to view their American "liberators" with contempt. He explained that many of the soldiers with whom he served felt they were in constant danger and, therefore, justified in using "oppressive and abusive tactics against Iraqis" to ensure their own survival. But he also came to the conclusion that they did not have to be there in the first place, an assessment that undermined his original belief that he was doing the proper thing by serving his country. Soon after his discharge, he met Cindy Sheehan at a "veterans for peace" meeting in Dallas. He and some friends quickly decided to accompany her to Crawford for several days to help "pitch her tent."[68]

In time popular support for a military strike on Iraq waned. The high-minded rhetoric of bringing freedom to Iraq and keeping America safe from future terrorist attacks could not survive the failure of the campaign to verify the Bush administration's rationales for war. More telling was the way an expanding tide of grief began to wash over the nation in the form of various protests and complaints. The normal reluctance of war-based patriots to dismiss the tragic implications of war and discredit the public expression of anguish did not go away. But increasingly political leaders, grieving parents, and even returning veterans attracted considerable attention when they refused to relinquish the role of bearing witness to the toll of human suffering that the invasion brought. In 2003 some 70 percent of Americans said they felt the move into Iraq was the right decision. By 2014 only 38 percent were willing to take such a stand.[69] As months of an American military presence in the Middle East turned into years, what was once celebrated as the Bush Doctrine became increasingly referred to as "the forever wars." War weariness, however, did not cause the debate over patriotism to wane. War-based patriots continued to disparage the empathizers. When television newsman Ted Koppel decided to read the names of American troops who had died in Iraq on his nightly news program on the ABC television network in 2004, stations owned by the Sinclair Broadcasting company prevented their viewers from watching his program at all. Some war-based patriots were not about to allow painful realities to seep into the airwaves if they could help it.

4 Visualizing the War

. . . .

The mounting tide of concern over death and suffering that helped turn many against the War on Terror was intensified not only by news reports and protests but by the circulation of images that exposed the war's bitter realities. In the earliest stages of the conflict, photos of planes striking the Twin Towers and the massive pile of rubble at Ground Zero, as a scholar of cultural communications such as Barbie Zelizer has argued, helped to nurture an aggressive patriotic template for understanding events that muted political criticism, fostered militarism, and reinforced the moral authority of the nation and its leaders. Iraq was certainly a more controversial issue but one that initially benefited from perceptions rooted in graphic images that flowed from the media coverage of 9/11. The decision of the government to label the invasion "Operation Iraqi Freedom" reflected a desire on the part of military planners and political officials to take advantage of this early consensus and the rhetorical power of the American veneration of liberty to mute the shock and trauma of the terrorist attacks and the damage that would follow in the Middle East.

Catchphrases like "Operation Enduring Freedom," the official designation given the attack on Afghanistan, or "The Good War" function to diminish or preclude the inclination people have to critique campaigns of state-sponsored violence, wallow in sorrow, or plead for a more caring society—basic tenets of an empathic patriotism. The persuasive power of high ideals can also help to stifle confusion. Brutality needs to be vindicated. Leaders need to be followed. Yet, the visualization of aggression and the mayhem of war itself can also challenge the dream of war-based patriots to turn trauma and death into noble deeds. The greater the assortment of horrifying pictures, the more difficult it becomes to manage the meaning of the entire enterprise. Dora Apel, who has written on how artists imagine wars, explains that the mass production of diverse images regarding warfare is driven, in part, by personal rebellions against government efforts to impose a "dominant logic on the oversupply of emotional reactions" that mass violence begets. This rebellion took place in powerful ways when it came to the global fight against terrorism and certainly helped to fuel the patriots' debate.[1]

There was nothing new in the quest to uphold American honor in wartime through the strategic use of metaphors and pictures. In the past the iconic photograph of an American flag-raising on Iwo Jima conveyed an illustration of victory and mitigated pervasive accounts of mass casualties in the later stages of World War II. Norman Rockwell's famous paintings of the Four Freedoms advanced the cause of World War II by picturing the American people as ideal types who loved their families and democratic values while putting aside any suggestions or images that might prove unflattering. Citizens themselves crafted likenesses of angels in 2001 to represent Americans who were killed on 9/11, reinforcing a larger ideal of American innocence and blamelessness. In a new century suddenly saturated with Internet connections and media images, however, the quest to protect laudatory depictions of American actions and identity became more difficult than ever. Any hope that the idea of a dignified concept like "Operation Iraqi Freedom" or honorable patriotic sentiments could be sustained in the face of a flood of pictures of death and wickedness soon collapsed. The implication here was about more than discrediting the agenda of George W. Bush; it was also about undermining the longer-term project to recast American violence and authority into a virtuous national identity.[2]

Abu Ghraib

The release of photographs in 2004 of American soldiers abusing Iraqi prisoners at Abu Ghraib prison in Iraq proved to be a momentous challenge to the hope of war-based patriots to cloak their aggression in honorable terms. In April the CBS program *60 Minutes II* televised photos and reports of soldiers physically and sexually abusing inmates at Abu Ghraib, an American penal complex that had formerly served as a prison where Saddam Hussein tortured and killed his enemies. This was the first time the general public saw the photographs and learned of a secret army investigation into the mistreatment of these captives by American forces. CBS commentator Dan Rather began the exposé by showing a photo of an Iraqi standing on a box with a hood placed over his head and holding wires. The inmate was told that if he fell off the box he would be electrocuted. This image was followed by one in which nude Iraqi men were stacked one on top of another in the form of a pyramid with U.S. Army soldiers laughing and posing next to them. Rather had prefaced the display of images by warning his audience that "they are difficult to look at." In the same program, the newsman interviewed army general Mark Kimmitt, who made it clear that he was appalled by these actions. He inferred the abuse was basically an aberration in the way Americans treated prisoners by claiming that these misdeeds were committed by only a small number of soldiers. Kimmitt also worried that such actions would make it difficult for Americans to expect that their troops, if captured, could be treated with respect. When Rather asked him if he had a message for the people of Iraq, Kimmitt said that he wanted to tell them that such ill-treatment was "wrong" but that they should not judge all American troops by the misdeeds of a few.[3]

Government and military officials moved quickly to contain the damage the photos did to their reputations and to the war effort. Secretary of Defense Donald Rumsfeld told the Senate's Armed Services Committee in the month following Rather's report that it was particularly difficult to fight a war in the "information age, where people are running around with digital cameras and taking these unbelievable photos and passing them off, against the law, to the media, to our surprise, when they had not even arrived at the Pentagon." Rumsfeld's remarks, sidestepping the fact that the photos revealed the horror of this war of choice, suggested that in no way could higher levels of leadership be connected to the torture and the dehumanization of these prisoners.

Military officials had already commissioned their own investigation of what happened at Abu Ghraib, a report that would hint at more complicated reasons for the scandal. The military account, written by Major General Antonio Taguba, revealed that between October and December 2003, "numerous instances of sadistic, blatant, and wanton criminal abuses were inflicted on several detainees" at Abu Ghraib. He even found evidence that Iraqi females were forced to witness the sexual humiliation of Iraqi men. Taguba located some of the blame for these misdeeds in the actions of military police sent to serve as guards at the penal complex who "intentionally perpetrated" abuse. He also made it clear that American intelligence units assigned to the site unduly influenced the police guards by insisting they produce "favorable interrogations of the witnesses" by any means. The objective was to secure information military officials deemed useful. Taguba also found what he felt was a basic lack of regulatory, doctrinal, and command requirements within the 800-member military police (MP) brigade responsible for the inmates at the prison site, a point that would suggest that the scandal emanated from more than the actions of a few misguided "people." The report concluded that Brigadier General Janis Karpinski, commander of the brigade, be relieved from command for failing to ensure that MPs under her control received the appropriate level of instruction for dealing with detainees.

Taguba had been ordered to investigate only the military police and not those above them in the chain of command and not military and civilian interrogators who also worked in the prison. He concluded, however, that because many of the MPs he interviewed had been forced to conduct interrogations, they were being asked to perform a task for which they were not trained. Taguba noted that this was clearly not consistent with army doctrine. He also affirmed that these MPs were placed into a terrible situation or, as he called it, a "hell on earth." He stressed that the entire operation at Abu Ghraib was infected by a cruel prison culture that had "migrated" from the American base at Guantánamo, Cuba where a pattern of abusing prisoners rounded up from the global fight against terror and sanctioned by the Bush administration had already been established.[4]

It is now clear that the Bush administration, including Donald Rumsfeld and Dick Cheney, had worked feverishly to construct a system of prisons outside the boundaries of the United States and the rule of law that sanctioned the use of torture and the abuse of inmates. Seeking to circumvent restrictions embedded in international laws and agreements such as the Geneva Convention of 1949, which stated that "combatants when out of the fight were not to be abused," American officials set up incarceration sites or secret detention centers in a number of foreign countries including Afghanistan, Libya, and Lithuania so that prisoners would not have access to American courts and "activist lawyers" who might be inclined to defend their legal rights. The American base at Guantánamo was one such site, as was Abu Ghraib. The administration also resorted to "euphemisms" like "enhanced interrogation" to describe some of the ways they treated prisoners, as historian W. Fitzhugh Brundage argued, in an attempt to forestall criticism that it had resorted to torture and abuse.[5]

Disclosures of cruel treatment at Abu Ghraib soon caused human rights organizations to gather information on their own and expand public awareness of what had taken place at the prison. In 2004 Human Rights Watch, an international nongovernmental agency, issued a report titled *The Road to Abu Ghraib*. This document took exception to Rumsfeld's assertions that the mistreatment of Iraqi prisoners was merely an "isolated incident" or the work of a "few bad apples" who acted without orders. Taguba's report, for instance, suggested the problem was systemic more than "isolated." Human Rights Watch argued that the only thing about Abu Ghraib that was exceptional was the fact that it was photographed. The report indicated that a number of news and human rights organizations including the BBC and the International Red Cross had also disclosed that prisoners were being tortured and beaten at the American airbase at Bagram in Afghanistan. Human rights activists argued strongly that "this pattern did not result from the acts of individual soldiers who broke the rules." Rather the report contended that abuse originated in decisions made by the Bush administration to bend or ignore existing policies that had been established for the fair treatment of prisoners. Human Rights Watch claimed that the severest abuses at Abu Ghraib occurred in the immediate aftermath of a decision by Rumsfeld to fortify the hunt for "actionable intelligence" among the Iraqis. In pursuit of that objective the American military sent the commander at Guantánamo, Geoffrey Miller, to Iraq to intensify interrogation practices at Abu Ghraib and make them conform to harsh methods already established in Cuba, including beatings with hard objects, placement in solitary confinement without clothes, and being hooded and made to stand in the sun for long periods of time. Even Taguba later admitted—after he was out of the army—that he was overwhelmed by the extent of bad behavior at Abu Ghraib and the fact that many of the prisoners were simply old men and teenagers taken off the streets of Baghdad.[6]

The photographs laid bare the contradictions between the righteous rhetoric of the Bush administration, which was supported by most war-based patriots, and the violation of human rights which troubled empathic patriots so much. The more virtue slipped from the hands of American leaders, the more the presumed innocence of American identity wavered in the wind. Insightful cultural critics like Susan Sontag saw immediately that if the mistreatment of prisoners was the result of official policy—violence perpetrated in our name—and not random acts by a few foolish individuals, then the "photographs are us," stark reflections of some thread within the fabric of the American character. Writing in the *New York Times* on Memorial Day in 2005, Bob Herbert opined that the mounting evidence of the atrocious treatment of terror suspects and detainees at Guantánamo was not advancing the cause of freedom in the world. Herbert believed that in the aftermath of 9/11 most of the world was ready to stand with the United States in a legitimate fight against terrorists, but in its lust for war with Iraq and its willingness to jettison every semblance of due process while employing scandalously inhumane practices against detainees, that opportunity was lost. In the *Cincinnati Enquirer* Richard Erlich worried that the use of torture by America was a danger to the nation's reputation for decency and threatened to turn its image into one of a "torture regime" instead of a "decent Republic." Roger Cohen, a columnist for the *New York*

Dennis Draughon, *Abu Ghraib 'Nam*, 2004. Used by permission of the artist.

Times, raised a fundamental point of the entire matter: "The world is asking what sort of liberation is represented by an American woman holding a prone naked Iraqi man on a leash?"[7]

Other media outlets were unrelenting in their attacks. Political cartoonist Dennis Draughon executed an image called *Abu Ghraib Nam* that connected the impact of American violence on civilians in Vietnam with the harsh treatment toward many Iraqis. In Draughon's famous cartoon, a photo of a young Vietnamese girl fleeing an American napalm attack was superimposed upon one of the hooded figures in the Abu Ghraib photos. On the CBS TV program *Meet the Press*, moderator Tim Russert said the world had been "shocked" by photos that showed such maltreatment. A number of guests on the program agreed and were willing to cast blame not only on Rumsfeld but on Bush as well for creating a mindset that disregarded international law. Senator John Warner, a Republican from Virginia and a guest on the program, tried to soften the blow to American virtue by insisting that the vast majority of the men and women in the American armed forces continued to perform "valiantly" and "loyally."

The *Washington Post* amplified the public criticism by publishing previously secret sworn statements by detainees at Abu Ghraib, documents that affirmed what the world saw in images with the words of the victims themselves. In one statement a man named Mustafa Jassim related how he saw guards at the prison strip the clothes of two prisoners and start to beat them. When one of the men started to bleed, the American guards called a doctor to attend to his wound. Once the physician completed his work, the guards started to beat the man again. Another inmate recalled being stripped of his clothes and forced to hold his penis and stroke it while guards took photographs "as if it was a porn movie." "They treated us like animals, not humans. . . . No one showed us any mercy," an Iraqi man recalled. Within weeks after the revelations by CBS, Bush had little choice but to offer an apology and admit that Abu Ghraib marked a "stain on our country's honor."[8]

"Riverbend," the young Iraqi blogger featured in chapter 3, was aghast at the appearance of the photos. She told her Internet audience that she felt "rage" when she saw them and had an incredible desire to break something. "Seeing those naked, helpless, hooded men was like being slapped in the face," she wrote. "I felt ashamed looking at them. . . . Any one of them might be a father or grandfather." This Iraqi witness received dozens of emails from Americans claiming that Abu Ghraib was an "isolated" incident, but she felt that whether it was or not was unimportant. In her mind the lives of many of the families and individuals abused at the prison would be changed forever. She reported, in fact, that in the aftermath of the release of the photos, many Iraqis gathered throughout Baghdad and even outside the prison protesting the atrocities and wondering about the fate of relatives who might still be incarcerated. She was quick to connect the horror stories from Abu Ghraib, in fact, with similar tales of brutal treatment emanating from Guantánamo and Afghanistan. After seeing American troops also break into Iraqi family homes and shoot innocent civilians, "Riverbend" could only conclude that torture and humiliation were simply business as usual for the Americans.[9]

Not everyone was outraged by the disclosure of human mistreatment by Americans or the fact that the photos showed soldiers taking delight in humiliating their captives. Much of the response by American officials, despite some apologies, was focused not on the maltreatment of Iraqis but on the damage the violent acts did to the myth of American honor and virtue. That was the point of Warner's remarks on *Meet the Press*. It was also a point President Bush made when after apologizing to the Iraqis he expressed regret that the photos prevented people from seeing the "true nature and heart of America." Radio commentator Rush Limbaugh actually dismissed the gruesome photos as little more than a college fraternity prank. Fox News commentator Sean Hannity claimed that that some people just could not accept what the military must do to win the war. Others attributed the outrage over Abu Ghraib to the misguided sentiments of the "liberal press." S. G. Mestrovic, a student of war crimes who served as an expert witness for the defense in the court-martial trials of several of the military police from Abu Ghraib, claimed that the army's prosecution of the soldiers held responsible was driven not by outrage over their acts of brutality but by the fear that such cruelty "smeared the honor of the Army." No Iraqi prisoners were brought before the trial proceedings at Fort Hood, Texas, to testify as to the suffering they endured. As Mestrovic wrote, their suffering and fate did not seem to matter. It was more important to blame a "few bad apples" for bringing dishonor to this branch of the service than acknowledge any form of human rights abuse or, for that matter, indict the higher ranks of army leadership.[10]

Public opinion revealed only some uneasiness over the incident. A Gallup Poll released immediately after the disclosures of abuse at Abu Ghraib indicated that 54 percent of Americans were "bothered a great deal" by the photos. One year later, however, that number had declined to 40 percent. The U.S. Congress later confirmed at least twenty-seven prisoner deaths at Abu Ghraib were homicides but issued no reports revealing the details of the killings. No soldier above the rank of staff sergeant ever received any jail time for the affair. A number of critics argued that there seemed to be something of a "moral blindness" or what Stephen Eisenman called the "Abu Ghraib effect" influencing much of the civilian population. Their collective reaction to evidence that America was capable of perpetrating barbarity seemed "blunted." It was well known that Secretary of Defense Rumsfeld saw the images as less about the brutal treatment of Iraqis— many of whom were innocents—and more about the threat they posed to upholding fabled versions of American honor and virtue. Eisenman suggested that it was possible that citizens had become somewhat numbed by the constant circulation of images of cruelties "perpetrated the name of American and British citizens in the War on Terror." Rumsfeld's view suggested, however, the power of a war-based patriotism to reject responsibility for the nation's cruelty also helped to explain some of the "effect" Eisenman had noticed. As a scholar such as Peggy Phelan has argued in relation to the images from Abu Ghraib, the photos provoked mostly "disavowal and defensiveness."

Disavowal and the projection of patriotic sentiments were also at the heart of Janis Karpinski's memoir of the incident. The brigadier general of the 800th Military Police Brigade, who was relieved of her command, recast the entire incident of prisoner abuse into a personal narrative focused on her honorable service and the very real problem of gender bias in the army. Karpinski explained how she had been raised in New Jersey in a household where "patriotism was not a slogan, or an issue, or a political touchstone; it was the fabric our lives." The pride she felt in America and the ideal of military service drove her to imagine herself as a soldier, specifically one who might parachute into "dangerous places" or "command soldiers where bullets were flying." Much of the lead-up to her discussion of the incident at Abu Ghraib concerns her arduous quest to succeed in an organization run by men, many of whom were resistant to the idea of female officers. For this dedicated soldier, a key reason she was singled out to take much of the blame for the actions of MPs at the Iraqi prison was due to the fact that she was a woman who was denied access to an "old-boy network" that might have spared her such punishment. Karpinski certainly detested the cruelty at the prison and argued, much like the report issued by Human Rights Watch, that the transgressions of the MPs were rooted in policies crafted by the Bush administration and "not the work of a few wayward soldiers and their female leader." In her reframing of the scandal, compassion for the victims was minimal. Yet, there was every reason to reaffirm faith in America and its struggle for the ideal of equality for all.[11]

Artists and Suffering

In 2007, numerous artists mounted their own challenge to the moral blindness they saw in war-based patriotism with an online venture called iraqimemorial.org, using images to dispute the idea that the Iraq invasion was necessary and noble. Launched by Joseph DeLappe, a professor interested in digital media at the University of Nevada at Las Vegas, the project issued an open call to artists, architects, and other creative individuals to submit proposals for memorials that would recognize the torment that American military actors brought to innocent civilians in Iraq. The public controversy surrounding the photos from Abu Ghraib had focused so much attention on the question of American honor that little was said of the suffering of the Iraqi people. DeLappe decided, in part, to initiate this venture after looking at the website that featured designs submitted for the World Trade Center (WTC) Site Memorial Competition in 2004. This competition resulted in 5,000 proposals from some sixty-three countries designed to commemorate, according to the competition's mission statement, "the thousands of innocent men, women, and children murdered by terrorists in the attacks of 1993 and 9/11." DeLappe claimed that the WTC competition made him think that "here we are in the process of carefully and respectfully working to remember and honor the innocents of 9/11 while simultaneously many thousands of people, arguably just as innocent, were being killed in order for us to "fight terrorism, protect our freedoms, and spread democracy.'" DeLappe began to consider issues such as who is mourned, who is responsible for the carnage, and "how do we, as artists, choose to respond?" Ultimately, he wanted to raise the matter of just what were the "true costs of the war."[12]

Seattle artist Mike McGrath responded to DeLappe's call with a series of images of Iraqis collectively titled *Lot's Tribe*. He conceived of this project as a memorial to "the other victims of 9/11" and cast life-sized figures that were placed in Occidental Park in downtown Seattle on the morning of September 11, 2006. Composed of white crystalline, the figures were meant to bring sudden incursions of unwelcome reality into our daily lives, "until the rain comes and slowly they dissolve away." McGrath said that he derived the idea for the images from news photos coming from the Middle East. To him the scenes were "shocking" and he wondered why they were not disseminated more widely. "They made me think about what it feels like to witness something so unexpected and vast; an explosion that will unexpectedly alter your life." Focused on the "unintended consequences of war," McGrath claimed that "this is what photojournalism once did more easily."

McGrath felt sculpture would have a more permanent effect than the barrage of images that came to America through the Internet and various media forms. In his view citizens were overwhelmed by a constant array of photos from car bombings to children being pulled out of some rubble in a distant land. For him it would be harder to "shrug off" the impact of sculpture—"It literally won't get out of the way." McGrath rejected the idea of a permanent memorial sculpture because he wanted to stress the idea of mortality and "personal tragedy" which figurative sculpture often lacked. His depictions, such as the one of a grief-stricken father carrying a limp child in Iraq, stood in the downtown park for about three months before they were destroyed completely by the weather and vandalism.[13]

Another artist who joined the online memorial project was Prince Varughese Thomas, a native of India who was a naturalized American citizen. Thomas has stated that because he was born in India, was raised in Kuwait, and became a citizen of the United States, he felt "outside" the dominant

Mike McGrath, *Pieta* from *Lot's Tribe*, 2006. Used by permission of the artist.

culture in which he now lives. It is this identity that explains, as he expressed it, his "conceptual concerns" and his art. Thomas titled his project on Iraq *Body Count* and aimed to raise awareness about the way warfare devalues human life. Since the U.S. government had taken countless lives in its War on Terror but had kept no record of the official count, this artist derived his own estimate of civilian deaths in Iraq from various reports. His creation presented piles of pennies with each coin meant to represent one civilian life. Like a single life, one penny may not have been able to make a significant impact. In total, however, piles of pennies brought greater attention to the cost of the fight against terrorism and demanded more attention.

Terry Rosenberg's *Women and Children* continued the assault on the notion of a virtuous American war by submitting to iraqimemorial.org a work that hoped to honor "the innocent dead" and remind people of the "injustice in Iraq." Rosenberg intended that his image would actually be reprinted on billboards and buses throughout the world. In the design the artist used a blend colors to present repeatedly the words "women and children." Troubled by all the rhetoric of war and news stories of cruelty and government corruption, Rosenberg meant in his art to remind all of the many whose suffering was lost amid the continual flow of reporting and information associated with violent confrontations throughout the globe. One critic wrote of Rosenberg's work that Rosenberg was attempting to force the viewer not only to consider alternatives but to make people realize that those who forced citizens to choose between simple binaries like good and evil may actually be enslaving rather than empowering public opinion.[14]

Danny Quirk was another artist who took up the project to record the human damage the War on Terror caused. Not part of iraqimemorial.org, Quirk had been interested in the war since his days in college. For a senior thesis, he interviewed troops to discover specifically how they felt about their tours of duty. For a time he even considered joining the military but his father talked him out of it, feeling that the fight in Iraq did not justify his son's sacrifice. As an artist and illustrator, Quirk focused clearly on what he called the "emotional toll" of the war" and the "vulnerability" it brought to many who served in it. He was especially drawn to suffering and issues such as post-traumatic stress disorder (PTSD) and, of course, death. When he executed his work titled 22, he said he was seeking to "make something hard hitting, something that got people thinking." This is why he produced an image of an American flag with twenty-two holes in it, a representation of the fact that some twenty-two American veterans of all wars committed suicide each day. Quirk felt that every time a veteran took his or her life, that veteran took a part of America with him or her.

The illustration of a flag with holes quickly drew comments on Quirk's Facebook page. Critics charged him with flag desecration. One wrote that "a true American would never consider destroying our flag under the guise of art." Another charged that America "doesn't deserve those bullet holes" and called the piece "ignorant shit." Supporters were numerous, however, even if they did not always like to see the flag torn. A marine veteran from Iraq who said he struggled "almost every day not to become one of the 22" thanked the artist. He said that Quirk had taken a symbol many revere and elevated it to almost holy status with its "cry for help." Another indicated that he did not like to see the flag with holes in it but he found it more troubling to have to attend funerals of friends who took their lives. "It makes you uncomfortable; that's the point."[15]

A number of photographers also attempted to capture the pain and helplessness of American soldiers who had fought in the war. Michael McCoy, an Iraq veteran as well as a photographer, drew upon his own battles with

Danny Quirk, 22, 2015. Used by permission of the artist.

PTSD to reimagine the war experience. Casting aside official explanations of what the war was about, McCoy used his camera to record images of Americans who were in anguish, whether they were African American protesters in his hometown of Baltimore or veterans back from the Middle East. After two tours of duty and a stay at Walter Reed hospital in Washington, D.C., for postwar stress, McCoy, plagued by sleeplessness and panic attacks, decided that his interest in photography could be a way to soothe the emotional confusion he felt. He insisted that the "only thing that comes across my mind when I have a camera in my hand is escaping the memories of being in a combat zone." The trauma of war left him with not only perilous memories but a heightened sense of the "vulnerability" others felt when they were put in dangerous situations. Thus, he began to snap pictures of veterans struggling with their postwar past and African Americans confronting the harshness of police brutality.[16]

Suzanne Opton, a New York photographer, also found a way to contest the proclivity of a war-based patriotic culture to elide the tragic view of military conflict. Challenging the supremacy of heroic motifs and rhetoric of patriotic honor, Opton elected to photograph American soldiers between tours of duty in Iraq and Afghanistan. Her approach was to focus her camera on the faces of young men in order to accentuate their individuality, a technique of resistance to speech that cast them into preordained molds of ardent patriots. Many of her photos showed the heads and shoulders of these warriors lying sideways on a flat surface, a move designed to illustrate their vulnerability rather than their capacity for valor.

Opton first exhibited her images in 2006, motivated in part by the fact that she had a son of her own. She very much hoped her photos would humanize the image of those who served. At best these images might force the public to think about what type of people these soldiers were or what they were feeling. Working at Fort Drum in upstate New York, the photographer-artist claimed that she was not antiwar but interested very much in what these warriors went through and how they would continue their lives with lingering memories of the war. Her challenge to the tenets of a traditional patriotic frame on the War on Terror was so powerful that a company in Saint Paul, Minnesota, canceled a contract to place her images on one of their billboards during the Republican National Convention held in the city in 2008. The company claimed that some of her photos showed soldiers who appeared to be dead, even though they were not, and that many might see them as "disrespectful." Opton disagreed with her critics, of course, and claimed her photos were not impertinent but merely intended to show the weakness of many of the men who served their nation. They could be anyone's son or brother or friend.[17]

Todd Heisler, another photographer drawn to the anguish the war generated, decided to accompany marine notification teams that brought the tragic news of a loved one's death to American homes. While working for the *Rocky Mountain News* in Denver, Heisler and fellow journalist Jim Sheeler felt a need to document for the paper's readers the impact the global struggle was having on small towns in the region. While Sheeler compiled texts on the impact soldier deaths had on families, Heisler snapped photographs. When published in the newspaper as a series titled Final Salute, both the stories and the photos won Pulitzer Prizes in 2006 and stand as another example of the pervasive empathy that marked the response of many Americans to the dreadfulness of the war itself. In the photo *Katherine Cathey Sleeping Next to Her Husband for the Last Time*, Heisler captured the mournful image of a grief-stricken widow sleeping beside a flag-draped casket that contained the remains of her spouse, Jim Cathey. During the night she opened her laptop computer and played soothing songs as fellow marines

Suzanne Opton, *Soldier: Claxton* (120 Days in Afghanistan), 2006. Used by permission of the artist.

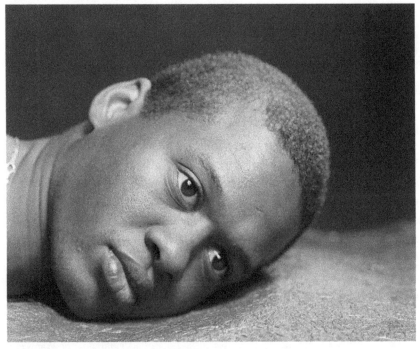

Suzanne Opton, *Soldier: Kitchen* (366 Days in Iraq), 2006. Used by permission of the artist.

Todd Heisler, *Katherine Cathey Sleeping Next to Her Husband for the Last Time.* 2006. Image from Denver Public Library. Used by permission of the artist.

stood guard nearby. When she first heard the news of Jim's death, as Sheeler reported, she screamed, ran to the back of her living room, and collapsed. She was particularly devastated by the fact that her fallen husband would never see the child she was carrying at the time.[18]

Jane Hammond's sensitive response to the war was a composition called *Fallen.* Beginning in 2004 she initiated this ongoing project to accumulate unique handmade leaves on a white platform hovering several inches above the ground. Each leaf contained the name of an American soldier killed in the Iraq War. Over the next eight years the work grew larger as the list of casualties increased. Hammond made it clear that the inspiration for her composition grew from the affective response she had to the loss of life in the war and her felt need to see this carnage not principally as a political issue but as a reminder of just how fleeting was the nature of life itself. She stressed that she envisioned herself in the role of "witness and recorder." Hammond wanted to memorialize dead soldiers in a manner that departed from many conventional memorials that were vertical rather than the horizontal and sought a degree of permanence in the face of loss rather than an aesthetic of gentleness and ephemeralness. The actual idea

Detail from Jane Hammond, *Fallen*, 2004–2012; Art Foundation, New York City, 2011. Color ink jet, printed from digital file recto and verso, on archival paper, cut, with matt medium, Jade glue, fiberglass strand, sumi ink, hand-made cotton rag paper and additional handwork in acrylic paint and gouache. Dimensions variable. Whitney Museum of American Art, New York. Purchased with funds from Sarah Ann and Werner Kramarsky, Mr. and Mrs. David Schiff, Melissa and Robert Soros, Marion C. and Charles Burson, Toby Devan, Larry Yocom, Ted and Maryanne Ellison Simmons, and the Stanley Family Fund of the Community Foundation of New Jersey. Used by permission of the artist.

for this artistic production came to her in a dream in which she saw herself walking through woods where leaves dropped to the ground, each inscribed with the name of a fallen soldier. When *Fallen* was exhibited in 2005 in New York, a grieving woman who had lost a son in Iraq would visit the installation each week and take a seat to spend time near the memorial that recognized her loss. In this work, Hammond remembers the sacrifice of Lance Corporal Casey Casanova, a woman killed in Iraq at the age of twenty-two.[19]

Symbols of War

Symbols of war that conveyed the tragic realities were deployed constantly during the conflict, offering a continual challenge to the hopes of those ardent patriots who hoped to keep the human cost of the conflict under wraps. Throughout the nation, everyday people forged their own version of events when they collected dog tags or drove crosses into the ground. The appearance of such emblems certainly did not evoke universal approval, a high standard in a culture divided over the human cost of the war. Yet, their pervasiveness indicated an empathic sensitivity to loss and an unwillingness to accept fully the tenets of a war-based patriotism. Stark photos of flag-draped coffins carrying the bodies of American soldiers returning to the homeland were for a time, for instance, censored from public view, a regulation stemming from the fallout to Vietnam. But in 2004 such repression was upended when the *Seattle Times* published a photo of coffins that had been loaded onto a cargo plane for a flight back to the United States. Within days the air force released several hundred additional images of caskets arriving at the air base at Dover, Delaware, in response to a Freedom of Information Act request. Public controversy ensued.

This depiction of bitter realities again challenged the hope that the true costs of American actions could be concealed. Many military families argued that publicizing the arrival of the dead even though they were accompanied by a military honor guard constituted an invasion of their privacy at a time when they were suffering the trauma of losing a loved one. A few felt their losses were being politicized, for such images would be used to critique the war itself. Others, of course, including some who sacrificed a family member, insisted that the American people had a right to know and see what the consequences of their policies entailed. A poll in 2003 indicated that 62 percent of the population agreed that such images should be circulated. In 2009, Barack Obama lifted the strict censorship by putting the decision to film the arrival of coffins at Dover in the hands of the Gold Star Families themselves.[20]

Citizens did not need official government photos, however, to help them visualize the war. They were fully capable of crafting their own symbols to signify how they saw the conflict and its consequences. Dog tags, for example, were used in a number of early attempts to memorialize the global contest. These emblems not only preserved the names of the dead but, when viewed in a large collection, reinforced the notion that the global struggle had disastrous human consequences, even if many saw the sacrifice they represented as honorable. One of the first attempts at memorializing the dead in this way was undertaken with the erection of the Iraq-Afghanistan Memorial in the memorial garden at the Old North Church in Boston. At the inception of the memorial in 2006, the dead were represented by a cross or

Army honor guardsmen remove a casket of a fallen soldier from a C-17 during a dignified transfer on Dover Air Force Base, Delaware, July 8, 2009. U.S. Department of Defense, http://www.defense.gov/observe/photo-gallery/igphoto/2001154180? (accessed July 7, 2020). The appearance of U.S. Department of Defense (DoD) visual information does not imply or constitute DoD endorsement.

a Star of David made of Popsicle sticks. Proving to be less than durable, the congregation soon erected a more permanent structure consisting of six tall posts planted in the ground connected by wires that held dog tags featuring the names of the dead. A plaque in front of the memorial simply expressed the wish that these fallen soldiers would "rest in peace." Elliott Ackerman, an Iraq veteran who visited the site, observed that most people who stop to ponder it appear "startled." He saw one young man burst into tears several times before he left. Several years later Joseph Howard, an Iraq veteran, fastened some 7,000 tags with the names of the dead within a twenty-eight-foot frame in a design that replicated an American flag at the Fallen Heroes Memorial in Richmond, Virginia. The flag is constructed in a way that allows it to be mobile and to be moved to other cities from time to time when people want to honor or consider soldier sacrifice. As in the memorial in Boston, death is cast within softer rhetorical tones of sadness and honor in these commemorations; in a culture torn between its noble and violent

Erik Patton, *Dog Tag Memorial*, Old North Church, Boston, 2020. Used by permission of the artist.

impulses, it is clear that the full reality of the human tragedy is that the war on terror brought could never be put completely away.[21]

White crosses were also deployed as metaphors for understanding the war as a human tragedy. In November of 2003 a chapter of an organization known as Veterans for Peace (VFP) began to drive homemade crosses into the sand on a beach in Santa Barbara, California, to honor each American soldier killed in Iraq. These vets felt strongly that the American public was not seeing the true human cost of the war, in part because the Bush administration was censoring photos of caskets arriving back in the United States. As more Americans were killed, additional crosses would be added to the site, which became known as Arlington West. The crosses were meant to be not only a visual reminder of the war's bloodshed but the focal point of a memorial site where family and friends could mourn and pay homage to their dead. Memorial services were held at the location on Sundays, and visitors would gather to honor and grieve. One young marine with tears streaming down his face told sociologist Lisa Leitz that he had come to the site to "say good-bye" to a fallen comrade. Periodically, people placed American flags near the crosses or dog tags, flowers, messages, or rosary beads. Within three years the number of crosses had risen to 3,000, and the installation covered a full acre of the beach.

In 2010 as the American involvement in Iraq diminished, the local board of the VFP decided to shift the focus of the memorial from Iraq to military deaths in Afghanistan. Steve Sherrill, one of the key creators of the original site, did not favor the move because he felt it would cause people to forget the bloody sacrifice in Iraq and weaken the powerful image that Arlington West had come to represent, although it had become more difficult for organizers to build and maintain the site as casualties rose in both war fronts. By 2016, the evolving memorial, now named "Costs of War," began to mount representations of other issues associated with war such as the rising rates of PTSD among returning soldiers and the turmoil the conflict brought to the Middle East. In one exhibit, wooden dollar signs were erected on the beach with names of corporations that were allegedly profiting from the War on Terror. Another display listed Middle Eastern nations like Iraq that had been destabilized by the conflict.[22]

A 2005 documentary film titled *Arlington West* recorded the views of visitors who trekked to the Santa Barbara location. Clearly the crosses attracted people with a diverse set of opinions, although the majority appeared to question the war and the level of sacrifice it required. One man claimed the United States had to stand up to Saddam Hussein; a nurse described the suffering she witnessed among vets who came home with PTSD. The film opens with shots of the crosses on the beach and the voice of Jane Bright, whose son Evan Ashcraft was killed in Iraq. Bright said that she had opposed the war from the beginning and that she held President Bush responsible for the man's death. She came to the Santa Barbara memorial to let others know how terrible it was to lose a child and expressed concern for the thousands of other "sons and daughters" still in Iraq. Knowing the misfortune of burying her oldest child, Bright did not want other parents to endure the same pain. She hoped only that more people would rise up against the war to "stop this madness." Interestingly the dead soldier's father, Asa Ashcraft, now divorced from his mother, saw honor in his son's sacrifice. He made it clear that Evan wanted to enlist in the military and found it an experience that helped him mature after a youthful period of drug use. Asa expressed real pride in seeing his son put a troubled past behind him and graduate from boot camp, and made it clear that the new soldier very much wanted to go with his unit to Iraq. After his son was killed when his Humvee was hit by a rocket-propelled grenade in northern

Iraq, Asa began to alter his early support for the war and came to see it as a "mistake." Yet, he continued to see his son as a "hero" who was willing to answer the call of his country, telling a reporter that there could be no outcome in Iraq that would ever change his view that his son had done something noble and praiseworthy.[23]

White crosses suddenly appeared again in 2006 on a hillside in Lafayette, California, a suburb of San Francisco. The location was a highly visible one, close not only to passing traffic but to passengers using a nearby commuter-rail station. The crosses were accompanied by a sign reading "Memorial of 2,839 troops killed in Iraq," a reference to the total number of American troops lost in the conflict up to that point. The entire venture was spearheaded by local peace activists such as Louise Clark, Jeff Heaton, and Lynn MacMichael. Clark, who owned the land upon which the crosses were erected, and Heaton's father had both opposed the Vietnam War and worked as draft counselors for the Mt. Diablo Peace Center in the 1960s. At the time of the Iraq invasion Heaton's thoughts often returned to a memory of his father marching in protest in Lafayette in the 1960s while some townsfolk ridiculed him. Drawing on his service in World War II aboard an aircraft carrier, the elder Heaton was affected by the death of close comrades and told his son that he should always question the "logic of going to war." MacMichael had also been active in antiwar protests during the Vietnam era and in Iraq as well in 2003 just before the American invasion, where she had joined a group called Voices in the Wilderness that was protesting the harsh impact of UN sanctions on Iraqi civilians.[24]

Clark and Heaton had tried to set up a smaller memorial consisting of just a few crosses three years earlier, but someone took them down, an act that left Heaton "disheartened." Clark felt that the soldiers represented on the hill had given "their lives for us" and "needed a memorial." Heaton explained that a central aim of the entire endeavor was to remind people that lives were being lost in Iraq and that families were being devastated. He explained that he felt the need to "chronicle the tragedy of the war." Certainly many of the activists who supported the mounting of this display of death did not back this war effort itself. Yet, Heaton insisted that everyone who planted these symbols in the ground, whether they were crosses that were simply painted white or adorned with Islamic crescents or the Jewish Star of David, were focused on offering a solemn tribute to the men and women who served in the military and not simply engaging in an antiwar protest. In fact, Heaton made it clear he was not interested in making overt attacks on the Bush administration itself.[25]

Nevertheless, and not surprisingly, the display drew immediate criticism. Initial passions were so strong that the Lafayette city council actually decided to hold public deliberations over the issue. Ultimately the council decided the crosses were not violating any existing statutes and refrained from trying to interfere with the commemorative rights of its citizens; Heaton recalled many in attendance also defended the mounting of the crosses as an act of free speech. One angry resident wrote the town manager, telling him that Heaton was an "un-American" who "spits on the real graves of our brave soldiers who have died to defend your right to make a fool of yourself and bring shame on your city in the process." Some felt the crosses on the hill were simply "anti-military." One person referred to the site as an "al-Qaeda scoreboard that is very negative" and felt it conveyed the idea that the United States was being defeated. Others referred to those who erected the emblems as "Jane Fonda types" or "despicable people." Early on, a retired marine officer, convinced the sign registering the mounting tally of U.S. war dead was a "disgrace to those who have sacrificed," simply tore it down. In 2007 at a pro-war rally in front of the hillside sponsored by a group of people who had lost a loved one in Iraq called Move America Forward, a speaker referred to the project as a "phony memorial." A fellow protester, continuing the vast project to disenfranchise grief, proposed a "big bonfire" to remove the symbols completely. Many simply saw the crosses as a sign of disrespect for the soldiers who served. "We know what it means to remain faithful to our sons and daughters while we remain faithfully here at home for them while they serve our great country," one critic exclaimed. At the same rally, as American flags waved, another member of the crowd issued a command to everyone who complained about the use of force by the American military: "Shut the hell up." Another Gold Star Father made it clear that he disapproved of crosses because they diminished the sacrifice of his son who he felt had died fighting for "freedom and justice for all" in Iraq.[26]

Proponents of the memorial site focused on the idea that the tragic aspects of the war simply could not be forgotten. A local lawyer argued that she supported the idea of making the public aware of how many "needless deaths of American soldiers there have been in Iraq." She believed that passing by the hillside "covered in white" was so dramatic that it drove home the point of how "costly and tragic this war has been." Another local citizen insisted that the crosses remain because so many people take the "blessings and freedoms" of America for granted. "Even though we know ultimately this war may be for oil or power," this man observed, "the memorial is a beacon of comfort for those families of fallen soldiers." Craig Cataline, a local carpenter and the father of a navy medic who had served in Iraq, took on the task of updating the sign that registered the growing number of American deaths. He said that at first he saw the venture as merely a protest against the war but eventually came to feel that it was a valid enterprise because it helped everyone to remember the soldiers who died. "Whether you believe the war is folly or not, these poor kids gave their lives for America," he insisted. Karen Meredith, whose only son was killed in the war in 2004, was actually glad the crosses were erected; she was convinced that people should pay attention to the reality that "children are dying in their name."[27]

The need to privilege heartbreak in the reframing of the war was reinforced by a series of solemn ceremonies that were held at the foot of the hill. For a time people would gather on the first Sunday of every month to meditate and pray in whatever religious form they desired. After the services volunteers would remove weeds and add new crosses. Laura Zucker, a local songwriter and storyteller, was so moved by the hillside commemoration that she composed her song "Memorial Day" in response to what she saw and started performing it at the site on the May holiday. Zucker's composition took a highly empathic perspective on the war and its cost by framing the death of soldiers from the perspective of a mother's loss rather than from the standpoint of patriotic sacrifice. Her tune exposes the incongruity of a mother attempting to instill values of love and kindness in her offspring only to see them forced to go off and kill or be killed. "How does a mother reconcile her pride," she asks, "with the news her child has just died?"[28]

Even George W. Bush eventually acknowledged the human cost of the war more openly. Taking up painting after his presidential term was completed, Bush began to execute portraits of wounded veterans and actually assisted in the rehabilitation of many by leading them in annual mountain bike treks and reaching out to the vets socially. His 2017 book, *Portraits of Courage: A Commander in Chief's Tribute to America's Warriors,* is meant to be an inspirational tome presenting Bush's portraits of veterans he had come to know. The president's concern for these men and women who served their country certainly appeared genuine. He is believable when he writes that he hopes these veterans "know he cares about them and will until the day he dies." Bush's empathy is real but modulated. It is designed ultimately to buttress a war-based version of patriotism because it seeks to mitigate the full extent of the damage the conflict caused. Most soldiers overwhelmed by the posttraumatic stress and traumatic brain injuries noted

Binh Danh, *Hillside Memorial of Crosses*, Lafayette, California, 2010. Used by permission of the artist.

in the book find a way to recover and move on with their lives in a purposeful manner. This is not to say that Bush's stories are untrue. In fact, they are moving. But the overall collection is also slanted in a way to encase the painful truths of war in a larger narrative that vigorously equates patriotism with military service and evades crucial issues such as veteran suicides, Iraqi civilian casualties, the anguish of Gold Star parents, and Bush's culpability in starting the war in the first place.[29]

Bush took a strong stand in reimagining the War on Terror and became a prominent defender of the idea of a war-based patriotism that permeated American culture in the early twenty-first century. Yet, as we have seen, justifications for the War on Terror were widely contested by Americans committed to using art to further a vision of patriotic empathy that resisted efforts to gloss over the full scope of human injury the global contest brought.

5 The Soldiers' Debate

. . . .

As in earlier wars, soldiers did not hesitate to write or talk about their experiences in the War on Terror. No matter their slant on the course of events, memoirs, novels, and biographies by and about combatants have become a staple in the reimagining of military conflict and an essential part of the discourse over what a war meant. This was certainly the case during the War on Terror as the literary output of those who served became an important part of the patriots' debate and its call for self-reflection. Those who sided with the ethos of an aggressive patriotism produced tales from the battlefield and the home front that validated the honor and courage of their combat, sometimes suggesting that their service to the nation had helped transform them into better and more mature individuals. Such accounts also featured tales of warrior proficiency, courage, and valor in defending the battle group.

Numerous veterans, however, produced a counternarrative based upon their direct participation in "the real war," joining the patriots' quarrel with the intent to safeguard evidence of emotional confusion and sense of loss many felt from witnessing the pain and death of others. They too took up projects of self-examination and inquiry, reflecting on how the war fit with the larger course of their lives and the nature of the country they served. In these versions the ambition of war-based patriots to smooth away strains of guilt and loss with the glories of patriotic sacrifice and moral redemption was thwarted by traumatic revelations. Heartbreak, stress, and critical reflection dominated such remembrances that not only mourned the loss of comrades but revealed the difficult years of readjustment that followed homecomings.

This dispute over feelings and interpretations found in writings by and about warriors was not like the literary fallout from Vietnam. In most cases soldiers who served in Southeast Asia reconstructed their experience as a narrative of declension or a loss of innocence; moral burdens were palpable. In these stories men steeped in a patriotic culture reinforced by World War II and the Cold War set off to defend their country with the attitude that they were embarking on a noble crusade. In the end—clear in the writing of veterans such as Philip Caputo and Ron Kovic—the initial enthusiasm to serve gave way to feelings of disappointment and a belief that the war was utterly meaningless. In Tim O'Brien's short story collection *The Things They Carried*, most characters lacked even a patriotic past and went to Vietnam mostly because they felt they had to or were embarrassed not to go. Seldom did they feel the pulse of patriotic honor at all. A few warriors, like James Webb, saw in the American fight in Vietnam the promise of demonstrating duty, sacrifice, and loyalty that was stirring. But the overall thrust in the Vietnam rewrite was centered on a tale of debasement, something noble patriotism worked to rebuff, and an inability to extract anything meaningful from service to the nation. In the War on Terror a traditional ideal of patriotic service as ennobling was at least able to regain a significant amount of literary space.[1]

The War-Based Patriots

Chris Kyle's bestselling memoir, *American Sniper*, revealed not only a heroic interpretation of the American war experience but a desire on the part of the public to embrace such a viewpoint in the aftermath of 9/11. Memoirs such as Kyle's and Mark Owen's *No Easy Day: The Autobiography of a Navy SEAL; The Firsthand Account of the Mission That Killed Osama Bin Laden* celebrated the skills of American special forces and reinforced the connection between valor and American national identity. The publication date of the story of SEAL Team Six authored by Owen and its mission to get bin Laden was actually moved up because of the "overwhelming excitement in the marketplace" for such a tale. Some have argued that these chronicles are popular because millions of Americans have served in the military and because they have a "fascination with heroism and hero archetypes." There is truth in such assertions, but it is also the case that heroic myths enjoy approval because they enable citizens to evade the moral implications and tragic consequences of their nation's ventures into brutality.[2]

No recent war memoir has sold more copies than Kyle's account of his expert marksmanship. At its rhetorical core *American Sniper* constituted an epic rendition of the soldier's experience and a robust defense of the war itself. In this book the actions of the veteran and the nation are cast as beyond reproach. George W. Bush's decision to go to war in 2001 and invade Iraq two years later is fully legitimated. Kyle's proficiency with a rifle is embedded in a moral framework in which the casualties he produced are justified because they protected American soldiers who otherwise could have been harmed and because they killed evil people who did not deserve to live. Patriotism here is mythical and proper, insulated from questions that might have come from the killing of innocent people or the decisions to go into Iraq in the first place. There is some dissent in this book, but it comes from Kyle's wife, Taya, who expressed the wish that the famous sniper should show more compassion for his family and not leave her and their children for successive tours abroad.

Kyle's portrayal of the war as an unequivocal crusade against wickedness permeates the entire memoir. He calls the fight in Iraq a struggle against "savage, despicable evil" and asserts that there is no way to describe properly what he and his comrades encountered there. Empathy, or the ability to walk in the shoes of another, is circumscribed; American violence becomes virtuous. In part his framing of the struggle was driven by his professed conviction that he was a Christian fighting a struggle against Muslim infidels who held a "twisted interpretation of religion." To demonstrate his religious fervor, Kyle got a tattoo in the shape of a cross on his arm and announced that he "hated the damn savages we were fighting." His faith also sanctioned his killing. In describing a moment when his role as protector of his comrades caused him to take the life of a woman he suspected might carry a grenade beneath her clothing, the sharpshooter expressed no regret.

"My shots saved several Americans whose lives were clearly worth more than that woman's twisted soul. . . . I can stand before God with a clear conscience about doing my job, but I truly, deeply hated the evil that woman possessed. I hate it to this day."[3]

Kyle's ethical frame on the war, a view that merged religion and nationalism, and his contempt for the enemy enhanced his reputation as the most lethal sniper in American military history, with some 160 confirmed kills. He viewed his opponents, who were often former Ba'ath Party officials or al-Qaeda partisans, as "whackadoos" and cowards who hid behind women and children. Borrowing from Robert McNamara's philosophy about the "Fog of War," he reasoned that a soldier had to kill the enemy over and over in order to protect not only himself but his comrades as well. "You do it until there is no one left to kill. That's what war is," he explained. This form of patriotic reasoning actually allowed him not only to take lives but to exalt in the aftermath of vanquishing enemy combatants. He called his service in Iraq the "thrill of his life." One night after a long firefight that lasted for almost two days, his unit was completely exhausted. Still, one marine managed to hoist an American flag and play a recording of the National Anthem. Kyle could still recall how satisfied this war memory made him feel and concluded that his military service had allowed him to live the "literal meaning of the land of the free and the home of the brave."[4]

When Kyle returned home for good after four tours, he had amassed an impressive record of service and was able to use his reputation to make important business contacts in Texas. He came to know President George W. Bush and J. Kyle Bass, a prominent hedge fund manager who admired the rigorous training the SEALs endured. Through his association with Bass, the American hero met other businessmen in the Dallas area and joined them on hunting trips. These men eventually helped Kyle to start Craft International, a consulting and training firm that offered instruction in the use of weapons and security measures to government and civilian agencies. Kyle not only headed the firm but used slogans such as "One of the top snipers in history of the American Armed Forces" or "Despite what your moma told you, violence does solve problems," as a way to promote his firm. At this time he also began to speak out for a strong defense of the Second Amendment and debunk calls for more gun controls in the United States.[5]

In a terrible and stunning turn of events, however, Kyle was killed in 2013 by a troubled veteran he was trying to help. The war hero had made a conscious attempt to assist such men who struggled with the emotional scars of war after their return home. Despite the tragic implications of the shooting, Kyle's memorial service in Dallas stoked traditional patriotic sentiments with its aspirations to minimize the damage Iraq had brought to many. Over 7,000 people attended ceremonies in the Dallas Cowboys' football stadium, where the fallen warrior's casket was placed at midfield. A brokenhearted widow, flanked by Navy SEALs, spoke tearfully of the loving relationship she had with her spouse and called him the "toughest and softest-hearted man on earth." Fellow SEALs spoke of his prowess as a shooter and the compassion he had for his fellow fighters, a reminder that this patriotic story was not without its human as well as national connections. From the stadium Kyle's casket was driven several hundred miles to his resting place south of Dallas as thousands of spectators lined the highway honoring him and the nation's military by waving American flags.

Reviewers were generally accepting of Kyle's memoir, which essentially offered an uncritical view of the Iraq conflict and a highly positive perspective on the warriors themselves. They were impressed with the rigor of SEAL training as he described it and the ease with which he approached the killing of hated enemies. In fact, a commentator in the *Washington Times* felt Kyle's depiction of the enemy was "revealing," since he described them as "cowards," parts of criminal gangs, or simply religious extremists.

One critic in the *Los Angeles Times* felt that Kyle deserved to be heard because he was really speaking for the "ground soldiers who did the fighting" and his book offered a reflection of the real "anger" these warriors felt and their "contempt" for most Iraqis. Another observer felt Kyle's direct and "blunt" perspective on the course of battle actually brought "honor to all those warriors who raise hell on the battlefield and also the ones who laid down their lives in the course."[6]

The honorable defense of a war-based patriotism is also upheld in Marcus Luttrell's book *Lone Survivor: An Account of Operation Redwing and the Lost Heroes of SEAL Team 10*. Americans have frequently used the language and imagery of traditional patriotism to claim the moral high ground in their in encounters with violence and brutality, a paradox that has helped them maintain a righteous identity even as they inflicted high numbers of casualties on innocent civilians as well as enemy combatants. Luttrell, another SEAL from Texas, is quick to adopt this approach, invoking ideals like his devotion to the traditional family, the love of God, and the basic goodness of the nation itself. Even more than Kyle, he sees the SEALs as exceptional warriors and rugged individuals imbued with nation-centered love and capable of powerful feelings of affection for each other. It was this love that explained their ability to fight heroically not only for the nation but for their battle group. SEALs are moral paragons not only because they endorse the nation's violent actions as just but because they are capable of unmatched deeds of selflessness.[7]

The SEAL fraternity dominates his rendition of the war and serves as a benchmark of male potency and courageous nationalism. To him SEALs certainly hold a love of country deep in their heart and "feel a slight quiver when they see Old Glory fluttering above the parade square" or listen to the strains of "Hail to the Chief." Luttrell was immensely impressed by the SEALs' sense of comradeship. To be a SEAL in his view is to know that your brethren would do all that they could to protect you and never let you down. Luttrell refers to this ideal as an "American Brotherhood" that has been "forged in blood" and is now "unbreakable." It is this adoration of solidarity, necessary for any battle group to fight and survive, that allows SEALs to rise from the bleakness and dreadfulness of war and stand as emblems of virtue and strength. Their reputation for unselfishness allows Luttrell to cast his stories from the war in honorable terms and uphold the virtuous core of a war-based patriotism. The death of a SEAL becomes more than simply a tragic loss. It represents a splendid ending to an admirable life. Surviving SEALs accompany the bodies of their fallen brethren home and offer to help surviving family members any way they can, thus continuing the performance of the ideal of brotherly affection. Luttrell actually opens his memoir with the story of the grief and feeling of survivor's guilt he felt while visiting the family of a fellow combatant who did not come home alive. In death the example of this dedicated but fallen soldier continues to serve his nation as he did in life.[8]

In *Lone Survivor*, Luttrell recounts his unlikely survival from a furious gunfight with Taliban forces in the mountainous regions of Afghanistan. Three fellow SEALs died in the confrontation and, sadly, another sixteen soldiers were killed in a helicopter crash while trying to rescue the trapped SEALs. Luttrell's good fortune was ultimately due to the intervention of local villagers who attended to his wounds while defying demands of the Taliban for information on his whereabouts. Although the skirmish was a catastrophe for these American forces, the retelling of the fight between SEALs and the Taliban mitigated the calamity by underscoring the bravery and courage of these highly trained special forces. The leader of their mission, Michael Murphy, actually exposed himself to direct fire in attempting to make a call for help for his entrapped men and was subsequently awarded the Medal of Honor.

Luttrell's rendering of the battle in Afghanistan becomes both a war remembrance and a political tract, upholding patriotic and warrior values and condemning liberal, antiwar voices in America who often referred to American troops as "brutal killers." Taking time to refer to the revelations of prisoner abuse at Abu Ghraib, Luttrell claimed that he could not understand the uproar over American cruelty when compared with "all of the death and destruction Muslim extremists have visited upon the world." That is why, in the end, he hated the rules of engagement that governed his behavior in battle. Such regulations inhibited the spirit of SEALs to do whatever it took to win. And he could never understand why the American media were continually "knocking us down" when all he and his comrades did was love their country and "everything it stands for."[9]

Five years after publishing *Lone Survivor*, Luttrell issued a second memoir based on his tour in Iraq, *Service: A Navy SEAL at War*. Having recovered from the injuries he sustained in Afghanistan, the dedicated soldier now joined counterinsurgency operations in Anbar province which had allowed American forces to forge a closer relationship with local Sunnis in an effort to blunt the influence of al-Qaeda. Wrapped in a highly patriotic and virtuous scaffold, this story is dominated by threads of devotion to the national cause and the ideals of SEAL brotherhood. SEAL bravery is front and center as these warriors dash about assisting wounded comrades and freeing those who are trapped. The death of a SEAL was always a momentous event that sparked furious acts of retaliation no matter the cost. Luttrell explained that he had learned from his experience in Afghanistan the necessity of extracting a price from the enemy for any damage they inflicted. It was this esprit de corps, this devotion to the well-being of the battle group, that drove much of the valor SEALs displayed. It was, in fact, a bond that the men missed very much when they finally returned home; intimate relationships with those outside the brotherhood were often difficult to maintain. Luttrell remarked that once back in Texas he often felt like a "dog looking for a home."[10]

Luttrell's writings garnered mostly laudatory reviews. One critic enjoyed not only the dramatic account of the SEAL's deadly mission in *Lone Survivor*, a highly successful best seller, but learning of Luttrell's story of his upbringing and family life. This reader did wonder at times how Luttrell ultimately survived his close encounter with death but quickly realized that he was saved by the incredible training he received as a SEAL. Another reviewer found much of Luttrell's tale from Afghanistan typical of war stories with their depictions of training camp and episodes of "remarkable heroism." But, taking the warrior's viewpoint, he sympathized with Luttrell's critique of rules of engagement that these SEALs operated under and felt they reflected poorly on "politicians safely ensconced in their Washington offices" who failed to understand what these men had to endure.[11]

Like Kyle, Luttrell continued to frame the war in terms of conservative politics in America after returning home. In 2008 he gave an address to the National Rifle Association in Louisville. He regaled his audience with a tale about being in a bar in New York City wearing a T-shirt with a Texas flag emblazoned on the back. A patron suggested to the former SEAL that if he wore such a shirt he must not be from America. Luttrell's accuser also had the misfortune of referring to him as a "cowboy" and apparently added some negative comments about America itself. Luttrell insisted that his normal response to such an affront was to light the perpetrator on fire or "slap him." In this instance, the brave warrior at first opted for the slapping option and pushed the man out of the bar. He claimed that he "was ready to rip his ear off" before security men stopped him. No one could be sure if this yarn was true or not. Luttrell made it clear, however, that the point he was trying to make to his enraptured audience was that if someone does not like America they should leave it.

He then proceeded to recount some of his battlefield exploits and feelings he had over losing some of the men with whom he fought. He insisted that he and fellow SEALs were not "heroes" but "patriots" who "bled on the flag to keep it red." He claimed that in the end he was only a "simple country boy," a statement that reinforced his claim to pure innocence and exceptional devotion. And he warned "politicians" that they had better make smart decisions when sending the likes of him into war again because "SEALs are about annihilating the enemy so we aren't attacked again." He might have added that in the process many of them suffered substantial pain.[12]

Mark Owen's depiction of his war experience also carried messages of patriotic devotion and personal integrity. Raised in Alaska, where his missionary parents taught him to hunt and trap in the wilderness, Owen participated in the raid in Pakistan that killed Osama bin Laden. Like his colleagues, he valued the rigorous standards of SEAL training and felt it was crucial to creating powerful warriors with "a limitless capacity to sacrifice our time and even our lives for a greater good." Like many of his brothers-in-arms, he, too, was initially motivated to fight because of the attacks on 9/11. He was looking for a "little payback."[13]

Owen provided a significant amount of detail on the bin Laden raid and saw it as momentous. For the project to get the al-Qaeda leader, the military erected a model of the compound that bi Laden inhabited in Pakistan. This allowed the American forces to plan exactly how they would circumvent his defenses and get to him. Owen and his comrades were even able to watch drone footage of the house and observe the movement of its inhabitants. Owen's team dropped into the compound after bin Laden had been shot. Part of his assignment was to clean up some of the blood that was shed so it would not be so visible in photos of the operation. For Owen this was personally an awesome experience and he not only rejoiced in the success of the mission but was amazed that "lying in front of me was the reason we had been fighting for the past decade."[14]

Like Luttrell, Owen also made an effort to attach SEAL heroics to a conservative political agenda by remaking tough soldiers into paragons of virtue. He stressed that SEALs sought no accolades for the heroics or any extra compensation. Their reward was in the attainment of excellence, their spirit of brotherhood, and their performance of duty. Owen made it clear that he saw men like himself as existing on a higher plane than "politicians" who sought only praise and "safely watch the war from a video monitor from thousands of miles away," a reference to news photos of President Barack Obama watching the bin Laden raid from the White House. Owen even insisted that none of the men in his outfit were "huge fans" of the president but did respect the position of commander in chief.[15]

Today Brendan Looney, a SEAL, and Travis Manion, a marine, are buried next to each other in Arlington National Cemetery, a placement meant to symbolize both their patriotism and their sense of comradeship. The men bonded while at the Naval Academy and were both motivated to fight by the collapse of the Twin Towers in New York. They were also inspired by the words of George W. Bush in 2001 that noted how the nation's grief had turned to anger and anger turned to determination "to bring justice to our enemies." At the time of 9/11, Manion gave his father a hat with a "Rescue 1 FDNY" logo emblazoned on the front and the inscription "9-11–01 Never Forget" on the back. He told his father that the hat would remind him "what we're fighting for."[16]

The terrible death of these two men is mitigated substantially in this story by an insistence from many who knew them that military service had led to personal growth. Manion's friends and family noticed when he returned from a tour of duty in Iraq that he carried himself with a new aura of seriousness and quiet self-confidence. Friends felt that he had shown a "hunger for success" at the Naval Academy but now felt that Iraq had changed him for the "better." In battle he had helped protect his fellow soldiers from improvised explosive devices (IEDs) and had acquired a mastery of "cruel tactics" of the enemy and a strong desire to retaliate against those who harmed the men he commanded. His deep desire to defend his battle group soon rivaled the motivation he initially had to fight just after 9/11. Men who knew Manion and Looney argued that they had the "uncanny ability" to focus on the big picture and not get drawn into political arguments, an apparent reference to squabbles back home over the reasons to invade Iraq in the first place.[17]

Looney is described as a war-based patriot as well, totally dedicated to the crusade to fight terrorism. Rejecting an assignment to navy intelligence after graduating from the academy, Looney opted instead for SEAL training as a sure way to get into the struggle against the terrorists. He also saw SEAL membership as a way to attain a greater degree of honor in his military career, for it meant that he would be learning to be "selfless" and to do "the right thing." When Travis was killed in Iraq, his parents gave his close friend the fallen soldier's knife and a bracelet that referred to him as a "Spartan Hero, and Leader." Ironically, when Looney fought in Iraq he used the bracelet as a good luck charm to help him feel safe. Unfortunately he was killed as well in Afghanistan.[18]

Brian Stann, another friend of Manion at the Naval Academy, also took up the cultural project to transform military service into a character-building experience. Raised on the rough-and-tumble streets of Scranton,

Pennsylvania, as he described them, Stann presented his childhood as a time when he used to "use his fists" and take care of himself. He maintained that he was a good enough student to get into an Ivy League university but his family could not afford the tuition. Besides, he claimed he was not interested in the "drinking and partying" of a "civilian college." He preferred a place such as the Naval Academy where he could drive himself to excel and "secure something significant in my life."[19]

Stann was devastated by the death of Manion. He had respected Manion's willingness to fight and felt Manion stood for "what was right." Attending Manion's funeral in Doylestown, Pennsylvania, proved to be emotionally overwhelming for this soldier, although Stann was comforted by the massive outpouring of public honor lavished on the dead marine. At Manion's funeral ceremonies, lines of police officers, firefighters, and Patriot Guard motorcyclists on Harley-Davidsons carrying American flags pledged to protect the fallen hero from any potential antiwar protest.

As a marine officer, Stann fought in Iraq as well and described in detail how he led men in ferocious combat. In one harrowing encounter, when his unit was completely surrounded, Stann earned the Silver Star, the nation's third-highest honor for bravery. Back home he disclosed that he continued to feel pangs of guilt for not saving some of the men who served under him. But ultimately his story was another example of how war could be redemptive or a boost to personal development. It was in battle and not in any classroom that this marine felt he realized part of his full potential by becoming a true leader.[20]

Many veterans framed their war-based patriotism along the lines of personal transformation, crediting their military service for their personal and professional uplift. Eric Greitens, a friend of Manion's who served with him in Fallujah, certainly saw his service this way and defended the war-based side of the patriots' debate unequivocally. A former navy SEAL who would eventually become governor of Missouri, Greitens reframed his experience as a warrior in terms of a patriotic catechism that offered hope for the future that sordid acts and brutal wounds could be left behind. Like Kyle and others, Greitens recast his military years into a larger life narrative as a gratifying experience that instilled in him a set of values that he deemed indispensable not only to his own life but to the moral life of the nation.

Greitens recalled that his parents had stressed the importance of education in his life. On a trip to China, however, he came to the conclusion that there was more value to be derived from real life experiences than reading books or living the "cushy life of a college student." He found particular satisfaction in the hard training demanded for boxing matches and came to enjoy the sight of blood on his hands and feeling of soreness in his jaw. "I began to learn that strength comes from working through pain and it felt good," he wrote.[21]

Despite his growing attraction to masculine pursuits, Greitens continued his studies by finishing a degree at Duke University and winning a Rhodes scholarship to Oxford. After reading about the rigors of SEAL training, however, he quickly understood that it could transform him into the type of rugged individual he wanted to become. "I realized also that if I stayed at Oxford or had gone to work for a Fortune 500 company," he wrote, "I could have lived my entire life with the same kinds of people who went to Duke or Oxford or worked at fancy law firms." Such privileged people in his estimation did not understand what it meant to depend "on the strength of your back." They considered themselves "global citizens," but SEALs like him considered themselves Americans. He knew such superior warriors, emblematic of a war-based patriotism, could inflict tremendous violence. What truly made them special, however, was their "thoughtful, disciplined, and proportional" use of force.[22]

After four tours of duty, including assignments in Iraq and Afghanistan, Greitens returned home impressed by the "love and muscular bonding that come with brotherhood under fire" that he had experienced in the SEALs. Despite the fact that he felt the invasion of Iraq was a misguided venture, he believed there was also a nonpolitical or personal dimension to war that actually served as an incubator of moral values. Impressed especially by his widespread exposure to ideals such as unselfishness that he experienced among the troops, he decided to sustain this self-sacrificing spirit by founding an organization called "The Mission Continues." The plan was to help returned vets struggling with issues like readjustment and post-traumatic stress disorder (PTSD) by assigning them specific missions or tasks that were altruistic. Greitens saw this venture as one that would not only help former soldiers but actually move society itself to a higher moral plane. He was struck by a visit to Washington, D.C., where he saw people living their lives in a self-absorbed fashion completely unaware of the plight of soldiers like his friend Travis Manion who were still in mortal danger in Iraq and Afghanistan at the time. In response to these concerns, the foundation began to place veterans into "platoons" with "squad leaders" that implemented a range of civic projects such as mentoring children, assisting homeless veterans, or even building sustainable agricultural networks that supplied fresh food to needy families.[23]

Redemption and growth also validated pain in David Bellavia's chronicle of his army life. In fierce urban fighting in Fallujah between American forces and Iraqi insurgents and foreign mujahideen troops, Bellavia felt that he found a true masculine and heroic identity for which he had longed. Far from fearing the battle to come, Bellavia had seen war as the "challenge of a lifetime," particularly because it provided an opportunity to engage in hand-to-hand combat and test his skills against another. He described a vicious struggle with a jihadist in which the two men were like "caged dogs locked in a death match." As Bellavia watched his adversary slowly die after stabbing him with his knife, Bellavia claimed he felt absolutely no sense of remorse—such was the attraction of this form of self-realization. For Bellavia, "close quarter combat" was really "intellectual," fought on the most animalistic level of the human brain. After vanquishing his foe, he recalled spitting blood and screaming at the top of his voice.[24]

The need to prove himself as ferocious warrior, as Bellavia told it, stemmed from his boyhood. Years before as two men burglarized his parents' home, his father stood in a doorway to protect David's mother, who lay ill in bed. The younger Bellavia was apparently frozen by the sight of the intruders and did not move. Later his father was quick to chastise him for not doing more to stop the home invasion. David claimed that he never forgot the look of disappointment on his father's face, a memory that helped shape his decision to join the army in the first place and seek the "heart and spirit" that he (and his father) felt he had lacked.[25]

Like soldiers before him, Bellavia not only found redemption in the killing of an adversary but reveled in the bonds of brotherhood he experienced in Iraq. At one point he felt so emotionally attached to his fellow soldiers that he passed on an opportunity to go home and reenlisted. Bellavia was awestruck by the sight of comrades firing their weapons until their hands bled. He was also astonished by the leadership qualities of men like Lieutenant Colonel Pete Newell. He recalled Newell's stirring speech to his men before the battle of Fallujah in November 2004. Invoking a moral frame on the fight to come, Newell proclaimed that the clash would be "as pure a fight of good versus evil as we'll probably see in our lifetimes." He told the men they needed not only to subdue the terrorists but to avenge the deaths of friends. "This is personal for me as it should be for you," he insisted as a way of rallying his forces.[26]

After leaving the army in 2006, Bellavia returned to Iraq as a reporter. He had already become critical of the American media which he felt had blurred the clear lines of distinction between good and evil that Newell and his president had affirmed and that he and some of his brethren had felt. As he walked along streets filled with Iraqis going about their daily business, he realized most of them had no idea of the heroism and courage men he knew had displayed. It bothered him that a remembrance of the honorable fight warriors like him had mounted was nowhere to be found. In this moment of reflection, he was brought to tears and began to grieve for his fallen brothers and place flowers at several spots where his friends had died. He admitted in his memoir, a deep exploration of his personal experience, that he still had flashbacks of the tragedies he saw. But he quickly let his mind return to another reality of Fallujah: the courageous fighting by American forces and the bravery they demonstrated in saving their own comrades. In Fallujah he felt he had "witnessed the best of the human condition—the loyalty, self-sacrifice, the love that brotherhood of arms evokes." For him the war itself was also justified because the Americans had fought to give the Iraqis the "basic human right" to be free of tyranny and oppression. He now lamented that such a "right" was lost.[27]

Joe Le Bleu, a highly proficient army sniper, also took up the quest to commemorate the War on Terror as primarily an exercise in warrior heroism with a deep passion. Like others, Le Bleu recalled his war more with honor than with anguish. He recited a proud tradition of military service in his family that included a great uncle who was a decorated army ranger in World War II. His sense of pride in serving the nation clearly explained the reaction he had to 9/11 as an attack similar to Pearl Harbor. For him the terrorist attacks brought not the tragedy of another war but only a rationale for revenge. In fact, he was so incensed by the fall of the Twin Towers that he re-enlisted in the Rangers six months after being discharged. He acknowledged that he also felt the pull of brotherhood that he had already known and the imperative to bring his expertise as a sniper to the new war.

Like those of other war-based patriots and defenders of a heroic tradition, Le Bleu's enemies were not only terrorists but fellow citizens who did not share his highly mythical view, an indication that tensions between honor and trauma were splitting the homeland. He was scornful not only of "bloodsucking liberals" but members of the media who, in his opinion, did not endorse the aggressive stance of warriors determined to kill as many of the enemy as possible. On one occasion he abruptly left the funeral of a fellow ranger because he was bothered by reporters who stood outside the church and seemed more interested in getting photos than in paying their respects to one of the first "Special Ops guys" to die in the war. While he was at it, Le Bleu also complained that many Americans lacked a killer instinct when it came to hitting back at the terrorists, a failure he labeled "politically correct bullshit"; he felt such a public attitude undermined the "warrior spirit" in the nation. His plan was clearly to maximize the deaths of al-Qaeda fighters: "I say we drop al-Qaeda terrorists from the trap doors of the cargo holds in jet passenger planes . . . and tell them to enjoy the ride down." In the same vein, he also became increasingly upset with some of his superiors in Iraq who attempted to enforce strict rules of engagement that hampered his inclination to inflict maximum damage whenever the need arose. He cited the "Greatest Generation" and their unrelenting effort to slay as many Japanese as they could and felt that soldiers should be free to "kill, kill, kill." He even leveled criticism at President George W. Bush and Dick Cheney. He was not against the decision to enter Iraq but thought that the invasion should have been delayed until the mission in Afghanistan was complete. His doubts about Cheney were based in his belief that the vice president was profiting in some way from his ties to defense contractors like Halliburton.[28]

Reviewers again showed an eager acceptance of tales that affirmed the valor and the superior fighting capabilities of American soldiers. Greitens's presentation of a compassionate warrior was especially well received. One observer felt his blend of courage and humanitarianism was "quintessentially American." In a blurb about the book, Tom Brokaw called him a "hero" and a reminder that "America remains the land of the brave and the generous." So inspiring was Greitens's story of virtue and violence that a special edition was produced for young adults in which the noted veteran encouraged teens to "serve their fellow man." Admiration was also evident for Bellavia and his chronicle of bitter fighting in Iraq not only because it was seen as a book that offered a realistic account of the war but because it demonstrated the "gallantry and sacrifice" of those who fought.[29]

The Witnesses

While war-based patriots downplayed the agony the war brought, empathic soldiers refused to let it slip away. Some, like Camilo Mejia, became so repulsed by seeing the suffering American forces brought to innocent people abroad that they actually deserted their army unit and suffered the consequences of imprisonment by military authorities. Many, however, like Dakota Meyer, pointedly rejected any inclination to infuse accounts of their tours of duty with themes that were uplifting or gallant. Calling himself a mere "grunt," Meyer was actually eager to get into the fight after watching the World Trade Center towers collapse at the age of thirteen. Growing up in Kentucky, where he played football and learned to hunt and shoot like many of his peers, he inevitably gravitated to the marines once he finished high school. Not surprisingly, the young man found boot camp gratifying and eagerly went on to sniper training, a move that he felt would ensure his assignment to a battle zone. Thrilled at attaining the status of a sharpshooter, he soon had a tattoo drilled into his chest with the Latin inscription "Vesti nex est meus vito" (Your death is my life).[30]

Becoming a highly trained warrior, however, did not ensure that Meyer would emerge from his battlefield exploits with a penchant for moralizing what he saw or felt. Meyer seemed unable to shake sensations of guilt that he brought home and prevented him from exulting over enemy kills. This brave warrior was awarded the Congressional Medal of Honor for his actions in the mountains of Afghanistan, where his unit fought Taliban insurgents entering the country from Pakistan. In September 2009, Meyer and his team of American and Afghan troops were ambushed and overrun. Using his wide experience with a variety of weapons, including a machine gun capable of firing several hundred rounds per minute and a grenade launcher, Meyer fought furiously and braved enemy fire in order to rescue his comrades. In the midst of what can only be described as a chaotic and frenzied fight, he later recalled that he felt neither fear nor anger. And not for a second did he think he would die. His sole motivation in continuing to shoot was to use his training to save his comrades-in-arms. At one point he even abandoned his powerful gun and killed a man with rock, hitting him again and again in what he called a "primal rage" until the man's head was crushed.[31]

Unlike some of his peers, Meyer could not veer into heroism because he was haunted by the memory of seeing so many of his brothers lying dead, their bodies "stiff and cold." He claimed that he never imagined that his unit would suffer such a fate and basically refused to accept it when they did. Carrying their bodies from the death zone left him "deflated and exhausted," and without any impulse at all to seek revenge. He simply went about the business of cleaning corpses, straightening uniforms and putting their remains in body bags with their names on them. Consumed by a sense of loss and a high regard for others, he felt no desire whatsoever to kill again.[32]

Back in Kentucky, nothing seemed right to the courageous but traumatized warrior. Despite hearing bluegrass music again and enjoying the sight of rolling hills and pretty girls, he actually felt like he had just "landed on the moon." Despite the best efforts of family and friends to comfort him, he was wracked with feelings of detachment, depression, and anger and soon sought treatment for PTSD at a nearby military facility. Meyer explained that after being under constant battle stress for a long period of time, it was hard to "reset your settings" back to what seemed normal before the war. He was haunted by the fact that he was not able to rescue his friends and plagued by a sense of utter failure which hit him like "a big dump truck." In an interview on the television show *60 Minutes*, he insisted that in Afghanistan you either got your comrades out or died trying. Unfortunately, a strong dose of survivor's guilt had convinced him that if he was now alive he must not have tried hard enough.[33]

One night during the winter of 2010, Meyer, now attached to his "new best friend," a bottle of Jack Daniels, pulled his truck over to the side of the road, put a gun to his head, and pulled the trigger. Fortunately the chamber was empty, but he claimed the experience sobered him enough to think that his fallen brethren would have disapproved of suicide as a way to die. He still missed his band of brothers terribly and even the thrill "of shooting thousands of rounds" and "not seeing the damage you inflicted." But there was nothing ennobling in Meyer's story of the war. Strains of heroism and patriotism were not to be found in his version of events. When Barack Obama presented him with the Medal of Honor, he could only tell the commander in chief he had no idea what he could now do with his life.

Meyer's impulse to take his life after coming home represented a growing problem that the American public slowly recognized during the war on terror. Veterans groups and especially critics of George Bush began to insist that the government do more to assist soldiers back from the battlefields in their efforts to deal with depression and PTSD. One result of this awareness was the fact that the Veterans Administration instituted a hotline in 2007 that allowed vets to seek help in their many moments of distress. Michael Anthony, a soldier trained to assist doctors performing surgeries in Iraq, focuses a good deal of attention on the problem of suicides in his own remembrance of his tour of duty and homecoming. Anthony describes not only his own call to such a crisis line and his postwar bout with drugs and alcohol once back in Massachusetts but talks incessantly of a friend who endured the same experience while in Iraq. Witnessing the carnage, amputations, and bloody wounds in a medical unit where American personnel tried to save the lives of not only their fellow soldiers but even Iraqi civilians and terrorists, Anthony came home feeling "hollow" and trapped in an "emotional abyss." One way he attempted to reconnect with the civilian world was to take classes on how to attract women. Such instruction helped a bit, but it did not ultimately prevent him from holding a lump of Ambien in his hand and coming close to swallowing it. He claimed that a deep desire to write about his experience was one reason why he put the pills down.[34]

Sean Parnell served as an army platoon commander in the mountains of Afghanistan. Like so many other combatants, he acknowledged in his war remembrance the powerful connection men charged with each other's well being felt. He was well aware of the moral quality of this bond, the way it valued unselfishness, but like Meyer he was still unable to turn his war story into a tale that was inspirational. The problem was not that Parnell was unable to recognize heroic acts on the part of men with whom he served. He was. The issue for this witness to human tragedy was that he was unable to wipe out the distress he felt over the death of his buddies.[35]

Parnell brought his feelings of connectedness to his comrades home. While on leave in the United States he worried continuously that they would be harmed while he was away. When he learned that a member of his platoon was killed, he not only mourned his comrade but empathized with the man's family and felt some of their pain. "Somewhere a woman's world had come apart," he thought, and wondered if she was holding her child when the tragic news of her husband's death arrived. There were even moments when his sympathies jumped over the boundaries of brotherhood. Early on in his mission in Afghanistan, he watched as a young girl killed by the Taliban died in his arms. Admitting that many of the more seasoned American soldiers serving with him had become "numb" to such events, this warmhearted patriot could only feel that part of him had died as well. He also recalled seeing an enemy combatant having his arm blown off and considered for a moment what the man might have wanted to do with his life. "Where is the human side?" he thought and wondered if the soldier in him could "coexist" with his sympathetic inclinations. And he especially lamented the death of an Afghan interpreter who served his battle group. Yet, soon he would feel an intense sense of rage and the "indescribable rush created by bloodlust" when some of his comrades were gunned down. Brotherhood not only lent a moral thread to the meaning of war but sanctioned its most decadent impulses.[36]

As a commander of a light armored company in Iraq, Benjamin Bush also pondered the human toll of war more than its inspirational possibilities. Bush had less to say about the benefits of comradeship and self-actualization and dwelled much more on the emotional toll war took. His mournful exploration of a war experience was unable to endorse a highly patriotic view because his narrative was basically one of declension centered on the loss of many things in his life, material and human. Unlike a number of stories authored by SEALs that twisted fragments of the war experience into a re-affirmation of noble sentiments, Bush folded his wartime episodes into a larger tale of heartbreak and death.

Once home from the battlefield, the former warrior revealed that he felt dejected and that his spirits were low. His cheerlessness was due not only to knowledge he brought back from Iraq but to recollections from his boyhood and the life he shared with his parents. "I have been welcomed home many times, " he reflected, "but I have never come all the way back from the places I have been." An encounter with war had prompted reflections on his boyhood and the elements of that past that had a military connection. Coming of age in upstate New York, he recalled with fondness playing among rivers and hills. He remembered well that his parents were opposed to the war in Vietnam but still allowed him to play with toy guns, although his mother was not pleased by this fact. He also loved building forts that he could defend. His mother wanted him to spend more time learning how to garden. He was also excited by a family trip to Gettysburg as a child and recalled looking at the site "where Pickett lost his division" and later loving books about the Civil War and Vietnam. When he went to college he drew upon these lifetime interests and joined a program that prepared him for marine officer candidate school after his junior year.[37]

Bush's tragic sensibilities were also shaped by the memory of the faces of Iraqi civilians who were forced to live with the violence he felt the Americans had brought to their lives. Indeed, his use of the metaphor "dust" in the title of his book, *Dust to Dust: A Memoir*, was in part to convey the sense of fragility of human life not only in Iraq but in his own family as well. While at war he wrote his mother about how everything in Iraq was always covered with dust. "The air turns opaque with an orange tan of migrating particles," he observed. He was struck by the sight of so many small villages sculpted from mud and sand and how easily they could "dissolve back into the desert." He saw old military barracks which Iraqis had used to fight an earlier war against Iran now buried below layers of sand. He even discovered cemeteries holding the remains of British soldiers from World War I that were now obscured under an endless sweep of sand particles. For this despondent soldier everything eventually reverted to the earth, even the life he knew with his parents as a boy. He recalled an old cemetery near his childhood home that had become buried under a sea of brush and soil. And dust was at the forefront of his mind when he had to spread his parent's ashes over a hill behind their homestead and on a beach in Maine where the family used to vacation. Faced with the reality that he missed the warmth of his parents' home and could take no satisfaction in bringing sorrow to Iraqis, Bush was left only with the somber reflection "that everything is recomposed from preexisting matter, that we are all fragments from earth and life blown apart and gathered up." "Pieces of us are in the stars and meteors, the ocean, dirt, and the dead," he mused. His war had left him with no trace of moral inspiration but only an immense sense of the tragedy and the gloom of human existence.[38]

While his son was still in the battle zone, Frederick Bush, Benjamin's father, published an article in *Harper's* (November 2005) that reinforced the feeling of distance both he and his son shared between the patriotic rhetoric they heard in America and their personal views. Frederick Bush's reservations about the conflict were not grounded in the sense of dejection that his son had derived from the war experience but were enmeshed in the concerns of a parent who waited for phone calls that proved his son was still alive and longed for the day when he would return home safely. In his published piece, the elder Bush recalled how his boy had played with guns as a child and protected his "tree fort." He reported that in his small town in upstate New York there were signs that read "God Bless Our Troops" and proud displays of American flags. But he insisted that nobody knew what others were feeling inside the confines of their respective homes. This parent was no supporter of the president and vice president and viewed with suspicion their assurances that the war in Iraq was nearing an end. He said he resented "ringing declarations" by political leaders that were "untroubled by the realities others endure." More to the point, the soldier's father argued that public proclamations of a war-based patriotism were obliterating the complex web of sensations that pervaded not only his private life but, he suspected, the home life of many others.[39]

Witnessing the war involved not only a preoccupation with the problems the conflict brought but doubts about its rationale. Colby Buzzell was one of a number of soldiers who expressed such disbelief. His memoir was essentially devoid of any high-mindedness and overflowing with distrust toward authorities that ran the war in the first place. In part, this may have been the result of his inability to find a suitable life as a young man. He did not re-create a portrait of an idyllic boyhood that many other soldiers described. Rather he chronicled only a list of "dead-end jobs" that left him miserable and open to joining the army as his only escape. By the time of his enlistment, he was sick of "living my life in oblivion where every fucking day was the same as the fucking day before." When his drill sergeant asked his unit how many had signed up because they loved their country, he said only a few raised their hand and that he was not one of them.

In Iraq Buzzell quickly began to shift the object of his disaffection from the economy to the war. He was livid with the American media for offering support for the invasion into Iraq and with officers who commanded him. He felt the notion that Americans were there to bring freedom to the country was totally false. Although he believed that Saddam Hussein could be a potential threat to America, he was convinced that the real motive for occupation was to secure more oil. Buzzell was not even complimentary when it came to describing his fellow fighters and did not hesitate to reveal accounts of female soldiers being raped or granting sexual favors to men of higher rank who could reward them in one way or another. He also noted how many infantrymen read nothing but "macho testosterone literature" about guns, ammo, and body building as a way to reinforce masculine images of who they felt they were.[40]

Eventually Buzzell expressed his dissatisfaction by setting up an Internet blog in 2004 called *Black Flag Fear and Loathing in Iraq*. "Black Flag" was a reference to a hardcore punk band known for their nonconformist attitudes. "Fear and Loathing" invoked Hunter Thompson's popular book *Fear and Loathing in Las Vegas: A Savage Journey in the Heart of the American Dream*, which was published in 1971. The novel featured a convoluted story of two men who go to Las Vegas in search of some vague version of improvement in their lives. In reality they end up in a series of drug-induced states that offer them only the bitter realities of what some lives in America can be like. In his blog Buzzell offered depictions of the ongoing war in Iraq that stripped the contest of any sense of dignity. The young soldier focused only on the harshness of the conflict such as the death of a comrade in a helicopter crash and stories of soldiers getting "waxed" on the day before they were due to go home. He even offered sympathy for Iraqis whose homes were subject to invasion by American forces.

Buzzell's unvarnished rendition of the war in Iraq startled many of his readers. He noted that some American soldiers were "bloodthirsty" and posted a photo of a dead Iraqi man with his eyes wide open and his tongue sticking out of his mouth, another image that subverted noble accounts of the invasion. Stories of Buzzell killing Iraqis or carrying their dead bodies in the back of his vehicle also appeared on the site. The young soldier also posted a conversation he had with the father of an American serviceman who was badly wounded. Buzzell offered a thick description of the firefight in which the man was injured. He also told the worried parent that he was praying for his son and that at least five warriors were still alive because of his son's actions. He even made a plea electronically for revenge and urged his followers who were able to "make these bastards pay" for wounding their comrade in the first place. Many who served with Buzzell praised him for "telling the truth," but army officials became so unnerved by his graphic version of events that they prohibited him from going on missions so he would not have anything to blog about. When he finally came home, Buzzell continued to produce versions of his unsavory view of the war and talked about "the bullshit brought upon me by the United States Army."

Matt Gallagher was another soldier-blogger who chose to use the Internet to denigrate rather than mythologize the war. He was convinced that the American presence in Iraq was foolish and disastrous. Beyond political policy, this soldier was troubled by the wide empathy gap he saw between an indifferent population on the home front and the suffering many of the soldiers endured in Iraq, something he referred to as the "suck" of the battle zone. "Soldiers died or they didn't; their families crumbled under the strains of deployments or they didn't," he cried out in anger. To Gallagher most Americans simply "followed the president's battle cry and continued to shop, squander, and flaunt." He had difficulty accepting the fact that America appeared to be a nation at peace while members of its military were slugging it out in war zones far away. To him the all-volunteer force was fighting for the nation but not "with" the nation.[41]

Other veterans opted to novelize their experiences. Kevin Powers, for example, elected to rebuff a war-based version of his experience in Iraq with a book titled *The Yellow Birds*. He told an interviewer that the story was more of an effort at capturing the emotions he and others felt in the war zone and less an attempt at offering a literal account of what he saw. A machine gunner who joined the army at age seventeen, Powers had fought in the northern Iraqi city of Al Tafar. He crafted his narrative around the personal relationship between two soldiers, Private John Bartle—a stand-in for Powers—and his good buddy, Daniel Murphy. Heroic patriotism has no place in this rendition of the war in which men of low rank struggle incessantly with their emotions and their constant exposure to human cruelty.[42]

Service in Iraq becomes a worthless exercise to Bartle. The endless repetition of missions into dangerous alleyways and dusty towns like Al Tafar or Mosul, the killing of enemy fighters, and even the gifting of candy to children begin to wear on him. He soon realizes that there is a sharp distinction between what officials had told him about the war and what he now thinks is true. His doubts are accentuated by the view he held of his grandfather's war in the 1940s and the sense of "destination and purpose" fighters of that era seemed to hold. His problem, in other words, was not tactical but cognitive. He was burdened by the disjuncture between rhetoric that was nation centered and patriotic and harsh certainties he saw and felt on the ground.[43]

Better than most tales authored by soldiers, Powers explores deeply the things warriors carry back home, including troublesome feelings of shame and regret. Back in Virginia, Bartle sleeps most of the time and avoids human contact as much as he can. He describes a typical day: "I had deteriorated more than one might expect in the short time I had been home. My only exercise was the two-mile round trip I made every afternoon to G. W. country store for a case of beer. . . . There is a fine line between not wanting to wake up and actually wanting to kill yourself and while I discovered you can walk that line for a long time without noticing, anybody around you surely will."[44]

His depression was rooted partially in the fact that he was haunted by the memory of death. He saw no justification for the killing of many Iraqi women who ended up in the line of fire of American troops. Even the death of Iraqi men did not sit well with him, especially when they were shot in the back or hit with more rounds than were necessary to put them down. "It was like just trying to kill everything you saw sometimes because it felt like acid seeping down into your soul," he recalled. "The whole thing fucking ravaged your spirit."[45]

Nothing bothered Bartle more than the death of his pal Murphy. The troubled veteran recalled how much his brother-in-arms had become disillusioned by the constant site of bloated bodies on Iraqi streets. He often visited the hospital on their base just to look at an attractive nurse who tended to the wounded and the dying. The young private was drawn to the woman not only because of her looks but because it became important to him to see that acts of compassion were still possible in a world that seemed bent on horror and destruction. One night, however, Murphy became so dismayed that he removed all of his clothes and wandered into the streets of Al Tafar unarmed, knowing that he would not return alive from such a foolish venture. When Bartle and his sergeant found Murphy's mutilated body the next day, they decided to dump it in a river where it could float away rather than return it to their base. Their logic was clear. They did not wish that the dead soldier's body be returned to a grateful nation that would heap patriotic honors upon it. To Bartle and his sergeant such tributes would mislead Murphy's family and those who knew him into thinking that the war was admirable rather than an unending succession of cruel events and that their friend's death was the result of a suicide.[46]

Near the end of his story Bartle indicated that his remembrance of war was fading. He even expected that Murphy's mother would give up her fight with the army to find out exactly what happened to her beloved son. Bartle also recalled another story that Murphy told him about his father, who had worked in the coal mines. One day the elder Murphy brought home some caged canaries and let them loose. The birds had been held captive underground in order to warn the miners of the presence of poisonous gases; dead birds were a signal that the miners needed to get out of their location as fast as they could. Murphy's father had assumed that the birds would welcome the chance to be free. He was mistaken. Once freed the birds only flitted around and returned to a perch on top of their cage. Like Bartle and Murphy the dreadful duty they were asked to perform left them bereft of a will to live.[47]

Roy Scranton's recasting of the fight in Iraq into an imaginary tale shared many of Powers's perspectives. Both veterans saw the violence as dehumanizing and the war of choice as a human disaster. Unlike Powers, however, who lamented the obliteration of the bonds of brotherhood among American forces, Scranton refused to reinforce any semblance of sympathy for the troops and focused more pointedly on their proclivity for aggression. The title of his book, *War Porn*, in fact, suggests that some American soldiers were not simply traumatized by the war but actually embraced opportunities it presented to harm others. Showing a regard for the suffering of others, Scranton also devoted much greater attention to the damage the invasion brought to ordinary Iraqis themselves.

A vet named Aaron is a key character in the book's critique of a war-based patriotism and its rejection of the need to hide viciousness. At an all-night party he attended once he was home, he spends a good deal of time showing civilians curious as to what the war was like photos of prisoners he and his comrades bloodied and abused. One shot revealed Aaron pushing an Iraqi man's skull into a metal bar. The vet admitted that "it's a weird thrill, having that much physical control over somebody, knowing what you are doing." Later that night at the same party Aaron continued his belligerent ways by turning an encounter with a woman into an act of sexual violence.[48]

Scranton does offer sympathy for the Iraqis themselves, realizing they are suddenly caught in a war not of their own making. In describing their collective lives, he writes that "as the bombing grew worse, the terror it brought stained every living moment. Sleep was a fractured nightmare of the day before, cut short by another raid. Stillness and quiet didn't mean peace, only more hours of anxious waiting—or death."

Qasim, a doctoral student in mathematics, is a key figure in this narrative of Iraqi victimization. Like many of his fellow citizens, he worries that the invasion will harm his own career and frets over what exactly would be the best course of action in his present circumstances. He wonders whether he should remain at his university and risk losing the position he enjoys there or return to his hometown and his wife and mother. At times he even harbors the hope that, perhaps, the Americans will make things better. Eventually, Qasim becomes an interpreter for American forces and finds what appears to be a vital role in the new Iraq. We learn later, however, his position was not as secure as it may have seemed; the Americans come to suspect that he is using his job to transmit whatever he might know to al-Qaeda. He is arrested and imprisoned. Ultimately readers discover that it was Qasim, the mathematician, who was the man Aaron was slamming into a metal bar in one of his photos of prisoner abuse. His career and the life of his family and relatives are essentially shattered by a military campaign that was supposed to bring them a new birth of freedom.[49]

Philip Klay, a former marine who served in Iraq, also attempted to undermine a sense of war-based patriotism by keeping alive memories of the emotional injuries that the war produced. In a series of short fictional pieces, he offered powerful testimony on the ineffectiveness of patriotic and nationalistic rhetoric to alleviate waves of disenchantment many warriors felt. The characters in Klay's stories, which are written from the viewpoint of ordinary soldiers, struggle mightily in their experience with human pain and loss.

In one tale titled "Redeployment," a man reflects upon his tour of duty after coming home. He recalled how the enthusiasm he felt coming out of boot camp to engage America's enemies quickly dissipated in the heat of battle. In one instance the narrator describes a scene in which an American officer slit the throat of a wounded insurgent who was already dying in order to put him out of his misery. Later when the same man arrived home and saw the father of one of his fallen comrades holding a sign that read "Heroes of Bravo Company," he felt perplexed. Heroism did not seem the appropriate term to describe what he and his fellow combatants had done. Feelings of confusion and estrangement intensified when the man's wife took him shopping. As he passed Americans, all he could think about was moving slowly down city streets in Iraq carefully scanning rooftops for potential snipers. He kept thinking they could never really know what it was like to lose your best friends the way he did in Fallujah. After a short time at home with his family, he actually decided that it might be better for him to return to his unit in the war zone.[50]

One of the most profound takes in Klay's reworking of the war was told from the viewpoint of a marine chaplain. The holy man was in a position to observe marines holding a memorial service for fallen comrades and noted how much their apparent toughness melted away in torrents of grief. Some of the troops sought a private meeting with the chaplain where they often expressed concern over the indiscriminate killing of civilians suspected of plotting attacks against U.S. forces. One soldier worried that he might be going to hell for his role in shooting some residents of Iraq and for his failure to stop comrades from doing the same thing. Another fighter, a lance corporal, confessed to the chaplain that he felt the war was "pointless." He complained that all the men do is go down the same street day after day looking for IEDs. "It's like you just keep going till you die," he remarked. This particular soldier eventually suffered extreme mood swings and found it difficult to sleep." The only thing that interested him anymore was "killing hajis."

When the chaplain himself began to experience a sense of hopelessness, he reached out to an elderly Jesuit that he had known for many years. In a long letter the older cleric expressed sympathy but did not see the chaplain's predicament as a crisis of religious faith. It was not that the fighters were engaging in sin and need to be forgiven, claimed the Jesuit. Rather he felt the chaplain was suffering in isolation and should share his feeling with those he counseled. Following the advice he received, the chaplain gave a sermon in which he related the story of an Iraqi man who sought medical help for his daughter from the Americans even though he held them in contempt for killing his son. The chaplain used the tale to stress the need for all to see the universality of human suffering even if it included the enemies American soldiers now fought. His plea did not go over well, however, and several marines refused to take Holy Communion that day, rejecting a humanitarian outlook for one that was deeply rooted in the need to defend their battle group.[51]

Soldiers who were compelled to restate the war in narratives that were highly critical found a receptive audience among reviewers as did those who featured courage and intense action. The fact that soldier stories were essentially accepted whether they attempted to uphold cherished myths or debunk noble sentiments of war reflected the fact that many readers of soldier tales had joined the multifaceted nature of the patriots' debate and its strained relationship with the viability of war-based myths. The highly favorable responses to Kevin Powers's novel illustrates the openness among the public to chronicles of suffering. One critic valued the novel's depiction of John Bartle's memory after the war or what he described as a "willful forgetfulness partnered with the inability to control images of so many bullets tearing through bodies." Caleb Cage, another evaluator, felt that the book's focus on the struggle of soldiers to survive the war and its aftermath challenged the "sanitized" narratives about the war that are often enjoyed by Americans at home. Writing in *The Guardian*, John Burnside argued that *The Yellow Birds* was a "must-read" not only because "it bears witness to this particular war, but also because it ekes out some scant vision of humanity from its shame and incomprehensible violence."[52]

Critical perspectives on the war and on the military itself were often embraced simply because they were seen as more authentic renditions of the conflict than those offered by war-based patriots or government leaders. Literary critic Michiko Kakutani liked *War Porn* because it captured the chaos of the American invasion of Iraq and the "misery it inflicted on Iraqi civilians." *Outlaw Platoon* was commended for offering a realistic portrait of American fighting units in which some could not stand up to the terror of combat and others excelled in their defense of their brothers-in-arms. Such admissions were needed, one reviewer felt, since such a small portion of the populace actually served.[53]

Women Warriors

As a consequence of the wider role that women played in the military during the War on Terror, stories about women soldiers also entered the cultural debate over patriotic sacrifice and the extent to which its harmful effects could be overlooked. This was obvious as early as 2003 when army private Jessica Lynch was captured as the result of an ambush of her convoy near Nasiriyah, Iraq. Riding in a Humvee that was hit by rocket-propelled grenades, the young soldier was badly wounded, suffering numerous injuries to her legs and two fractures to her spine. Bodily damage was not at the center of news reporting on the attack that wiped out a good deal of her unit, however. Rather the American media immediately turned her trial by fire into a gallant defense in which she fired her guns to the end to stave off an overwhelming force of Saddam loyalists. The heroic narrative was reinforced when it was reported that she was rescued from an Iraqi hospital by U.S. troops. To sustain the quest for a positive spin on something that was tragic, the army added a dramatic quality to the entire affair by releasing a "green-tinged night vision video" of their daring assault to liberate the badly wounded private.

Ultimately, it was Lynch herself who tamped down the patriotic zeal of the original reports, something many soldiers did when it came to telling their story, by revealing that her weapon jammed and that she was never able to fire a shot in the entire skirmish. Her unit was actually defenseless because as a supply team rather than a combat unit it was not equipped with grenades and rocket launchers. Jessica was knocked unconscious in the melee, waking up much later in a hospital where she was treated by Iraqi physicians who acted to save her life. She would later emphatically tell all who listened that she was a not hero but a "survivor."[54]

The epic story of American valor and courage did not fully take hold in Lynch's hometown of Palestine, West Virginia. In this rural place, people who knew her were shocked and devastated by the initial reports that she was missing in action. Certainly local residents supported many of the ideas central to a war-based patriotism and were proud of the service some of their own had rendered to the nation. Young people in this region of West Virginia had depended on the military for a path out of the economic hardship that plagued their towns and hollows for decades. Thus, news of Lynch's precarious fate certainly caused some residents to fly the flag. But traditional threads of patriotic feelings were simultaneously balanced by a proliferation of yellow ribbons and the organization of candlelight vigils at the local courthouse, signs that worry and agony were blunting simple knee-jerk responses of pride. A special assembly was called at the local high school to announce that "a student from this community is listed as M.I.A," causing some students to break into tears. In the Lynch household Jessica's mother would periodically "shriek" and simply run out the front door "barefoot and shaking." The rest of her family suffered grievously not knowing her fate. Citizens from throughout the country wrote to the Lynch family expressing their sympathy for what the family was enduring.[55]

Jessica's eventual return to West Virginia became a joyous civic event that actually masked much of the pain and suffering she endured. Realizing the public relations values of a "heroic" female warrior, the army flew her and several family members from Washington to Palestine in a Black Hawk helicopter after awarding her a Purple Heart and the Bronze Star for meritorious combat service. Scores of television crews covered the helicopter landing as thousands of local residents came out to welcome home their native daughter. Lynch's first stop was a huge press tent where she told reporters how thankful she was to all who helped her survive, from the army troops who rescued her to the Iraqi medical staff who tended to her wounds. She also made it clear that "it hurts" to know that some of her comrades did not make it home, including her best friend in the army, Lori Piestewa, a single mother with two children. Jessica then rode in a motorcade through local communities adorned with American flags and yellow ribbons and under a banner that proclaimed "Welcome Home PFC [Private First Class] Jessica Lynch America's Hero." A hometown newspaper even printed a special edition with Jessica's photo and expressed appreciation for all of America's troops who were making immense sacrifices for the benefit of others.

Even as she waved at throngs happy to see her and know that she had returned safely, Lynch later admitted that "her back throbbed and her legs—the parts of them she could feel—ached." One foot, held together with a metal screw, was especially bothersome despite the fact that doctors had given her painkillers. After the crowds went home, Lynch struggled to restore some degree of order to her life. She eventually fulfilled a long desire to go to college and become a school teacher. And she often appeared at patriotic rituals such as flag raisings at a local high school football game. But cheering crowds and patriotic fervor never quelled the pain she endured. Doctors performed twenty-two surgeries on her, as she continued to wear a brace on one of her legs. Twelve years after her homecoming, she told a reporter that she had seldom talked about her postwar suffering because people were more interested in her "war story" and wanted "to hear the positive stuff." She was also reluctant to discuss the extent of her injuries so as not to upset her parents. "I saw the photos of my parents when I was missing. I know how much they hurt," she explained; "I didn't want them to feel hurt again." She also admitted that she never saw a mental health professional in the years after her ordeal, thinking she could will her way out of continuing bouts of depression. In 2015 she did acknowledge, however, that her tour of duty had left her with nightmares and immense feelings of vulnerability. Each night before she went to bed she would still walk around her house locking and rechecking doors and windows to make sure they were secure. "I do that 200 times a night before I lay down to go to bed."[56]

The war stories of Kayla Williams also challenged the precepts of a war-based patriotism by reflecting deeply on difficulties women faced both in the military and once they were home. Williams was a veteran of the Iraq campaign, and her experiences, like those of Lynch, made it difficult to place pure and simple frames of virtue on military service. In Love My Rifle More than You: Young and Female in the U.S. Army, Williams revealed what it was like to be a woman in a man's army. Serving as an Arabic interpreter, she did manage to escape some of the rigors of the frontline battles and missions sent to break into Iraqi homes in a quest for insurgents and weapons. As she tells her story, however, her military experience was basically shaped not by her particular assignment but by her gender. On the one hand she felt the need to continually prove herself to be as capable as the men. She actually joined the army in part to prove to a boyfriend that she could actually handle the task. More frequently, she was subjected to leering eyes, suggestive comments, and sexual harassment. Some men, of course, took kindly to her, but many were reluctant to view her as a comrade. Rather than constantly fearing an enemy, Williams needed to be alert to what men thought about her and even to direct sexual advances. "Sex is key to any woman soldier's experiences in the American military," she wrote.

Williams presents herself as a dedicated soldier willingly serving her country but like Lynch does not endorse the mission of traditional patriotism to screen wartime truths. Her tour of duty is filled with reports of boredom and meaningless tasks as well as sexual tensions. She is also forthright in expressing her opposition to the American entry into Iraq in the first place. She recalled that at one point, upon hearing about worldwide protests against the invasion, she thought about the friends who marched in those rallies and felt that she did not want to die in the desert for a campaign she considered dubious. Williams claimed a strong bond with fellow soldiers in her unit but not to the government that had sent her to war. In her opinion only the "most messed-up-patriotic-head-up-his ass-blind-faith-in-my-country-right-or-wrong-soldier" could believe the "lies" that put America in Iraq.[57]

Her rendition of the war especially demonstrated a deep sensitivity to the plight of female soldiers and contained a powerful thread of empathy. In her story officers insulted her military performance for no reason other than she was a female and some men shunned her completely because of her gender. One male comrade told her he wanted to have sex with her and the "rougher the better." When she told him she was not interested, he revealed that many of the men were constantly aroused by the sight of women in their ranks: "We see you girls in your T-shirts. We can see your boobs. You know we're watching." She also commented on the cruel way some American troops treated Iraqi civilians: "I heard all sorts of horror stories, soldiers busting down civilian doors and dragging people into the streets . . . shooting up entire cars of people as they approached a manned checkpoint (women, children, whatever) because they didn't stop in time." About the only reason she had for going to war as she told it was to prove that she could do what most men thought impossible.[58]

Reviewers generally appreciated her effort to divulge the pressures exerted on female soldiers who were faced with a "continual barrage of misogynist slang and jokes." Curiously, however, some readers felt she could have expanded more on this point and not rehash familiar tales of the tedium of army life. One reviewer, who valued her point that women were devalued in the military, felt her best contribution was her firsthand description of the abuse of Iraqi prisoners. In short, the critical tone of her memoir was generally accepted along with similar points made by other combatants debunking the promise of redemption through national service.[59]

When investigative journalist Helen Thorpe listened to the stories of three women from Indiana who served their nation during the War on Terror, she actually heard little about traditional combat or intense encounters with the enemy. The War on Terror for these National Guardswomen was viewed more as an intrusion into their private lives than a chance to sign on to a crusade to rid the world of the terrorist threat. Wartime for these three women was primarily a time of personal hardship and familial turmoil more than an exercise in virtue and heroism, although they also faced a number of dangers in serving their country. All three, Michele Fischer, who served only in Afghanistan, and Debbie Helton and Desma Brooks, who both served in Afghanistan and Iraq, came from working-class backgrounds and enlisted chiefly to get badly needed economic benefits. (Thorpe alerts her readers that she used a pseudonym for one of the women but does not indicate which one.) Fischer, who recalled that her mother had depended on food banks and saw her siblings fall into drug use, joined the National Guard for college tuition benefits. She was not even keen on supporting the War on Terror and expressed admiration for Barbara Lee, a congresswoman who had voted against the Authorization for Military Force just after 9/11. Brooks, who grew up in a small town in southern Indiana, was raised in foster homes and had a child when she was seventeen. Helton was the manager of a beauty salon in Bloomington.[60]

Like other women serving in the military, these Indiana soldiers faced the constant pressure of sexual harassment. Brooks claimed the man who recruited her to the National Guard sexually assaulted her after she signed her enlistment papers. All three learned to be on high alert for unwanted advances from male comrades when they were stationed at Camp Phoenix in Afghanistan and felt that rape was a constant threat. It was not safe to walk around the base late at night, especially if they had been drinking. Zones given over to all-male infantry units were considered especially dangerous for women soldiers. They noted that male soldiers in their Indiana support battalion, now separated from wives or girlfriends back home, often competed to see who could drink the most beer and sleep with the most women. This male culture was also evident in the pictures of scantily clad women they hung in their tents. Thorpe's reporting also indicated that some of the battalion's senior leaders were having affairs with young subordinates, which went afoul of regulations. It was understood in the culture of the moment that "nobody was supposed to get caught."

Sexual assault, of course, was becoming a major problem in the modern military with as many as one-third of the women who served in Afghanistan and Iraq reporting that they had been the victim of some form of sexual aggression. Michelle and Desma felt the potential for such violence was stronger, however, from men who served outside their mixed-gender battalion. Sometimes sex was consensual. Both Michelle and Desma struck up relationships with married men while in Afghanistan, a fact that put a strain on a number of relationships in their lives. Sexual liaisons could also prove disruptive within military units with some religiously minded soldiers looking with disfavor on such activity while others were willing to shrug it off as a consequence of wartime conditions.[61]

Back home in Indiana, these women faced problems of adjustment. Only Desma had sustained a battle-related injury. The other two guardswomen were able to perform their support roles in relative safety. Still, Michele felt vulnerable and suffered from panic attacks. At times her heart "thudded in her chest" and she began crying uncontrollably. Desma endured bouts of anxiety as well but also faced more serious issues because she had been hurt in an explosion while riding in an army truck in Iraq. She was eventually diagnosed with a traumatic brain injury and had a very difficult time focusing and remembering how to perform various tasks. This proved problematic at work where a supervisor often had to remind her how to do her job. At home her children often thought she was "crazy" because she would forget to do things she had promised them or even lose money if she was not careful. Every day she was forced to take a substantial supply of pills to help her sleep and pain killers. Not surprisingly when the three of them would gather to consider their experiences in the war, they generally concluded that its cost was too high not only in terms of human life but in terms of dollars spent and the high rates of substance abuse and depression it had brought to many who served.[62]

Soldier stories from the War on Terror had much more to say about Americans than the enemies they faced, a reminder of how much the pervasive discussion about the war's meaning turned on the need to reexamine the nation's character. Vets diligently invoked motifs of traditional patriotism to explain what involvement in the war felt like. Certainly Navy SEALs played a central role in this remembrance of the global struggle and carried a significant cultural burden in the vast project to sustain a highly moral view of the entire American campaign. They became the embodiment of the masculine hero and the dream of many after Vietnam to imagine America's enormous military power as a force for good in the world. SEAL narratives and those of other fighters eagerly mobilized a number of symbolic points that included the veneration of a rugged form of manhood, the bonds of comradeship, and faith in a Christian God. These dedicated soldiers promulgated versions of the war that affirmed not only their muscular patriotism, moreover, but their belief that war could be a character-building exercise as well. In this reenactment, mourning was minimized, liberals were castigated, and empathy was essentially restricted to a loyal band of brothers. Remedial acts were not necessary. In a sense these exemplary warriors became worthy heirs to the memory of World War II as a "good war" fought by the "greatest generation" and antipodes to the victimized vets who returned from Vietnam, all images that helped to sustain their popularity even as news of human tragedy permeated the culture.

To a striking extent, however, the generation that fought this war was fractured. Promises of maturation and redemption were seen as meaningless by many who served. For the veterans willing to challenge patriotic myths with recitations of inconvenient truths, the War on Terror became simply a crucible of turmoil riddled with anger, pain, and regret. Soldiers committed to the task of witnessing opted to mount a pervasive critique of the war and a war-based patriotism by stressing its tragic consequences whether it was the loss of close buddies, sexual harassment, or the harm done to innocent civilians in other lands. In addition to taking up the long-standing review of military authority that veterans from many wars have expressed, they carefully detailed their own battles with postwar trauma and the feeling many had that, far from feeling noble, some American troops derived little satisfaction from their tours of duty. Threads of honor punctuated the soldier remembrance. Troops fought bravely and instinctively sacrificed themselves for the welfare of the battle group. In the end, however, their stories made it clear that the righteous sentiments of a war-based patriotism were often unable to encase the real human cost of the conflict. This vast output from soldiers from both sides of the patriots' debate would provide rich fodder for a raft of films that would seek to reenact both the terrorist attacks and the wars that followed.

· ·

American filmmakers, both producers of feature films and documentaries, were quick to jump into the debate over the War on Terror. In the aftermath of the 9/11 attacks, a number of movies quickly endorsed the imperatives of a war-based patriotism by infusing the dramatization of American suffering and sacrifice with themes that were highly moral and inspirational. In these features the bond between the nation and its citizens was firm; the reasons for the nation's responses were unassailable. Images of America's virtuous heroes and victims would remain part of the imaginative reconstruction of this global struggle for years to come not only because of their authenticity but because they were crucial to safeguarding the rhetorical power of American righteousness and binding feelings of personal and public love. It was such a patriotic mindset that led an entertainment company like Miramax Films to delay the release of two motion pictures in the fall of 2001, *The Quiet American* and *Buffalo Soldiers*, because they cast American military activities abroad in an unflattering light.[1]

The project to recast the war into an admirable crusade against wickedness, however, was again effectively contested. A fundamental truth about the cultural debate over the War on Terror was that the force of a compassionate patriotism, willing to chronicle the wide scope of personal suffering and doubt the war created, could not be contained. In this time of turmoil a torrent of filmmaking redirected public perspectives away from the didacticism of traditional patriotism and the moral authority of the nation toward the trials and tribulations of ordinary people, family members who struggled with loss, soldiers haunted by the death of comrades or even of innocent civilians, and Iraqis whose homes and lives had been destroyed. In these features ideas that suffering could be redemptive faded. Meditations on why we fought were less noticeable. In their place a sense of "moral instability" and personal trauma emerged to challenge the honor and power of the nation and its leaders. Patriotic rituals and public flag displays, of course, could seldom reveal the private turmoil war brought to people the way melodramas and documentaries could. In part, it was the ability of melodrama to recognize the struggles of individuals—women dominated by men or men striving to succeed in society—that explained Hollywood's rise to prominence in the first place. This focus on personal destiny was tailor-made to resist easy assumptions that the real moral center of life was grounded in the assertions of higher authorities or patriotic myths. In such a format, war on film became a debate rather than a campaign; politics began to give way to the tumult of human emotions it had hoped to discipline or conceal.[2]

Attack on America

American heroism was constantly imagined and deployed as an important part of the film version on the War on Terror, especially when it came to terrorist attacks on the homeland. Essentially these narratives were reassuring because they centered their attention on ordinary Americans who possessed exemplary traits of courage and bravery, from passengers on a plane to first responders. These features suggested that the nation's military crusade against terrorism was imbued with an irrefutable and honorable purpose because many of the nation's citizens responded reflexively and immediately to threats they encountered at home. Although the depiction of heroism was usually based on actual deeds, it was also mythical in that it projected a picture of a nation filled with brave civilians who had the potential to save America in a world growing more dangerous by the moment. Concerns that the costs of fighting terrorism could be catastrophic for the people the heroes loved was evident in these pictures, but a more positive patriotic narrative was still able to hold its own in these stories, in part because people appeared undeterred by the sacrifice that was required. Images of gallant citizens also tended to reinforce an ideal of the nation as virtuous and the hope that private and public affections could stand in perfect alignment.

Heroism was at the center of *United 93* (2006), a film that reconstructed the struggle that took place on the ill-fated flight from Newark to San Francisco on 9/11. The story largely eschews the political controversies that came to dominate the public debates over the war in favor of a straightforward presentation of civilian valor. The motivations of the hijackers are consigned to a dim background; they chant prayers but it is never clear that they are part of some well-orchestrated plot. American global politics and the extent to which it may have been implicated in such a conspiracy are also erased from the presentation, which focuses on the confrontation between ordinary citizens and the unexpected arrival of evildoers.

The battle that emerges on the plane is largely between two contending forces: dedicated terrorists and unassuming Americans with exceptional potential who suddenly find themselves in an extraordinary situation. When these passengers board their flight to California, like their fellow citizens everywhere, they have no inkling of what is about to transpire. The morning sky is blue and the early moments of the flight are smooth. In short order, however, terrorists kill a stewardess, break into the plane's cockpit and take over the flight. The film makes it clear that the objective of the hijackers is to crash the plane into the U.S. Capitol Building in Washington, although to this day the precise target of the terrorists remains unknown. As Flight 93 heads for the nation's capital, passengers with access to phones learn that the World Trade Towers have been destroyed and realize they are now caught up in a larger terrorist plot. They have no other option than attempting to retake control of the plane, a plan that seems possible when they discover that one of the passengers has piloting experience.

Before the plane crashes in a field in Pennsylvania, these everyday Americans mount a gallant charge to enter the cockpit and regain control. The story suggests that their motivation to attack is not only about protecting the Capitol Building but finding a way to return to their loved ones again, a nod to the importance of personal relationships in their conception of loyalty to the larger community. We never get a full portrait of the life of any American here, but the film shows countless attempts by distraught passengers to call or get heartfelt messages to loved ones prior to making their charge. When the plane goes down the narrative confirms their sacrifice; clearly they wanted to vanquish the terrorists who invaded their homeland. But their brave response was also driven by emotions grounded in their daily lives and the feelings they had for those who meant the most to them.

Appearing in the same year as *United 93*, Oliver Stone's *World Trade Center* again offered the reassuring message that the devastation and trauma present on 9/11 could be overcome by the innate courage of average Americans. In this reality-based story of the rescue of two New York Port Authority policemen buried under the debris of the fallen towers, director Stone—known for his highly politicized films about historical subjects—avoids large-scale political controversies. Stone's depiction of civilian strength and virtue works feverishly to temper deep strains of fear and traumatic memories that were incited by the horror of the event itself and offers some hope that things will turn out all right in the end.[3]

This film reframes the terrorist attacks from an assault upon America to one that primarily impacts the "silent majority," residents of tightly knit working-class enclaves. The policemen trapped under the rubble suffer greatly and the loved ones who await news of their fate endure nearly unbearable anguish. The opening of the story signals that the dedication these blue-collar men have to both their families and their jobs will be featured. Nicholas Cage's character, John McLoughlin, is awake before sunrise crossing from the New Jersey side of the George Washington Bridge into the city as he does every workday. As he gathers with his fellow Port Authority officers, a supervisor reminds the men of something they already know: "Protect yourself and watch each other's back." When the time comes, these men do not hesitate to enter the danger zone of lower Manhattan to save anyone they can. Unfortunately McLoughlin and a colleague become trapped under falling debris. Loved ones maintain a vigil in a filmic representation of the powerful bonds of family life—a key facet of an imagined noble American character. McLoughlin's young son is so distraught that he wants to drive to Ground Zero to help find his father. For their part, the trapped men constantly talk about their families as a means to survive. McLoughlin wants to get out of the rubble so he can finish remodeling his kitchen. He recalls that his wife's pregnancy will bring an additional economic burden to their household, but both he and his wife are determined to meet the responsibility of parenthood. These everyday Americans are models of diligence and reliability, symbols of national hope in a period of darkness.

The big politics of the War on Terror captures only background attention in this family melodrama. George Bush appears briefly on a television set to affirm that the resolve of the nation is being tested but that Americans "will pass the test." A former marine, trained to serve his country, dons his old uniform and travels to Ground Zero to help recover bodies. Policemen from Wisconsin, who also travel to New York to assist recovery efforts, express anger toward the "bastards" who engineered the attacks and, along with others, talk about avenging America's losses.

The film ends not in war of revenge, however, but in the joy of family reunions. McLoughlin tells his wife, "You kept me alive." It was also clear that efforts of those who rescued the trapped man were immense. McLoughlin reflected that 9/11 demonstrated that some human beings are capable of evil. Yet, he was quick to note that when it came to Americans, it revealed the "goodness" within us and how people can take care of each other. "It is important for us to talk about that goodness and remember it," he mused. Actor Nicholas Cage had it about right when he said he did not want to attach politics to the film. He saw it more as a "triumph of the human spirit" and about survival and courage. Yet, clearly the film was taking a strong stance in the political quest to position virtue on the American side of the war.[4]

There are no heroic patriots in Spike Lee's narration of post-9/11 New York City, *25th Hour* (2002), a film narrative that resists the reassurance so prominently displayed in other dramatic accounts of domestic attacks. The movie opens with a lingering view of the shafts of blue light that lit the nighttime sky in New York to commemorate the loss of the Twin Towers. Additional scenes show the devastation at Ground Zero and the ongoing work of the cleanup. Residents of the city do not stand united in the face of adversity in this story, however. The focus is actually on the plight of drug dealer Monty Brogan (played by actor Edward Norton). Brogan is an angry and frustrated man on the verge of a seven-year prison term for peddling drugs throughout the city. When he is arrested by police for his misdeeds, he begins to rant about his life and the frustrations that led him to commit criminal acts. As he sees it, New York, and by implication American society, is saturated with people on the make trying to exploit anyone they want for their own good and indifferent to the needs of others. In such a milieu, Brogan became resentful of the self-serving nature of society and concluded that he was justified in embarking upon his own unbridled quest for personal gain. He was simply doing what everyone else was.

His bitterness knew no boundaries. He made it clear he hated Sikh cab drivers he felt were "terrorists in training." He detested gay men in his neighborhood, Korean grocers who still could not speak English after living in the country for ten years, and Russian mobsters in Brighton Beach for being simply "thugs." He also despised Wall Street brokers who were "figuring new ways to rob people blind," Puerto Ricans for "swelling the welfare rolls," and rich ladies on the "Upper East Side." He certainly abhorred Osama bin Laden for killing innocent people but clearly declined to draw a dividing line between terrorists who were evil and Americans who were virtuous—a line that was indispensable for the nurturing of a war-based patriotism. In the character and thought of Brogan, the Lee film serves as a rejection of American innocence in the wake of the attacks at Ground Zero. At the end of the tale, as Brogan's father drives him to prison, the two men temporarily imagine what it would be like to turn left across the Hudson River and flee to somewhere in the interior of the nation where Monty could find a safe place to build a new life and escape incarceration. Yet, an ideal American dream is not possible in a nation bearing the brunt not only of terrorism but of a massive commitment to selfishness. The future for Brogan and his fellow citizens appears bleak.[5]

War without Honor

With a few exceptions, movies about fighting the war in Afghanistan and Iraq were not only "toxic" at the box office but lethal when it came to upholding themes of patriotic virtue. The moral certainty that framed George Bush's call to war after 9/11 and the legacy of America as a respectable power failed to persuade most filmmakers to ignore the emotional mayhem the global contest brought to ordinary people. Soldiers, for instance, could attain a degree of respect for their service and professionalism in these films, but some American warriors were also shown to be victims of government decisions or even perpetrators of evil deeds. These feature films were also therapeutic in the way makeshift memorials and somber memoirs were—willing to push painful memories out into the open so they could be assessed rather than squelched.

In the Valley of Elah (2007) is a good example of the imperative to expose trauma. It not only sees the war in Iraq as damaging to those caught in its embrace but also offers strong critiques of the military and some of the men who fought. The main character, Hank Deerfield, played by Tommy Lee Jones, is an upstanding Vietnam vet who is illustrative of a trusted and proud warrior. Soldiers home from Iraq, however, clearly fail to meet the standard of honor Deerfield represents. They are not only indifferent to the attractions of a war-based patriotism but inherently cruel—capable of perpetrating all kinds of misdeeds—including the killing and dismembering of Deerfield's soldier-son, Mike. The problem in this framing of the War on Terror is not so much the decisions of Bush and Cheney, which are certainly not endorsed, but the fundamental nature of the American character. In this story the military does not always tell the truth and those who serve prove to be capable of committing atrocities. On this battleground valor appears unattainable.

The title of the movie itself suggests the aspirations of the filmmakers to force Americans to come to terms with darker aspects of their own identity—the other enemy—and worry less about terrorists and more about their own capacity for violence. *In the Valley of Elah* references a biblical battle where David fought Goliath. The reason a young David could take on the giant where others had failed was because he came to terms with his own fears and drew upon an inner reserve of courage. Hank Deerfield tells a young man in the film that the biblical tale offered a lesson in how a person (and a nation) can fight their personal demons: "You look them in the eye, let them get close to you, and then you smack them down."[6]

Deerfield, the father of two American soldiers, reveres the American flag. He is troubled, however, when the army informs him that his son, Mike, has gone AWOL. This is a complete surprise to him because he believed that his offspring was still in Iraq. Deerfield drives to an army base in New Mexico to learn more about the fate of his son but finds that he cannot get straight answers regarding the man's whereabouts after he had just "spent the last eighteen months bringing democracy to a shithole country and serving his country." Deerfield and his wife had already endured the sorrow of losing another son who died in a helicopter crash while serving in the army.

The case of the missing soldier turns out to be more of a murder mystery than a heroic tale. To make matters worse, the perpetrators were American soldiers who served with Mike. Apparently they stabbed him to death after a bout of drinking and cut his body into pieces to hide their crime. Men who knew Mike tell Hank that he loved the army and "could not wait to get to Iraq and get the bad guys and save the good guys." The film makes it clear that the problem for these soldiers—the reason they became so brutal—was not that they lacked patriotic sentiments but that they were dehumanized by the nature of warfare in Iraq, where it was never clear who the enemy was and where—"Everything there is fucked up."

Scenes of the horror in Iraq are revealed piecemeal to Hank (and the audience) in scattered videos from Mike's cell phone—a nod to the way digital technology could bring home the horrors of the war. There are no dramatic beach landings or air drops in this war film, which offers only the dreadfulness of burning body parts and the running over of Iraqi civilians. Hank learns of one incident where Mike's Humvee killed a child, a death that haunted the young warrior. By this time Mike's mother is livid with Hank for encouraging his sons to be soldiers in the first place; there is no possibility in the narrative of gaining any form of redemption for anyone through military service or in assenting to claims of American virtue. At the end even Hank is so downhearted that he stops at a flagpole in his hometown to turn the emblem upside down—a distress signal indicating that the viability of patriotic honor, an ideal that he held dear, was in serious jeopardy. Reviews of the film invariably accepted this dark portrait of the nation's venture into this part of the global contest against terrorism and saw it for what it was—a "raw, angry, earnest attempt to grasp the moral consequences" of what Americans were doing.[7]

War as tragedy is also at the heart of *Stop-Loss* (2008), a story emphasizing Iraq as destructive to the troops who serve and to the aspirations of those who would wrap it in patriotic virtue. The film begins with the spectacle of a parade honoring a contingent of vets returning to Brazos, Texas. Cheering crowds, a high school band, and banners proclaiming pride in local heroes impart a positive frame to the war and those who served in it. Ceremonies awarding the Purple Heart and Bronze Star to native son Brandon King generate an even greater sense of admiration and local pride over what these vets have accomplished. Yet public respect does not adequately reflect what King himself was feeling. When asked to give a short speech, Sergeant King can only say, "I was over there as everyone else trying to bring my men back safe." In fact, King's speech is so prosaic that a fellow vet feels the need to interrupt his modest rendition of events and offer the crowd a staunch defense of the War on Terror, claiming that the men were overseas "killing them in Iraq so we don't have to kill them in Texas."

King originally looked forward to his return not only because he was leaving the war zone but because he was due to end his army service. When informed that he was now subject to a "stop-loss" order or a forcible extension of his military service and a return to Iraq, he was furious and refused to abide by the command. His first thought was to visit his senator in Washington to see if something could be done to fix the situation. His mother pleaded with him to go to Mexico instead and offered to take him herself. Ultimately, with the help of a female friend, King went AWOL. In his desperate flight through the back roads of America, the film turns ethnographic and shows King discovering a wider wave of dissent from both the war and military policy than he realized. In one town he encounters a group of vets who are planning to mount a lawsuit against the policy of stop-loss and learns of a lawyer in New York who is helping some soldiers move to Canada. He also observes human suffering up close when he makes a painful visit to the family of a man who was killed in Iraq while serving under his command, a death that hurts him deeply. Time spent with other wounded warriors who had served with him and who were struggling to adjust to life with missing limbs further amplified the intent of this narrative to empathize with the common soldier and reveal his travails rather than endorse ideas that sought to conceal the damage the war brought.

King is also bothered by the unusual nature of the war in Iraq. Soldiers energized to fight evildoers suddenly found themselves barging into the homes of ordinary Iraqis and having to shoot innocent women and children as well as insurgents. King claimed he had signed up for the army because he wanted payback after 9/11. Sensitive to the suffering of others, he was disenchanted to find in Iraq that the "enemy" was not out in the desert but in hallways, kitchens, and bedrooms. "Nobody knows who is who," he lamented; "the only thing you can believe in is surviving."

In the end he decides not to run away and returns to the army. He hates the policy of stop-loss or what was often called a "back door draft" but gives no evidence of having patriotic aspirations. He is receptive, however, to pleas from buddies who are going back that they need him as they return to battle—a reminder of the feelings of brotherhood that help all soldiers survive. He also feels that he is trapped in a larger vortex of war and military policy that has limited his options to joining the fight again or living a life on the run. Reviewers inevitably saw the film as an effort to evade a larger discussion of the reasons Americans were in Iraq in the first place. But a story dominated by warriors caught on the horns of a dilemma was actually a direct critique of the war itself and far from being evasive. Reviewers also picked up on the fact that in real life stop-loss had become so unpopular that the army was eventually forced to drop the program completely.[8]

Films such as *The Messenger* (2009), *Good Kill* (2014), and *Last Flag Flying* (2017) sustained the effort to disclose the extent the war brought trauma and discontent to Americans. In *The Messenger* two servicemen are assigned to a "Casualty Notification Team" charged with the task of informing next of kin with the news of a soldier's death. Both men find their assignment debilitating as they witness the utter grief and anger their messages bring to civilians who cared deeply for the deceased. Upon hearing the news of his son's death, one distraught father spits in Montgomery's face—a startling display of protest against the war, its leaders, and the logic of a war-based patriotism. Stone and Montgomery also turn increasingly to alcohol as the cumulative effect of their duty becomes overwhelming.

The demoralization of American soldiers who never leave the homeland is also at the center of *Good Kill* (2014), a feature film that aims the camera at the use of drones as weapons of human destruction. American combatants destroy suspected enemy targets and a good number of innocent civilians in distant lands from the comfort of a high-tech base in Nevada. Since they are able to return home each night to their families in suburban Las Vegas, these troops realize their assignment is cushy. But this narrative stresses that seeing the horrors of war on a video screen thousands of miles from the action can still be psychologically devastating. As the War on Terror dragged on, in fact, public protests over the use of drones emerged throughout the United States and in foreign countries as well over the fact that they had led to the death of civilians. In this film such casualties weigh heavily on the drone operators themselves, forcing them to deal with emotional stress and bouts of heavy drinking. Illustrations of how their personal turmoil adversely affected their family life further contribute to the evidence that the global war had no redemptive possibilities.

Generational reckonings are also at the center of *Last Flag Flying* (2017), where death and trauma again overwhelm the ideal of noble sacrifice. "Doc" Shepherd, a Vietnam vet, travels to Dover Air Base in Delaware to receive the body of his son, a marine killed in Iraq. He asks former marine buddies Sal and Muller to accompany him to provide moral support for his dreadful task. When the men arrive at an airplane hangar at Dover where flag-draped coffins containing bodies of American soldiers reside, Shepherd is informed by an officer that his son was a "hero who served his country" and "an inspiration to fellow marines."

Soon "Doc" learns from another soldier, however, that his son's death was not so valorous. Indeed, he was shot in the back of his head while purchasing goods in a Baghdad store. The force of the shot actually blew away his face. To make matters worse, the men learned that the dead soldier's comrades had opened fire on innocent civilians in response to the killing of one of their own.

Concerned over the discrepancy between two conflicting accounts of his son's death, Shepherd insists on seeing the body. He is understandably shaken by the experience and now upset by the fact that the government had lied to him. Immediately he rejects a marine plan to bury his son at Arlington with full military honors and demands that he be allowed to take the body back home to New Hampshire. The promise of patriotic honor and ritual cannot console the Gold Star Father and prevent him from grieving and taking possession of the son whom he loved. With the help of his Vietnam friends, the man rents a truck to carry the casket, despite pleas from the marines that his son deserved the honor of a burial beneath the "sacred soil" of Arlington. Shepherd laments, "We send him off to a godforsaken desert, why? Who knows? It wasn't to protect America. It's like that jungle they sent us to. It was no threat to us."

These vets also remain haunted by their war, frequently expressing disbelief in the official rationale for Vietnam, which was to stop the spread of communism. And they regret that they did not do more to save the life of another comrade in Southeast Asia who never came back. On the way to New Hampshire, they make a stop in Boston at the home of their friend's mother to express condolences. It is clear to them that the falsehoods Doc heard at Dover are similar to the deception they felt they heard from the government when they served in Vietnam.

The film narrative backpedals from its powerful critique of a war-based patriotism, however, by the time it gets to Larry's funeral. Sal, who was a constant critic of Vietnam and the government's war policies, and Mueller don marine uniforms and present Doc with a folded flag, a nod to the idea of honor in military sacrifice. And Shepherd reads a letter Larry had written in case he never came back alive. He tells his father that he was prepared to die for his country and was "honored to die in this way," an assertion that revealed how the patriots' debate divided families themselves. The desire of empathic patriots to clamor for a true acknowledgment of harsh truths is sustained in this story but tempered as well in a last-minute demonstration of honor and pride. Yet it is Shepherd's quest to insulate the sphere of personal love, like that of some Gold Star Mothers and 9/11 widows, from the intrusion of official and patriotic practices that can rupture loving relationships that ultimately commands most of the attention in this reflection on the War on Terror.[9]

Thank You for Your Service (2017) furthers the collective unveiling of pain and suffering at home by re-creating the real-life experiences of several veterans who served in Iraq. Based on the investigative journalism of David Finkel, the film exposes the struggle some soldiers had with post-traumatic stress disorder (PTSD) once back in the United States. Tragic memories obliterate any attempt here to frame the conflict in an admirable way. The entire mood of the movie (and the book upon which it was based) is somber and unrelenting in its absorption with the way veterans struggle with emotional stability and personal relationships. These soldiers are simply unable to put their traumatized feelings behind them.[10]

The film never invokes the term "brotherhood" but still centers much of its attention on the affectionate ties that soldiers had forged with each other. Honor counts for little in their encounter with war. Men here are primarily concerned with the fate of their fellow warriors. Three brothers-in-arms—Adam Schumann, Tausolo Aieti, and Billy Waller—gather in a bar once back in the United States to drink and sing, unwilling to let go of the attachments that had sustained them in Iraq. Longing for the closeness of the battle group, a sentiment that at times impeded their ability to reestablish other relationships once home, also magnifies the sense of loss they feel over those who could not come home at all. Waller's postwar readjustment is short-lived as he takes his own life after being rejected by a girlfriend. Tausolo actually feels that he does not even belong at home and longs for a return to his battle group. Schumann is burdened by feelings of guilt because he felt responsible for causing a fellow fighter to suffer a severe brain injury, and considers ending his life. In Finkel's book, but not in the film, Schumann's wife actually did find him one day holding a shotgun to his head. Inner demons possess these vets; discussions of such matters with friends and lovers prove difficult at best.[11]

The American public was not always open to evidence of soldier suffering, however, preferring to let its warriors live in a mythic world of patriotic honor. The gap between citizen idealism and soldier trauma was at the heart of *Billy Lynn's Long Halftime Walk* (2016). Lynn and his fellow soldiers who served in Iraq are brought home to a rousing ceremony at a Dallas Cowboys game. The men are recognized for their service in Iraq, with the owner of the Cowboys declaring that the War on Terror "may be just about the purest fight between good and evil we are ever likely to see." As fans and cheerleaders celebrate the men, Lynn and his buddies grow increasingly uncomfortable with all of the adulation. They are haunted not only by the loss of comrades but the devastation they had brought to Iraqi families. Most reviewers of the movie embraced the importance of showing the contrast between the "grisly reality" of the men's battle experiences and the "jingoistic spectacle" of the celebration in Dallas—really a cultural representation of the nation's patriotic debate. They wrote approvingly of the way the film held up for critical review the hyperpatriotism of many Americans and the need to see it as the human tragedy it really was.

The Return of Honor

More overt messages of war-based patriotism could be found in the highly popular film version of Chris Kyle's autobiography, *American Sniper* (2014). The film version of Kyle's story generally lines up with his autobiography except that it actually exposes more forcefully his serious bout with PTSD upon his return home. In the film's final moments, live footage of the huge public funeral held in his honor in Texas after he was shot by a veteran he tried to help is also presented. Thousands of people are seen lining the highways waving American flags as his body is driven to its final resting place. Clearly many citizens framed his service in reverential sentiments that were generally accepting of the human cost of the struggle.

Although the film was an immense financial success, it did produce a flurry of controversy. Critics of George Bush's policies saw the celebration of the American sharpshooter as right-wing propaganda defending the invasion of Iraq and warmongering. Prominent personalities actually discounted Kyle's deeds. Bill Maher, taking note of the killing, called Kyle a "psychopathic patriot" intent on shooting anyone in his way; filmmaker Michael Moore charged that snipers were basically "cowards," shooting only from a safe distance. John McCain, however, called Kyle a "noble American warrior," and many said they liked the film because it allowed them to express "pride in our defenders" and see the domestic struggle that military families endure. Film critics noted that Clint Eastwood, the movie's director, had again returned to an oft-repeated theme in his work of violence becoming a "moral necessity" in confronting "evil" in the world, a premise that was prominent in Kyle's book as well and in the original rationale for the War on Terror. But Muslim students on a number of college campuses complained that the film actually denigrated Muslims and threatened to promote more violence against them in the homeland.[12]

In *Zero Dark Thirty* (2012) Navy SEALs entered the compound in which Osama bin Laden lived in Pakistan and killed the man who organized the 9/11 terrorist plot. This film not only re-creates the quest to find bin Laden but centers more attention on a dedicated female named Maya (played by actress Jessica Chastain) who works for the Central Intelligence Agency (CIA) than it does on rugged warriors or even terrorists. Driven by a sense of dedication to her task and revenge over 9/11, this patriotic woman is unrelenting in searching for the leader of al-Qaeda even when others in the CIA doubt the validity of her leads. She and her fellow agents will use any resource at their disposal, including controversial torture techniques, to get what they want. Her life is on the line as well; she narrowly escapes a terrorist bombing at a hotel she is staying at in Islamabad that kills several fellow agents. Finally, her ardor and diligence pay off when she is able to pick up the cell phone signal of a courier who serves the terrorist leader. It is Maya who relays the pivotal information of bin Laden's whereabouts to SEALs who are finally able to get him. And it is Maya who identifies bin Laden's body when it is brought back to an American base in Afghanistan. This narrative of courage and dedication truly supports the ideals of a war-based patriotism. Maya does shed some tears at the end, but it is only for agents who were lost in the quest and, perhaps, from an emotional letdown now that she has to let go of the mission itself.

The film did reignite the public debate over the use of torture that had raged since 9/11 with its depiction of waterboarding and its inference that such methods ultimately helped find bin Laden. Critics felt such techniques did not generally produce useful intelligence, and others claimed that its value was clear given the outcome of the bin Laden raid. Senator John Mc-Cain, a victim of torture in Vietnam, was repulsed by the film. He agreed with critics of the Bush administration's practice that such torment seldom produced helpful information and reflected poorly on the image of the United States as an honorable nation. Many Americans also feared that a resort to torture would diminish the nation's ability to convey moral censure in its fight against terrorist groups and enhance the possibility that when captured, American soldiers would be more susceptible to such cruelty themselves. Public opinion polls since 9/11 have repeatedly revealed Americans to be badly divided on the issue, with about half the nation feeling the fear of future attacks warranted such extreme measures and others expressing revulsion that such brutality could be inflicted in their name. Kathryn Bigelow, the movie's director, argued that her depiction of torture did not constitute a statement of support on her part for the practice, although the dramatization of this method certainly added to the larger cinematic project to question the moral certainty of the War on Terror and the myth of American virtue.[13]

Like Bigelow's other film dealing with the war, *Hurt Locker* (2008), her main point was to admire the incredible focus and dedication America's war agents brought to their assigned task. The earlier film is less supportive of an aggressive patriotism, however, because it directs its attention mostly to the dangers faced by those who served and does not end with any positive outcome like the capture of bin Laden. In this story, dedicated warriors simply try to survive given the harrowing task of defusing explosive devices in Iraq that might harm fellow soldiers. Some soldiers actually see little merit in taking such risks, but the film's hero becomes so addicted to the task of defusing bombs that he returns to Iraq for another tour. The film is not about to wave the flag, but it does grant respect to fighters who show courage in the face of sudden death.

The Global War

Feature films probed not only the personal experiences of Americans caught in the turmoil of the War on Terror but the larger political implications of its worldwide dimension. As the camera attempted to span the globe, the moral basis of American patriotism withered and the nation's war leaders came under intense scrutiny. *Rendition* (2007) was one of those movies that pushed outward and challenged the nation's foreign policy by recognizing the suffering of others throughout the world, especially those hurt by the harsh effects of American-sponsored torture. The subject of numerous reviews because of its focus on persecution, the film evoked a wide range of comment. Critics valued its effort to say that the nation had "forfeited the moral high ground" by resorting to such brutality. Writers more accepting of the need to fight terrorists by any means possible generally felt the film was "unbalanced" and "too negative" in its depictions of America's torture policy. Far from reaffirming American innocence and courage, this feature presents an American CIA agent who has doubts about his nation's use of torture and even shows some regard for a Muslim family somewhere in North Africa that struggles with the impact of terrorist activities in their own lives.[14]

CIA operative Douglas Freeman is assigned the task of finding a suicide bomber who caused the death of a fellow agent in Africa. Freeman's boss (played by actress Meryl Streep) has given orders for an extraordinary rendition, or the illegal transfer of a prisoner to a country where torture is allowed to help Freeman in his quest. This procedure allowed the United States to deny that it had resorted to such brutal techniques because others performed the task on its behalf. Freeman is repulsed by what he sees in the torture chamber, where an Egyptian national named Anwar El-Ibrahimi (who in the film is actually married to an American woman in Chicago) is subjected to various forms of punishment such as waterboarding in an effort to find out what he knows about the perpetrator of the attack. The torture in this case is orchestrated by a local security chief named Abasi Fawal, who is trying to stem Islamic radicalism in his region. Unlike the official refutations about the use of torture that came from the Bush administration, this movie version of the war actually presents reenactments of the suffering caused by cruel interrogation techniques and beatings in its effort to discredit American denials of culpability. Departing from the notion of an American consensus on the War on Terror, Freeman is so repelled by the pain Anwar endures that he frees him from his jail and finds a way to get him back to his wife and family. Freeman goes even further by calling the *Washington Post* in order to expose the illegal practice of extraordinary rendition that he witnessed.

American exceptionalism is further undermined in the movie's portrayal of a Muslim family in Africa. While trying to combat terrorist activity, Abasi Fawal is faced with a rebellious daughter named Fatima. Much to her parent's chagrin, she has rejected her father's authority to select a mate for her and has become involved with a young terrorist. Audiences get to see the other side of the War on Terror with the reenactment of a meeting of Muslim men who are told they have a "sacred duty" to fight the "infidel" and that "Jihad is the only path to freedom." Unfortunately for Fatima, her boyfriend chooses to become a suicide bomber who not only blows himself up but her as well in a misguided attempt to kill her father. In this film grieving families are not only relatives who lost loved ones at Ground Zero but Muslims who mourn the loss of their daughter—a dramatic turn in the call for empathy. Americans themselves question their own government and are shown as capable of orchestrating violent acts as much as their enemies.

In the 2007 film *A Mighty Heart*, Mariane Pearl is another woman mourning the loss of a loved one in a distant land. In this dramatization of a real-life episode, she is the wife of Daniel Pearl, a correspondent for the *Wall Street Journal* who was kidnapped and beheaded in Pakistan early in 2002 by terrorists supportive of the 9/11 attacks. Mariane's story, told in *A Mighty Heart*, focuses on the worry and suffering she endured during the period when American and Pakistani intelligence officials tried to find her spouse. Her circumstances are made more difficult by the fact that she is pregnant at the time.

This narration of the war makes it clear that al-Qaeda and similar groups not only hate America but are capable of extreme forms of brutality. Yet the feature does not offer a ringing endorsement of America's military strategy. Terrorists are clearly upset over U.S. bombings in Afghanistan which have killed innocent people. The controversial detention program the United States initiated at Guantánamo, Cuba, is also held up for review by revealing that it was one reason why terrorists in Pakistan captured Pearl in the first place. At one point they offered to trade Pearl for the release of some of those incarcerated in Cuba. In one email sent by the terrorists, they claim that Pearl is being kept in "inhuman circumstances similar to the way Americans are keeping captives in Cuba." A photo attached to the note shows Pearl in chains. His capturers contend that if the Americans improve conditions for detainees in Cuba, they will do the same for Pearl. The story also stresses that he was a terrorist target because some of his enemies felt he might be a secret agent for the CIA or even the Israeli Mossad; the fact that Pearl is of Jewish descent is also held against him. The implication is that the United States was attacked in part because of political decisions such as its support for Israel and, therefore, its failure to embrace Muslim interests.

Despite the brutality of Daniel Pearl's death, the film does not end in with a patriotic endorsement of the War on Terror or a suggestion that further acts of revenge may be needed. Rather, audiences see Mariane giving birth to a son, as life follows death, and watch as she stated the belief that her encounter with violence had not destroyed her but had actually given her the courage to face anything that life throws at her.

Syriana (2005) subverts the entire notion that America was simply an innocent and blameless actor in the war. In this feature 9/11 is seen not so much as the consequence of radical terrorism but the result of pervasive scheming on the part of American corporations and government interests trying to acquire oil and gas rights in the Middle East long before 2001. The stars in the film are not soldiers dedicated to the defense of the homeland but operatives working to expand America's economic influence. Actor George Clooney plays Bob Barnes, a CIA agent, and Matt Damon portrays Bryan Woodman, a partner in an energy company. Clooney's character excels at causing mayhem in the Middle East by selling explosives to whatever political group suits the interests of the United States at the time. When Barnes attempts to interest a leader of Hezbollah in Lebanon in a business proposition, he is abducted by men speaking Arabic and is threatened with torture. His captors want the names of everyone who has taken money from him—an obvious effort to discover the extent of American deal-making in the region.

Damon's character is more interested in making democratic reforms in an Arab nation that has its own oil monopoly. He attempts to get the oil-rich state to reinvest its profits in social programs in its homeland. His plan is stymied, however, by the machinations of a large American energy corporation and the CIA, which kills a pro-democracy leader in the oil-rich kingdom. Soon a greater share of the oil profits is flowing out of the Middle East and into the accounts of the energy company. In response, Muslim voices in this feature offer a moral critique of the West and its ravenous appetite for money and power. An Arab character argues that the "pain of modern life cannot be cured by deregulation, privatization, economic reform, and lower taxes." And, inferentially, the American actions prior to the War on Terror are seen as a source of Muslim anger.

A few films undermined beliefs central to a war-based patriotism by offering critical appraisals of American politicians who led the War on Terror. *W*, a feature film directed by Oliver Stone that appeared in 2008, raised serious questions of George W. Bush's decision to invade Iraq. Rather than seeing Bush's actions as a legitimate extension of the war against terrorists, Stone cast the controversial decision in terms of Bush's personal development. This narrative argues that Bush, failing at a number of jobs as a young man and unable to please his father, saw Iraq as a chance to demonstrate his decisiveness and leadership, especially after his father had failed to topple the dictator in the aftermath of the Gulf War. Stone makes it clear that a religious conversion earlier in life had left the president with the idea that in using American military power in the world—no matter how many were harmed—he was not only fighting threats to the nation but carrying out the will of God. Iraq is a failed venture in this movie not only because the United States never found any weapons of mass destruction but because its president was consumed with a complex private agenda that did not serve the best interests of the nation he led.

Bush's vice president, Dick Cheney, is also consumed with his own agenda in *Vice*, a 2018 dramatization. In this feature film, Cheney and his wife are seen as a couple obsessed with attaining power in Washington over several decades. The opportunity to become George W. Bush's running mate in 2000 gives Cheney the ultimate opportunity to consolidate his influence in the highest reaches of the American government. Cheney becomes so entrenched, in fact, that he is able to read intelligence reports even before the president sees them and approve the production of official memos that authorize the use of torture. In this feature the vice president is portrayed as singularly responsible for convincing Bush to take the leap into Iraq, although Bush has a definite interest in doing so. Cheney is certainly motivated by 9/11 to protect America, but his resort to controversial moves such as taking out Saddam Hussein is clearly seen as the result of an ambitious man bent on the acquisition and use of power at all costs and indifferent to the potential human damage his actions might entail.

Documentaries

Documentary filmmakers joined the patriots' debate over the significance of the war on terror as eagerly as motion picture companies did. Although some validated the nobility of the American cause, most joined their better-funded counterparts in offering a withering critique of the war and the war-based patriotism that framed it. Some of these productions challenged the moral declarations and bellicosity of the Bush administration directly. Yet, the bulk of these films based their assessments on compassionate glimpses into the lives of those adversely affected by the brutality more than they did on simple antiwar diatribes. They revealed a deep compassion for everyday people trapped in the swirl of events beyond their control—grunts tasked to fight a battle in which they often did not know who the enemy was, families suffering from the burdens of extended tours of duty, and even Muslim families vulnerable to military forces that upended their lives. In this sense the abundance of documentary films that probed the War on Terror, driven in part by the availability of handheld cameras and inexpensive digital media, offered not so much a definitive view of the real war but a perspective that was more thoroughly based in human sensibilities and empathic feelings. As such these productions were part of a widespread resistance movement to efforts to encase the war in traditional patriotic and noble terms. On such a cultural battleground redemption and honor did not disappear but were now tempered continually by a stream of dark images of what the global contest was really like.[15]

Brothers at War was a 2009 documentary that depicted this entwinement of patriotism and emotional disorder by looking at one family and its commitment to serve the nation. The feature was directed by Jake Rademacher, who was not a soldier but interested in investigating the experience of his two brothers who served tours of duty in Afghanistan and Iraq. Actor Gary Sinise, long a staunch supporter of veterans, served as executive producer of the film. In an interview Sinise made it clear that he wanted to raise awareness of the struggles that military families endured in general and the "integrity of the people" he knew who were serving their nation.[16]

The documentary moves back and forth between the home front and the front lines in an effort to examine the impact of military service on this family of seven children who were raised in Decatur, Illinois. Isaac and Joe Rademacher are brothers serving in the war when their sibling Jake starts to question their sense of duty, especially because of the extended tours the men have had to serve. In an attempt to understand them, Jake takes off for the war zone to "find his brother's war."

Jake moves directly into harm's way. He actually stays with Isaac at a forward operating base in Mosul and joins several missions to the Syrian border with his brother and without him in order to understand the larger conflict and what it is that drives his siblings' participation. Jake experiences both the boredom of military service and the heightened sense of danger of being in a theater of operations. On one mission he is bothered by the heat and tedium of looking for insurgents in a remote desert area. Hanging out with the troops, he is able to detect a range of sentiments.

Some men feel that they do not really know why they are fighting, while others believe their sacrifice will benefit relatives in America and offer them a better life. During his second trip, Jake finds his way to the Sunni Triangle, where he is shot at during a mission in which one of the soldiers near him barely escaped being hit by flying shrapnel. By this time Jake claimed that not only had his appreciation of the American soldiers grown but also he had gained a deeper understanding of the Iraqi people and what they were enduring.

The Rademacher family is fully supportive of their soldiers, despite the emotional burdens they endure. In Iraq Isaac tells Jake that he regrets the time he is away from his daughter. Isaac's wife confirms that this is a problem at home and that the young girl hardly knows her father. But she supports the warrior's deeds and says he is "sacrificing everything" to make the world a better place for his daughter and others to grow up in. The spouse feels that it is actually her job to explain to the little girl why her father needs to be away but that he still loves her very much. The Rademachers' parents back their sons as well. The father of Isaac and Joe saw military experience as a defining event in the lives of his two warrior sons that would help transform them into mature men. Joe's fiancée does admit that she cried a lot when he was gone and was depressed but felt that she could be as strong as Joe wanted her to be. She also reinforced the family ideal that military service, while dangerous, had a positive outcome, for it made Joe and men like him "more brave and independent"; she now felt Joe was able to stand up to her in ways he did not in the past. At the end of the story a message on the screen expresses thanks to the "American troops who have served in Iraq and Afghanistan and the families that support them."

Patriotic service is transformed into a difficult bout of familial and personal struggle in *Off to War: From Rural Arkansas to Iraq*, a seven-and-one-half-hour documentary on the deployment of the Thirty-Ninth Infantry Brigade of the Arkansas National Guard that was sent to Iraq for eighteen months in 2004. In this feature redemptive images of warfare are undermined by extensive documentation of the troubles the families of guardsmen encounter with their breadwinners stationed abroad. The film follows the experiences of these working-class people as they negotiate the tense relationship between the home front and the war zone. *Off to War* opens with a talk by Arkansas governor Mike Huckabee asking every Arkansan to give "one-hundred percent support" for the 3,000 guardsmen from his state who were being sent overseas. As men are filmed boarding military trucks, however, doubts are quickly raised about the entire venture. Some soldiers lament the possible loss of their jobs, and a female spouse sheds tears worrying about how she will have to care for her children alone.

In this take on the War on Terror, stories of family turmoil blunt the rhetoric of patriotic honor and the moral high ground of the American military struggle. One woman joins a support group while her husband is away at war and affirms the need for the women to support each other because outsiders could never understand their plight. She is particularly concerned that her husband may not be faithful to her while he serves overseas. Another woman is forced to quit her job to run the family farm while her spouse is in Iraq, a task she finds daunting. Sergeant Joe Betts and his wife struggle mightily while he is away. When he is sent home from Iraq early due to back pain, he finds their family finances have hit rock bottom. At the beginning of his assignment Matt Hertlein thought it was "cool" that so many from his small community came out to shore up the morale of the troops as they departed for war by waving American flags and holding signs proclaiming "God Bless." In time, however, Hertlein acquires a highly disparaging view of the war, claiming that Saddam had nothing to do with 9/11 and feeling disappointed that the aggression of American troops brought to Iraq had only incited much hatred toward the United States.

The *American Widow Project* (2008) extended the empathic thrust of the documentarian by focusing on the plight of women who lost their spouses in the war and were struggling to rebuild their lives. In the documentary six women recount their stories of falling in love, seeing their husbands off to war, and trying to put their lives back together after they were shattered by death. The pattern of expressing a wide and contradictory range of sentiments evident in other family features is evident here as well. Traditional patriotism is a thread in this account of the war on terror, often shown in the form of public rituals or military funerals, but it struggles for narrative space in tales that are more about the emotional damage these women endured than about the honor of serving one's country. Clearly the producers of such stories were moved more by a sensitivity to suffering than a war-based patriotism would normally allow.

Consider the case of Nina Carr, the wife of Sergeant Robert Carr of Warren, Ohio, who was killed in Iraq from the blast of an improvised explosive device (IED). Nina explained that she was already crying in the days before he left on his deployment. Sidestepping the enormity of the upcoming separation in her life, she began to concentrate on little things like whether she had packed Chap Stick for his trip. Minutes after he had left for his deployment, she had a distinct feeling that she "had already lost him." She recounted that in their long-distance phone calls, he would always assure her, however, that he knew he was "supposed to come home."

On the day she received the news of his death, she heard dogs barking outside her home. Looking outside, the woman quickly spotted a white van with two soldiers in it. "My heart dropped to the floor," Nina recalled. "It was the weirdest feeling in your body, just numbness." She soon started screaming. "You lose all self-control" and do not know what to do. "I didn't want to talk to anyone."

For Nina, the day she saw his flag-draped casket was harder than the actual funeral. "All I could remember was seeing the casket and thinking that he was in there." His presence actually seemed to comfort her despite the fact that he was dead because, as she told it, he had been away for so long. She kept thinking maybe they could still go camping. During the funeral she felt that she was just "going through the motions" of living amid a crowd of people lining the streets that included the Trumbull (Ohio) Veterans Honor Guard. When military representatives handed her a folded flag, she could only remember feeling "like a zombie." "You see it on TV and you don't think it's going to be you. You try to be dignified about it," she indicated, but "I don't know what got me through it." The days after the public ceremonies were especially hard for Nina. "I didn't want people to give me hugs. I just wanted to be alone," she felt. She recalled thinking that other people go back to their jobs and lives but "here I am with all this grief."

In the time after Robert's burial, Nina explained that she struggled with heartache and her status as a widow. "I felt cheated out of being young," she explained. "I feel so old. I feel like I have been through so much." Widowhood made her feel that she could never be happy again. Rituals of honor could neither heal nor sufficiently explain everything for her; she still talked to her dead husband at night. In visits to the cemetery, she would often attempt to re-create conversations they had about what their future would be like. In part she was angry over the fact that she never received a graphic account of his passing, a point that inferentially critiqued traditional ceremonies meant to soothe and explain. Nina thinks a good deal of the day he was killed and what he might have looked like at the time. She even studied closely the personal effects that were returned to her for some clue "of what happened that day but they kind of erase all that stuff. It's kind of methodical, fold this up, wash this, here's your stuff."

Other widow stories supported the basic narrative of loss and anguish revealed by Nina Carr and the attempts by the living to find a way forward after traumatic ruptures and even attempts to communicate with the dead.

Deb Petty, the widow of Captain Chris Petty, had to deal not only with the death of her spouse but with the responsibility of raising two young sons. She felt the news of his passing in Iraq was "creepy." "I went to sleep and woke up the next morning thinking maybe it hadn't happened," but seeing flowers throughout her house and her brother sleeping on the couch confirmed for her the bitter reality.

Like Nina Carr, the aftermath was torturous. She felt numb a good deal of the time and "did the minimum of what I had to do in the house to keep it running, keep the kids alive." Little things like a doorbell ringing set her off. "You don't want to answer it. Don't knock on my door. I heard of people pulling out their doorbells because they don't want to hear them anymore." She still regrets that her fallen warrior can no longer see his sons and participate in activities at their school. She described one encounter at the school where a woman actually said to her that if her husband had not been "so fucking stupid to get killed he would still be here." Stunned by the affront, she struck the impertinent individual.

As she recovered, Deb often took her boys outdoors at night so they could "kiss" a special star that she had picked out in the sky to honor her husband—a personal ritual she invented. And she planned to co-write a children's book about grief. In the text a young boy makes a wish upon a star and is able to have his father come back to earth for one hour so the boy can tell him things he feels still needed to be said.

The documentarian's attraction to victimization was revealed in features not only about troubled families but about soldiers in the field as well. Deborah Scranton took advantage of an offer to become embedded with soldiers from the New Hampshire National Guard who were headed to Iraq in 2004 and produced *The War Tapes* (2006). Willingly sharing her directorial authority, she placed cameras in the hands of several soldiers in order to get what she felt was a more "immediate" view of the reality these men faced. The result was a complex portrait that was the very antithesis of a war-based patriotism because it was filled with conflicting experiences and feelings.[17]

These citizen-soldiers certainly suffer in this descent into battle. Many feel helpless as they patrol, knowing they could be hit at any moment by an enemy they cannot always see. Intense firefights erupt after IED explosions. After one such encounter, a soldier exclaims that he had now for the first time shaken a man's hand that was not attached to his arm. Indeed, pulling the bodies of Iraqis and Americans from burning trucks became a gruesome routine. Anger grows among the guardsmen as they increasingly come to resent Iraq and its people. One soldier makes the point that nothing will ever be solved in the round of constant missions the men undertake. Drawing on his rage over the loss of American soldiers, he concludes that the only solution here is "nuking this fucking country." Especially traumatic for the warriors was an episode in which their Humvee hit a young woman and tore her body apart. A soldier exclaimed, "We are supposed to help the Iraqi people and we just killed one of them."

Captain Michael Moriarty, a central figure in the documentary, confirmed that true patriotic sentiments adequately reflected the feelings of most of the troops in his unit when they entered Iraq but that such emotions had been ground to dust in the mess that they encountered. Moriarty claimed that he was a "substantially patriotic person" who took 9/11 very hard. The terrorist attacks on the United States felt to him like someone had "hit my house." In the aftermath he took time from work to travel to Ground Zero to see it burning. It was then that he decided to enlist in the army. Another man felt most guys in his company identified with what he called "Bush macho," a reference to President George Bush's plan to invade Iraq in the first place. Near the end of the deployment, however, many of the men are more disdainful. A few insist that the United States was only in Iraq for the oil. Moriarty claims that the war affords the Iraqis a fantastic opportunity to become a free and democratic society and then adds, "After that happens maybe we can buy everyone in the world a puppy."

The men from New Hampshire receive the traditional hero's welcome upon their return. Scenes of loving family reunions are genuine. But the aftermath of war is as troubling for some as the war itself. Moriarty's wife says Moriarty is not the same person that he was before his deployment. She revealed that he tends to lose his temper more frequently and is haunted by flashbacks of hitting the woman in the road. The couple also struggle with the fact that each does not feel the other truly understands what they endured during the long weeks of being apart.

Restrepo (2010) shifted the focus on soldiers from recollections of their viewpoints to intense coverage of an actual encounter with the enemy. Concentrating on the deployment of a platoon of American troops in Afghanistan's Korengal Valley, this film, in the words of one of its directors, Sebastian Junger, sought to capture "purely a soldier's-eye view of combat." Junger was adamant that he wanted to document the effects of war on people and had no intention of trying to advocate any "political position" for or against the American involvement in Afghanistan. In a sense Junger's aspirations are impossible to realize; documenting personal perspectives and feelings inevitably undermine the lofty aspirations of leaders and patriots to encase state-sponsored violence in frameworks that are highly moral.[18]

Soldiers in this film make it clear that their outpost in the valley, named after one of their fallen comrades, Private First Class (PFC) Juan "Doc" Restrepo, was simply a wretched place. One soldier called it a "shit hole" where troops were not only faced with incoming fire constantly but forced to burn their feces and live in tents. Captain Dan Kearny, one of Junger's subjects, said he felt like he was living like fish in a barrel. And the loss of comrades continually weighed on the men who survived, especially the memory of Doc Restrepo, who was shot twice in the neck and "bled out."

The men were also charged with the responsibility of winning the friend-ship of local villagers as a way of preventing them from gravitating to the side of the Taliban. This is a constant struggle and Kearny is forced to con-tinually meet with local leaders to undertake projects such as improving roads that might help the local economy. Their effort to achieve some good-will, however, is made more difficult by the fact that they are forced to search local homes for Taliban sympathizers; they do not want to see the power of the Islamic group restored to levels that pertained before 9/11. Indeed, it is not always possible to figure out just who is on the side of the Taliban and who is not. When the actions of American forces inadvertently lead to the death of some villagers, the quest to befriend locals becomes even more chal-lenging. At times the only incentive that sustains the troops is simply to seek revenge for their own losses; the war at this point has no wider meaning.

Most documentaries centering attention on the trials and tribulations of ordinary folks caught in the trap of war seemed not only to defy the impact of patriotic moralizing but to evade the political controversies that raged in the homeland as well. Some have argued that the immense amount of pa-triotic rhetoric in American society during the war that encouraged people to "support the troops" might have led to such an avoidance. Yet, it would be difficult to deny that the vast body of filmic material on the fight against terrorism did not in itself constitute both a powerful display of sympa-thetic support for those who fought and suffered and a potent rebuke of both the decisions of the Bush administration that led the war and its human toll that was certainly political. In highly critical documentaries like Michael Moore's *Fahrenheit 9/11* (2004), in fact, politics and sympathy are woven into caustic analysis.

Moore's immensely popular film unabashedly went after Bush, but it also invoked the sorrow and pain of Americans adversely affected by the bloody struggle. It took sides in the raging political debates of its time in a more explicit manner than most documentaries or feature films but also stayed true to a melodramatic tradition of highlighting the emotional chaos politics brought to ordinary lives. Moore wanted ordinary people to speak, as did most of his fellow documentarians, but was less interested in letting their voices stand alone. His film was a determined attempt to mobilize them into a narrative that was firmly planted on one side of the patriots' debate—the side that refused to be consoled and comforted by the tenets of a war-based patriotism.

Moore's presentation of the war focused considerable attention on the citizens of Flint, Michigan, a town that has been severely injured by the devastation of plant closings. Here his antiwar agenda is astutely tied to a critique of corporate policies sanctioned by many in Bush's party; his film is not only about the war and the invasion of Iraq but about a political class and a party he despises. Interviews with marine recruiters and high school students in the depressed city strongly suggest that the pitch the military makes to these young working-class kids is essentially dishonest. Because these kids lack opportunity for advancement, military recruiters present them with chances for world travel or even playing on sports teams in the Marine Corps as a way of downplaying the darker possibility of being sent off to dangerous terrains like Afghanistan and Iraq.

Lila Lipscomb is an important voice in *Fahrenheit 9/11*. Lipscomb, the mother of a man killed in Iraq and the sister of four brothers who had served in previous wars, was a longtime Flint resident who had proudly flown the American flag at her home. Lipscomb told how she put the flag on her porch every day when her daughter served in the Gulf War in the hope she would come home safely. And she did. Moore choose to feature Lipscomb, however, not because of her traditional patriotic attachments but because she had acquired a decidedly critical perspective on Iraq. Intent on challenging Bush, Moore flooded the screen with Lipscomb's story where he could.

Moore's retelling of Lipscomb's grief over the loss of a son in the war is a central part of the entire feature. The young man had felt that it was his duty to serve. But nothing can assuage the Gold Star Mother's heartache when she gets the news that he was killed in a helicopter crash. Informed by phone of his death, she exclaims, "The grief grabbed me so hard that I literally fell on the floor . . . remember screaming. Why did you have to take my son?" The film shows the distraught mother's unsuccessful attempt to visit the White House in an attempt to convey her anger and pain to George Bush. Lipscomb makes it clear she has not lost her love for America but only respect for its president and the decisions he made.

Moore also sustains his overall critique of political leaders by showing unflattering images of the president and by attempting to speak with members of Congress. Along with a marine who had refused to return to Iraq, Moore approaches lawmakers and urges them to have their children enlist for military service, challenging the degrees of separation they enjoy from the war's bitter realities. Most ignore the documentarian, but Moore, of course, succeeds in his twin goals of discrediting Bush in advance of the 2004 election bid and drawing attention to the various levels of inequality in a nation and the harmful effects of many of its policies.

Not surprisingly *Fahrenheit 9/11* proved controversial. Traditional patriots and Bush supporters deeply resented Moore's appraisal. Conservative commentators called the film "un-American." Melanie Morgan, a radio talk show host in San Francisco, saw the film as "crap" and felt it was "undermining the war on terrorism." Morgan even joined an effort to get theater owners not to schedule showings. Dan Bartlett, a White House official, called the feature pure "fiction." But others like Zbigniew Brzezinski, Jimmy Carter's national security advisor, thought the film was a powerful statement that "raised fundamental issues of morality and trust." A movie reviewer praised the use of Lila Lipscomb for her testimony on the "inhumanity of the war." And a fan of the film wrote Moore to say that his account had "brought the war home to me" and that "Americans had too often put the flag before people."[19]

Body of War (2007) also constituted a direct political assault on Bush and his decision on Iraq. The presentation is focused on two key figures: a prominent member of the U.S. Senate and a wounded warrior who was shot in Iraq. Robert Byrd of West Virginia, who took a very public stance against the plan to invade Iraq in part because the War Powers Clause of the U.S. Constitution had invested Congress with the power to declare war and not the president, plays a key role in this feature. This documentary not only features Byrd's campaign against the decision to occupy Iraq but presents parts of the actual roll call of senators voting on an authorization that would grant the president the power to use military force there—a vote that Byrd vehemently opposed. Byrd, an elderly man at this time, whose hands now trembled from illness, is shown speaking in the Senate. In eloquent fashion he argued that it was leaders who were pushing for war but not "common people" and that he felt it was a "shame" that many senators backed such an initiative. He was especially suspicious of appeals political leaders made that exploited the fears people had by telling them that if the nation did not strike first they would be attacked. And he regretted attacks on pacifists that simply dismissed their views as anti-patriotic.

In this film Byrd's statesmanship is joined to a soldier's story. Wounded in Iraq and confined to a wheelchair, Tomas Young offers evidence that Byrd's reservations about Iraq were justified—and not just on constitutional grounds. Like many U.S. soldiers, Young was originally inspired to fight by the 9/11 attacks. Coming back from Iraq in a wheelchair, however, he was angry enough to join the Iraq Veterans against the War and Cindy Sheehan at her protest in Crawfordsville, Texas. This documentary actually offers not only riveting accounts of Byrd and Young but live coverage of the Sheehan protest. In one scene Sheehan introduces a very weary Young, who speaks about the need of wounded vets for stem-cell research, a project that raised hopes that regenerative medicine would heal battlefield injuries. Such remarks were aimed directly at Bush, who had prohibited such studies if they involved the use of human embryos. At other points in the story, Tomas relays how he is forced to sit in his room at times crying uncontrollably. His mother bitterly complains that elites like the president simply do not care enough about people like her son who suffer from their war service. Young even gets to appear on the television program *60 Minutes*, where he declares the war was unnecessary. This statement provoked a question from his interviewer on the program asking if he felt that expressing such opinions undermined American troops now in the war zone. Young responded that it bothers him when people say he is not patriotic just because he does not agree with aspects of the war on terror and notes that his family continues to worry because his brother was still serving in Iraq. At the end of the film Byrd is seen walking down a hallway in the Capitol with Young riding in his wheelchair beside him—emblems of a frame on the War on Terror that was both patriotic and empathic.

The willingness to consider human pain in accounts of the war opened the way to the critique of not only political policy but the mindset of intolerance and division that was required for the fight at hand. It was not always difficult to extend compassion to Americans who suffered, but it was a much harder proposition to acknowledge the distress Americans brought to others in Afghanistan and Iraq. *Ghosts of Abu Ghraib* (2007) continued to sustain a disparaging view of the Iraq based not so much on the actual decision to invade or the harm it brought to American soldiers but on the contentious practice of torturing Iraqis. The intent of the film was to refute the army's Taguba report that blamed the controversial mistreatment of Iraqi prisoners on the action of few misguided soldiers as a way to insulate the nation's leaders from culpability. Taguba reported no evidence that the abuse came from a policy shaped by officials and blamed a few "bad apples" in the lower ranks. Filmmaker Rory Kennedy, disgusted at the sight of the photographs of prisoner abuse at the Abu Ghraib prison in Iraq, interviewed not only American soldiers who mistreated the inmates but some of the Iraqi prisoners themselves. Most commentators shared Kennedy's outrage over the way American leaders had been spared from criticism in the official response to the abuse. More conservative voices, however, did express resentment that the film and the public indignation over Abu Ghraib tended to ignore that Saddam Hussein had committed many more atrocities at the same site.[20]

The film blames Donald Rumsfeld, the U.S. secretary of defense, for the use of torture and the degradation of Iraqi prisoners. Rumsfeld is portrayed as being so agitated that he was not getting useful intelligence regarding the insurgency in Iraq that he sent Major General Geoffrey Miller to assess the situation. Miller had already been running prison operations in Guantánamo, Cuba, where he had resorted to "extreme" techniques to gather the intelligence that was needed. The use of such techniques—such as "sexual humiliation and forced nudity" was approved by Rumsfeld and carried out by Miller. It was Miller who told Americans in charge at Abu Ghraib that if they did not "treat prisoners like dogs" they would lose "control" of the interrogation. The Kennedy documentary claims that, in fact, it was Miller who shaped policies at Abu Ghraib that resulted in an increase in harsh treatment and extreme techniques.

Dramatically it is Iraqi prisoners themselves who describe the callous treatment they received, as the documentary extends its sympathetic gaze. These men explain how they were hung by their hands to inflict unbearable pain or told that if they did not offer information, close relatives would be harmed. One Iraqi described how he saw bruises over the back of his father who was also incarcerated and pleaded with guards to have him examined because he had trouble breathing. His pleas were ignored, however, and his father died. The film also documented some of the actual abuse with video and words. American guards are seen forcing naked Iraqis to form a pyramid of human bodies or being sexually humiliated by having women's panties placed over their heads.

American actions in the war on terror were questioned again in *Taxi to the Dark Side* (2007). This documentary sustained the project to assign responsibility for America's controversial use of torture not to a few ill-advised soldiers but to the highest echelons of the nation's leadership and maintained the emerging wave of sympathy for its victims. The story is built around the death of an Afghan taxi driver named Dilawar. Audiences learn that Dilawar was a "good and honest man" who was suddenly arrested in 2002 and imprisoned at the huge Bagram air base run by the Americans. Five days after his incarceration he was found dead with multiple bruises covering his body. Military police commenting on his death in the film express uncertainty as to exactly how he died.

Carlotta Gall, a *New York Times* reporter stationed in Kabul, was troubled by claims made by General Dan McNeill, commander of coalition forces in Afghanistan in 2002, that it was not the intent of U.S. forces to kill prisoners deemed to have important intelligence. Suspicious, Gall began to investigate the death of Dilawar and another inmate at the same facility. Eventually she found Dilawar's family, who showed her a death certificate that was given to them with his body that actually stated that his demise was the result of a "homicide" and that he had suffered "blunt force trauma to the legs." McNeill had claimed there was no indication of homicide.

Other reporters soon picked up the story and its obvious contradictions. Tim Golden, another *Times* reporter, uncovered hundreds of pages from the official army investigation of testimony from soldiers involved in the matter that documented that Dilawar was hung "by his arms" with a hood over his head and beaten severely. Other witness statements confirmed the fact that many prisoners at the Bagram facility were forced to endure sleep deprivation and long hours of "loud music" and barking dogs.

Already skeptical of efforts to assign blame to soldiers on the ground, the film suddenly becomes instructional and presents an analysis of the origins of American policies that sanctioned the use of enhanced torture. Dick Cheney, the American vice president, described how interrogation policies were about to change after 9/11. He told a television interviewer that it would now be necessary to "work the dark side" in terms of intelligence because that is how the terrorists operate. The role of John Yoo, who crafted this policy for the Bush administration in the earliest days after 9/11, is also examined. Working in the Department of Justice, Yoo prepared memos that argued that the outlawing of torture to gain information from prisoners of war under the Geneva Convention (1949) did not apply to enemy combatants in Afghanistan and at Guantánamo Bay.

Taxi to the Dark Side is effective in its critique because it captured direct testimony from many American soldiers themselves. Carolyn Wood, an army captain who served in intelligence at Abu Ghraib after a tour of duty at Bagram, said she felt pressure to use enhanced techniques to gather information. Another MP (military police officer) at the Afghan base, Thomas Curtis, actually recalled the brutal techniques used against Dilawar. Other information was presented to suggest that not only was a green light given for such treatment by the Bush administration but that some of the ideas for torture migrated from Guantánamo to Bagram in the early days of the War on Terror, including practices of sexual humiliation and sleep deprivation.

Dilawar had been charged specifically with driving a group of terrorists to a point where they could fire rockets at an American base. Glendale Walls, an American soldier at Bagram who actually interrogated Dilawar, thought it was possible that Dilawar did not know the intent of his passengers and that prison officials really had no information of any kind on what he might or might not have done. Yet Walls was chastised by a superior for being "too nice" and was ordered to "put more pressure" on the Afghan, including hanging him by his hands from the ceiling. It was later that Walls learned that Dilawar had died and that the passengers in his taxi had been sent to Guantánamo.

Eventually several military police were charged in the beating deaths of Dilawar and another Afghan. Walls, for one, spent several months in jail for his role in the affair. This film, of course, rejected the idea of blaming the troops and exonerating their military and political superiors. At its end it even presented an Afghan point of view by allowing Dilawar's brother, Shapoor, to speak about his dead sibling. He noted that he often prays for his deceased brother at a local cemetery and insisted that his brother was not only innocent of any wrongdoing but "barely more than a child" when "they killed him."

Sympathy and critique were also evident in documentaries that directed their prime attention to the viewpoints of citizens of countries adversely impacted by American military forces. Thus, the appearance of a production like *The Dreams of Sparrows* (2005) that chronicled the efforts of ordinary Iraqis struggling to live in the time after the fall of their dictator and the arrival of American soldiers was not surprising. Appearing on the screen, director Hayder Mousa Daffar, a onetime night clerk at a Baghdad hotel, said that he intended to show the world the truth about the situation in Iraq—a truth that would refute any effort by Americans to moralize their global war.

Saddam Hussein does not fare well in this production. A few Iraqis longed for his return. Most rejoiced over his fall. Images appear of celebrations in the streets after he was deposed. Members of the Communist

Party of Iraq gleefully stomped on a photograph of the former Iraq leader. Others testified to all the deaths that resulted from wars he had started. The brutality of his sons and of his secret police forces left an indelible mark. One former Iraqi army officer called Saddam's regime a terrorist organization itself.

The main problem Iraqis faced in this film, however, was not the former dictator but the presence of the Americans and the actions of George Bush. People in the street rejected Bush's argument that the Americans came to liberate and "nothing more." Their anger and displeasure were palpable. Some claimed the invasion was illegal and that the matter of finding weapons of mass destruction was a ruse. "I want to say to George Bush enough of this deception and soap opera," one Iraqi shouted. At one point the camera enters a shelter for homeless children. Many of the inhabitants were rendered homeless by the American attacks and forced to live in the streets for a time. Some lived in another shelter called the "House of Mercy" before it was bombed by the Americans and they had to come to their present location. This story is followed by images of children playing among piles of rubble and gathering junk in the streets. It is clear that many Iraqis now have no jobs and one unemployed resident wonders whether George Bush would allow this to happen to his own people. A few insist that the Americans proved not to be "liberators" but a "menace."

One citizen of the new Iraq related the story of a friend named Sa'ad, who was delighted that Saddam had been overthrown but was soon killed by American forces as he unknowingly drove toward one of their positions at night. Observers were able to count over 100 bullet holes in his car. The narrator of the story lamented "that he was not supposed to die." Another of Sa'ad's acquaintances, distraught over the loss of his friend and over the entire American invasion, declared that "Baghdad is hell, really hell. And you in New York are in paradise." He felt that the American soldiers stationed in the city were simply "hard hearted" and acted like they were in a "Clint Eastwood movie," just shooting all the time for no good reason.

Finally, the filmmaker elected to cover not only the situation in Baghdad but Fallujah. The site of fierce fighting in 2004, the city was a site of immense destruction. Families saw their homes completely leveled; surviving members insisted they had not been part of any resistance or they possessed no weapons of any kind. "This is what Bush did. Let him come and see," one individual asserted. Images of burned-out minivans, Iraqis with missing feet, and civilians carrying their dead to cemeteries, burying corpses, and crying over the remains of those they loved are not only distressing but add weight to larger claims Iraqis made that the Americans turned out to be anything but liberators.

Andrew Berends's documentary *Blood of My Brother* (2005) continued the vilification of the American occupation of Iraq and the ideal of a militant patriotism by focusing, in part, on the pain of the family of Ra'ad Fadel al-Azawi, an Iraqi portrait photographer killed by an American patrol. The family of Ra'ad, who had been the breadwinner of a large extended family, is devastated by his loss. He and his friends were guarding a holy mosque one night in their neighborhood so that it would not be harmed by either Americans or insurgents. Ra'ad felt the American forces in the area knew him well enough that they would not shoot at him, but unfortunately that assumption proved to be a miscalculation.

The film actually opens with a view of his brother Ibrahim mourning his loss, and men carrying his coffin in the streets. Ibrahim seems delirious as he wanders through the funeral procession talking of Ra'ad as a martyr and, at the same time, claiming his brother's blood was "squandered." Later women related to Ra'ad visit his grave and wail in grief, beat their fists against their chests, and talk to their dead relative, telling him how much his absence hurts them. His mother exclaims that she wishes she had died in his stead. His sister explained that "two birds had come to her" and that one remained while the other flew away. She saw this as a way that Ra'ad still spoke to her. In her mind the fact that one bird remained was Ra'ad's way of saying that he remained nearby.

The Forgotten War (2010) offers a rare perspective on the impact of the War on Terror on civilians in Afghanistan. In part it provides a history lesson on the long history of foreign invaders occupying the nation, including the Russians in the 1980s. In the current era Afghan citizens are squeezed between the arrival of anti-terrorism troops from America and Canada and the local Taliban units that seek to prevent people from cooperating with soldiers from the West. There seems to be no way out for these people—including alignment with Western troops. A narrator asks, "What does it mean for the West to come back here? His respondent says that his people are simply destined to fight invaders and die in "another forgotten war." Evidence of Afghan suffering is widespread. Images are presented of Afghan children crying over the bloodied body of their big brother who was killed in a suicide bombing. Afghan men have incredibly poor employment prospects, a fact that makes them susceptible to financial offers to side with the Taliban. Children in school suffer because of the deaths of parents and disease. The nation's illiteracy rate is one of the highest in the world. And the only real cash crop for farmers is opium, a fact that causes them to resent soldiers who destroy their crops as a way to cut off financial flows to the Taliban insurgents. They gladly accept Taliban military security for their plantings. There is a War on Terror going on in Afghanistan, but while it may or may not bring some security benefits to the West, it does not seem to promise much life improvement for these civilians caught in a trap between contending forces.

Sara Ahmed has raised the important question, "How does pain enter politics?" Certainly the diligent work of empathic filmmakers willing to register the trauma and suffering of the War on Terror and indifferent to the need to conceal the damage contributed to that infiltration. The excessive focus of melodrama on human emotions—deeply embedded in many feature films about the war and in the sentiments chronicled in documentaries— worked incessantly to undermine proclamations of moral righteousness and the hope of war-based patriots to see that private and public feelings of love were in perfect alignment. Traces of support for a war-based version of patriotism could certainly be found in the film version of the war, but they were vastly outweighed by the relentless effort of filmmakers to capture the tragedy and suffering of soldiers, families, and innocents abroad who bore the brunt of American military power. And to a significant extent, commentators on these cultural productions tended to support the project to rework the war in terms of its most ghastly truths.

The political world orchestrated by powerful American business and political leaders was also held up for review in these features. The nation's quest for oil and the controversial decisions of the Bush administration— topics one could follow in the press—were certainly part of this filmic record. Yet, it was the private sphere of personal life—the ongoing distress of shattered families, bands of brothers, beleaguered drone operators, and blameless civilians—that captured the attention of those who aimed the camera's eye on this global struggle and upended hopes that the war could remain clothed in noble patriotic dress. Outside the screening room, however, war-based patriots were not ready to give up the fight, even if it meant resorting to violence committed against one's neighbors at home.[21]

War-based patriots always carried an unstable mix of loving and hateful emotions. Less troubled by evidence of human torment to begin with, some of these loyal Americans had no problem seeking retribution against evildoers and even innocents emanating from outside the nation's borders. Their version of patriotism always held the potential to undermine its ethic of love with cannons of loathing and aggression—a potential that could infect adherents permanently or temporarily. In the new global war, moreover, this violence was unleashed against not only foreign adversaries but residents of the United States itself. In a climate in which a belligerent patriotism attempted to throttle dissent and serve as a litmus test of who could be trusted, Muslims living in America and people who looked like them were suddenly seen as potential threats to the body politic and, for that matter, easy targets. A surge of bias attacks and waves of intimidation swept American soil, even before the government launched retaliatory attacks abroad. Arabs, Muslims, and South Asians living in America—often for decades—were now suddenly subjected to the anger of patriots intent upon waging their own version of a homeland defense. At least 1,000 "bias incidents," including some nineteen murders and the burning of mosques, were reported in the weeks after the terrorist attacks.

This wave of grassroots hostility was reinforced by the enactment of the Patriot Act in October 2001, which facilitated the widespread roundup of immigrants by allowing for warrantless searches of private residences and indefinite detentions of individuals—especially from the Middle East—who had not committed any serious crime. When George Bush folded the Immigration and Naturalization Service into a new Department of Homeland Security, the situation of these newcomers to America became even more precarious, for they were now seen not as potential citizens seeking a better life but as a danger to national security based mostly on their appearance or background. More than 5,000 males were picked up for interrogations. Others were thrown into detention for no apparent reason. By 2002 the Department of Justice began to move to the top of a list for expulsion men who had come from countries "in which there has been an Al Qaeda terrorist presence." Attorney General John Ashcroft, who had launched secret raids to arrest Muslims in America, even instigated a pattern of racial profiling when he announced "Operation Tips," a program that tasked all Americans to look for suspicious people in their neighborhoods who might be connected to some form of terrorist activity, a decree that immediately placed American Arabs, Muslims, and South Asians in a dangerous position. Despite the fact that President Bush had visited a mosque in Washington six days after 9/11 to remind citizens that Muslims in America needed to be treated with respect, his administration appeared to be moving in the opposite direction.[1]

War-based patriotism has always had a troubled relationship with the liberal ideal that all men and women merited respect under the law. Any potential for sustaining ideals of egalitarianism and tolerance was inherently challenged by its preoccupation with enemies and its tendency to sanction violence inflicted in its name. Studies have shown that in the climate of fear that marked the aftermath of 9/11, Americans clearly expressed high levels of national pride or "an affective attachment" to the larger political community. But fear, as Michael Welch has suggested, can lead to a search for "scapegoats" or subversives who were often neighbors thought to be less devoted to the nation or incapable of ever joining its ranks of ardent compatriots. Patriotism as a basis for unity can be real but disingenuous if its goals are reactionary or "war-based" and heavily contingent upon the debasement of others. Thus, Darren Davis found that "high levels of patriotism after 9/11 were associated with negative evaluations of Islamic fundamentalists and Arabs." Conversely, Davis discovered that highly positive reputations were granted to "whites" and "Christian Fundamentalists," apparent exemplars of an authentic American identity. This preoccupation with the threat of strangers not only enhanced a narrower view of who constituted a true American but fostered a strain of xenophobia that was not only exclusionary but racist.

Anti-immigrant sentiment, of course, was not new to the United States. Nativism, which historian John Higham defined as a fear of influences originating abroad that threatened the life of the nation from within, flourished at the end of the nineteenth century. He noted that the "most characteristic complaint" of the nativist was the belief that a particular group was not sufficiently loyal or patriotic. Historically this was true when native-born Americans attacked Catholic newcomers in the nineteenth century on the presumption that they were more faithful to the Vatican than to Washington. It was also the case during World War II when the government removed

Japanese-Americans from their homes and put them in detention camps throughout the West on the unfounded fear that their true allegiances resided with Tokyo.[2]

In the days after 9/11 long-standing strains of nativism meshed with an endemic racism that had long characterized American society. Traces of this merger were already evident in the 1990s in the campaign for Proposition 187 in California, a measure state voters approved to deny social services and nonemergency health care to Mexican immigrants.[3] In this retreat from a liberal vision of human equality, hostile racial attitudes nurtured by an expanding call for "white rights" after the 1960s blended with older xenophobic fears of an invasion to produce a victory for anti-immigrant forces. The Muslim origins of the 9/11 perpetrators quickly cast an even greater shadow of mistrust over certain foreigners who appeared to be true outsiders in terms of their appearance and their religion. Muslims, Arabs, and South Asians now bore not only the weight of their racial markings but the burden of nativist dread.[4]

Hatred in the Homeland

In the aftermath of 9/11 Arab-Americans, Muslims, and South Asians were extremely vulnerable wherever they lived in the United States. A Muslim college student in Manhattan named Maya recalled her experience on the day of the attacks. She heard about the towers falling while visiting the Muslim Students Association at her campus and rumors that the assault may have been engineered by Islamic extremists. Conventional wisdom among her friends was that women like Maya who wore the traditional headscarf or "hijab" might be in danger. Gripped by uncertainty, the young woman did not want to remain at her school but was fearful of venturing into the streets and taking public transportation. Instead, she decided to remain on campus and call her family, a difficult undertaking, as most phones were not working properly. Eventually she reached her father, who put her in touch with two Muslim men who agreed to escort her home. In what became one of the most frightening trips of her life, she recalled being spit upon and hearing people proclaim that they were going to kill Muslims.[5]

Hate crimes and threatening speech permeated American cities in the fall of 2001. Practicing Muslims and people who simply seemed to have some sort of Muslim or Arabic appearance now faced possible harassment and severe forms of violence. The American-Arab Anti-Discrimination Committee reported over 700 bias incidents against people deemed to be

Muslim or Muslim presenting in the first nine weeks after the Twin Towers fell. They counted an additional 165 such events in the first ten months of 2002. The FBI noted a fifteenfold increase in reported "anti-Islamic" attacks between 2000 and 2001. On September 11, 2001, in Ronkonkoma, New York, Brian Harris, age twenty-nine, was charged with a hate crime after he allegedly held an "Arab-American" at gunpoint while making anti-Arab threats. The following day Adam Lang was charged with first-degree reckless endangerment after he tried to run down a Pakistani woman with his car in South Huntington, New York. In San Diego, two men opened the car door of Swaran Bhullar, a video store owner, as she was stopped at a red light and threatened to slash her throat "for what you have done to us." The Indiana Advisory Committee to the United States Commission on Civil Rights reported that on September 14th a man drove a car into the Evansville Islamic Center and told police he was "getting the Muslims back for what they did." In Bloomington a Hindu man who was mistaken for a Muslim was beaten up and a Muslim woman wearing a traditional headscarf was punched in the face. In Fort Worth, Texas, two Ethiopian men were stabbed while visiting a botanical garden. Mosques also became prime targets for vandals. Some were riddled with bullets or defaced with "obscene graffiti" and swastikas. A bag filled with "pig's blood" was thrown at the door of a mosque in San Francisco.[6]

No region of the country offered a safe haven from such hostility. The Orange County, California, Human Relations Commission reported thirty-seven hate crimes against "Middle Easterners" in the three weeks following 9/11. This sudden surge dismayed local officials, since there had been a downward trend in such acts since 1999. Most of the reported incidents in the county took place in Anaheim, which had a fairly large concentration of Muslims. The most serious incident reported by the commission was the severe beating of a man of "Asian Indian descent." In nearby Los Angeles, authorities reported that there were seven times as many bias incidents against "Middle Easterners" in the first three weeks after 9/11 than during the entire year of 2000. The 1,031 alleged hate crimes recorded by the Los Angeles County Human Relations Commission was the highest number recorded in the twenty-one years such records were kept. One of the incidents in the city was the murder of Adel Karas, a Coptic Christian grocer, who was killed in his store in San Gabriel.[7]

Hate crimes and violent incidents surged in Chicago as well. Forty-nine such transgressions against people of "Arab descent" were reported in 2001, up from only nine the previous year. Most of this tension was centered in the southwestern suburbs of the city, which contained a concentration of

Muslim residences and small businesses. Ironically, the incidence of hate crimes was higher in these suburbs than in the neighboring southwest section of the city itself, where many Muslims also lived. One apparent reason for the difference was that in the city Muslims were more integrated into a diverse social fabric of minorities that included African Americans and Latinos. In the suburban setting, people of "Arab descent," whose numbers had been increasing before 2001, stood out as a distinct minority in a sea of white residents. In this suburban conflict zone, as in much of America, stress between natives and newcomers had been building for some time, so it was not surprising to learn that there was political opposition to the establishment of a new mosque in the suburb of Palos Heights in 2000. The town council actually approved a measure to force a buyout of Muslim property owners in order to stop the mosque project completely, a decision that forced local Muslims to abandon the idea altogether.[8]

The day after 9/11 several hundred young students gathered at Oak Lawn High School, encouraged by the ravings of a radio commentator, and organized a protest march to the Mosque Foundation of Bridgewater, about two miles away. Louise Cainkar, who has studied post-9/11 bigotry in the Chicago area, noted that the protesters draped their cars with American flags and yelled "Death to Arabs." Police formed a human barrier around the neighborhood to protect citizens inside. The entire episode incited so much fear among Muslim families living nearby that many took to "hiding behind curtains" in their homes. Police actually cordoned off the area and created check points for several days after the protest in order to limit accessibility to the neighborhood to local inhabitants only. One Arab-American expressed the point that the protection was appreciated but "at the same time you feel isolated. It's a mixed feeling. . . . It could have been much worse." In a collective strike against intolerance and anger, the Southwest Organizing Project (SWOP), an association formed to promote open-mindedness in the area, mobilized its members to form a "circle of peace" around the mosque in order that Muslims could pray without disruption. A few days later students at a nearby Catholic high school sent handwritten notes of "concern, compassion, and prayer" to the local Muslim congregants. One of the organizers of the protective circle was quoted as saying, "We stand up for the Muslim community and they stand up for us."[9]

Distrust of Muslims lingered, however. In 2004 plans for the construction of another mosque near suburban Orchard Park again induced fierce opposition. Resistance to the idea was so strong that the city council decided to hold hearings on the matter. Although the mosque was eventually built, public comments made it clear that many citizens had conflated in their own minds the terms "Muslim" and "terrorist." Cainkar reported that the minister of a local Baptist Church evoked loud applause at the city council meeting when he said, "The Radical Muslims kill every day. Moderate Muslims do not kill people. Moderate Muslims supply the cash to militant Muslims."[10]

Police protection and support from tolerant citizens could not shield all Arabs and Muslims in the Chicago region. Cainkar's study found that biased individuals still found ways to vent their fear and anger by targeting specific individuals, especially Muslim women wearing a hijab. In true nativist fashion, these women were seen as residing outside the dominion of authentic patriots and probably incapable of ever gaining entry into such a select group. Some were subjected to not only verbal attacks, moreover, but physical assaults as well. One Arab woman told Cainkar that she was too scared to leave her home because she feared for her life. "When I did go out, I would have things thrown at my car. . . . People who used to be friendly were not so friendly," the woman explained. Eventually Muslim families began to wave the flag themselves and place it on their cars and on their front lawns. In contrast to xenophobes who used the flag as a symbol of segregation, these newcomers waved it instead to signal their intent to make the American homeland more inclusive.[11]

Well before 9/11 the Detroit area had been a center of Arab settlement in the United States, especially concentrated in Dearborn. At the time of the attacks it was estimated that several hundred thousand Lebanese, Yemenis, and Iraqis—most of them Muslims—resided in the region. In part because they could live within a large mass of Arabs and Muslims, many potential victims of bias attacks were protected from harm. The main threat to these residents came not so much from neighbors but from the belligerent actions of federal authorities who looked upon the Detroit region and its large Muslim population as a potential breeding ground of terrorist activity. In the aftermath of 9/11 Detroit became a focus of government efforts to ferret out potential terrorists as federal agencies rounded up thousands of Arab, Muslim, and South Asian men who were suspected of planning more attacks. Six days after 9/11, for instance, the FBI raided a home in the city looking for Nabil Almarabh, whose name appeared on a pre-9/11 terrorist watch list. Almarabh was not found at the site, but four of his "noncitizen housemates" were detained after false identity papers were discovered in their apartment. Attorney General Ashcroft soon made this Detroit group a national story by referring to them as a "sleeper cell" capable of inflicting more damage upon the nation. Eventually charges against the men were dropped, but the entire case revealed not only the hysteria that now gripped the United States but the peculiar situation in which Arab and Muslim men in Detroit and elsewhere found themselves. It comes as no surprise to learn that by 2003 the FBI headquarters in Detroit was home to the largest counterterrorism investigation in American history.[12]

The size and wealth of Muslim Detroit actually allowed it to mount a strong public relations campaign against those who threatened them. The Arab American National Museum (AANM) opened in Dearborn in 2005, although plans for its construction predated 9/11, as one effort to cast the entire Arab and Muslim immigrant community into a traditional, pro-American narrative of immigrants coming to America for greater opportunity—a tale that would ostensibly moderate fears of terrorism and make the newcomers appear to be incipient patriots. The museum's project to establish legitimacy for these newcomers received a boost when it was able to partner with a cooperative program that allowed museums to share collections, exhibitions, educational strategies, and research agendas with the Smithsonian Institution in Washington, D.C. Rachel Yezbick, a scholar who examined the AANM project, demonstrated that overall the new museum made a clear argument that Arabs had settled in the United States just as Italian-Americans and Mexican-Americans had done before them. Museum officials also insisted that their tale was the "story of people who come to this country for better lives for themselves and their families." After examining exhibits and attending museum-sponsored workshops, Yezbick concluded that the entire venture was generally shaped by a desire on the part of its creators to reject the "post 9/11 politics of fear" by affirming the contributions of Arabs as "patriotic, ethnic American citizens." This positive rendition of Arab-Americans was also reinforced in the museum by images and stories of their service to the armed forces of the United States.[13]

Yezbick also attended a workshop sponsored by the museum on the topic of "cultural competency." In this setting she was able to listen to conversations between visitors and museum staff on cultural values held by many Arab-Americans. One curious visitor asked why many Arab women wear the hijab. Interestingly the staff response was not simply that these women were carrying on a cultural tradition pertaining to female modesty but that some Arab women actually found the practice "liberating," a word designed to appeal to American values. Another staff member hastily added that in America many Arab women begin to work outside the home—another suggestion aimed at enhancing the prospects of their assimilation. In another exchange, a member of the public wondered why they had often seen Arab-American men standing on street corners talking. A museum educator tempered the suspicious implications of the question by explaining that there had recently been much conflict in Lebanon (2008) and that these men were most likely discussing that situation.[14]

Assaults on Arab-Americans tapered off somewhat by the end of 2002 but by no means disappeared. A report in 2008 by the American-Arab Anti-Discrimination Committee (ADC) affirmed the fact that the rate of violent crimes against Arabs and Muslims declined from the "post 9/11 surge," although the rate was still higher than the period before the terror attacks. The report made clear that these people continued to feel "a heightened sense of vulnerability not only from biased citizens but from continued "defamation" in the media and the aggressive attempts of federal officials to deport them, an effort that frequently violated their civil rights. Arabs and Muslims were also cast into a difficult position in 2003 because most were "deeply opposed" to the Bush administration's invasion of Iraq. The report hastened to add, however, that for many Arab-Americans the United States remained a place where they could live and prosper and that most were "personally unmolested" after 9/11.[15]

One reason the report cited to explain the continuing harassment of this minority was the evidence of terrorist activity abroad. News of beheadings in the Middle East by terrorists under the command of Abu Mussab al-Zarqawi triggered a new surge of hate crimes in America. Terrorist bombings in London and elsewhere in 2005 produced similar results. Thus, in 2004 a pregnant Arab-American woman wearing a hijab was beaten unconscious in Massachusetts when she asked a man to restrain his dog because it frightened her child. Two years later in Michigan an Arab-American man in Detroit was battered in front of his wife and children allegedly because of his "religious and ethnic background." At airports throughout the country during this period the Transportation Security Administration resisted calls to enforce a policy of racial profiling in processing airline passengers but still detained some people simply because they wore hijabs or turbans. And Arab and Muslim immigrants continued to encounter problems at points of entry, especially at the Canadian border near Detroit.[16]

Employment discrimination was another lingering problem. The American-Arab Anti-Discrimination Committee reported numerous instances of Arab-Americans and Muslims encountering hostile work environments. Many heard abusive comments focusing on their ethnic, racial, or religious identity.

Some employers refused to allow Muslims the time they needed to pray during the workday. In 2003 an Arab-American working for the Federal Bureau of Prisons in Kingsport, Tennessee, experienced discrimination at work in the form of racial slurs such as "terrorist" and "camel jockey." In the same year, Mohammad Pharoan, a waiter at the Hyatt Regency Hotel in Baltimore and an American citizen, was sent home from his job because President Bush would be attending a fundraiser at the hotel. Secret Service agents informed him that because his name was Mohammad he would not be allowed to be in the hotel when the president arrived and escorted him out of the building. In Los Angeles in 2005 a Muslim American was fired without explanation a day after he took issue with accusations that most Muslims were terrorists. His boss told him that he was being dismissed not because he failed to meet expectations on the job but because he was not a "cultural fit" for his company. And in 2006 an instructor at Blackfeet Community College in Montana encountered bias when colleagues asked him if he was a terrorist and if he was going to "blow us up." The man was forced to publicly proclaim in front of a group of teachers that he had no aspirations to perform such an act.[17]

Arabs and Muslims had long been plagued by the negative way in which they had been portrayed in American culture. It was a problem that the American-Arab Anti-Discrimination Committee insisted had actually gotten worse since 2001. The committee claimed that the source of this denigration had shifted, however, from feature films to the field of politics, particularly from rhetoric coming from the "evangelical Christian right." Arab-American leaders were deeply concerned that attacks from this sector of patriots, which were increasingly aimed at Islam as a religion, were not only growing but capable of instigating an even greater level of hate crimes and assaults on civil liberties. In fact, in this moment Muslim and Arab organizations in the United States began to intensify the defense of their civil rights despite the continuing threat of more reprisals. In Silicon Valley, for instance, such groups sponsored "Know Your Rights" workshops designed to inform Muslims and South Asians about how they could defend themselves from unwarranted arrests or verbal attacks. The Massachusetts chapter of the Muslim American Alliance that had been concentrating on voter registration drives now became more involved with the peace movement and protesting the invasion of Iraq.[18]

It was difficult not to notice that many of the discriminatory moves against Arabs and Muslims were mounted by conservative Christian spokespeople and other religions after 9/11. White evangelical Christians had been huge supporters (some polls registered 87 percent) of Bush's thrust into Iraq. In a television appearance in 2007, the late Reverend Jerry Falwell argued that the Prophet Mohammed was a "terrorist" and claimed that Islam was not a religion but a political movement bent on world domination and the spread of Sharia, or Islamic religious precepts. Falwell warned that Sharia could eventually supersede the U.S. Constitution as the law of the land and lead to the legalization of wife-beating in the United States and even beheadings. Another evangelical leader, Pat Robertson, called Mohammed "a killer" and claimed Islam was inherently violent. Franklin Graham, son of noted preacher Billy Graham, referred to Islam as a "very evil and wicked religion" and actually persisted in spreading a politics of fear based on anti-Muslim diatribes and homophobia. Graham was upset that Islamic clerics from throughout the world had failed to apologize for 9/11 and issue statements reassuring Americans that terrorism was not a part of "true Islam." Even a Catholic spokesman like Robert Spencer, who headed a Muslim-bashing website called Jihad Watch, called for a complete ban on Muslim migration to the West and argued that Islam was merely a "false religion." The American-Arab Anti-Discrimination Committee was not only troubled by the rhetoric of these militant patriots but furious that the Bush administration directed federal funds to evangelical Christian organizations despite clear evidence of their "open bigotry."[19]

Conservative political pundits and commentators also took up the cause of a belligerent patriotism to demonize Muslims. Ann Coulter attracted considerable attention just a few days after 9/11 with an essay in the *National Review* that called for an immediate war against the countries from which the terrorists came. Coulter's remarks not only inflamed anti-Arab and anti-Muslim feelings but also cast aspersions on Islam itself. Coulter felt there was no time to conduct exacting studies to determine exactly who had just attacked America. She preferred that bombs start falling as soon as possible. And she railed against immigration policies that hesitated to conduct racial and religious screenings. For her the only legitimate response to 9/11 was to invade the countries of origin of the terrorists and "kill their leaders and convert them to Christianity." "We weren't punctilious about locating and punishing Hitler and his top officers," she asserted. "We carpet bombed German cities; we killed civilians. That's war and this is war."

In television specials and interviews, radio talk show host Glen Beck also contributed to the anti-Muslim assault. He famously told the first Muslim elected to Congress, Keith Ellison, that he felt that Ellison was "one of our enemies" and indicated that many Americans shared his outlook. In

2004 right-wing columnist Michelle Malkin published a book titled *In Defense of Internment: The Case for Racial Profiling* that claimed the incarceration of Japanese-Americans in World War II was justified due to the danger Japan posed to America at the time; she now called for the outright discrimination of Muslims in the United States. Malkin denied she was actually advocating a roundup of all Muslims but felt the threat they posed, which she labeled "Islamofascism," was so widespread and hard to detect that it might be impossible to imprison all of them. At the very least she advocated a program of "systematic discrimination" that required all Muslims to face special scrutiny and be prevented from serving in the military or gaining access to classified information.[20]

Patriots Who Murder

In the hostile climate that followed 9/11 a number of Arab, Muslim, and South Asian men in America were even killed because their appearance resembled those who flew the terrorist planes. Some of the victims were neither Arab nor Muslim, but such distinctions made little difference to citizens whose patriotism was fully imbued with anger and hate and bent upon exacting revenge. The number of these murders has never been firmly established, but estimates range from eight to nineteen. There are disputes in the matter because in some cases police were not convinced that the motive for murder was intolerance and posited alternative reasons. For instance, in Los Angeles a Palestinian-born salesman was shot while making door-to-door rounds. His family called it a hate crime, but police felt robbery may have been the motive.[21]

Mark Stroman, who worked in a body shop in Dallas, committed two of the "anti-Muslim" murders in the aftermath of 9/11 and badly wounded a third individual. On September 15, 2001, he shot Waqar Hasan as Hasan grilled hamburgers in his Dallas convenience store. Six days later he wounded Raisuddin Bhuiyan, another convenience store operator. Not finished, he continued his spree in early October by taking the life of Vasudev Patel. He later admitted that during his vendetta he also contemplated going to a shopping mall and taking shots at as many "Middle Eastern people" as he could find. Upon arrest he readily acknowledged his misdeeds but refused to admit that he had committed a hate crime. Stroman believed that he was simply doing his duty and called his deed "an act of passion and patriotism." At his trial a fellow prisoner testified that Stroman told him he was angry over 9/11 and felt that America had not retaliated sufficiently against Arabs and Muslims living in the homeland, an attitude that caused him to think that he had to take such matters into his own hands by killing people of "middle eastern descent." In a series of letters he authored while in pretrial detention, Stroman actually made the false claim that he had a sister who was killed at Ground Zero. He further elucidated the volatile mix of revenge and patriotism he felt after 9/11. He wrote: "I began to feel a great sense of rage, hatred, loss, bitterness and utter degradation. . . . I wanted the Arabs to feel the same sense of insecurity about their immediate surroundings. I wanted them to feel the same sense of vulnerability and uncertainty upon American soil much like the chaos and bedlam they were already accustomed to in there [sic] home country. How dare they come to America and be at peace and find comfort in our country, my country America."[22]

Just before he was executed in 2011, Stroman did express misgivings over the amount of hatred in the world but still insisted that he was a "proud American, Texas loud." In fact, he seemed to retain his patriotic mix of love and hate until the end. On his "death blog," which he maintained from prison, he claimed on the day before he died that "the Spirit flows through these Texas veins, red, white, and blue" and that he was "unbroken and anxious to get this show on the road." In her study of wounded veterans, Nancy Sherman has explained how anger often fueled a desire on the part of veterans she studied to join the War on Terror in the first place. For the suffering vets she met just back from the war front, their inability to control their fury proved to be a problem because it impeded their ability to grieve or come to terms with losses they experienced in war, especially the death of close comrades. For Sherman, grieving helped to detoxify rage. Sherman also noticed that frequently feelings of anger and rage could "mingle deeply with patriotism." While we can only speculate on Stroman's full emotional makeup, he was certainly driven by a powerful mix of hatred and national loyalty that circulated widely through American culture at the time.[23]

The three men that Stroman shot shared a different version of American patriotism, one rooted not in the past or in the mindset of a native son of the Lone Star State but in a glimpse of the future and the hope for a better life. Waquar Hassan was a Pakistani immigrant who originally moved his family to New Jersey. Later he went to Dallas to run a convenience store with the intent of eventually having his family join him. Vasudev Patel was a native of India and a Sikh, not a Muslim. He settled in Dallas in 1982; his wife, Alka, followed him five years later. Eventually, they opened a Shell gas station in the suburb of Mesquite and worked it together. Most mornings Vasudev would arrive early to open the station and call his wife around 6:30 A.M. to wake her so she could get the children off to school. Consequently, she was not at the station when Stroman walked in around 7 A.M. to murder her husband. The loss of male breadwinners proved to be devastating for both immigrant families. Hassan had applied for a green card but it was not yet granted, a fact that left his wife and children subject to deportation. They were finally able to continue their immigrant dream only because of the intervention of a sympathetic congressman. Patel's wife was a citizen when she lost her spouse, but she struggled after his death because of the need to work longer hours at the station, raise her kids, and care for elderly parents.[24]

Fortunately Raisuddin Bhuiyan did not die when Stroman shot him in the face at the Buckner Food Mart, although he was blinded in one eye. Emigrating from Bangladesh in 1999, where he had been raised in a Muslim family and trained as a military pilot, he spent two years in New York City rooming with other men from his homeland and working in a gas station. From this post in the American lower class, Bhuiyan had a close-up view of the reaction many Americans had to 9/11. He frequently overheard some of his customers ranting that immigrants were taking over this country and expressing a desire to kill Muslims.[25]

Surprisingly, Bhuiyan eventually sought to show Stroman mercy by launching an effort to save him from the death penalty. The immigrant from Bangladesh reasoned that such a move would help even in a modest way to reduce the level of distrust and animosity between Muslims and the larger American society. Bhuiyan's first step was to publish an article in the *Dallas Morning Herald* titled "Why My Attacker Should Be Spared the Death Penalty." In this essay he publicly granted Stroman forgiveness for shooting him. He then mounted a campaign that ultimately proved unsuccessful to have Stroman's death sentence commuted to life with no parole. He explained clearly that his motivations were based on the fact that his parents had adhered to an adage that "he is best who can forgive easily." He also felt strongly that no one had the right to take another person's life. And he made it clear that he wanted to bring solace to the wives of Hassan and Patel and Stroman's children, who he felt were also victims in this tragic episode.[26]

Frank Roque, another self-proclaimed American patriot, shot and killed Balbir Singh Sodhi on September 15, 2001, while Sodhi was arranging American flags in front of his gas station in Mesa, Arizona. Many American citizens displayed the flag after the attacks, but for Sikhs like Sodhi, waving the flag also became a defensive move aimed at forestalling nativist assaults. After Roque shot Sodhi, he proceeded to a home that he had just sold to an Afghan family and fired at least three shots into the residence, although no one was hurt. Finally, he headed over to a convenience store and fired seven shots through the store window, barely missing Anwar Khalil, a clerk of Lebanese descent. Ironically, just days before his death, Sodhi and members of the Phoenix Sikh-American community were attempting to organize a press conference to condemn attacks on Muslims, Arabs, and South Asians in the United States and prevent assaults on their own members.[27]

At first Mesa police did not consider the murder a "hate crime" and felt the shooter's motive was unclear. The Sikh American community quickly rebutted this assertion. A day after the shooting, Janet Napolitano, Arizona's attorney general, held a press conference and stressed that "acts of bigotry" against any Arizona citizen would not be tolerated, confirming that she agreed with the Sikh community's position. It soon became clear that Roque, like Stroman, loathed anyone he felt resembled the men who flew the hijacked planes and considered any form of retaliation he might take as a patriotic act. At his arrest he proclaimed, "I am a patriot. I stand for America all the way."[28]

Roque was at work as an aircraft mechanic at a Boeing repair facility in Mesa on 9/11 when he learned of the collapse of the Twin Towers. According to court records, he began to cry uncontrollably and babbled incoherently after returning home as he watched news coverage of the day's events. The next day he skipped work and told a colleague that he planned to shoot some "rag heads," a reference to individuals who wore turbans. On the morning of 9/15, Roque went to the Wild Hare sports bar to drink before setting out on his shooting rampage. Later at his trial a bouncer at the bar recalled that many customers that day talked about seeking some sort of vengeance against anyone wearing a turban. Other accounts noted that Roque had been seen at other taverns in the area ranting at the continuing televised news coverage of the terrorism. When police arrived at his home on the night of the murder, he put his hands in the air and declared, "I am a patriot and an American. I'm American. I'm a damn American." Inside the patrol car, he complained that the officers were arresting him and letting the terrorists "run wild." He expressed the wish that as punishment he be sent to Afghanistan with a "lot of weapons." During an interrogation Roque's wife, Dawn, said that he had threatened to "slit the throats" of "Iranians, maybe forty or fifty of them." And she recalled he kept saying that there were many more people who felt just as he did.[29]

Balbir Singh Sodhi, like many other Sikhs and Muslims, was part of an extensive migration network that had forged specific strategies to establish a foothold in the United States. Family connections have always proved foundational in helping newcomers move to this country by providing motivation, shared resources, and crucial information on jobs and housing. As Balbir's brother Rana tells it, the Sodhi family's move from India centered on the plans of five brothers who lived in a small village in the Punjab region. In 1984, Indian prime minister Indira Gandhi was assassinated by her two Sikh bodyguards, an act that triggered widespread retaliation against members of this religious group. Because Rana's parents wanted their children to find a safer place to live, they decided to send two of his brothers to Arizona. Soon they opened a restaurant and reported back to their kin in India that they had found the state to be hospitable and a place where all types of people were respected. Balbir soon became the third member of the household to follow this migration chain.[30]

In interviews, Rana revealed that Sikhs in the Phoenix area were shaken by the backlash after 9/11. He recalled that "everyone was scared" and noted how quickly many South Asians began to realize that their position in the United States was becoming more and more defenseless. In a scene from the documentary *A Dream in Doubt,* Sodhi family members discuss Balbir's shooting and express their view that he was attacked solely because of his appearance. They were convinced that anyone who looked remotely like Osama bin Laden was likely to be targeted. Rana even divulged that after 9/11 his young children were called names in school and often referred to as "bin Ladens."

One year after Balbir's death, another brother, Sukhpal, was shot and killed while driving a taxi in San Francisco. The immigrant was hit by gunfire while stopped at a red light at 4 A.M. Like his brothers, Sukhpal was not only trying to establish himself in a new city in order to bring his wife and children to join him but was also sending remittances back to them in India. His brother Lakhwinder, living in Phoenix, related that family members in India had a difficult time informing the family patriarch about the loss of another son. Lakhwinder said that his father was the one who had originally encouraged the men to move in the first place because he thought it would be better than India, but he now felt that America was the "worse place."[31]

When documentary film maker Valarie Kaur went to India to interview Balbir's wife several years after his death, she found the woman still mourning. "Everyone tries to console me, but I do not have one moment of

peace," she disclosed. "Everything is empty to me." She particularly regretted that her husband was planning a return trip to India to see her and
their children at the time of his death. Kaur asked the grieving woman what
message she would like to send to the American people. Balbir's widow
revealed that her heart was "in deep pain" but that she appreciated the
kindness she received when she attended her husband's funeral in Arizona.
She was struck by the fact that people from so many different backgrounds—
Hindu, Muslim, and Christian—offered her condolences. The woman affirmed that she did not hate America and concluded simply that "it was not
his fate to come back."[32]

Many loyal citizens in Arizona moved quickly to express their sorrow
over the murder of Balbir Singh Sodhi and affirm the public need for compassion and tolerance to supplant hatred in America. An impromptu memorial filled with candles, flowers, a Christian cross, American flags, and a
photo of the decedent appeared at the gas station where he was gunned
down. A sign was also placed at the station that read, "In Memory of Balbir
Singh Sodhi. We will all truly miss you. The memory of your kindness will
live with us forever." At a memorial service representatives of various
faiths spoke and strongly condemned prejudice and intolerance. Members
of the local Sikh community brought many of the letters they had received
in the wake of the tragic killing. One spokesman read a passage from a letter written by a woman whose father had served in Vietnam. She expressed
the opinion that Sodhi demonstrated as much courage as any soldier by
trying to raise a flag at such a dangerous moment for him. She wrote,
"nothing I can say will be of much consequence or comfort. Please know
that this violent act against Mr. Sodhi is beyond my comprehension and as
you know does not represent how most Americans feel or what our country
stands for. I checked back tears as I read that Mr. Sodhi had tried to find a
flag at his business so that others would not only see that he was patriotic
but that he too was touched by the horrible events of September 11."[33]

On the first anniversary of 9/11 Mesa held a ceremony honoring all of
America's victims of terrorism, including those killed in the backlash against
Arab-Americans, Muslims, and South Asians. Empathic patriots carried
torches for the dead and "for the cause of peace and freedom." Sikh women
in mourning and in tears participated along with other citizens, and a local
attorney spoke, stressing that he was honored to have come to know many
Sikh families in the area. He also promised that justice would be served in
the case of Frank Roque, who at that time had been charged with Sodhi's
murder. A few of the dead man's relatives also addressed the gathering,

making it clear that Balbir did not deserve to die but also affirming their loyalty and calling upon God to bless America.[34]

In 2006 Arizona dedicated a state memorial to 9/11 in Phoenix called "Moving Memories." The design of the memorial consisted of a flat metal ring with written statements cut into the surface in a way that allowed sunlight to shine through and project the words onto a concrete base. Designers intended that the text would reflect not only an actual timeline of the day's events but various viewpoints people held on the attacks and on acts that followed such as the ensuring war. Drawing on newspaper accounts of the time, the final design included phrases such as "Patriotism Peaks" and "Multiple Funerals in a Day." The state's governor, Janet Napolitano, lauded the memorial and stated that "the thoughts and remarks etched in stone will serve as learning tools for all of us, our children, and our children's children."[35]

The memorial design soon sparked outrage from those who felt it did not recast the terrorist attacks and the War on Terror in sufficiently patriotic and mythical tones. Inscriptions such as "You don't win battles of terrorism with more battles" were seen as a direct rebuke of the decision of George W. Bush to invade Iraq. A quote that referred to the killing of innocent civilians in Afghanistan, "Erroneous US Air Strike Kills 46 Uruzgan Civilians"—also upset those who felt it took attention away from the American victims of terror. Other quotations included "Fear of Foreigners" and "Foreign-Born Americans Afraid." A conservative pundit took issue with the inscription "09 15 01. Balbir Singh Sodhi, A Sikh Murdered in Mesa." Mary Katherine Ham acknowledged that the crime was tragic but that it really was not part of the way in which most Americans reflected on 9/11 and that "its placement on the memorial is absurd." In fact, she called the inclusion of the reference to Sodhi "a slap on the wrist for the dreaded widespread 'backlash' which for the most part never materialized."

Soon a chorus of critics filled the blogosphere with denunciations of the state's remembrance. Largely conservative voices maintained that the memorial was inappropriate because it included references to events outside the deaths of civilians in New York, Shanksville, and Washington and contained ideas critical of America, making it both "unpatriotic" and "overly liberal." Bloggers mounted a particular critique against a school curriculum project that was meant to accompany the memorial by providing lessons suggesting how teachers could discuss 9/11 at several grade levels. These opponents objected to the insertion of the Singh episode in the instruction guidelines or the idea that part of the teaching would focus on the denial of civil liberties under the Bush administration. A Republican candidate wanting to unseat Napolitano called the memorial a "blame America monument" and argued that it did not properly honor the victims of 9/11 and those who served in the military. One representative in the Arizona legislature wanted to destroy the memorial altogether. Ultimately the commission in charge of the memorial did remove several references to American air strikes killing innocent people in Afghanistan. Commissioners also added the phrases "Let's Roll" and "God Bless America" as the vast cultural debate over the meaning of American loyalty continued.[36]

Several years later, in 2011, an inscription on the memorial again stirred controversy. John Kavanagh, a representative in the Arizona legislature, pushed for passage of a bill to remove the reference to Sodhi. "It's part of the myth following 9/11," Kavanagh asserted, "that Americans went into a xenophobic rage against foreigners." He insisted that America's response was in the end "commendable." Rana Singh strongly objected to Kavanagh's plans and charged that some people were again in a "hate crime" mode in an effort to remove the trace of his sibling at the memorial. The local Sikh community even mounted a petition drive in an effort to defeat the legislation. The bill did pass both houses of the state legislature along party lines, with Republicans supporting the motion for removal. Kavanagh argued that Balbir was the victim of a "madman" but not the 9/11 attacks. The legislator also wanted additional messages removed that he felt were overly critical of President Bush and which he thought were simply examples of "America bashing." Despite this push for alterations, considerable public opinion opposed the bill, a point that made it easier for Arizona governor Jan Brewer to veto it.[37]

"The Ground Zero Mosque"

The ability of some war-based patriots to restrain their aggressive impulses when it came to Muslims and Islam was tested again with the proposal to build a mosque in lower Manhattan. In 2009 Feisal Abdul Rauf publicized plans to construct an Islamic Center containing a mosque mere blocks from Ground Zero. Rauf, a well-known imam, had already attracted public attention by leading the Cordoba Initiative, a project aimed at educating Americans about the similarities between Islam and the West. Scholars like Rosemary Corbett have explained that Rauf's fundamental message was that Islam was part of an ethical tradition originating with Abraham, a biblical patriarch common to Judaism and Christianity. He argued that

Islam actually contained tenets similar to multiculturalism and "democratic capitalism." Even after 9/11, in fact, it was not unusual to build such centers and mosques in the United States. By the end of 2011 there were an estimated 2,106 such facilities in the nation.[38]

The project quickly became controversial, however, despite the fact that it met all building and zoning requirements and was endorsed by Barack Obama. At a White House dinner celebrating the Muslim holiday of Ramadan, Obama stated that as a citizen and as a president, "I believe that Muslims have the same right to practice their religion as anyone else in this country. That includes the right to build a place of worship and a community center on private property in lower Manhattan." The problem was that despite the fact that it remained undeveloped at the time, Ground Zero had come to be seen as a sacred space in the mind of most Americans. Human remains were still embedded in its soil. Many believed that to build a Mosque so close to this piece of land constituted an affront to the dead and to those who grieved for them. It also held symbolic importance for American patriotism, since many first responders died there in selfless efforts to help fellow citizens. Some even imagined it might serve as a possible site for another terrorist attack on America.

By the spring of 2010, an organization called "9/11 Families for a Safe and Strong America" adamantly rejected the idea. They charged that Rauf's intent was "shockingly insensitive" to the memory of the dead because it aimed to "leverage" the site's proximity to a place they held in reverence only to "grow the Muslim community." Debra Burlingame, a co-founder of the family-based organization, argued that demands now made by Rauf for religious tolerance were nullified by earlier statements he made in 2001 that blamed 9/11 on America's mistreatment of Muslims. Burlingame's group also refuted promises that the new Islamic center would promote interfaith dialogue. They felt the imam was simply too invested in Sharia, or Islamic law, which would oppose man-made rules such as the constitutional doctrine of the separation of church and state. Families for a Safe and Strong America made it clear that in their view the attempt to "use our loved ones' death and the painful legacy of 9/11 still felt by New Yorkers to engage in a campaign to reverse America's core doctrine of religious freedom . . . is a gross insult to those who were killed on that terrible day."[39]

The Anti-Defamation League, a Jewish organization, also opposed the idea of a mosque so close to Ground Zero. Members of the league shared the feelings of others that it would tarnish a hallowed site where many friends and relatives had been killed. But they also explained that they had countered plans to establish a Catholic convent near Auschwitz in 1980 out of respect for Jews who grieved for loved ones and who did not want the Jewish legacy of the death camp diminished in any way. Opinion polls showed that most Americans rejected the idea of the Ground Zero mosque as well. A *Time Magazine* survey revealed that some 61 percent of those responding felt "it would be an insult to the victims of the attacks." The results of the report also revealed a lingering animosity against all things Muslim. Nearly one-third of Americans thought that adherents to Islam should be barred from running for the presidency. Some one-fifth of Americans at the time even believed that Obama was a Muslim, a figure that had risen since he assumed office, despite his frequent pronouncements that he was a Christian.[40]

To be sure, many citizens rallied to support the ideal of tolerance expressed by Obama, including some who had close ties to the Ground Zero victims. Public rallies held in lower Manhattan around the time of the ninth anniversary of 9/11 actually supported both points of view. The September 11th Families for Peaceful Tomorrows backed Rauf's vision and helped organize one of the rallies along with Common Cause, an activist group for progressive causes. At this gathering, speakers called for opposition to bigotry and racism and support for a version of loyalty supportive of "multiculturalism." At a competing rally, participants waved American flags in support of "anti–Ground Zero Mosque messages" and doubts about the peaceful nature of Islam itself.[41]

Soon the idea of a mosque near Ground Zero was enveloped by the national politics of the day. A coalition of conservative right-wing leaders and Tea Party adherents began to mount a scathing attack on the plan not only because it seemed to dishonor the victims of 9/11 but also to discredit Obama, whose support for the center and for a broadminded outlook on Islam ran counter to their xenophobic nationalist policies. Newt Gingrich, a Republican leader and a prominent critic of the president, charged that those who supported the mosque were nothing but "radical Islamists" who wanted to prove that they can build a mosque "next to a place where 3,000 Americans were killed." "Nazis don't have the right to put up a sign next to the Holocaust museum in Washington," the former Speaker of the House proclaimed in an appearance on Fox News. "We would never accept the Japanese putting up a site next to Pearl Harbor." New York real estate developer Donald Trump even offered to buy the site of the proposed mosque and strike an agreement that would prohibit it from being built within five blocks of Ground Zero.

Gingrich and his wife, Callista, actually produced a documentary film in 2010 titled *America at Risk: The War with No Name* that argued that plans for the mosque were not only insulting to Americans but part of a long-term Muslim war on the West. The film featured a number of speakers including the Gingriches and Debra Burlingame. All made the claim that Americans and particularly the Obama administration had been slow to recognize the threat posed by radical Muslims throughout the world. To the former Speaker of the House, the idea for a mosque 600 feet from Ground Zero was part of a "Holy War" that aimed to bring Sharia to the United States and other Western societies. Regarding the concept of a mosque near Ground Zero, the film made the point that the idea of religious freedom in the United States was being exploited and that Rauf was nothing more than an agent of what Burlingame called a "soft jihad" that aimed to achieve its goals by clever tactics like building Islamic centers rather than through violent acts. Burlingame asserted that Muslim extremists plan to "take down this country" and worried that the next attack might be "catastrophic." At the end of the film the Gingriches become patriotic warriors in the battle against terrorism and are seen looking at the Statue of Liberty and calling for "courageous action" that will be needed to achieve "victory."[42]

Pam Geller, a political activist who along with Robert Spencer co-founded Stop Islamization of America in 2010, an anti-Muslim group, also joined the effort to discredit plans for the mosque and Obama at the same time. Geller promoted her brand of patriotic hatred through a website named Atlas Shrugged that warned of the threat "Muslim militancy" posed to America and Israel and called the president a "third worlder" and a coward who is only interested in appeasing "Islamic Overlords." *New York Times* reporters who visited with Geller wrote that she awoke each morning to "wage a form of holy war through Atlas Shrugged" and actually referred to herself as a "racist-Islamophobic-anti-Muslim-bigot," a sign of how much the public expression of intolerance was becoming normalized after 9/11. The writers compared her view of Islam to the outlook of many in 1950s America who saw communism as a "stealthy global threat creeping into nodes of power that must be opposed at all costs."[43]

Geller and Spencer raised their public profile considerably by joining efforts to oppose the Ground Zero mosque. Driven by a war-based patriotism fixated on enemy threats and suspicious of calls for tolerance, they made it clear that they saw the planned center as the beginning of a long-term Islamic war on the West and the next step in a subversive plot to undermine American freedom and impose Sharia, a legal system based in part on the Koran, upon the United States. In the preamble to a documentary film Geller produced in 2011, she promised that her production would expose "the insidious Islamist agenda to use a massive mosque built at Ground Zero as a base to infiltrate and eventually control America." The documentary also insisted that liberals in America such as the "media" and Obama had not taken the Islamic threat seriously and, therefore, were aiding and abetting the danger it presented. Spencer, in particular, was outraged that Obama had refused to equate terrorism with Islam, preferring to argue that terrorist groups such as al-Qaeda had simply perverted Islamic teaching. He charged the president with actually aiding and abetting "Islamic supremacist, pro-Sharia regimes."

Geller's documentary also preserved valuable film footage of protesters and speakers who attended anti-mosque rallies. Some demonstrators carried American flags or signs that debunked Obama and insisted that Ground Zero was a "burial site" that should not be violated in any way. At one gathering Geert Wilders, a leader of the right-wing Party of Freedom in the Netherlands, warned again about the threat posed by Islamic law and how incompatible it was with the symbolic importance of New York City as a place that for him represented freedom, openness, and tolerance. Wilders contrasted New York to the Islamic city of Mecca, where according to Wilders if you were not Muslim, you were not welcome. At one rally, the crowd directed chants of "Shame on you" toward Obama for being willing to dishonor the victims of 9/11 by supporting the building of the mosque. Another rally featured Spencer accusing the imam behind the project in lower Manhattan with plotting to bring Sharia to the United States. After he makes such an assertion, the film immediately cuts to footage of a woman being beaten in the Sudan as an example of Muslim brutality and statute. Another feature of the documentary displayed an alleged "captured internal document of the Muslim Brotherhood" and suggested this group was obsessed with the goal of destroying Western civilization. Andrew Breitbart, publisher of Breitbart.com, also appeared in the feature and demanded that people must stand up to "radical Islamists" and show them we have the backbone to fight. And Nelly Braginskaya, who lost a son when the Twin Towers collapsed, evoked sympathy when she spoke to anti-mosque supporters and told them many like her do not even have a grave to visit and only received a small amount of body parts after their loved ones died at Ground Zero. For her and for others, Ground Zero was their "burial place," and it would be disgraced by the building of a mosque nearby. She was supported by the mother of a New York fireman who died at the site and who felt it was much too soon to talk about building a mosque in the vicinity.[44]

City leaders debated the issue as well. New York's mayor, Michael Bloomberg, among others, made it clear that he felt Muslim citizens had the same rights to free speech as all Americans and could build a house of worship wherever they chose. Timothy Dolan, the Catholic archbishop, and David Paterson, New York's governor, offered a compromise solution that would have involved support for the construction of a mosque but at somewhat greater distance from the sacred site of Ground Zero. In the end developers dropped their plans for the mosque and began to explore other options for the use of the property, although the entire episode revealed the mounting challenges Muslims faced in America to their basic civil rights.

The storm that emerged over the mosque in New York was actually part of a renewed wave of anti-Muslim and anti-immigrant sentiment that had fallen off a bit after the violent eruptions just after 9/11. Attacks at mosques actually spiked sharply between 2008 and 2012. Polls in 2002 showed that about one-quarter of Americans held an "unfavorable" view of Muslims. Eight years later, similar polling showed that about one-half of the nation's citizens held such outlooks. And the Federal Equal Opportunity Commission reported increased levels of workplace discrimination against Muslims in America after 2009.

One reason for this renewed loathing was the election of Barack Obama and the racist backlash it evoked. Right-wing elements circulated false rumors during the 2008 election campaign that he was actually a Muslim who had refused to salute the American flag. Others, notably future U.S. president Donald J. Trump, contested the fact that he was even born in America. Christopher Bail's incisive research has also documented the rise of a number of anti-Muslim fringe organizations around this time whose influence was amplified by the use of social media and the proclivity of news organizations to feature sensationalist charges and warnings of Muslim takeovers of America. This growing hysteria led to fears that the U.S. Constitution may eventually be eclipsed by Islamic law. In 2010 voters in Oklahoma passed a "Save Our State Amendment" to their constitution that forbade the use of Sharia in their state courts. Although not a credible threat to Oklahomans, legislators who supported this change argued that the American people were in a fight for their survival and that Muslims eventually wanted to take away the "liberties and freedom of our children." The following year protesters in Yorba Linda, California, showed up at a dinner sponsored by an American Muslim relief organization to raise money for women's shelters and homelessness in the United States. An angry crowd of patriots waved large American flags and shouted catchphrases like "Go back home," "We are patriotic Americans," and "We don't want Sharia law" at those attending the charity event. A local councilwomen speaking to the protesters called the gathering of Muslims "pure unadulterated evil." Later a report from the Southern Poverty Law Center explained that the rally was fostered by a number of hate groups, including ACT! for America, a Muslim-bashing organization that claimed that the Koran fostered violence, and other far-right organizations. ACT had actually been formed in 2004 by Brigitte Gabriel, a woman who believed deeply that many Muslims living seemingly peaceful lives in the United States were actually working secretly to destroy the nation. Gabriel argued that Americans in general had become too tolerant of their Muslim neighbors and that "Patriotic Americans" needed to stand up to what she felt was a threat of domestic terrorism.[45]

Deportations

The grassroots surge of violence and hatred directed toward Arabs, Muslims, and South Asians after 9/11 by ordinary citizens was matched by the cruel and often racist actions of the federal government. Federal authorities, including deportation officers and criminal investigators from U.S. Immigration and Customs Enforcement (ICE) launched a "neo-nativist" purge in the homeland that brought fear and panic to many immigrant families who had no connection to terrorism at all. This wave of repression not only violated the legal rights of Muslims and others but buttressed long-standing bigoted and xenophobic attitudes in American culture that had often been used to deny legal rights to minorities and intimidate them as well. In this theater of suppression, nearly all immigrants came under the gaze of suspicion, although those who looked like the men who flew the planes on 9/11 attracted the most attention of all.

The groundwork for this oppressive campaign had actually been put into place prior to 2001 due to a dramatic increase in the number of undocumented newcomers. The government began to expand significantly its "punitive enforcement apparatus" in order to find greater numbers of unauthorized immigrants and remove them from the country. Congress passed laws in 1996, for instance, that increased the number of crimes for which a new arrival could be expelled. After the terrorist attacks the Patriot Act, drafted by the Bush administration in 2002, greatly expanded the ability of law enforcement to monitor the activities of both natives and newcomers living in the United States. The official title for this piece of legislation, "Uniting and Strengthening America by Providing Appropriate Tools Required to Intercept and Obstruct Terrorism," does not convey the full extent to which it weakened civil rights protections for private citizens. Those living in the United States whose visas had expired were now more likely to face this more belligerent use of government power. The fact that the act authorized indefinite detentions of immigrants revealed not only the law's potential for violating traditional civil rights but also helped to stigmatize large numbers of immigrants as possible terrorists. The Patriot Act also allowed law enforcement to search homes and businesses without the consent of owners and the FBI to gather private phone, e-mail, and financial records without a court order. Several months after the act passed, the Department of Justice issued instructions under the Alien Absconder Initiative for law enforcement to round up over 300,000 people who had deportation orders but who had failed to surrender themselves. The same agency also initiated a "call-in program" for male noncitizens from mostly Arab and Muslim countries to register with immigration authorities.[46]

Government crackdowns on these immigrants quickly drew the attention of human rights advocates. Amnesty International (AI) reported in 2002 that in the two months following 9/11 more than 1,200 "non-US nationals" were taken into custody in the United States, mostly of "Arab or South Asian" origin. Through interviews with attorneys and even some detainees, AI learned that a significant number of those arrested were denied rights under international law. There was evidence as well that the United States was actually using its immigration system to conduct criminal investigations, a method that allowed officials to circumvent rights people normally enjoyed in the criminal justice system. Thus, the Immigration and Naturalization Service (INS) was not only profiling Arabs, Muslims, and South Asians but denying them the basic right to attorney representation and even minimal contact with relatives. The INS had actually been granted increased powers after 9/11 to arrest individuals without any specific charge for up to forty-eight hours or even longer in "extraordinary circumstances." In its tour of jails and detention centers, AI discovered numerous instances in which detainees were not advised of their right to a lawyer or were even prevented from contacting one if they expressed such a wish. A Pakistani man arrested in Florida told AI that his request to see an attorney was denied while he was handcuffed to a chair after hours of interrogation. One detainee in New York on a visa overstay claimed he had asked twice for a lawyer but was refused both times. Many other detainees complained of their inability to even speak to next of kin.

The relatives of two Pakistani men held in Chicago contacted the human rights organization because they could not even find out where their loved ones had been taken. Eventually they learned that the men were being held at the Metropolitan Detention Center in New York but were still forced to wait several months before they were granted visitation.[47]

The consequences of aggressive moves and "sweeps" on the part of federal authorities brought a reign of fear and uncertainty to Muslims living and working in the United States. This was certainly true for Abdullah and Sukra Osman, a couple that had just reunited in Minneapolis in 1999 after years of separation. Abdullah had left their native Somalia first and found a job driving school buses for the city's public schools by day and taxis in the evenings and on weekends. Sukra followed him and quickly became fluent in English, securing a position as an education specialist in an elementary school. The Osmans were part of a large Somali community that had begun, ironically, with government support when the State Department arranged for refugees from Somalia's civil war to resettle in Minnesota. Most were, in fact, grateful for the opportunity to escape the ravages of war and acquire resources that would allow them to send remittances to relatives still trapped in refugee camps in Kenya. Abdullah expressed satisfaction in 2001 that he had a family, a job, "money to pay the rent," and the ability to help kinfolk in Africa.[48]

Some of the horror the couple faced in Somalia suddenly confronted them again in the United States in the form of government roundups. American officials were particularly wary of newcomers from countries they felt might harbor terrorists and likely to arrest many of them on immigration violations and treat them as potential threats to national security. This certainly happened to Somalis in the Twin Cities. Already familiar with feeling vulnerable, Sukar began to worry a great deal that Somalis would be targeted. She later recalled that she became so frightened she refused to step out at night after the 9/11 attacks. Her dread was not without justification. In Minneapolis within weeks of the terrorist assault, Ali W. Ali, a "Somali elder," was punched in the head while waiting for a bus and fell to the ground, apparently hitting his head with such force that he died. The day he was assaulted, the *Minneapolis Star-Tribune* reported that local Somalis had been unintentionally funding al-Qaeda through remittances sent to relatives.[49]

The couple's situation deteriorated when Abdullah was arrested for getting into a fight with a man who had tried to rob him. His lawyer suggested that he probably had little to worry about if he pleaded guilty to felonious assault because his assailant had a prior history of such attacks. However, the lawyer also made it clear that his Muslim identity could make his legal position more precarious due to the prevailing climate of the times. Following the advice of his legal adviser, Abdullah entered a guilty plea on the assumption it would most likely result in him spending only eight months in a work-release program. Once in the hands of law enforcement, however, Abdullah faced a much more dangerous situation. He was thrown into a lockdown in a county jail in Minnesota, where he was denied medical help of any kind and allowed to see Sukra only on weekend visits. He was then shuttled from prison to prison throughout the United States in a cruel system of detention which was designed to deny detainees access to family, friends, and legal counsel. While incarcerated he discovered that under a 1996 federal statute, noncitizens convicted of "aggravated felonies" were subject not only to detention but to expulsion. Eventually an immigration judge helped to turn his rather innocuous guilty plea into a nightmare and ordered his deportation. In 2003, after spending twenty months in various jails and state prisons, he was told he would be sent home under supervision until his final removal from the United States.

Life in America also became terrifying for Anser Mehmood and his wife, Uzma, in the fall of 2001. The couple had emigrated from Pakistan along with their three children on "visiting visas" in 1994. Another son, Hassan, was later born in the United States. Political violence and turmoil in Karachi had forced the family to sell its business and seek a safer life in Bayonne, New Jersey, where the couple soon established a small trucking business, bought a home, and sent their children to local schools. "My life was great before September 11," she told interviewers. "My family did not have any problems with anyone and never felt any discrimination." Uzma was impressed that in her neighborhood people of different backgrounds, religions, and races all appeared to respect each other. She particularly cherished the fact that her children could attend a school across the street from her home and that she could watch them go to classes each day. For their part, her offspring valued the fact that everyone seemed friendly and that each child had his or her own bedroom.

Everything changed after 9/11. Neighbors began to look at them with suspicion. Even their children felt more uncomfortable at school with some students calling them "Muslim terrorists." Anser recalled that a few residents "taunted" Uzma because she wore a headscarf. She remembered standing outside her home one day hearing young people yell at her family, "They did it. They did it." For a moment she actually felt a tinge of responsibility for the dead at Ground Zero. On the morning of October 3, 2001, a large group of FBI agents and other government officials abruptly appeared at the family's front door. One burst into Uzma's bedroom as she slept and told her to join her husband in another room. Initially agents wanted to take Uzma in order to gain information on her brother, who was already under arrest due to an expired visa. Anser pleaded with the investigators not to take her away, for she was needed to care for their children, and offered to go in her stead. Law enforcement then charged him with having an expired visa as well and placed him under arrest, telling him that this was a minor violation that would most likely be resolved in a day or two after paying a small fine.

Nothing could have been further from the truth. Once Anser was in FBI custody, as with the case of so many immigrants rounded up after 9/11, Anser's status changed abruptly. He was thrown into a border patrol van with another Pakistani and two Tunisians and beaten by guards who broke both of his hands. He was also told not to ask any questions or "you will be dead." And his captors declared that he was not being arrested for any visa violation but because of the "World Trade Center attack." He was taken to the Metropolitan Detention Center in New York City, where he was thrown into solitary confinement for several months.[50]

Uzma and her children were left in turmoil. She had no word of her husband's whereabouts for days and was forced to go to a local police station in Bayonne to find any information she could. Finally she hired a lawyer who discovered the details of his detention in New York. The government still denied her a chance to see him for months. When she was finally able to meet with him again she discovered that he had been shackled. Both Uzma and Anser were reduced to tears. Broken and financially desperate, the woman now made arrangements to move back to Pakistan with her children. On the day she left, some children from her neighborhood came to watch their departure. A few seemed sad. But others—riddled with contempt rather than empathy—jeered at them and screamed that they were terrorists; "It's a good thing you are leaving."[51]

Uzma returned to Pakistan in February 2002; Anser met up with her three months later. In 2005 he still had no job and complained that the U.S. government had frozen his bank assets and equipment from his business. He described what a "shock" it was for him to absorb all that happened but felt something good came from the experience since he now felt "closer to Islam and Allah." He recalled that in America he had started to skip his prayers and drift from his religious beliefs. Uzma was bitter. She recalled how hard her spouse had worked in the United States to build his business and then they lost everything. She complained that they were not even allowed time to liquidate the assets they had. "What kind of justice system is that?"[52]

In January 2004 the American Civil Liberties Union (ACLU) filed a petition with the United Nations Working Group on Arbitrary Detentions alleging that the U.S. government had detained petitioners as suspected terrorists even where there was no evidence that they had engaged in criminal activity of any kind. The men had been imprisoned under a "hold until cleared" policy that presumed they were guilty until proven innocent. Yet, in many instances, they were still kept in confinement even when the FBI had cleared them of all charges. It goes without saying that the vast majority of such arrests after 9/11 were made against individuals of South Asian and Middle Eastern descent. The ACLU also charged that the government incarcerated the petitioners in inhumane conditions that included the wearing of hand and leg shackles and solitary confinement. After traveling to Pakistan to collect accounts from several Muslim men who had been deported, the ACLU publicized their charges and presented them to UN officials in Geneva.[53]

One of the cases publicized by the ACLU in its filing with the United Nations was that of Khaled Abu-Shabayek. Arriving in the United States in 1994, Abu-Shabayek applied for political asylum as a Palestinian living in Jordan. His application was denied, but he decided to remain in America with his wife and two children working in construction and running a small business on the side. The family rented a home in Raleigh, North Carolina, and his children were soon attending public schools. When he was arrested in 2002 he had an application for permanent resident status pending but was quickly sent to a series of detention centers for a period of five months before being sent back to Jordan. His wife and children had no choice but to follow him back to the Middle East.

Once they were back in their homelands, life for deportees like Abu-Shabayek became a daily struggle. Trained as an electrician, Abu-Shabayek found little work in Amman and ended up spending his days either looking for employment or hanging out in his brother's electronics store. A son dropped out of high school because he had trouble learning a new language after growing up speaking English in North Carolina. Savings from the United States allowed the family to get by for about a year, but soon the money was gone, and at the time he was interviewed by the ACLU, they were behind on their rent. They had to sell their car just to get some ready cash. A daughter exclaimed that the family was very worried about their finances and that "it's really hard to get money over here." She had even experienced harassment in school in Jordan for "being American." "Over there in America, you'd see us 24/7 happy," she said. "But over here we're really frustrated and angry."[54]

The War on Terror was fought in combat zones at home and abroad. The domestic campaign—steeped more in anger than in grief over casualties—was waged by belligerent patriots like police forces, immigration agents, and ordinary citizens who physically attacked and, in some instances, murdered people who were Muslims or looked like they were. It was not only bodies that were assaulted, moreover, but civil rights as well. Immigration roundups often led to the breakup of Arab and Muslim households in America on baseless charges. Plans Muslims had to build houses of worship were adamantly resisted, sometimes with rhetoric from well-educated Americans that can best be described as fear-mongering. Certainly there were those who joined the patriots' debate to resist this descent into racism and nativism and continued to strive for a more tolerant and caring version of what the nation should be. But the patriots who sought to avenge 9/11 and promote a right-wing version of American nationalism proved just how much the threads of love embedded in patriotic talk could be refashioned to sanction waves of fear and animosity.

Conclusion

A House Divided

· ·

Patriotism in America after 9/11 became a distinct theater of operations in the global war on terror pitting conflicting impulses of hatred and love against each other. Energized by the terrorist attacks, war-based patriots led by powerful political leaders launched an offensive not only to protect the homeland but sheathe it in a cultural cloak woven with threads of devotion, rectitude, anger, and fear. Enemies were annihilated, innocents were killed, and legal rights were abrogated. The result was a highly aggressive version of national loyalty intent upon turning violent actions into honorable deeds, dehumanizing others, and masking the tragic impact of the damage it produced. The American dream of these hostile patriots was no smokescreen; its adherents held real visions of a mighty and virtuous nation inhabited by exemplary citizens and heroic actors whose actions were moral in every way. Their belief in this century as it had been in previous ones was that excursions into episodes of brutality would in no way discredit the nobility of their venture.

Empathic patriots also wanted to safeguard their nation from further attacks, but they could not always countenance the aspirations of their more bellicose countrymen and countrywomen to inflict widespread viciousness in the world, unleash anger, and minimize the traumatic consequences of such actions. They came from all walks of life and were genuinely intent upon resisting efforts to rework the reality of human loss into noble deeds or harsh reprisals. Their mournful appeals were unsettling to more belligerent loyalists because their empathic inclinations threatened to undermine the position that violent actions were admirable, that the exercise of American power was solely a force for good in the world, and that the suspension of civil rights was acceptable. Expressions of bereavement and pain by those willing to bear witness to the tragedy of the war actually constituted an appeal for a more caring and compassionate society, a call that undermined assumptions about America's goodness. The voice and action of witnesses to the painful realities of war were often dismissed because the deployment of tragic memories, even the public mourning of the dead, raised the specter of the need for remediation or the implementation of liberal ideals such as due process, tolerance, and a deep concern for others.[1]

Most Americans were initially baffled by the attacks of 9/11. They had never heard of al-Qaeda and were not exactly sure what was taking place when the news of the planes hitting the Twin Towers appeared on their television screens. The decision of the Bush administration to launch a war on terrorism was not only an act of anger and retaliation for the brutal destruction visited upon the homeland but an attempt to replace this confusion with a coherent understanding of what had happened and what needed to be done to protect the nation in the aftermath of such a traumatic rupture. Instinctively the president turned to authoritarian solutions like the Patriot Act which enhanced the government's ability to curtail the civil rights of individuals and round up immigrants. He also invoked motifs of traditional patriotism and moral rectitude that readily legitimated military action against evildoers and celebrated the heroic acts of brave first responders and warriors.

This turn to a war-based patriotism reverberated throughout the culture. Large numbers of citizens rallied to the president's call to war and did not hesitate to write their representatives to let them know they backed their commander in chief. Impressive memorials were erected to diminish the human cost of the struggle at key sites of remembrance associated with 9/11; makeshift memorials replicating the emotional disarray of the attacks and the war were eventually taken down. News of the torture and killing of innocent people abroad by Americans was sometimes brushed aside and the dangerous designs of the terrorists were duly acknowledged. Soldiers back from battle fronts wrote memoirs and accounts of their experiences that endorsed the battle at hand and recounted the heroic exploits of courageous comrades. Many exalted over the vanquishing of enemies and the thrill of defending the land that they loved. Moviemakers sometimes cast a supportive glance at Americans who tracked down terrorists or braved danger to serve their country. Angry nativists attacked fellow residents in the homeland simply because they looked like the individuals who hijacked the planes on 9/11.

This surge of war-based patriotism was nurtured not only by the appeal of righteous rhetoric and nativist angst but by other factors as well. Certainly the existence of an all-volunteer military played a role. As Andrew Bacevich has argued, the all-volunteer force relieved most citizens of the obligation to contribute directly to the defense of the country and insulated them from the grim realities of that burden on a daily basis. Only a small portion of the populace now send loved ones directly into harm's way. Most families are spared the horrors of waiting for relatives to come home, caring for the traumatized, and burying their dead. Citizens can now fulfill patriotic duties by simply thanking soldiers for their service, which Americans do profusely. Bacevich makes the insightful point that the relationship between society and the military now rests more on symbolic slogans and gestures such as the surprise reunions of soldiers and loved ones at sporting events that allow citizens to "feel good" about a war with bitter realities. Others have suggested that the overflow of pornographic images in American culture with its emphasis on sex and violence—key themes in the photos from Abu Ghraib—has nurtured a fascination with and even some enjoyment in viewing human degradation which is at the heart of so many representations of war. We are simply used to seeing brutality enacted in all kinds of formats all the time. This might mean there is an exhaustion of empathy, although that is hard to measure. It certainly means, as historian Carolyn Dean has made clear, a failure on our part to contemplate and reflect upon a vital issue of our times: whether we have collectively failed to meet "the expectations of our own humanity" that are inscribed in an ethics of caring and concern for others.[2]

Divided by Terror argues, however, that the American public was not as insulated from grim realities as some have argued or devoid of empathic instincts. Even before the existence of the all-volunteer force and certainly since the experience of Vietnam, many citizens have demonstrated a deep connection with the fallout from American warfare and wrestled with the implications of trauma and tragedy. If the public had been as quiescent as many assumed, war-based patriots would not have had to mount the aggressive tactics that they did to mute expressions of confusion, pain, and sorrow or romanticize violent acts. It was the frequency of the empathic response that signaled not only the fact that Americans were split over the war and its implications but also that they were not immune to recognizing its human cost. Even among families that experienced the weight of war more directly, studies like those of anthropologist Zoe Wool at Walter Reed Hospital found a distinct split among veterans between those who accepted highly patriotic symbols and rhetoric as valid explanations of what they had endured or why they had to suffer and others who could not be comforted by such traditional rhetoric.[3]

Traumatic ruptures stood at the heart of the empathic patriots' rebellion and the patriots' debate itself. They explained why there was so much resistance to the calls of war-based patriots to see the nation's excursion into war in purely honorable and virtuous ways. Millions of citizens readily accepted the need to defend an innocent nation, the redemptive promise of its military actions, and aspirations of a right-wing nationalism. It was never the case, however, that this more aggressive version of the war and the nation itself completely captured the political and cultural landscape. In an era steeped in the legacies of a failed war in Southeast Asia, revelations of racism and sexism in the American past and present, and a constant news cycle featuring images of the fallen towers and human tragedy in Iraq, trauma reverberated throughout the culture. Citizens who did not experience harrowing events directly still managed to feel they had been affected by the horror and suffering around them. In a sense they joined the ranks of a "second order" of witnessing and were moved to reject the rhetoric of a redemptive war and its possible numbing effects. They passionately pitted their mood of heartbreak and disillusionment against those who preached the virtue of our violence or even the need for retaliation. The result became a massive cultural exercise in introspection.

Even as Americans marched in a collective patriotic parade after 9/11, well before the invasion of Iraq, individuals devastated by personal losses or those who sympathized with them assembled altars in their homes, stuck figures of angels and white crosses in the ground, wept in church, and wrote their representatives to stop the war and the carnage it produced. Soon soldiers back from the fronts in Afghanistan and Iraq penned numerous memoirs and novels attesting to the sorrow they felt over the loss of comrades and the inability of patriotic rhetoric to soothe their souls. Filmmakers crafted scores of feature films and documentaries that detailed the relentless cost of the war in terms of shattered families and injured people in other lands. Artists and photographers backed this effort by producing an array of images designed to question the human cost of the entire enterprise. Defenders of a more empathic patriotism realized all citizens were in the war together and envisioned a nation focused more on the need to be compassionate, to consider the feelings and rights of others, than one riveted to visions of power and supremacy.

Always inherent in American political culture, the debate over patriotism and American identity takes center stage in times of crisis, especially foreign wars. But it can also sound its battle call during a domestic crisis such as in August 2017, when citizens violently clashed in the streets of Charlottesville, Virginia. Far-right extremists, a loose association of radical groups cobbled together under the term "alt-right" and captivated by notions of white supremacy, anti-Semitism, and anti-immigrant animus clashed with progressives intent on preserving a version of America sympathetic to the needs of all citizens regardless of their race or religion. The immediate cause of the fight was not the War on Terror but the existence of Confederate monuments in the city and the legacy of intolerance they represented. Alt-right marchers carrying Nazi images saw the memorials as cultural props supporting a heritage of white racism in America. They were opposed to the appeals of empathic patriots intent on forging a more tolerant sense of national identity rooted in a real regard for others. Certainly not all supporters of a war-based sense of patriotism who supported the global fight against terrorism sympathized with the white nationalists who were at the center of the Virginia riot. Millions of citizens supported the campaign against terror that was waged at home and abroad and were not disposed to dismiss entirely the ideal of civil rights for all to the extent many agitators at Charlottesville did. They simply felt the homeland needed to be defended and the troops supported whatever the costs. But the dominant logic and symbolism that drove the war and war-based patriotism did convey support for ideas the extreme right and white identity zealots found attractive, including an unwillingness to confront the violent and hateful side of American culture and a contempt for human-centered ideas and those who advocated them. A glimpse of this disdain can be grasped in memoirs by Navy SEALs that constantly made negative references to a "liberal press" and Barack Obama and in the frequent attacks upon citizens who mourned in public and who insisted on exposing the trauma American actions brought to the world.[4]

President Donald Trump created an uproar when he failed to support the compassionate patriots by declining to condemn the racist outburst at Charlottesville in unequivocal terms. His 2016 election campaign, marked by an utter disdain for immigrants and anyone else who did not rally to his cause, had already breathed new life into the alt-right movement. Watching the commotion in Virginia from his golf resort in New Jersey, the chief executive at first did tweet an appeal for calm and proclaimed that "there is no place for this kind of violence in America." He quickly retreated from this stand, however, when he declared that there had been an "egregious display of hatred, bigotry, and violence on many sides," a statement that suggested an equivalency between the views of white supremacists and the defenders of civil rights for all. He added to the controversy when, speaking at a press briefing, he claimed that the "alt-left came charging" at the rally and proved to be "very violent." And he insisted that many in the crowd were at the rally simply to prevent the removal of the statue of Robert E. Lee and carried no hostile intent. According to the president, when it came to violence, "blame both sides."[5]

Critical responses to the racist rally and Trump's remark were widespread. Empathic patriots like Barack Obama chastised the president for not standing up to discrimination. Senator John McCain called the turmoil a "confrontation between our better angels and our worst demons." He felt that "white supremacists and neo-Nazis are by definition opposed to American patriotism and the ideals that define us." Cory Gardner, a Republican senator from Colorado, tweeted that the president needed to call "evil by its name." Orrin Hatch, a senator from Utah, argued that his brother did not give his life in World War II for "Nazi ideas to go unchallenged here at home." David Duke, however, a former head of the Ku Klux Klan who attended the rally in Virginia, claimed that white supremacists were bent upon taking back "our country" and cautioned Trump about being too critical of the alt-right because people like them had helped put the president in power much more than "radical leftists."[6]

Trump's election in 2016 had in many ways sanctioned the type of belligerent patriotism unleashed by the War on Terror. His political dream of making the nation "great again" rested on hostile impulses more than empathic ones and drew its oxygen from the constant pursuit of enemies—a hint of how far militarization had seeped from the field of battle into the broader society—and a dream of authoritarianism rather than human equality. Using cruelty and anger as "bonding mechanisms," the president—who famously hugged the American flag at a meeting of the Conservative Political Action Conference in 2019—urged his supporters at spirited rallies to wave the flag and draw upon their most belligerent impulses to attack protesters who differed with them, jail political rivals, and mock women who marched against sexual harassment. He had based a good deal of his election campaign on the need to keep immigrants out of America and demonizing Arabs and Muslims—ideals already nurtured by the immediate response to 9/11. In one moment he even falsely claimed that he recalled seeing "thousands and thousands" of "Arabs" in New Jersey cheering the fall of the Twin Towers. His "America First" agenda sought to reinforce the nation's power in the world rather than its "better angels" and stoked sentiments of fear and hatred—emotions better suited to fostering division rather than cohesion and compassion. Not surprisingly the number of neo-Nazi groups in the United States rose in the year after Trump's election. In 2017 the number of anti-Muslim organizations reached its highest level ever in America and at least thirteen states introduced anti-Sharia legislation. There was also a marked rise in anti-Semitism including the shooting of eleven Jewish-Americans in Pittsburgh by a man who harbored fears of an immigrant invasion he thought was being assisted, in part, by Jewish relief organizations.[7]

The early years of Trump's reign saw not only the continued unfolding of his aggressive patriotism, however, but an intensification of the patriots' debate with a renewed pushback from empathic citizens committed to visions of a more compassionate society. When African American football players like Colin Kaepernick chose to kneel at National Football League games starting in 2016 during the playing of the national anthem, Trump called for their teams to fire them. Howard Bryant, who has studied the relationship between black athletes and dissent over time, concluded that since 9/11 such opposition has drawn more criticism because patriotism has increasingly become conflated with militarism and authoritarianism. When asked about the controversy over the football players, however, Barack Obama acknowledged that it was important to honor the flag and the national anthem because they helped hold Americans together, but also insisted that the athletes were simply exercising their constitutional rights to express their opinions. More to the point, Obama asked for understanding from both sides. He called upon the protesters to appreciate the pain that relatives who lost loved ones in the war might feel when they saw someone refusing to stand for the national anthem. Realizing that everyone hurts, however, he also asked all citizens to consider the pain racial minorities have encountered as well. Clearly, the forty-fourth president and millions of other citizens did not want a patriotism devoid of empathic sentiments.[8]

Empathic patriots rose again in a tidal wave of support for a more caring and just society in 2020 in the aftermath of the killing of George Floyd, an African American man whose air supply was cut off by the force of a policeman's knee. Public protests deriding police brutality and affirming the fact that "black lives matter" were immediate and widespread. Massive marches called for an end to systemic racism in America, a painful reality whose exposure always threatened to undermine the noble view of America and reveal the brutality it often inflicted at home and abroad. War-based patriots like Trump and Senator Tom Cotton of Arkansas quickly struck back. Trump debunked the protesters, choosing to see them as threats to law and order rather than advocates for a more just society. Cotton, who served in the infantry in both Afghanistan and Iraq and who was moved to join the War on Terror after seeing news coverage of 9/11, joined

Trump in dismissing the legitimacy of those who marched and even called for a show of military force to tamp down public pleas for compassion and justice. Trump and Cotton joined a long line of belligerent patriots who had already been quick to reject protests and highly visible pleas for a more empathetic society from Gold Star Mothers, traumatized veterans, and citizens horrified by Trump's harsh immigration policies. Trump even threatened to send American troops to Seattle to quell protests in the aftermath of Floyd's killing, calling those in the streets nothing more than "domestic terrorists." Seattle's mayor, Jenny Durkan, quickly rebuked the president, however, and joined the patriots' debate by arguing that what the people in the streets were doing was not terrorism but "patriotism."

Belligerent patriots cannot survive without fostering hatred and fear toward enemies; hostility trumps compassion for them every time. And so to celebrate the Fourth of July in 2020 Trump stood in front of Mount Rushmore and told the American people that they were now threatened not by terrorists from abroad but by a homegrown movement dedicated to a "far left fascism" that was intent upon destroying "our beloved American way of life" and teaching children "to hate America." Not surprisingly, as he promised to do battle with loyalists who clamored for an end to racism and injustice, he kept silent about the thread in "our history" that was filled with the voices of those who have suffered, have grieved, and now faced the terrorism of a dangerous virus that was rapidly infecting the homeland. Concerns for those Americans would be left to loyalists with more sympathetic inclinations.

Acknowledgments

It might not take a village to write a book, but the effort certainly requires a support group. I would like to thank Dr. Barbara Truesdell of Indiana University for helping me in numerous ways throughout this venture. Early in the research Nancy Ashley of the university's history department scanned thousands of pages on my behalf. At the Library of Congress, Ann Hoog and Peggy Bulger assisted me in using the library's vast collection of material dealing with the public response to the 9/11 attacks. At the University of Virginia's Small Special Collections Library, Elizabeth Wilkerson and Lauren Work patiently helped me navigate the papers of John Warner. I also received expert aid from Jody Brumage in using the papers of Robert Byrd at Shepherd University. Similar assistance was offered by Ashley Taylor with the John Murtha papers at the University of Pittsburgh. At the National Park Service offices at Shanksville, Pennsylvania, Barbara Black provided space for me to read visitors' responses to the site commemorating the crash of Flight 93. Jan Seidler Ramirez also helped to further my work at the 9/11 Memorial and Museum collections in New York. Wendy Chmielewski facilitated my access to materials at the Swarthmore College Peace Collection. Edward Linenthal and Marita Sturken proved to be cooperative scholars by reading drafts of my manuscript. I appreciated their remarks. At the University of North Carolina Press, Debbie Gershenowitz demonstrated her superior skills as both an editor and a scholar through steadfast support and insightful suggestions. Finally, my wife, Donna, again helped me in numerous ways as she has throughout my scholarly career.

Notes

Introduction

1. On the immediate response of George W. Bush and Dick Cheney to the 9/11 attacks, see Mayer, *Dark Side*, 3–8, 101–10, 292; Holloway, *Cultures of the War on Terror*, 4–7, 43, 60. On the motives of al-Qaeda and its deep-seated anti-Semitism, see Kuntzel, *Jihad and Jew-Hatred*; Mark Danner, "Taking Stock of the 'Forever Wars,'" *New York Times*, September 11, 2005.

2. On the tension between patriotic myths and mourning, see Connerton, *Spirit of Mourning*. See Margalit, *Ethics of Memory*, 31, on mourning as a form of caring. Johnston, "Patriotism Which Is Not One," 285–312; Johnston, *Truth about Patriotism*, 2, 13–16; Johnston, *American Dionysia*, 3–7; Butler, *Precarious Life*, 19–21; Faludi, *Terror Dream*, 13, 165–95.

3. For a discussion on uncritical versions of patriotism as opposed to those containing a "democratic critique of political, economic, and social injustice," see Hansen, *Lost Promise of Patriotism*, xvii. Kopecek, "Human Rights," 570–602; Lyons, "Fragmented Nationalism," 377–418; Bacevich, *New American Militarism*, 147; Bryant, *Heritage*, 100–107; Betz, "Contemporary Right-Wing Radicalism," 209–16; Nandy, "Patriotism and the Left"; Nussbaum, *For the Love of Country?*, ix–xiv, 4–5. On the need for mourning the dead to temper aggressive forms of nationalism, see Butler, *Precarious Life*, 19–21. On the idea of "virtuous victimization," see Eagle, "Virtuous Violence, Visceral Violence," 148. For a perceptive account of the struggle between political and personal love during World War I, see Huebner, *Love and Death*.

4. George W. Bush speech of September 14, 2001 at www.presidencyucsb.edu /ws/?pid=63645. See Noon, "Cold War Revival," 75–99. Noon argued that for "neoconservatives" military power was fundamental to a sense of what Americans were as a nation and that our values and ideals had to be imposed upon the rest of the world.

5. Collins, *Homeland Mythology*, 17–19; Haberski, *God and War*, 1–3, 197–203; Slotkin, *Gunfighter Nation*.

6. My understanding of the impact of trauma on nation-states has been influenced by Edkins, *Trauma and the Memory of Politics*, xiii–xv, 1–7. For a discussion of "numbness" and "empathy fatigue," see Dean, *Fragility of Empathy*, 1–15. Ahmed, *Cultural Politics of Emotion*, 2–15; Mathy, *Melancholy Politics*, 11; Roger I. Simon, Sharon Rosenberg, and Claudia Eppert, "Introduction," in Simon, Rosenberg, and Eppert, *Between Hope and Despair*, 1–8.

7. Stowe, "Pericles at Gettysburg and Ground Zero," 686–87; LaCapra, "Revisiting the Historians' Debate," 81–82. Butler, *Precarious Life*, xiv, 19–23, makes the

case as well for the need for critical reflection on acts of aggression and brutality. Vasi and Strang, "Civil Liberty in America," 1716–64.

8. Lawson, *Patriot Fires*, 2–7, 11–14. Faust, *Republic of Suffering*, 24–25, 165, explains the rising religious overtones contained within patriotic expressions in the era of the Civil War. See the insightful discussion on levels of engagement between American citizens and the reality of death in the various wars they have fought in Dudziak, "'You Didn't See Him Lying,'" 1–16.

9. Blight, *Race and Reunion*, 300–305; Haas, *Sacrificing Soldiers*, 2–6.

10. Blight, *Race and Reunion*, 8, 132; Janney, *Remembering the Civil War*, 5–9; Stowe, "Agonistic Homecoming," 681–91; Foster, *Ghosts of the Confederacy*, 88–103.

11. Gerstle, *American Crucible*, 8, 88–92. On the expansion of government authority, see Capozzola, *Uncle Sam Wants You*; O'Leary, *To Die For*, 59–66.

12. Capozzola, *Uncle Sam Wants You*, 12–13; Higham, *Strangers in the Land*, 264, 281.

13. McElya, *Politics of Mourning*, 2–3, 187–89.

14. Trout, *On the Battlefield of Memory*, 218.

15. Borgwardt, *New Deal for the World*, 28–29.

16. Bodnar, *"Good War" in American Memory*, 200–202; Fried, *Russians Are Coming!*, 87–92.

17. Bodnar, *"Good War" in American Memory*, 35–36.

18. Appy, *American Reckoning*, xvii–xviii.

19. Hass, *Carried to the Wall*, 1–3, 17; Savage, *Monument Wars*, 272–83.

20. Hagopian, *Vietnam War in American Memory*, 16–17.

21. Hagopian, *Vietnam War in American Memory*, 233–68.

22. Booth, *Communities of Memory*, 15–25; 70; Stow, "Pericles at Gettysburg and Ground Zero," 195–208.

Chapter 1

1. Woodward, *Bush at War*, 170–71. See Nathan Guttman, "Two Years after 9/11, Anti-Semitic Theories Are Still Going Strong," *Haaretz*, April 9, 2003, http://www.haaretz.com/1.5370338 (May 5, 2019).

2. Updegraff, Silver, and Holman, "Searching for and Finding Meaning," 1–51; Schuster, "National Survey," 1507–21.

3. Michael G. Long and Tracy Wenger Sadd, "Introduction: Why Rethink Christianity and Patriotism," in Long and Sadd, *God and Country?*, 1–3, argue that there is a conservative version of U.S. patriotism that is uncritical of the nation and tied closely to the exercise of military power. On the conflicting emotions after 9/11, see Gross and Snyder-Korber, "Introduction," 368–84; "Madison Avenue Rises a Wave of Patriotic Fervor," *New York Times*, October 8, 2001, C10; "The Stuff of Patriotism and Cheap Too," *New York Times*, October 14, 2001, WK7. On the confusion generated by the attacks, also see Dudziak, *War Time*, 95–101.

4. Damon Wilkinson, Personal Account, September 11 Digital Archive, Library of Congress, the September 11th Digital Archives, Library of Congress, archived at the Library of Congress Web Archives, www.loc.gov. This archive was created by a

merger of several different projects aimed at collecting firsthand accounts of 9/11. Ann Hoog and Peggy Bulge, folklorists at the American Folklife Center, started asking people trained in anthropology and folklore to conduct interviews with citizens about their reactions. Hoog was motivated partially by the fact that the Folklife Center had undertaken similar interviews in 1941 just after the attack on Pearl Harbor. Later, similar material gathered by the Roy Rosenzweig Center for the History and the New Media at George Mason University and the American Social History Project was merged with the materials the Library of Congress had gathered.

5. Laura Barti, Personal Account, September 11 Digital Archives, Library of Congress, archived at www.loc.gov.

6. Cynthia Fukami, Personal Account, September 11 Digital Archives, Library of Congress, archived at www.loc.gov.

7. Written statements submitted to the Library of Congress from West Georgia College, box 10, September 11th Documentary Project, American Folklife Center, Library of Congress.

8. Recorded interviews with Janet Freeman, November 10, 2001; Jessica Kardon, October 10, 2001; Maureen Delaney, November 11, 2001; Sound Recordings 139, 144, 153, September 11 Digital Archives, Library of Congress, archived at www .loc.gov.

9. Recorded interviews with Carol Reed, Peter Rouderbush, and Lorna Tuck, Iowa Sound Recordings 113, 160, American Folklife Center, September 11 Digital Archives, Library of Congress, archived at www.loc.gov.

10. Chico State University interviews, box 10, September 11 Documentary Project, American Folklife Center, Library of Congress.

11. Knoxville Writers Guild Wall of Unity files, box 11, September 11 Documentary Project, American Folklife Center, Library of Congress.

12. Bennett, *Why We Fight*, 10–14.

13. *Indianapolis Star*, September 16, 2001, D6–D7; Francis X. Cline, "The Shooting Range," *New York Times*, October 5, 2001, B9; Jim Ruktenberg, "Fox Portrays a War of Good and Evil and Many Applaud," *New York Times*, December 3, 2001, C1.

14. Brian Gilmore, "Stand by the Man," 38–45; Cheryl Poinsette Brown, "I Pledge Allegiance," 29–38; and Karin L. Stanford, "The War Within: African-American Public Opinion on the War against Terrorism," 95–113, all in Malveaux and Green, *Paradox of Loyalty*. Louis Menand, "Faith, Hope, and Clarity," *New Yorker*, September 16, 2002, 101; Goldstone, "African-American Professor Reflects," 29–34; Charles Whitaker, "Black America and the U.S. Crisis," *Ebony* 57, December 2001, 164–70; Shaw, "'Two Warring Ideals,'" 20–37; Jesse Jackson, "No Test, No Testimony," September 16, 2001, in Simmons and Thomas, *9.11.01*, 104–15; Sharpton, *Al on America*, vii–xii; John Edgar Wideman, "Whose War," *Harper's Magazine*, March 2002, 33–39; Mathilde Roza, in "America under Attack: Unity and Division after 9/11," in Rubin and Verheul, *American Multiculturalism after 9/11*, 105–7.

15. Janet Elder, "The Poll: Public Voices Overwhelmingly Support the Use of Force against Terrorism," *New York Times*, September 17, 2001, A15. For a contrary view, see Elizabeth Becker, "Marchers Opposed Waging War against Terrorists,"

New York Times, October 1, 2001, B17, which describes a march in Washington, D.C., sponsored by the Washington Peace Center, which felt that "our grief is not a cry for war" and that perpetrators of the attacks should be tried as criminals for crimes against humanity, not be used as a reason to wage military conflict.

16. Louis, *United We Stand*, 1–20; *Herald-Falls* (Fall River, MA, September 3, 2001), 3; Gallup Poll, http://gallup.com/poll/1740/Post9/11-Patriotism-Steadfast.apsx (accessed August 1, 2016); Michael Ross, "Poll: U.S. Patriotism Continues to Soar," www .nbcnews.com/id/8410977/ns/us_news/t/poll-patriotism-continues-soar-#/WSHZN ylgpo (August 1, 2016).

17. Charlton Heston, "President's Column," *American Rifleman*, January 2002 14; Wayne LaPierre, "Standing Guard," *American Rifleman*, September 2002, 12. Heston supported LaPierre's point about arming pilots in "President's Column," *American Rifleman*, June 2002, 12. LaPierre, *Guns, Freedom, and Terrorism*.

18. Aaron Brune, Personal Account with email responses from Jennifer Worsham and Joan Abbot, September 11 Digital Archive, Library of Congress, archived at www.loc.gov.

19. John Kotzian and Lulie Loiseau, Personal Accounts, September 11 Digital Archives, Library of Congress, archived at www.loc.gov.

20. Kotzian and Loiseau, Personal Accounts, Iowa Sound Recordings, 113, 156, 166; interview with Adam Gospodarek, September 13, 2001; interview with Lai Bic Ha Olsen, November 7, 2001; and interviews with students at West Georgia State University, box 10, all in September 11 Documentary Project, American Folklife Center, Library of Congress.

21. "Letters for Flight 93 Heroes," Personal Accounts, September 11 Digital Archives, Library of Congress, archived at www.loc.gov.

22. Beata Suranyi, Personal Account, September 11 Digital Archives, Library of Congress, archived at www.loc.gov.

23. See http://usatoday30.usatoday.com/news/sept11/poll-result.htm (accessed January 7, 2018). See also E. J. Dionne and Thomas E. Mann, "Polling and Public Opinion: The Good, The Bad and the Ugly," 2003, www.brookings.edu/research /articles/2003/06/summer (January 7, 2018).

24. On Tom Brokaw and Dan Rather, see Eisman, "Media Manipulation," 55–72. Edy and Meirick, "Wanted Dead or Alive," 119–41. Edy and Meirick found two competing frames dominating the nightly news coverage in October 2001: the war frame and the crime frame. The war frame was supported strongly by those who wanted vengeance; those who supported the crime frame wanted the perpetrators brought to justice tended to be motivated by a concern over harming innocent civilians. Overall, the network news, in their study, generally supported going to war rather than looking for criminals. Robert Jensen, "The Problem with Patriotism: Steps toward the Redemption of American Journalism and Democracy," in Artz and Kamalipour, *Bring 'Em On*, 67–83.

25. Rumsfeld, *Known and Unknown*, 114; Woodward, *Bush at War*, 17–18, 49, 60, 205; Haberski, *God and War*, 201–3. On the cultural power of the idea of war and its ability to upset normal moral and legal standards, see Dudziak, *War Time*, 3–7. Rice, *No Higher Honor*, 80.

26. *Selected Speeches of President George W. Bush, 2001–08,* http://georgebush -whitehouse.archives.gov; Ivie and Giner, *Hunt the Devil,* 12–18.

27. *Selected Speeches of President George W. Bush, 2001–08.*

28. Bacevich, *New American Militarism,* 1–3, 147.

29. Bush, *Decision Points,* 3–4, 30–34.

30. Bush, *Decision Points,* 127, 146–48.

31. Bush, *Decision Points,* 204.

32. Keen, *Endless War,* 4, 25, 97, uses the term "magical thinking" and suggests that it tends to blunt rational discussions of what happened on 9/11 and what could be done about it. On the tendency of Bush and Dick Cheney to use references to the "old West," see West and Carey, "(Re)enacting Frontier Justice," 379–412. Sen, *Identity and Violence.*

33. Frank Newport, "Overwhelming Support for War Continues," Gallup Poll, November 29, 2001, http://gallup.com/poll/5083/Overwhleming-Support-War -Continues.

34. Robert Worth, "In Three Languages Urgently Chanting for Peace," *New York Times,* October 8, 2001, B12.

35. See *New York Times,* October 9, 2001, A24; September 21, 2001, A24.

36. *New York Times,* September 22, 2001, A24.

37. Potorti, *September 11 Families for Peaceful Tomorrows,* 26, 31–33; Rita Lazar, "Opinion Essay," September 11 Families for Peaceful Tomorrows Papers, box 3, Swarthmore College Peace Collection.

38. Potorti, *September 11 Families for Peaceful Tomorrows,* 13–22.

39. Potorti, *September 11 Families for Peaceful Tomorrows,* 24–25.

40. See the documentary film *In Our Son's Name* (Lightfoot Films, 2015). Angela Alaimo O'Donnell, "In Our Son's Name," *National Catholic Reporter* (May 18, 2015).

41. Potorti, *September 11 Families for Peaceful Tomorrows,* 54; Potorti, "Transforming Personal Grief into Global Healing: Survivors of Violence Converge to Advocate Peace," *Peacework* 33 (September 6, 2006), copy in box 6, Families for Peaceful Tomorrows Papers, DG 244, Press Clippings file, 2006, Swarthmore College Peace Collections. See "Afghans Portraits of Grief: The Civilian/Innocent Victims of U.S. Bombing in Afghanistan," peacefultomorrows.org/wp-content/uploads /2012/01/AfghanPortraitsOfGrief.pdf (August 15, 2016).

42. Potorti, *September 11 Families for Peaceful Tomorrows,* 144–45. See emails to Potorti, Correspondence File, 2002, September 11 Families for Peaceful Tomorrows Papers, DG 244, box 3, Swarthmore College Peace Collection.

43. See Rory Carroll, "Bloody Evidence of US Blunder," *The Guardian,* January 6, 2002, http://www.theguardian.com/world/2002/jan/07/afghanistan.rorycarroll (July 7, 2017).

44. Maney, Woehrle, and Coy, "Harnessing and Challenging Hegemony," 357–81. This study looked at the official statements of nine "recognized peace movements" between September 11, 2001, and March 31, 2002. The authors found in these statements a desire to see in the emotions of the era a chance for the nation to reassert "its true values" and draw on a "humanitarian heritage" to work for social improvements rather than embark upon a violent war.

45. The letter to George W. Bush can be found in *Pax Christi International Newsletter*, December 2001. Chiba and Schoenbaum, *Peace Movements and Pacifism after 9/11*.

46. U.S. Conference of Catholic Bishops, "Pastoral Letter: Living with Faith and Hope after September 11," November 14, 2001, www.usccb.org/resources/pastoral -message-living-faith-and-hope-after-September-11 (November 14, 2001).

47. "Angry Letters to One Member of Congress Who Voted against the War on Terror," www.theatlantic/Politics/Archive/2014/09/the-vindication-of-barbara-lee -38084 (August 4, 2016) (accessed August 4, 2016).

48. See Dower, *Cultures of War*, 94–101, 299–301. Anderson, *Bush's War*, 94; Bodnar, *"Good War" in American Memory*, 243; King and Wells, *Framing the Iraq War Endgame*, 33.

49. Sound Recording 6358A (Washington, DC), 636A (Burlington, NC), 6360A (Bloomington, IN), "After the Day of Infamy: Man in the Street Interviews," American Folklife Center, Library of Congress, archived at www.loc.gov.

50. Sound Recordings, 6361B (Nashville, TN), 6358A (Washington, DC), "After the Day of Infamy: Man in the Street Interviews, American Folklife Center, Library of Congress, archived at www.loc.gov.

Chapter 2

1. Kirk Savage, "Trauma, Healing, and the Therapeutic Monument," in Sherman and Nardin, *Terror, Culture, Politics*, 103–20; Savage, *Monument Wars*, 272–83. Erika Doss also argues that contemporary American memorials have been more likely to reflect "historical trauma" rather than conceal its existence. Doss, *Memorial Mania*, 3–7, 47–49, 122, 159.

2. Sherman, "Naming and the Violence of Place," in Sherman and Nardin, *Terror, Culture, Politics*, 121–45, argues that the names of the dead at Ground Zero have been expropriated by political interests. Maureen Dowd, "Unbearable Lightness of Memory," *New York Times*, November 30, 2003, WK9.

3. On sanctification, see Foote, *Shadowed Ground*, 5–15; Barthes, *Mythologies*.

4. On the idea of "strategic remembrance," as opposed to coming to terms with a more difficult past, see Roger I. Simon, Sharon Rosenberg, and Claudia Eppert, "Introduction," in Simon, Rosenberg, and Eppert, *Between Hope and Despair*, 1–8.

5. See Glen Collins, "Vessels of a City's Grief," *New York Times* (March 8, 2002), B1. See *Portraits 9/11/01*, 133, 146–47; Snyder-Korber, "'Portraits of Grief,'" 451–78.

6. Greenspan, *Battle for Ground Zero*, 10–12. Paul Christopher Johnson, "Savage Civil Religion," *Numen*, 52, no. 3 (2005), 289–324, argues that the "popular religiosity" manifested at the site "proffered no political objective" and would give way to a more "instrumental civil religion" with specific goals such as the invasion of Iraq.

7. Low, "Memorialization of September 11th," 326–39.

8. Sally Jenkins, "9/11 Memorials: The Story of the Cross at Ground Zero," *Washington Post*, September 3, 2011, http://www.washingtonpost.com/politics/9-11/-memorials (July 11, 2016); Simko, *Politics of Consolation*, chap. 7.

9. Skita, "Patriotism or National Understanding," 1995–2005; *Lincoln* (Nebraska) *Journal*, October 15, 2001, D2; *New York Times*, October 1, 2001, E1. The term "civic piety" is drawn from Hariman and Lucaites, *No Caption Needed*, 93–136.

10. Giuliani, *Leadership*, 121–31; Goldberger, *Up from Zero*, xiii; Nobel, *Sixteen Acres*, 12–19; Aronson, *Who Owns the Dead*, 10.

11. Greenspan, *Battle for Ground Zero*, 22.

12. Nobel, *Sixteen Acres*, 138–40.

13. Libeskind, *Breaking Ground*, 19–51; Rosenfeld, *After Auschwitz*, 180–89; Bodnar, *"Good War" in American Memory*, 219–23.

14. Greenspan, *Battle for Ground Zero*, 33–34; Young, *Stages of Memory*, 32; Sturken, "Aesthetics of Absence," 311–25; Nobel, *Sixteen Acres*, 235; Aronson, *Who Owns the Dead*, 9–10, 43. Aronson, 48, 234–35, also describes the controversy over dumping debris filled with human remains from Ground Zero at the Fresh Kills landfill on Staten Island. Many members viewed this site and what it contained as an affront to the memory of dead loved ones. Steps were taken to minimize such an insult. A Disaster Mortuary Operational Response Team was created to sift through the rubble using DNA to search for any trace of human remains. The remains were then identified (some 8,000 pieces were never identified) and eventually placed behind a wall in the new museum at Ground Zero where grieving kin could visit them in a special room removed from public view. Many relatives never accepted this solution and continued to complain that the LMDC had "usurped" the right of the next of kin to determine the final resting place of their loved ones.

15. Levitt, "Speaking Memory, Building History," 65–78; Greenspan, *Battle over Ground Zero*, 131–43; Debra Burlingame, "The Great Ground Zero Heist," *Wall Street Journal*, June, 7, 2005.

16. Nobel, *Sixteen Acres*, 248–51.

17. Young, *Stages of Memory*, 25, 62–63. Also see Young's essay, "The Stages of Memory at Ground Zero," in Stier and Landres, *Religion, Violence, Memory, and Place*, 214–34. Goldberger, *Up from Zero*, 228.

18. Goldberger, *Up from Zero*, 206–7; Sturken, "Aesthetics of Absence," 311–25; Sturken, *Tourists of History*, 7, 221, 229, 248, 252.

19. Patricia Cohen, "At Museum on 9/11: Talking through an Identity Crisis," *New York Times*, June 2, 2012; Sturken, "9/11 Memorial Museum," 471–90; Greenspan, *Battle for Ground Zero*, 205–17; Adam Gopnik, "Stones and Bones: Visiting the 9/11 Memorial Museum," *New Yorker*, July 7 and 14, 2014; Sarah Capko, "Tasteless Photo," *Chicago Tribune*, September 14, 2001, 30; Tom Junod, "The Falling Man: An Unforgettable Story," *Esquire*, September 9, 2016, http://www.esquire.com/news-politics/a48031/the-falling-man-tom-junod (December 3, 2018). See the documentary film "9/11: The Falling Man." Seidler-Ramirez, "Collecting the National Conversation," 79–111. Seidler-Ramirez offers an insightful discussion of the decision to remove photos of people jumping from the towers from the "central

visitor pathway" of the museum. For a review of the museum and the observations on the presentation of the photos of the victims, see Sodaro, *Exhibiting Atrocity*, 153.

20. Manning, *Unmeasured Strength*, 182.

21. Manning, *Unmeasured Strength*, 14–15, 113.

22. Fontana, *Widow's Walk*, 1–10, 31.

23. Fontana, *Widow's Walk*, 35–37, 57, 81–87.

24. Fontana, *Widow's Walk*, 156–67.

25. "New York Voices: Eulogy by Marian Fontana delivered at the Memorial Service at St. Francis Church, Oct. 17, 2001," New York Voices, http://www.thirteen.org/nyvoices/transcripts/eulogy.html (June 14, 2016).

26. Fontana, *Widow's Walk*, 340, 350.

27. Kemper, *Rubble*, 86–87.

28. Kemper, *Rubble*, 86–87; "Among the Angels," *New York Post*, December 12, 2002, 27; Dennis McKeon Interview with Wendy Pellegrino, April 14, 2005, copy in National September 11 Memorial and Museum, Oral History Archives; Seidler-Ramirez, "Collecting the National Conservation," 110.

29. Gabrielle Glaser, "Father's Day after 9/11," *New York Times*, June 16, 2002, WE1; *Westchester Journal*, September 11, 2011, 1.

30. Sheehy, *Middletown*, 53, 101.

31. Sheehy, *Middletown*, 63, 76, 117.

32. Sheehy, *Middletown*, 134.

33. Breitweiser, *Wake-Up Call*, 48–49.

34. Sheehy, *Middletown*, 291–93.

35. Kevin Coyne, "Remembering from a Distance," *New York Times*, September 10, 2006, M1; "New Jersey Selects Its Memorial," *New York Times*, July 1, 2004, E3; "Empty Sky Memorial Opens in Jersey City Emotional Ceremony," *Newark Star Ledger*, September 10, 2011, www.N.J.com/news/index.ssf/2001/09/911_memorial_Jersey_city.html (January 8, 2018).

36. Cheney, *In My Time*, 4.

37. "Secretary Salazar, Governor Rendell, Senator Casey and Others Break Ground," U.S. Dept. of Interior, http://www.doi.gov/news/photoss/2009_11_07-photo (November 7, 2009); Sean Hamill, "After 8 Years Work Starts at a Sept. 11 Site," *New York Times*, November 8, 2009, 30.

38. Riley, *Angel Patriots*, 4–10. The impact of religion and patriotism in framing the site is also discussed in Thompson, *From Memory to Memorial*, 138.

39. See oral history interview with Wallace Miller, July 19, 2007, by Kathie Schaffer, National Park Service Collections, Shanksville, PA.

40. These messages are taken from "Temporary Memorial Book and Ambassador Log Books, 2003–2004," and the "National Memorial Visitor Book, November 11, 2003," National Park Service (NPS) files, Shanksville, PA. The messages were often not signed, in part because the NPS officials suggested visitor signatures were not required.

41. "Temporary Memorial Book and Ambassador Log Book," 2003–04, NPS, Shanksville, PA.

42. Quotations taken from "National Memorial Visitor Book," November 11, 2004; "Box of Visitors Comment Cards," August 7, 2004–May 29, 2005; box of "Leave Your Message Cards," August 30, 2010 to September 23, 2011, NPS, Shanksville, PA.

43. See Britton, "Face of What Came After," 123–36. Durbin, "Expressions of Mass Grief and Mourning," 22–47; Doss, *Memorial Mania*, 100.

44. Gardella, *American Angels*, 6; Riley, *Angel Patriots*, 97–99.

45. National Park Service, Flight 93 National Memorial, *Final General Management Plan/Environmental Impact Statement* (Somerset, PA: National Park Service, 2007), 1–9; "Leave Your Message Cards," August 30, 2010 to September 30, 2010, NPS, Shanksville, PA.

46. Quotations taken from "Mission Statements Public Comments," 2004, box 1, NPS, Shanksville, PA.

47. National Park Service, Flight 93 National Memorial, *Final General Management Plan*, 10–28.

48. "Public Comments, Final Design from Archives of Design Competition, Stage II," NPS, Shanksville, PA. See Philip Kennicott, "9/11 Memorial at Shanksville Is Minimalist but Evocative and Compelling," *Washington Post*, August 26, 2011, 3. See Thompson, *From Memory to Memorial*, 110, 131, 137. A visitor's center was opened at the Shanksville site in 2015 that tells a more complete story of the event. It includes photos of the dead passengers and the crew and recordings of phone calls some passengers made to loved ones before they charged the cabin. Human remains, kept by the coroner of Somerset Country, Pennsylvania, were finally buried at the crash site in 2011. See Katharine Q. Seelye, "At a 9/11 Site, a Last Funeral," *New York Times*, September 9, 2011, A10.

49. Glick and Zegart, *Your Father's Voice*.

50. Glick and Zegart, *Your Father's Voice*, 30.

51. Glick and Zegart, *Your Father's Voice*, 59, 61, 211.

52. Glick and Zegart, *Your Father's Voice*, 1–2, 63–64, 142, 213.

53. Beamer, *Let's Roll*, 41–58, 105.

54. Beamer, *Let's Roll*, 55, 166, 220.

55. Beamer, *Let's Roll*, 171, 224–25.

56. Beamer, *Let's Roll*, 232–33, 247–48, 300.

57. Greenspan, "Spontaneous Memorials, Museums, and Public History," 129–32; McElya, "Remembering 9/11's Pentagon Victims," 51–63. Margaret R. Yocom, "We'll Watch Out for Lisa and the Kids," in Santino, *Spontaneous Memorials*, 57–97, noted that she saw model airplanes, replicas of fighter jets, and photos of dead passengers at the Pentagon's makeshift memorial.

58. See Nick Miroff, "From Families' Grief, a Symbol of Loss and Hope," *Washington Post*, September 11, 2008, A01; Allen Freeman, "Light Touch," *Landscape Architecture*, March 2003. The view of "memorial officials" who said they wanted no "flames, no bodies" is reported in *National Post* (Canada), January 13, 2003, AL1. The views of Beckman and Kaseman offered in 2011 are found at http://www.cbsnews.com/news/pentagon-memorial-designers-look-back/.

59. U.S. Forest Service, "Living Memorial Project Summary: Final Report," July 2007, at www.livingmeorialsproject.net (accessed May 30, 2018).

60. U.S. Forest Service, *Living Memorial Project Summary, Final Report*, July 2007, at www.livingmemorialsproject.

61. Hyman, "Public Face of 9/11," 183–88. See Burnett, *Fighting Back*. See "Bush Library: Brazen Attempt to Rewrite History," *People's World* (Continuing the Daily Worker), April 26, 2013, at http://www.peopleworld.org/article/bush-library-brazen -attempt-to-write-history (accessed January 10, 2018).

62. Svendsen and Campbell, "Living Memorials," 318–34. White, "National Subjects: September 11 and Pearl Harbor," 293–310, discusses what he sees as a "vibrant civic environmentalism" in the creation of landscape memorials.

Chapter 3

1. Woodward, *Bush at War*, 339–41; Woodward, *Plan of Attack*, 162–63.

2. Woodward, *Bush at War*, 339–41; Woodward, *Plan of Attack*, 162–63.

3. Anderson, *Bush's War*, 42–43; Woodward, *Plan of Attack*, 1–4, 21.

4. Anderson, *Bush's War*, 42–43; Woodward, *Plan of Attack*, 1–4, 21.

5. Pew Research Center, "Trends in Public Opinion about the War in Iraq, 2003–2007," http://www.pewreserch.org/2007/03/15/trends-in-public-opinion-about-the war-in-Iraq-20032007/.

6. Adel Iskandar, "The Great American Bubble, the 'Mirage' of Objectivity and the Isolation of American Public Opinion," in Artz and Kamalipour, *Bring 'Em On*, 153–73; Jim Rutenberg, "Cable's War Coverage Suggests a New 'Fox Effect' on Television Journalism," *New York Times*, April 16, 2003, B9; Dennis J. Bernstein, "Silencing Donahue and Anti-War Stories," Consortiumnews.com at http://consortiiumnews .com/2012/01?15/silencing-donahue-and-anti-war/voices/. See "Dixie Chicks Pulled from Air after Bashing Bush," CNN.com, March 14, 2003, http://www.cnn.com/2003 /SHWOBIZ/Music/03/14/dixie.chicks.reut/.

7. Farber, "Fighting (against) the Wars," 194–219.

8. Carty, "Anti-War Movement," 17–38. See Thomas, *Battle in Seattle*, 11–12, 53, 70. Ruppert, "Globalizing Common Sense," 181–98; T. V. Reed, "Globalization and the 21st Century Peace Movement," in Chiba and Schoenbaum, *Peace Movements and Pacifism after Sept. 11*, 183–99; Acuff, "Battle in Seattle," 30–34. See Brown, *Undoing the Demos*.

9. Lofy, *Paul Wellstone*, 113–21. On neoliberalism and patriotism, see Scott, *Neoliberalism and Foreign Policy*, chap. 5.

10. Jodi Wilgorer, "In Word, Song, and Sign: Demonstrators Across the United States Say No to War," *New York Times*, February 16, 2003, 21. Ishaan Tharoor, "Viewpoint: Why Was the Biggest Protest in World History Ignored," February 13, 2003, http://world.time.com/2013/viewpoint-why-was-the-biggest-protest-ignored (August 8, 2016).

11. Jodi Wilgorer, "In Word, Song, and Sign: Demonstrators Across the United States Say No to War," *New York Times*, February 16, 2003, 21.

12. "Ulster Says No to a Bush Bomb Blitz," *Irish News*, February 20, 2003, 6.

13. Steffan Walgrave and Dieter Rucht, "New Activists or Old Leftists," in Walgrave and Rucht, *World Says No to War*, 78–97.

14. The material on the response of Catholic bishops is drawn from http://www .usccb.org/issues-and-dignity/global-dignity-issues-and-actonhuman-life-and -dignity/global-dignity-issues-and-actionhuman-life-and-dignity/global-issues /middle-east/Iraq/sheet-on-bishops-positions-on-war-in-Iraq-2003–05.cfm and Powers, "U.S. Bishops and War," 73–96.

15. Potorti, *September 11th Families*, 74–78, 193, 199–200, 22. The letters cited are reproduced in this book.

16. Larry Syverson, "Personal Statement," Syverson Correspondence, Military Families Speak Out Records, DG253, box 2, Swarthmore College Peace Collection; Tina Eshleman, "Speak Softly, Carry a Big Sign," *Richmondmag*, August 28, 2016, http://richomondmagazine.com/news/sunday-story/speak-softly-carry (April 15, 2018).

17. Letters and emails to Larry Syverson are found in "Larry Syverson File, 2003," Military Families Speak Out Records, DG 253, box 2, Swarthmore College Peace Collection.

18. See Lisa Pollak, "After the War," *Baltimore Sun*, July 11, 2003, http://www .baltimoresun/bal-to-vigiljul11-story.html (April 15, 2018). S. Gallimore to Larry Syverson, December 4, 2004, Kate Foster to Syverson, September 27, 2003; Larry Syverson Files 2003 and 2004, Military Families Speak Out Records, DG 235, box 2, Swarthmore College Peace Collection.

19. John Warner to Larry Syverson, October 23, 2003, and George Allen to Larry Syverson, March 2, 2004, Larry Syverson Files, 2003 and 2004, DG 253, box 2, Military Families Speak Out, Swarthmore College Peace Collection.

20. "In Fighting Troop Increase Senator Finds Old Allies," *New York Times*, February 1, 2007, A8.

21. The constituent correspondence of John Warner is located in the Senator John Warner Papers, Special Collections, University of Virginia. Letters cited here are drawn from a CD dated October 8, 2002 to December 10, 2002 and a CD holding letters from February 27, 2003 to April 7, 2003. The University of Virginia specifies that no identifying information pointing to specific individuals, families, or organizations be divulged in the use of this material. The quotations used here come from a sample of some 1,000 letters. Certainly in this vast amount of materials citizens expressed a number of viewpoints. My disclosure of material supportive of George Bush or critical on the move into Iraq on humanitarian grounds is among the most prominent opinions, with the latter far outnumbering the former. Another frequently cited view was that the United States should work with the United Nations and other nations in order to find a diplomatic solution to the issue.

22. Citations are taken from constituent correspondence in the Senator John Warner Collections, Special Collections, University of Virginia, CDs dated October 8, 2002 to December 10, 2002 and February 27, 2003 to April 7, 2003.

23. Jason Cherkis and Sam Stein, "Have We Learned Anything from the Iraq War Vote?," *Huffington Post*, September 23, 2017, http://www.huggintonpost.com/entry /candidate-confessional (April 20, 2018); Byrd, *Losing America*, 172–77, 187, 190.

24. Byrd, *Losing America*, 172–77, 187, 190.

25. Letters to Robert Byrd are located in the Byrd Congressional Papers, Shepherd University, Shepherdstown, WV. Terms of use for the collection prohibit the disclosure of the names of letter writers. See box 27, letters from Frankfort, WV, January 27, 2003; from Charleston, WV, March 12, 2003; from Salem, WV, November 19, 2003; from Shepherdstown, WV, September 2, 2003; from Depot, WV, July 29, 2990. See box 28, letter from Bluefield, WV, April 25, 2004; from Parkersburg, WV, March 31, 2003; from Benwood, WV, June 30, 2004; form Romney, WV, April 25, 2004; from Vienna, WV, September 12, 2004.

26. Byrd Papers, box 27, letter from Morgantown, WV, September 16, 2003; from Clarksburg, August 8, 2003; from Dellslow, WV, November 7, 2003; from Middleway, WV, May 6, 2004; box 29 from Morgantown, WV, September 16, 2003; from Middlesex, WV, May 6, 2004.

27. Byrd Papers, box 27, letter from Huntington, WV, December 3, 2003; from Beckley, WV, September 3, 2003. See box 28, letter from Charleston, WV, March 26, 2003.

28. Byrd Papers, box 27, letter from Charleston, WV, September 25, 2003; box 28, letter from Charleston, WV, June 12, 2003; from Bluefield, WV, March 22, 2003; from Morgantown, WV, January 18, 2003.

29. Byrd Papers, box 27, letter from Culloden, WV, March 18, 2003; from Clarksburg, WV, March18, 2003; from Charleston, WV, October 18, 2003. Box 28, letter from West Union, WV, May 10, 2003; from Morgantown, WV, May 7, 2003, from Point Pleasant, WV, May 6, 2004; box 29, letter from Charleston, WV, January 22, 2004.

30. Copies of Byrd's standard letter of response are attached to many of the letters he received in Byrd Papers, boxes 27, 28, and 29.

31. Abrahamson, *Sweet Relief*, 59–70.

32. Abrahamson, *Sweet Relief*, 89–90, 136.

33. Abrahamson, *Sweet Relief*, 162–81.

34. Sarah Holewinski, "The True Costs of War," *Washington Post*, January 15, 2006, A15; Trudy Rubin, "Marla Ruzicka's Life and Death Drew Attention to Iraq Issues," *Philadelphia Inquirer*, April 21, 2005, 4.

35. Riverbend, *Baghdad Burning*, 8, 10, 46, 144.

36. Eric Ringham, "A Slaughter of Innocents," *Minneapolis Star-Tribune*, December 26, 2004, 1A. Norman Burdick letter is from the *Berkshire Eagle* (Williamstown, MA), November 9, 2004. See "U.S. Denies Most Iraqi Compensation," *Dayton Daily News*, October 24, 2004, A1.

37. See Les Roberts et al., "Mortality Before and After," 1857–1868; Burnam, Lafta, Doocy, and Roberts, "Mortality After the 2003 Invasion," 1421–28; Iraq Body Count (IBC), "IBC Response"; IBC, "Total Violent Deaths." IBC felt the *Lancet* study was problematic because it was based on a projection from a small sample of Iraqi households. IBC used actual news reports and other data such as Department of

Defense files released by WikiLeaks only about "specific" deaths. See also Fischer, "Iraqi Civilian Casualties Estimates." American Civil Liberties Union, "The Human Cost—Civilian Casualties in Iraq and Afghanistan," "ACLU Releases Navy Files on Civilian Casualties in Iraq War," July 2, 2008, http://www.aclu.org/news.adu -releases-navy-files-cililian-casualties (April 24, 2018); John Sloboda et al., "Iraq Body Count: A Case Study in the Uses of Incident-Based Conflict Casualty Data," Oxford Scholarship Online (2013). Tirman, *Death of Others*; Mitchell, *So Wrong for Losing*.

38. Kucinich, *Prayer for America*, 57–59, 75–76.

39. Juan Cole, "Kucinich Cole Congressional Hearings," December 13, 2006, at http://www.juancole.cem/2006/12/kucinich-paul-congressional-hearings (accessed January 20, 2018); Renita Jablonski, "Ohio Town Mourns Marines Lost in Iraq," National Public Radio, *All Things Considered*, August 3, 2005, http://www .npr.org/templates/story.pbp?story/ID=r784380 (August 10, 2018); "Marine's Death Has Steep Impact on Ohio Town," National Public Radio, *All Things Considered*, August 16, 2005, http://www.npr.org/templates/story/story.php?storyId=4802262, (August 10, 2018). See *USA Today*, August 3, 2005, 1.

40. Clemenson and Penna, *Murtha War Fighter*, 11–26; Deborah Sontag, "Injured in Iraq: A Soldier Is Shattered at Home," *New York Times*, August 5, 2007, A12; November 22, 2005, A14; April 5, 2007, A13. "John Murtha's Johnstown," *The Nation*, December 5, 2005, http://www.thenation.com/article/john-murhtas-johnstown/ (May 31, 2018).

41. "Congressman Walter Jones Writes to Families of Dead Troops, Penance for the Iraq War Vote," *Newsday*, October 23, 2017, http://www.newsday.com/new /nation/iraq-war-soldiers-killed-cond (January 20, 2018); "Republican Who Broke Ranks on War Is an Outcast No More," *New York Times*, June 6, 2011, A1.

42. "John Murtha's Johnstown," *The Nation*, December 5, 2005, http://www .thenation.com/article/john-murthas-johnstown/ (May 31, 2018).

43. These letters are located in the John Murtha Congressional Papers, University of Pittsburgh. The terms of use for this collection prohibit researches from divulging the names of letter writers. See box 282, letters dated November 17, 2005, November 19, 2005, November 21, 2005, November 29, 2005, November 30, 2005, December 12, 2005.

44. See Murtha Papers, box 285, letters dated November 5, 2005, November 19, 2005, November 18, 2005, November 21, 2005, December 7, 2005.

45. See Murtha Papers, box 287, letters December 1, 2005, December 16, 2005.

46. See Murtha Papers, box 287, letters dated November 21, 2005, November 23, 2005, December 18, 2005.

47. See Murtha Papers, box 287, letters dated November 21, 2005, December 1, 2005, December 2, 2005, December 6, 2005, December 21, 2005, December 16, 2005, December 19, 2005.

48. See Murtha Papers, box 287, letters dated November 23, 2005, December 1, 2005, December 7, 2005, December 26, 2005.

49. Sheehan, *Peace Mom*, 37–63. See also Moy and Morgan, *American Mourning*. This book contrasts Sheehan's story with an account of a father who lost a son in

Iraq and went there to gain revenge and kill those who took his son's life. "Interview with Gold Star Mother Cindy Sheehan," August 1, 2005, http://www.dailykos.com/story/2005/08/02/135210/interview-with-Gold-Star-Mother-Cindy-Sheehan.

50. See the YouTube video "Real Time with Bill Maher," August 26, 2005 (accessed January 9, 2018). Bush never met with Sheehan at the Crawford site. She and her husband had actually met him in Fort Lewis, Washington, in June 2004 with other parents who were grieving for the loss of their loved ones in the war. Bush recalled that in this meeting some of the parents did lash out at him but the vast majority of the group expressed pride in the service their offspring gave to the nation. In his memoirs, Bush said that he felt sympathy for Sheehan and understood that her grief had "consumed her life." He was hopeful, however, that someday those that grieved would be comforted to see a free Iraq and a "more peaceful world as a fitting memorial to the sacrifices of their loved ones." Bush, *Decision Points*, 357–58.

51. Celeste Zappala's speech to the Truth Commission on Conscience in War, March 21, 2010, is on YouTube at http://video.search.yahoo.com (accessed November 20, 2017). Lia Lipscomb is featured in Michael Moore's documentary *Fahrenheit 9/11*. See Slattery and Garner, "Mothers of Soldiers in Wartime," 429–45.

52. A transcript of Celeste Zappala's online discussion can be found at "Antiwar Mother," *Washington Post*, August 15, 2005, http://www.washingtonpost.com/wp-2yn/content/discussion/2005/08/18.

53. Pershing and Bellinger, "From Sorrow to Activism," 179–217; Leitz, *Fighting for Peace*, 167–68. The recitation of the rosary at Camp Casey is noted in Smith, *Vigil*, 40–41, 160. A copy of Larry Syverson's article in the Richmond Peace Education Center News is in Syverson file, Military Families Speak Out Records, box 2, Swarthmore College Peace Collection.

54. Smith, *Vigil*, 50–51, 86–87; Moy and Morgan, *American Mourning*, 150–56. Morgan was a cofounder of "Move America Forward." "Thousands Protest at Crawford," http://www.foxnews.com/story/2005/08/38/thousands-protests-in-crawford.

55. *Waco Herald Tribune*, August 27, 2005, 6.

56. *Waco Herald Tribune*, August 27, 2005, 6.

57. *Waco Herald Tribune*, August 27, 2005, 6.

58. On a "hierarchy of grief," see Butler, *Precarious Life*, 33–36. Bill O'Reilly's condemnation of Cindy Sheehan is to be found at YouTube, August 9, 2005, http://www.youtube.com/watch?t+III-GW-OTH-CDI (October 26, 2018). Letterman's rebuttal of O'Reilly is at http://video.search.yahoo.com/Search/video?for+mcafee&p=letterman+defends+cindy+sheehan (accessed April 26, 2018). See also "The Swift Boating of Cindy Sheehan," *New York Times*, August 21, 2018, 4, 11, for an illustration of the "character assassination" that Sheehan's opponents used against her. Also see "Walking the Wrong Way," *New York Times*, August 21, 2005, C9, for a discussion of how the Bush administration worked to screen the true costs of the war by taking actions such as prohibiting photos of flag-draped caskets used to return dead soldiers back to the United States.

59. Franklin and Lyons, "From Grief to Grievance," 237–45. These authors concluded that attacks on Sheehan appeared to be "excessively nasty." Don Van Natta,

"Bid Coffers and a Rising Voice Lift a New Conservative Group," *New York Times*, September 30, 2007, 1.

60. Prewitt's reflections on the tour are found in "Jean Prewitt Statement," November 9, 2015, Military Families Speak Out Papers, National Office file, box 1, and Stacy Bannerman's statement in Military Families Speak Out Papers, National Office file, box 1, Swarthmore College Peace Archives. See also Bannerman, *When the War Came Home*. In 2009 Bannerman's husband returned from Iraq suffering from PTSD and prone to violent behavior, a situation that led to the end of their marriage. See also Gold, *Mother's Tears*, 37–41, 87, 94.

61. Mike Memmott, "About 100,000 Anti-war Protestors Rally in Capital," *USA Today*, September 26, 2005, 1; Michael Janofsky, "Antiwar Rallies Staged in Washington and Other Cities," *New York Times*, September 24, 2005, 26; Joe Racdie, "Symbol of Protest Is Arrested," *New York Times*, September 27, 2005, A16.

62. Levinson, *War Is Not a Game*, 4–6, 134.

63. Gantz, *Winter Soldiers*, 24–26.

64. Gantz, *Winter Soldiers*, 63.

65. Gantz, *Winter Soldiers*, 74–77, 91–93.

66. Gantz, *Winter Soldiers*, 155–58.

67. Gutmann and Lutz, *Breaking Ranks*, 2–6, 105, 110, 137–41, 168–69.

68. Gutmann and Lutz, *Breaking Ranks*, 176.

69. "More Americans Say U.S. Failed to Achieve Its Goals in Iraq," Pew Research, June 12, 2014, http://www.pewresearch.org/author/BDRAKE (July 17, 2017).

Chapter 4

1. Anderson, *Bush's War*, 100–101; Barbie Zelizer, "Photography, Journalism and Trauma," in Zelizer and Allan, *Journalism after September 11*, 55–71; Apel, *War, Culture*, 1–2. Butler, *Frames of War*, xiii–xviii, argues that attempts to manage the diverse responses to violence always fall short.

2. Kozol, *Distant Wars Visible*, 5–13.

3. The *60 Minutes II* program is available at http://www.cbsnews.com/news /abuse-at-abu-ghraib/ (January 8, 2018). See Giroux, *Against the New Authoritarianism*, 41–42, 109–12.

4. Donald Rumsfeld quoted in Kennedy, "Soldier Photography"; "AR-15-6, Investigation of the 80th Military Police Brigade," Investigating Officer, MG Antonio M. Taguba (2004), 16, 44, 176, 189, http://www.thetourturedatabase.org/document /AR-15-6-investigation-800th-Military-Police-Investigating-officer-mg (August 8, 2017); Giroux, *Against the New Authoritarianism*, 116–18; Seymour M. Hersh, "Torture at Abu Ghraib," *New Yorker*, May 10, 2004, 43–46.

5. Forsythe, *Politics of Prisoner Abuse*, 2–3, 32–33, 44; Brundage, *Civilizing Torture*, 289–335.

6. Human Rights Watch, *The Road to Abu Ghraib*, June 2004, http://www.hrw .org/reports/2004/USA0604/USA0604.pdf (August 7, 2017). See "Alleged Methods of Ill Treatment, National Public Radio report, February 2004, http://www.npr.org /iraq/redress/abuse_report.html (August 7, 2017). See Seymour Hersh, "The General's

Report," *New Yorker*, June 25, 2007, http://www.newyorker.com/magazine/2007/06/25/the-generals-report (December 3, 2018).

7. Susan Sontag, "Regarding the Torture of Others," *New York Times*, May 23, 2004, sec. 6, 25; "On Torture and American Values," *New York Times*, October 7, 2007, C13; Bob Herbert, "America, a Symbol of . . ." *New York Times*, May 30, 2005, http://www.NYTimes.com/2005/05/30/opinion/America-a-symbol-of (November 16, 2018); Richard D. Erlich, "The America Worth Saving Is One that Doesn't Condone Terror," *Cincinnati Enquirer*, May 20, 2007, E2; Roger Cohen, "They've Apologized. Now What?," *New York Times*, May 9, 2004, 4. The *Boston Globe* editorial was published on May 7, 2004. Anthony Lewis, "Guantanamo's Long Shadow," *New York Times*, June 21, 2005, A21.

8. Iraqi victim testimony can be found at www.washingtonpost.com/wpsru/world/iraq/abugraib/swornstatement04104.html; Sontag, "Regarding the Torture of Others," 26–28. For a discussion on the Abu Ghraib photos, see the transcript of *NBC News: Meet the Press*, May 9, 2004, at www.nbcnews.com/id/4938258/ns_the_press/t/transcript-May/#,W8iJ-PMIQ-po (August 11, 2017).

9. Riverbend, *Baghdad Burning*, 259–62.

10. See A. Davis, "Unveiling the Rhetoric of Torture," 114, 137.

11. Eisenman, *Abu Ghraib Effect*, 5–16. Butler, "Photography, War and Outrage," 822–27, looks at the overall lack of "moral outrage" over the revelations at Abu Ghraib. Peggy Phelan, "Atrocity and Action: The Performative Force of Abu Ghraib Photographs," in Batchen, Miller, Gidley, and Prosser, *Picturing Atrocity*, 51–61; *Standing Operating Procedure*, documentary film by Erroll Morris (2008) Susan Sontag, "Regarding the Torture of Others," *New York Times Magazine*, May 23, 2004, 26–28; Karpinski, *One Woman's Army*, 2, 5, 63, 73, 201, 221.

12. DeLappe's views are stated online at iraqimemorial.org (accessed October 17, 2018).

13. See Regina Hackett, "This Memorial Destined for Oblivion," *Seattle P-I*, September 10, 2006, http://www.seattlepi.com/ae/article/This-memorial-destined-for-oblivion-1214219.php (January 18, 2017).

14. See Richard Shusterman, "Colors of War and Colors of Words," at www.terryrosenberg.blogspot.com.

15. John Bodnar interview with Danny Quirk, December 20, 2019. According to the U.S. Department of Veterans Affairs, the annual number of vet suicides exceeded 6,000 from 2008 to 2017. See *2019 National Veteran Suicide Prevention Annual Report* (Washington, DC: U.S. Department of Veterans Affairs, 2019), 8, at http://www.mentalhealth.vagov/docs/data-sheets/2019/2019National_Veteran_Suicide_Prevention_Annual_Report_508.pdf (April 13, 2020).

16. See Jon Sham, "Mike McCoy, Baltimore Street Photographer," *Baltimore Sun*, November 9, 2015, http://darkroom.baltimoresun.com/2015/mike-mccoy-baltimore-street-photographer (November 11, 2011).

17. *New York Times*, "Battles over Billboard Space Preceded G.O.P. Gathering," August 30, 2008, A10; Paul Moakley, "Soldier Down: The Portraits of Suzanne Opton," *Lightbox*, November 11, 2011, http://lightbox.time.com/2011/11/23/soldier-down-the-portraits-of-a-soldier (accessed August 9, 2015); Edkins, "Politics and Personhood," 139–54.

18. John Bodnar interview with Todd Heisler, January 11, 2020; Sheeler, *Final Salute*, 16–19.

19. Jane Hammond to John Bodnar, email, April 20, 2015. Hammond and Porter, "Collecting Leaves," 66–77.

20. Katharine Q. Seelye, "Coffins Arrive from War an Issue," *New York Times*, February 21, 2009, 22.

21. Elliott Ackerman, "How Should We Memorialize Those Lost in the War on Terror," *Smithsonian Magazine*, January 2019, http://www.smithsonianmagazine.com/history/how-should-memorialize-those-lost-terror-180971006 (January 11, 2020).

22. Keith Hamm, "Arlington West Evolves into Costs of War," *Santa Barbara Independent*, August 26, 2016, http://www.independent.com/news/2016/Apr/26/arlington-west-evolves-costly-wars/ (October 17, 2018). A copy of discussion questions to accompany the film can be found in "Arlington West: A Curriculum Guide," Military Families Speak Out Records, box 11, Swarthmore College Peace Collection. Leitz, *Fighting for Peace*, 201–10. "Eyes Wide Open" was another project using symbols of death—in this case empty combat boots—to illustrate the human cost of the war. The traveling memorial was organized by the American Friends Service Committee. See "Eyes Wide Open Dramatizes Human Cost of Iraq War," http://www.peoplesworld.org/articles/eyes-wide-open-dramatizes-human-cost-of-Iraq-war (February 22, 2019).

23. See *Arlington West* (2005), a documentary film produced by Peter Dudar and Sally Marr. Asa Aschcroft's views are expressed in an interview with Steve Lopez, "Iraq's Legacy Includes Heroes," *LA Times*, December 22, 2010, http://articles.latimes.com/2010/dec/local/la-me-12222-lopezcolumn-20101222 (October 17, 2018).

24. "Americans Stage Protest Hussein Is Happy to Allow," *New York Times*, October 27, 2002, 8.

25. Jason B. Johnson, "Iraq War Memorial Sets Tempers Ablaze/Creators Say Display a Gesture of Respect," *San Francisco Chronicle*, November 26, 2006, A1; John Bodnar phone interview with Jeff Heaton, August 18, 2018.

26. See http://lafayettecrosses.blogspot.com/search/label/crosses (August 2018). To see a video of the Move America Forward Rally, see http://lafayetecrosses.blogspot.com/search/chris's video (August 8, 2018). John Bodnar phone interview with Jeff Heaton, August 18, 2018.

27. Peter H. King, "On California: Essays from the Golden State," *LA Times*, November 10, 2008, at latimes.com/2008/nov/10/local/local/me-oncal10/2 (October 12, 2018).

28. John Bodnar phone interview with Laura Zucker, August 7, 2018; Hannah Pellissier, "Crosses of Lafayette," *New York Times*, October 24, 2010, A31 B.

29. Bush, *Portraits of Courage*, 28, 48, 174.

Chapter 5

1. Sherman, *Untold War*, 4–5; Haraj, "Martial Illusions," 43–72. James Dawes explains that in the modern era large military and bureaucratic organizations attempted to assume the moral responsibility for launching large-scale projects of

violence and draw such burdens away from the individual combatant but were not always able to do so. Dawes, *Language of War*, 157–91. See Bodnar, *"Good War" in American Memory*, 34–59, 240–41; Herzog, *Vietnam War Stories*, 31, 69; O'Brien, *Things They Carried*, 62; Caputo, *Rumor of War*; Kovic, *Born on the Fourth of July*. On the notion of a memoir as an inquiry, see Murdock, *Unreliable Truth*, 11–18.

2. See Juan Martinez, "Words of War: Military History and Memoirs," *Publishers Weekly*, August 24, 2009; Julie Bosman, "A Wave of Memoirs with You Are There Appeal," *New York Times*, March 19, 2012, C1.

3. Kyle, *American Sniper*, 4–5, 250.

4. Kyle, *American Sniper*, 7, 95–96.

5. Michael J. Mooney, "The Legend of Chris Kyle," *D Magazine*, April 13, 2013—a monthly magazine devoted to issues in the Dallas and Fort Worth area. Mooney noted that Kyle acquired a reputation of telling tales that tended to sustain his heroic status but that were basically unbelievable. One such story recounted an incident where two men ostensibly approached Kyle at a gas station south of Dallas and demanded money and the key to his truck. In short order Kyle pulled a gun and shot the men dead before they could realize what had happened. Police never arrested him because they realized they were in the presence of a legitimate American hero.

6. Tony Perry, "American Snider: The Most Lethal Sniper in US Military History," *Los Angeles Times*, March 5, 2012, at http://www.latimes.com/books/la-xpm -2010-Mar-05-la-et-book-2010-story.html; "American Sniper—Book Review," http:// serioiusreading.com/book-reviews/history/681-american-sniper-book-review-html (August 13, 2015); Joshua Sinai, "Book Review: American Sniper," *Washington Times*, January 13, 2012, https://www.washingtontimes.com/news/2010/jan/13/book-review -american-sniper/ (August 13, 2015).

7. Wesley, "Hero of the Hour," 109–24.

8. Luttrell, *Lone Survivor*, 59–60.

9. Luttrell, *Lone Survivor*, 197, 232–36.

10. Luttrell, *Service*, 144, 224.

11. Luttrell, *Service*, 227, 302–5.

12. See the National Rifle Association's Digital Network, Video of Marcus Luttrell Speaking to NRA Convention, Louisville, Kentucky, 2008, at http://www .nratv.com/videos/retired-navy-seal-marcus-luttrell-2008-meetings (August 8, 2018).

13. Owen, *No Easy Day*, 39. "Owen" is a pseudonym used to protect the "security" of the author.

14. Owen, *No Easy Day*, 193, 241.

15. Owen, *No Easy Day*, 20.

16. Sileo and Manion, *Brothers Forever*, 25, 74.

17. Sileo and Manion, *Brothers Forever*, 63–66, 91.

18. Sileo and Manion, *Brothers Forever*, 64, 181, 227.

19. Stann, *Heart for the Fight*, 1–11, 391.

20. Stann, *Heart for the Fight*, 33, 89, 275, 293.

21. Greitens, *Heart and the Fist*, 27–36.

22. Greitens, *Heart and the Fist*, 150, 189.

23. See Kline, *Charlie Mike*, 90–93, 123, 133. Kline made it clear that the families of Greitens and of Travis Manion were upset by critical news coverage of the battles in Iraq because they felt it devalued the sacrifices soldiers made.

24. Bellavia, *House to House*, 113, 128.

25. Bellavia, *House to House*, 47.

26. Bellavia, *House to House*, 20, 50, 59–64, 149, 175–78.

27. Bellavia, *House to House*, 290–300. For more on the attainment of honor in Fallujah, see West, *No True Glory*, 184–85, 319–24, 344.

28. Le Bleu, *Long Rifle*, 20–21, 38–39, 102–3, 134, 169.

29. "The Heart and the Fist," http://www.politics-prose.com/book/9780547424859 (January 16, 2020); Anicka Edwards, "Thursday Book Review: House to House," Buffalo Public and Erie County Library, April 22, 2010, http://www.buffalorising.com /2010/04/thursday-book-review-house-to-house-by-david-bellavia; "Book Review: Carnivore by Dillard Johnson," The Truth About Guns, http://www.thetruthaboutguns .com/book-review-carnivore-by-dillard-johnson (October 22, 2019).

30. Meyer and West, *Into the Fire*, 26, 31; Mejia, *Road from AR Ramadi*, 55, 117, 213–14.

31. Meyer and West, *Into the Fire*, 145.

32. Meyer and West, *Into the Fire*, 159–60.

33. Meyer and West, *Into the Fire*, 179–204.

34. Meyer and West, *Into the Fire*, 188–92; Anthony, *Civilianized*.

35. Parnell, *Outlaw Platoon*, 83, 89, 154, 210, 289.

36. Parnell, *Outlaw Platoon*, 13–15, 69–70, 117, 314.

37. Busch, *Dust to Dust*, 5–15, 35.

38. Busch, *Dust to Dust*, 278–81, 295.

39. See Frederick Bush, "Don't Watch the News: A Marine Family Lives from Phone Call to Phone Call," *Harper's*, November 2005, 33–41.

40. Buzzell, *My War*, 20–33.

41. Buzzell, *My War*, 81–106, 244–70, 284, 300. Wright, *Generation Kill*, 5–6, 346.

42. See "Conversation with Kevin Powers, Author of 'Yellow Birds,'" *PBS News Hour*, October 4, 2012, http://www.pbs.org/video/pbs-newshour-kevin-powers-author -of-the-yellow-birds/ (August 9, 18). In this interview Powers says most of the emotions expressed in his novel were emotions he felt himself.

43. K. Powers, *Yellow Birds*, 60–91.

44. K. Powers, *Yellow Birds*, 131–35.

45. K. Powers, *Yellow Birds*, 144–45.

46. K. Powers, *Yellow Birds*, 164–65; 206–7.

47. K. Powers, *Yellow Birds*, 139.

48. Scranton, *War Porn*, 320–22.

49. Scranton, *War Porn*, 214, 320–25.

50. Klay, *Redeployment*, 1–16.

51. Klay, *Redeployment*, 140–60.

52. Benjamin Percy, "On the Ground: The Yellow Birds," *New York Times*, October 4, 2012, http://nytimes.com/2012/10/07/books/review/the/yellow-bird (October 23, 2019); John Burnside, "The Yellow Birds by Kevin Powers," *The Guardian*, August 31, 2012, http://www.theguardian.com/books/2012/aug/31/the-yellow-birds-kevin-powers-reviews (October 23, 2019).

53. Michiko Kakutani," Review: War Porn Widens the Field of Vision about the Costs of Iraq," *New York Times*, August 8, 2016, http://www.nytimes.com/2016/08/09/books/review-war-pron-roy-scranton-iraq.ntml?auth-login-emai&login=email (October 2, 2019); Gary Anderson, "An Army Commander Weighs In," *Washington Times*, March 20, 2012, http://www.washingtontimes.com/news/2012/mar/20/an-army-commander-weighs-in (July 12, 2018); "Snapshots from the Front," *Wall Street Journal*, February 5, 2016, http://www.wsj.com/articles/snapshot-from-the-front-1454706975 (July 12, 2018).

54. Bragg, *I Am a Soldier Too*, 5, 152–58; Frank Rich, "Saving Private Lynch," *New York Times*, May 16, 2004, AR1. See "Jessica Lynch Fast Facts," http://www.cnn.com/2013,07,17/US/Jessica-Lynch-fast-facts/Index.html (accessed August 23, 2018); Buttsworth, "Who's Afraid of Jessica Lynch?," 42–62.

55. Bragg, *I Am a Soldier Too*, 86, 94–95.

56. Bragg, *I Am a Soldier Too*, 191, 201. See Ashley Frantz, "For Years Former POW Jessica Lynch Kept the Hurt Inside," at http://www.cnn.com/2015/07/20/us/Jessica-lynch-where-is-she-now/index.html.

57. Williams, *Love My Rifle*, 14–18, 40, 70. Williams also authored a second memoir detailing her postwar struggles and those of her spouse, who was also an Iraq war vet. See Williams, *Plenty of Time*.

58. Williams, *Love My Rifle*, 72, 123, 141, 165.

59. See Carol Burke, "Bitch or Slut," *Wellesley Review of Books*, http://www.wewonline.org/WRB-Issues/273, (October 30, 2019); Carole Cadwalladr, "My Life as a Bitch," *The Guardian*, January 28, 2006, http://www.theguardian.com/books/2006/jan/29/biography.features3 (October 31, 2019); Williams, *Love My Rifle*, 14.

60. Thorpe, *Soldier Girls*, 28–47, 65.

61. Thorpe, *Soldier Girls*, 156–59, 162–63, 223.

62. Thorpe, *Soldier Girls*, 242–43, 366–67.

Chapter 6

1. Shelton, "Rituals of Mourning and National Innocence," 35–48; Weber, *Imagining America at War*, 7. On aligning individuals to notions of political love, see Ahmed, *Cultural Politics of Emotion*, chap. 6.

2. Eagle, "Virtuous Victims, Visceral Violence," 139; Bayles, "Portraits of Mars," 19; Shelton, "Rituals of Mourning and National Innocence," 40–48; Weber, *Imagining America at War*, 8–10; Riegler, "9/11 on the Screen," 155–65.

3. Karen Randell, "It Was Like a Movie: The Impossibility of Representation in Oliver Stone's World Trade Center," in Birkenstein, Froula, and Randell, *Reframing 9/11*, 141–52.

4. Randell, "It Was Like a Movie," 144–52.

5. See Jeff Birkenstein, Anna Froula, and Karen Randell, "Introduction," in Birkenstein, Froula, and Randell, *Reframing 9/11*, 2–4.

6. Kellner, *Cinema Wars*, 224. "Goliath" in the movie is seen as a stand-in for the military justice system. Baker, *"Toxic" Genre*, 3, 32; Carruthers, "No One's Looking," 71–77.

7. See A. O. Scott, "Seeing Clues to a Son's Death and a War's Meaning," *New York Times*, September 14, 2007, E1.

8. Peter Travers, "Stop-Loss," *Rolling Stone*, March 28, 2008, http://www.rollingstone.com/movie-reviews/stop-loss-101722 (October 27, 2019).

9. Brian Tallerico, "Last Flag Flying," November 3, 2017, http://www.rogerebert.com/reviews/last-flag-flying-2017 (October 27, 2017).

10. See *Thank You for Your Service* (2017).

11. *Thank You for Your Service* (2017), 103. See Ben Kenisbert, "Thank You for Your Service: The War at Home," *New York Times*, October 27, 2017, C9.

12. See Sarah Latimer, "Everything You Needed to Know about 'American Sniper' Culture War Controversy," *Washington Post*, January 30, 2015, http://www.Washingtonpost.com?arts-and-entertainment/wp/2015?01/26a-guide-to-the-americansniper (October 26, 2019). A. D. Scott, "Review: 'American Sniper,' a Clint Eastwood Film with Bradley Cooper," *New York Times*, December 25, 2014, C12.

13. Manhola Dargis, "By Any Means: Jessica Chastain in 'Zero Dark Thirty,'" *New York Times*, December 18, 2012, C1. See Alan A. Stone, "The Price of Vengeance: Settling the Cinematic Torture Debate," *Boston Review*, March 1, 2013, http://www.bostonreview.net/BR38'alan_stone_kathryn_bigelow_zero_dark_thirty (August 8, 2016).

14. Westwell, "Regarding the Pain of Others," 811–34. See Holloway, *Cultures of the War on Terror*. See, for instance, reviews of Rendition in "MovieGuide," http://www.movieguide.org/reviews/rendition.html (November 8, 2019); *New York Times*, October 19, 2007, E10.

15. Kellner, *Cinema Wars*, 199–218; Conovan, "Patriotism Is Not Enough," 413–32. Aufderheide, "Your Country, My Country," 55–65, argues that American documentaries about Iraq are important because they "are active interventions in public life" and also attempted to fill perceived gaps in media coverage of the war which was deemed by many not honest and prone to bow to official views. Also see Gaines, "Production of Outrage," 36–55, who stresses that the use of American violence is often justified in films about Iraq because it is being used to destroy evil enemies—a point that may be somewhat overstated.

16. Gary Sinise interview in *Huffington Post*, May 2, 2009, at http://www.huffingtonpost.com/brad-balfour/q-a-actor-gary-sinise-hel_b_181749.html (August 16, 2018).

17. See "An Iraq War Movie Crowd-Sourced from Soldiers," TED blog at http://www.ted.com/talks/Deborah_scranton_on_her_war_tapes (August 17, 2018).

18. See Sebastian Junger, "The Right and the Left Are Wrong about My Movie," *Daily Beast*, July 21, 2010, http://www.thedailybeast-junger-on-war-and-restrepo-in-afghanistan (August 17, 2018).

19. Bill Schneider, "'Fahrenheit 9/11' Sparks Controversy and Wins Attention," June 25, 2004, CNN.Com, http://www.cnn.com/2004/ALLPOLITICS/06/25/moore .film/index (August 17, 2018); Moore, *Official Fahrenheit 9/11 Reader, Part III*; Top-lin, *Michael Moore's Fahrenheit 9/11*, 71–77; Weber, "Fahrenheit 9/11," 113–31. For a discussion of how mass culture can diminish the political import of war, see Stahl, *Militainment*.

20. See Robert Alt, "The Horrors of Abu Ghraib," *National Review*, May 17, 2004, at http://www.nationalreview.com/2004/05/horrors-abu-ghraib-robert-alt/ (No-vember 8, 2019). For another documentary detailing how American soldiers killed innocent civilians in Afghanistan, see *Kill Team* (2013) and Mark Boal, "The Kill Team: How U.S. Soldiers in Afghanistan Murdered Innocent Civilians," *Rolling Stone*, March 28, 2011.

21. Ahmed, *Cultural Politics of Emotion*, chap. 6; DeWeese-Boyd and DeWeese-Boyd, "Flying the Flag of Rough Branch," 214–32. In Wendell Berry's writings these authors find a patriotism based on "the love of one's place and those that dwell there." They see this as different from the veneration of the abstract idea of the state. They argued that Berry's version is "more democratic" because it is concerned with the needs of people one knew and less likely to turn into simply a celebration of national power.

Chapter 7

1. Ahmad, "Rage Shared by Law," 1261–70; Volpp, "Citizen and the Terrorist," 1575–86; Karam, *9/11 Backlash*, 3–10. See Bakalian and Bozorgmehr, *Backlash 9/11*. On the use of the term "homeland" in this era, see Kaplan, "Violent Belongings," 1–18. On the Ashcroft raids, see Rothschild, *You Have No Rights*, 9–20.

2. Higham, *Strangers in the Land*, 3–5; Welch, *Scapegoats of September 11th*, 7–8. D. Davis, *Negative Liberty*, 178–79, 183, 210, suggests how the type of patriotism emerging after 9/11 was a more "restrictive" conception of what it means to be an American and "more emotional than evaluative."

3. Ngai, "Architecture of Race," 67–92. Ngai argued that the 1924 law helped to construct the idea of a "white American race" in which persons of European de-scent shared a "whiteness that made them distinct from those deemed not white" and facilitated their assimilation. Jacobson, *New Nativism*, xiii–xxvii. Jacobson stresses the racist side of anti-immigrant policies directed against Mexicans in California.

4. Salita, "Beyond Orientalism and Islamophobia," 245–66; Simpson, "After 9/11," 193–206; David Niose, "Is American Patriotism Getting Out of Hand," *Psy-chology Today*, http://psychologytoday.com/our-humanity-naturally/201503/is-Ameri can-patriotism-getting-out-of-hand (September 9, 2016).

5. Maya's story is drawn from Peek, *Behind the Backlash*, 61–62. Peek's book is based upon some 140 interviews with Muslim Americans conducted between 2002 and 2003.

6. "Anti-Muslim Incidents since Sept. 11, 2001," at http://www.splcenter.org/news /2001/03/29/anti-muslim-incidents-sept-11-2001 (accessed September 24, 2017); J. Kaplan, "Islamophobia in America?," 15. The Bhkullar incident is described in the

documentary film *Divided We Fall: Americans in the Aftermath* (2008). American-Arab Anti-Discrimination Committee (ADC) Research Institute, *Report on Hate Crimes and Discrimination*, 11; "Aftermath of 9/11 Attacks," www.religioustolerance .org/reac_teri htm. "For Arab Americans a Familiar Backlash, Threats Prompt Police to Provide Extra Security for Mosques, Islamic Centers," *Washington Post*, September 13, 2001, A26; "Briefing on Civil Rights Issues Facing Muslims and Arab Americans in Indiana Post September 11 before the Indiana Advisory Committee to the U.S. Commission on Civil Rights (May 30, 2002)," in U.S. Commission on Civil Rights, *Federal Civil Rights Engagement with Arab and Muslim Communities*, 11–30; U.S. Commission on Civil Rights, "Briefing on Boundaries of Justice," 5–13.

7. "Orange County Crimes against Muslims Multiply," *Los Angeles Times* [Orange County edition], December 11, 2001, B2; "Los Angeles: Suspected Hate Crimes Rise 11% in County," *Los Angeles Times*, September 10, 2001, B3. There was some disagreement between the police and the family of Adel Karas over whether this murder was a hate crime. The police said there were no witnesses inside his store, suggesting his death was the result of an attempted robbery. Karas's wife was convinced that even though he was a Coptic Christian, he was mistaken for a Muslim. She noted that his store was just two blocks from a mosque that had been vandalized two days before his death. She also said there was no money taken from the store. See "Backlash Murders and the State of Hate between Families and Police," *Washington Post*, January 20, 2002, AO3.

8. The material on the Chicago area is drawn from Cainkar, *Homeland Insecurity*, 197–205.

9. Cainkar, *Homeland Insecurity*, 215–17.

10. Cainkar, *Homeland Insecurity*, 219.

11. Cainkar, *Homeland Insecurity*, 247.

12. See Sally Howell and Andrew Shryock, "Cracking Down on Diaspora: Arab Detroit and America's War on Terror," in Abraham, Howell, and Shryock, *Arab Detroit*, 67–89.

13. Rachel Yezbick, "The Arab American National Museum: Sanctioning Arabness for a Post 9/11 America," in Abraham, Howell, and Shryock, *Arab Detroit*, 287.

14. Yezbick, "The Arab American National Museum: Sanctioning Arabness for a Post 9/11 America," in Abraham, Howell, and Shryock, *Arab Detroit*, 290–312.

15. ADC Research Institute, *Report on Hate Crimes*, 2–8.

16. ADC Research Institute, *Report on Hate Crimes*, 20–25.

17. ADC Research Institute, *Report on Hate Crimes*, 34–38, 75–97.

18. Certainly American films had presented unflattering images of Arabs for decades prior to 9/11. A leading scholar on the subject, Jack Shaheen, referred to these images as "malevolent stereotypes" that equated Arabs and Islam with violence and felt they prevailed both before and after 9/11. See ADC Research Institute, *Report on Hate Crimes*, 76; Maira, *Missing*, 233; Maira, *9/11 Generation*.

19. ADC Research Institute, *Report on Hate Crimes*, 82–85; *New York Times*, October 4, 2002, 17. For Franklin Graham, see *New York Times*, August 15, 2002, A14. "Muhammad a Terrorist to Falwell," *New York Times*, October 4, 2002; Charles Marsh, "Wayward Christian Soldiers," *New York Times*, January 20, 2006, A17.

20. Ann Coulter, "This Is War," *National Review,* September 17, 2001. See Malkin, *In Defense of Internment;* ADC Research Institute, *Report on Hate Crimes,* 85–92.

21. Ahmad, "Rage Shared by Law," 1258–59; U.S. Commission on Civil Rights, *Briefing on Boundaries of Justice,* 5–13. Sukhpal Sodhi is treated extensively in the documentary film *A Dream in Doubt,* 2007, directed by Tami Yeager.

22. Stroman's letters from jail are at www.clarkprosecutor.org/html/death/us /stroman1262.html (September 17, 2018). Also see the documentary film *An Eye for an Eye* (2016). Giridharadas, *True American,* 49–51.

23. Stroman's thoughts are expressed at "Mark Anthony Stroman," http://www .clarkprosecutor.org/html/death/US/stroman1265.htm (September 16, 2018). Stroman's "death blog" quotes are drawn from the documentary *An Eye for an Eye* (2016) directed by Llan Ziv.

24. Giridharadas, *True American,* 125–27; Robert E. Pierre, "Victims of Hate Now Feeling Forgotten," *Washington Post,* September 14, 2002, 1.

25. Giridharadas, *True American,* 2–48.

26. Bhuiyan secured legal assistance in his attempt to gain clemency for Stroman, but the effort failed in the end. See "Why My Attacker Should Be Spared the Death Penalty," at http://wwwdallasnews.com/opinion/commentary/2011/05/20 /rais-bhuiyan-why-my (accessed September 18, 2018). Giridharadas, *True American,* 207–17.

27. Sikh American Legal Defense and Education Fund, "The First 9/11 'Backlash' Fatality: The Murder of Balbir Singh Sodhi," saledf.org/wp-content/uploads/2011 /08/Balbir_Sodhi_First_Backlash_Murder.pdf (September 20, 2017).

28. Sikh American Legal Defense and Education Fund, "First 9/11 'Backlash' Fatality."

29. See the documentary film *A Dream in Doubt* (2007). See also Transcript of the Supreme Court of Arizona at State v. Frank Roque at http://caselaw.findlaw .com/az-supreme-court/1429284.html (October 9, 2020). Roque was eventually spared the death penalty. In a telephone interview from prison, he claimed he had a "mental breakdown" after 9/11. He said that the terrorist attacks were the most "horrific" thing he had ever witnessed in his life and that he was not a "racist person." Simran Jeet Singh, "A Unique Perspective on Hate Crimes: The Story of a Convicted Killer," *Huffington Post,* September 12, 2012, http://www.huffington.com /sirman-jeet-singh/a-unique-perspective-on-hate-crime-the-story-of-a-convicted -killer (September 17, 2017).

30. *Dream in Doubt* (2007).

31. Jaxon Van Derbeken, "American Nightmare / Sukhpal Singh Sodhi Came to S.F. to Help His Village in India. Now, a Year after His Brother's Death, His Family Mourns Again," *SFGATE,* August 6, 2002, http://www.sfgate.com/news/article /American-Nightmare-Sukhpal-Singh-Sodhicame-to-2813583.php (September 18, 2017).

32. See the documentary film *Divided We Fall* (2008).

33. *Divided We Fall* (2008).

34. *Dream in Doubt* (2007).

35. See Bishop, "United We Stand?," 502–11.

36. Mary Katharine Ham, "Arizona 9/11 Memorial: Another 'Blame America' Monument," *Tipsheet* (September 24, 2006), https://townhall.com/tipsheet/mary katharineham/2006/09/24/arizona-911-memorial-another-blame-america -monument-n679460 (September 18, 2018); Beth Lucas, "Sept. 11 Inscriptions Spark Outrage," *East Valley Tribune*, September 23, 2006, http://www.republic.com/focus /f-news/1707070/posts (October 9, 2020); C. Smith and McDonald, "Arizona 9/11 Memorial 123–39; Randal C. Archibold, "Effort to Rework Arizona 9/11 Memorial Fails," *New York Times*, April 17, 2008, A20.

37. The bill was vetoed on April 29, 2011. Jim Walsh, "Erasure: Arizona Bill Wipes Sodhi's Name from the 9/11 Memorial," *Valarie Kaur* 26 (April 2011) at http:// valariekaur.com/2011/04/erasure-arizona-bill-wipes-sodhis-name-from-9/11 -memorial (September 17, 2018); Jim Walsh, "Arizona September 11 Memorial Legislation Draws a Veto," *Arizona Republic*, April 29, 2011, http://www.azcentral.com /election/azelections/articles/2011/29/201429 (September 16, 2017).

38. Corbett, *Making Moderate Islam*, 1–3; "Controversies over Mosques and Islamic Centers across the U.S.," Pew Research Center on Religion and Religious Life, www.pewforum.org/files/2012/09/2012-mosque-map.pdf.

39. Abby Phillip, "Obama Defends Ground Zero Mosque," *Politico*, August 13, 2010, http://politico.com/story/2010/08/obama-defends-ground-zero-mosque 041060 (September 18, 2019); Kilde, "Park 51/Ground Zero Controversy," 297–311.

40. Jacob Gershman, "Sides Dig in over Ground Zero Mosque," *Wall Street Journal*, August 2, 2010, A15; Alex Altman, "TIME Poll: Majority Oppose Mosque, Many Distrust Muslims," *TIME Magazine*, August 19, 2010, http://content .time/nation /article/0.8599.2011799.00.html (September 16, 2018); Pew Research Center, "Growing Number of Americans Say Obama Is a Muslim," August 18, 2010, http://www .pewforum.org/2010/08/18/growing-number-of-americans-say-obama-is-a -muslim (September 16, 2016).

41. Michael Grynbaum, "Proposed Muslim Center Draws Protestors on Both Sides of the Issue," *New York Times*, August 23, 2010, A14; Moustafa Bayoumi, "Between Acceptance and the Legacies of September 11," *OAH Magazine of History*, 25 (July 2011), 15–19; Annie Gowen, "Near Ground Zero: Mosque Supporters Gather to Show Their Support," *Washington Post*, September 11, 2010, A15.

42. *America at Risk: The War with No Name* (2010), documentary film produced by Citizens United. The film featured Newt and Callista Gingrich. Obama's support was articulated at a White House dinner in 2010, although he actually backtracked a bit on his comments the next day when he said he would not make a statement on the wisdom of placing a mosque near Ground Zero. See Richard Cohen, "Obama Muddles His Mosque Message," *Washington Post*, August 17, 2010, A15. On Trump's offer, see *Wall Street Journal*, September 9, 2010.

43. Andy Barr, "Newt Compares Mosque to Nazis," *Politico*, August 16, 2010, http://www.politico.com/story/2010/08/us/newt-compares-mosque-to-nazis -041112 (September 10, 2017); Corbett, *Making Moderate Islam*, 185. See Anne Barnard

and Alan Feuer, "Outraged, and Outrageous: Pamela Geller Attacks Park 51 as the 'Monster Mosque' and Calls Herself, Ironically, a 'Racist-Islamophobic-anti-Muslim-bigot," *New York Times*, October 10, 2010, NJ1.

44. See the documentary *The Ground Zero Mosque: The Second Wave of the 9/11 Attacks*, produced and directed by Pamela Geller, at http://gellerreport.com/2018/09/groundzeromosque-2.html/ (October 22, 2018); see Spencer and Horowitz, *Obama and Islam*.

45. Kilde, "Park 51/Ground Zero Controversy," 298; Ali, "Shariah and Citizenship," 1027-68, 1061-63; Bail, *Terrified*, 33-52, 109-30; YouTube video, "Hate Comes to Orange County," http://www.youtube.com/wtch?tv+NutFkykjimbM (October 22, 2018); Leah Nelson, "After Vicious Anti-Muslim Rally, A Defining Silence," *Hatewatch* (Southern Poverty Law Center, March 4, 2010), 1; Gabriel, *Because They Hate*, 145.

46. Hing, "Misusing Immigration Policies," 195-224; Buss, "Deportation Terror," 523-51; Nguyen, *We Are All Suspects*, xviii-xix; Welch, *Scapegoats of September 11th*, 9; Gonzales and Raphael, "Illegality," 1-17.

47. Amnesty International, "United States of America: Amnesty International's Concerns Regarding Post September 11 Detentions in the USA," May 4, 2002, http://www.Amnesty.org/en/documents/AmR51/044/2002/en.

48. Nguyen, *We Are All Suspects*, 28-44.

49. Nguyen, *We Are All Suspects*, 33. On Ali's beating, see Boyle and Busse, "Institutional Vulnerability," 947-74.

50. The story of Anser Mehmood and Uuzma Naheed is drawn from Shiekh, *Detained without Cause*, 8-9, 93-121. Shiekh's book demonstrates that young males from Middle Eastern countries became a focus of the intelligence community after 9/11 and government officials used immigration issues to round them up and charge them with links to terrorism.

51. Shiekh, *Detained without Cause*, 104-21.

52. Shiekh, *Detained without Cause*, 116-17.

53. American Civil Liberties Union, "Worlds Apart," 12-15; "How Deporting Immigrants After 9/11 Tore Families Apart and Shattered Communities," December 2004, http://www.aclu.org/report/worlds-how-deporting-immigrants-after-911-tore-families-apart-and-shattered-communities.

54. American Civil Liberties Union, "Worlds Apart," 13-14.

Conclusion

1. Margalit, *Ethics of Memory*, 26-33.

2. Bacevich, *Breach of Trust*, 4-5, 7, 13-14, 105; Bacevich, *New American Militarism*, 108, 219; Dudziak, *War Time*, 132; Dean, *Fragility of Empathy*, 17.

3. Wool, *After War*, 13, 100-105, 175. On cultural trauma, see Gross and Snyder-Korber, "Introduction," 369-84. Beauchamp, "Detached Literature."

4. See United States District Court for the Western District of Virginia, Charlottesville Division, Elizabeth Sines, et al. plaintiffs v. Jason Keller, Richard Spencer, Loyal White Knights of the Ku Klux Klan et al. defendants, http://www.integrity

foramerica.org/sites/default/files/FirstAmended Complaint-as-filed.pdf. (October 3, 2018); Johnston, *Truth about Patriotism*, 2, 13–16; Spencer, *Summer of Hate*, 6; Brenkman, *Cultural Contradictions of Democracy*, 4, 9; Jeffrey Isaac, "Right-wing Patriotism: What William Bennett Doesn't Understand," *Dissent* (Spring 2003): 64–70. See Hawley, *Alt-Right*, 4–14, 138–39.

5. Woodward, *Fear*, 239, 243–46.

6. "Donald Trump under Fire after Failing to Denounce Virginia White Supremacists," *The Guardian*, August 13, 2017, http://www.theguardian.com/us-news/2017/aug12/charlottesville-protest-trump-condemns-violence-many-sides (June 6, 2020).

7. "2017: The Year in Hate and Extremism," *The Intelligence Report* (Southern Poverty Law Center), Spring 2018; "Donald Trump Is no Patriot," *The Atlantic*, July 19, 2018, http://www.theatlantic.com/ideas/archive/2018/07/the-unpatriotic-nationalism-of-donald-trump/565607? (June 6, 2020); Jonah Goldberg, "Commentary: The Problem with Trump's Doctrine of Patriotism," *National Review*, September 27, 2018, http://www.nationalreview.com/2018/09/the-problem—with-trumps-doctrine-of-patriotism/ . The phrase "bonding mechanism" is quoted from Adam Serwer, "The Cruelty Is the Point," *The Atlantic*, October 3, 2018, http://www.theatlantic.com/ideas/archive/2018/10/the-cruelty-is-the-point/572104/ (January 30, 2019).

8. Bryant, *Heritage*, 100–107; Graham Vyse, "Obama Redefined Patriotism: Trump Is Trying to Erase That Too," *New Republic*, September 26, 2018, http://newrepublic.com/article/145014/obama-redefined-patriotism-trump-trying-to-erase-that-too (October 12, 2018).

Bibliography

Manuscript Sources

Charlottesville, VA
  University of Virginia
    John Warner Papers
Pittsburgh, PA
  University of Pittsburgh
    John Murtha Congressional Papers
Shanksville, PA
  National Park Service Archives
    "National Memorial Visitor Book, 2004–2005"
    "Temporary Memorial Book—Ambassador Log Books, 2003–2004"
Shepherdstown, WV
  Shepherd University
    Robert C. Byrd Congressional Papers
Swarthmore, PA
  Swarthmore College Peace Collection
    Military Families Speak Out Papers
Washington, DC
  Library of Congress
    American Folklife Center, Man in the Street Interviews
    American Folklife Center, September 11th Documentary Project
    The September 11 Digital Archive: Saving the Histories of September 11, 2001

Documentary Films

America at Risk: The War with No Name. 2010. Kevin Knoblock, dir. Citizens United Productions, video.

The American Widow Project. 2008. Taryn Davis, dir. American Widow Project, video.

Arlington West. 2005. Peter Dudar and Sally Marr, dirs. Laughing Tears Productions, DVD.

Blood of My Brother. 2005. Andrew Berends, dir. Storyteller Productions, video.

Brothers at War. 2009. Jake Rademacher, dir., video.

Divided We Fall: Americans in the Aftermath. 2006. Sharat Raju, dir. New Moon Productions, video.

A Dream in Doubt. 2007. Tami Yeager, dir. Center for Asian American Media (CAAM).

Dreams of Sparrows. 2005. Haydar Daffar and Hayder Mousa Daffar, dir. Harbinger Productions, video.

An Eye for an Eye. 2016. Ilan Ziv, dir. Indie Rights (dist.).

Fahrenheit 9/11. 2004. Michael Moore, dir. Miramax.

The Forgotten War. 2010. Paul Johnson, dir. Paul Johnson Films, video.

Ghosts of Abu Ghraib. 2007. Rory Kennedy, dir. HBO Documentary Films, video.

Gunner Palace. 2004. Petra Epperlein and Michael Tucker, dirs. Nomados Productions.

In Our Son's Name. 2015. Gayla Jamison, dir. Lightfoot Films, TV movie.

Iraq in Fragments. 2006. James Longley, dir. Daylight Factory films, DVD.

The Kill Team. 2013. Dan Krauss, dir. Motto Pictures.

9/11: The Falling Man. 2006. Henry Singer, dir. Darlow Smithson Producers, TV movie.

Off to War: From Rural America to Iraq. 2004. Brent Renaud and Craig Renaud, dirs. MMV Downtown Community TV Center, DVD.

Restrepo. 2010. Sebastian Junger, Tim Hetherington, dirs. Outpost Films.

Standard Operating Procedure. 2008. Errol Morris, dir. Sony Pictures Classics, 2008, video.

Taxi to the Dark Side. 2007. Alex Gibney, dir. Velocity/Thinkfilm, DVD.

The War Tapes. 2006. Deborah Scranton, dir. SenArtFilms.

Feature Films

American Sniper. 2014. Clint Eastwood, dir. Burbank, CA: Warner Home Video, 2015, DVD.

Billy Lynn's Long Halftime Walk. 2016. Ang Lee, dir. Sony Pictures, video.

Body of Lies. 2008. Ridley Scott, dir. Warner Bros. Pictures.

Good Kill. 2014. Andrew Niccol, dir. Paramount, video.

Hurt Locker. 2008. Kathryn Bigelow, dir. Summit Entertainment, video.

In the Valley of Elah. 2007. Paul Haggis, dir. Burbank, CA: Warner Independent Pictures.

The Kingdom. 2007. Peter Berg, dir. Universal Pictures, video.

Last Flag Flying. 2017. Richard Linklater, dir. Amazon Studios, DVD.

Lions for Lambs. 2007. Robert Redford, dir. MGM Distribution Co., video.

Lone Survivor. 2013. Peter Berg, dir. Universal Pictures, video.

Memorial Day. 2011. Samuel Fischer, dir. Image Entertainment.

The Messenger. 2009. Oren Moverman, dir. Oscilloscope Laboratories, video.

A Mighty Heart. 2007. Michael Winterbottom, dir. Paramount, video.

Patriots Day. 2016. Peter Berg, dir. Lionsgate Films, video.

Rendition. 2017. Gavin Hood, dir. New Line Cinema, video.

Stop-Loss. 2008. Kimberly Peirce, dir. Paramount Pictures, video.

Taking Chance. 2009. Ross Katz, dir. HBO Films, video.

Thank You for Your Service. 2017. Jason Hall, dir. Universal Pictures, video.

25th Hour. 2002. Spike Lee, dir. Buena Vista Pictures, video.

Syriana. 2005. Stephen Gaghan, dir. Warner Bros. Pictures, video.

United 93. 2006. Paul Greengrass, dir. Universal Pictures, video.

Vice. 2018. Adam McKay, dir. Annapurna, video.

W. 2008. Oliver Stone, dir. Lionsgate, video.

World Trade Center. 2006. Oliver Stone, dir. Paramount Pictures, video.

Zero Dark Thirty. 2012. Kathryn Bigelow, dir. Sony Pictures, video.

Memoirs

Beamer, Lisa. *Let's Roll: Ordinary People, Extraordinary Courage.* Carol Stream, IL: Tyndale House, 2006.

Bellavia, David. *House to House: An Epic Memoir.* New York: Pocket Star Books, 2007.

Breitweiser, Kristen. *Wake-Up Call: The Political Education of a 9/11 Widow.* New York: Warner Books, 2006.

Busch, Benjamin. *Dust to Dust: A Memoir.* New York: HarperCollins, 2012.

Bush, George. *Decision Points.* New York: Broadway, 2010.

Buzzell, Colby. *My War: Killing Time in Iraq.* New York: G. P. Putnam's Sons, 2005.

Cheney, Dick. *In My Time: A Personal and Political Memoir.* New York: Simon & Schuster, 2011.

Fontana, Marian. *A Widow's Walk.* New York: Simon & Schuster, 2005.

Gallagher, Matt. *Kaboom: Embracing the Suck in a Savage Little War.* New York: Da Capo, 2010.

Giuliani, Rudolph. *Leadership.* New York: Hyperion, 2002.

Glick, Lyz, and Dan Zegart. *Your Father's Voice: Letters for Emmy about Life with Jeremy—and without Him after 9/11.* New York: St. Martin's Griffin, 2004.

Greitens, Eric. *The Heart and the Fist: The Education of a Humanitarian; The Making of a Navy SEAL.* Boston: Houghton Mifflin Harcourt, 2011.

Johnson, Dillard. *Carnivore: One of the Deadliest American Soldiers of All Time.* New York: William Morrow, 2013.

Kyle, Chris. *American Sniper: The Autobiography of the Most Lethal Sniper in U.S. Military History.* New York: William Morrow, 2010.

Le Bleu, Joe. *Long Rifle: A Sniper's Story in Iraq and Afghanistan.* Guilford, CT: Lyons, 2007.

Libeskind, Daniel. *Breaking Ground: Adventures in Life and Architecture.* New York: Riverhead Books, 2004.

Luttrell, Marcus, with Patrick Robinson. *Lone Survivor: The Eyewitness Account of Operation Redwing and the Lost Heroes of SEAL Team 10.* New York: Little, Brown, 2007.

———. *Service: A Navy Seal at War.* New York: Little, Brown, 2012.

Manning, Lauren. *Unmeasured Strength.* New York: Henry Holt, 2011.

Meyer, Dakota, and Bing West. *Into the Fire: A Firsthand Account of the Most Extraordinary Battle in the Afghan War.* New York: Random House, 2013.

Owen, Mark. *No Easy Day: The Autobiography of a Navy Seal; The Firsthand Account of the Mission That Killed Osama Bin Laden*. New York: Dutton, 2010.

Parnell, Sean. *Outlaw Platoon: Heroes, Renegades, Infidels, and the Brotherhood of War in Afghanistan*. New York: William Morrow, 2012.

Rice, Condoleezza. *No Higher Honor: A Memoir of My Years in Washington*. New York: Crown, 2011.

Riverbend. *Baghdad Burning: Girl Blog from Iraq*. New York: Feminist Press, 2005.

Rumsfeld, Donald. *Known and Unknown: A Memoir*. New York: Penguin, 2011.

Sheehan, Cindy. *Peace Mom: A Mother's Journey through Heartache to Activism*. New York: Atria Books, 2006.

Stann, Brian. *Heart for the Fight: A Marine's Hero's Journey from the Battlefields of Iraq to Mixed Art Champion*. Minneapolis: Zenith, 2010.

Williams, Kayla. *Love My Rifle More than You: Young and Female in the U.S. Army*. New York: W. W. Norton, 2005.

———. *Plenty of Time When We Get Home: Love and Recovery in the Aftermath of War*. New York: W. W. Norton, 2014.

Newspapers and Periodicals

American Rifleman

The Atlantic

Baltimore Sun

Chicago Tribune

Ebony

Esquire

The Guardian

Harretz

Harper's Magazine

Indianapolis Star

Irish News

Lincoln (Nebraska) *Journal*

Los Angeles Times

Minneapolis Star-Tribune

The Nation

National Catholic Reporter

National Review

New Republic

New York Post

New York Times

New Yorker

Philadelphia Inquirer

Politico

Rolling Stone

TIME Magazine

USA Today

Waco Herald Tribune

Wall Street Journal

Washington Post

Westchester Journal

Novels

Abrams, David. *Fobbit*. New York: Grove Atlantic, 2012.

Caputo, Philip. *A Rumor of War*. New York: Houghton-Mifflin, 1977.

Klay, Philip. *Redeployment*. New York: Penguin, 2014.

O'Brien, Tim. *The Things They Carried*. New York: Houghton-Mifflin, 1990.

Powers, Kevin. *The Yellow Birds: A Novel*. New York: Little, Brown, 2012.

Scranton, Roy. *War Porn*. New York: SOHO, 2016.

Secondary Works

Abraham, Nabeel, Sally Howell, and Andrew Shryock, eds. *Arab Detroit 9/11: Life in the Terror Decade*. Detroit, MI: Wayne State University Press, 2011.

Abrahamson, Jennifer. *Sweet Relief: The Marla Ruzicka Story*. New York: Simon Spotlight, 2006.

Acuff, Stewart. "The Battle in Seattle and Where Do We Go from Here." *New Labor Forum* (Spring, Summer, 2000): 30–34.

Ahmad, Muneer I. "A Rage Shared by Law: Post-September 11 Racial Violence as Crimes of Passion." *California Law Review* 92 (October 2004): 1261–70.

Ahmed, Sara. *The Cultural Politics of Emotion*. New York: Routledge, 2015.

Ali, Yaser. "Shariah and Citizenship—How Islamophobia Is Creating a Second-Class Citizenry in America." *California Law Review* 100 (August 2020): 1027–68.

Anderson, Terry. *Bush's War*. New York: Oxford University Press, 2011.

Anthony, Michael. *Civilianized: A Young Veteran's Memoir*. San Francisco: PULP, 2016.

Apel, Dora. *War, Culture, and the Contest of Images*. New Brunswick, NJ: Rutgers University Press, 2010.

Appy, Christian. *American Reckoning: The Vietnam War and Our National Identity*. New York: Viking, 2015.

Aronson, Jay D. *Who Owns the Dead: The Science and Politics of Death at Ground Zero*. Cambridge, MA: Harvard University Press, 2016.

Artz, Lee, and Yahya R. Kamalipour. *Bring 'Em On: Media and Politics in the Iraq War*. Lanham, MD: Rowman & Littlefield, 2005.

Aufderheide, Pat. "Your Country, My Country: How Films About Iraq Construct Publics." *Framework: The Journal of Cinema and Media* 48 (Fall 2007): 36–55.

Bacevich, Andrew. *Breach of Trust: How Americans Failed Their Soldiers and Their Country*. New York: Metropolitan Books, 2013.

——. *The New American Militarism: How Americans Are Seduced by War*. New York: Oxford University Press, 2005.

Bail, Christopher. *Terrified: How Anti-Muslim Fringe Organizations Became Mainstream*. Princeton, NJ: Princeton University Press, 2015.

Bakalian, Anny, and Meddi Bozorgmehr. *Backlash 9/11: Middle Eastern and Muslim Americans Respond*. Berkeley: University of California Press, 2009.

Baker, Martin. *A "Toxic" Genre: The Iraq War Films*. New York: Pluto, 2011.

Ball, Christopher. *Terrified: How Anti-Muslim Fringe Organizations Became Mainstream*. Princeton, NJ: Princeton University Press, 2015.

Bannerman, Stacy. *When the War Came Home: The Inside Story of Reservists and the Families They Leave Behind*. New York: Continuum, 2006.

Barthes, Roland. Mythologies. New York: Hill and Wang, 1972.

Batchen, Geoffrey, Mick Gidley, Nancy K. Miller, and Jay Prosser, eds. *Picturing Atrocity: Photography in Crisis*. London: Reaktion Books, 2012.

Bayles, Martha. "Portraits of Mars." *Wilson Quarterly* 27 (Summer 2003): 12–19.

Bayumi, Mustafa. "Acceptance and Rejection: Muslim America and the Legacies of September 11," *OAH Magazine of History* 25 (July 2011): 15–19.

Beauchamp, Scott. "The Detached Literature of Remote Wars." *American Affairs* (August 16, 2017). http://americanaffairsjounral.org/2-17/08/detached -literature-remote-wars/.

Bennett, William. *Why We Fight: Moral Clarity and the War on Terror.* New York: Doubleday, 2002.

Betz, Hans George. "Contemporary Right-Wing Radicalism in Europe." *Contemporary European History* 8 (1999): 299–316.

Bishop, Sarah C. "United We Stand? Negotiating Space and National Memory in the 9/11 Arizona Memorial." *Space and Culture* 19 (2016): 299–316.

Blehm, Eric. *Fearless: The Undaunted Courage and Ultimate Sacrifice of Navy SEAL Team Six Operator Adam Brown.* Colorado Springs, CO: WaterBrook, 2002.

Blight, David. *Race and Reunion: The Civil War in American Memory.* Cambridge, MA: Harvard University Press, 2001.

Bodnar, John. *The "Good War" in American Memory.* Baltimore: Johns Hopkins University Press, 2010.

Booth, W. James. *Communities of Memory: On Witness, Identity, and Justice.* Ithaca, NY: Cornell University Press, 2006.

Borgwardt, Elizabeth. *A New Deal for the World: America's Vision of Human Rights.* Cambridge, MA: Harvard University Press, 2005.

Boyle, Elizabeth Heger, and Erika Busse. "Institutional Vulnerability and Opportunity: Immigration and America's 'War on Terror.'" *Law and Social Inquiry* 11 (Fall 2006): 947–74.

Bragg, Rick. *I am a Soldier Too: The Jessica Lynch Story.* New York: Vintage Books, 2003.

Brenkman, John. *The Cultural Contradictions of Democracy: Political Thought since September 11.* Princeton, NJ: Princeton University Press, 2007.

Brier, Stephen, and Joshua Brown. "The September 11th Digital Archive: Saving the Histories of September 11, 2001." *Radical History Review* 111 (Fall 2011): 101–9.

Britton, G. Robert. "The Face of What Came After: Memorialization of September 11 in News Images and the Shanksville Site." Unpublished Ph.D. diss., University of Missouri, 2008.

Brown, Wendy. *Undoing the Demos: Neoliberalism's Stealth Revolution.* Brooklyn, NY: Zone Books, 2015.

Brundage, W. Fitzhugh. *Civilizing Torture: An American Tradition.* Cambridge, MA: Harvard University Press, 2018.

Bryant, Howard. *The Heritage: Black Athletes, a Divided America and the Politics of Patriotism.* Boston: Crown, 2017.

Burnett, Deana. *Fighting Back: Defining Moments in the Life of an American Hero, Tom Burnett.* Altamont Springs, FL: Advantage Books, 2006.

Burnham, Gilbert, Riyadh Lafta, Shannon Doocy, and Les Roberts. "Mortality after the 2003 Invasion of Iraq: A Cross-Sectional Cluster Sample Survey." *The*

Lancet 368, no. 9545 (October 12, 2006): 1421–28. https://doi.org/10.1016/S0140 -6736(06)69491-9.

Bush, George W. *Decision Points.* New York: Random House, 2010.

———. *Portraits of Courage: A Commander in Chief's Tribute to America's Warriors.* New York: Crown, 2017.

Buss, Rachel Ida. "The Deportation Terror." *American Quarterly* 60 (September 2008): 523–51.

Butler, Judith. *Frames of War: When Life Is Grievable.* London: Verso, 2009.

———. "Photography, War and Outrage." *PMLA* 120, no. 3 (2005): 822–27.

———. *Precarious Life: The Powers of Mourning and Violence.* London: Verso, 2004.

Buttsworth, Sara. "Who's Afraid of Jessica Lynch? Or One Girl in All the World? Gendered Heroism and the Iraq War." *Australasian Journal of American Studies* 24 (December 2005): 42–62.

Byrd, Robert C. *Losing America: Confronting a Reckless and Arrogant Presidency.* New York: W. W. Norton. 2004.

Cainkar, Louise A. *Homeland Insecurity: The Arab American and Muslim Experience after 9/11.* New York: Russell Sage Foundation, 2009.

Capozzola, Christopher. *Uncle Sam Wants You: World War I and the Making of an American Citizen.* New York: Oxford University Press, 2008.

Carruthers, Susan. "No One's Looking: The Disappearing Audience for War." *Media, War, and Conflict* 1 (2008): 70–76.

Carty, Victoria. "The Anti-War Movement versus the War against Iraq." *International Journal of Peace Studies* 14 (2009): 17–38.

Chiba, Shin, and Thomas J. Schoenbaum, eds. *Peace Movements and Pacifism after 9/11.* Northampton, MA: William Pratt House, 2008.

Christi, Muzaffr, and Claire Bergeron. *Post 9/11 Policies Dramatically Alter the U.S. Immigration Landscape.* D.C.: Migration Policy Institute, 2011.

Clarke, Richard A. *Against All Enemies: Inside America's War on Terror.* New York: Free Press, 2004.

Clemenson, Brad, and Jim Penna. *Murtha War Fighter: Fighting for the Soul of America.* Parker, CO: Outskirts, 2012.

Collins, Christopher. *Homeland Mythology: Biblical Narrative in American Culture.* State College, PA: Penn State University Press, 2007.

Connerton, Paul. *The Spirit of Mourning: History, Memory, and the Body.* Cambridge: Cambridge University Press, 2011.

Conovan, Margaret. "Patriotism Is Not Enough." *British Journal of Political Science* 30 (July 2000): 413–32.

Corbett, Rosemary. *Making Moderate Islam: Sufism, Service, and the "Ground Zero Mosque" Controversy.* Stanford, CA: Stanford University Press, 2017.

Davis, Amanda Jean. "Unveiling the Rhetoric of Torture: Abu Ghraib and American National Identity." Unpublished Ph.D. diss., University of Texas, Austin, 2008.

Davis, Darren. *Negative Liberty: Public Opinion and the Terrorist Attacks on America.* New York: Russell Sage Foundation, 2007.

Dawes, James. *The Language of War: Literature and Culture in the U.S. from the Civil War through World War II.* Cambridge: MA: Harvard University Press, 2002.

Dean, Carolyn J. *Aversion and Erasure: The Fate of the Victim after the Holocaust.* Ithaca, NY: Cornell University Press, 2010.

——. *The Fragility of Empathy after the Holocaust.* Ithaca, NY: Cornell University Press, 2004.

DeWeese-Boyd, Ian, and Margaret DeWeese-Boyd. "Flying the Flag of Rough Branch: Rethinking 9/11 Patriotism through the Writings of Wendell Berry." *Civics* (Winter 2005): 214–32.

Doss, Erika. *Memorial Mania: Public Feeling in America.* Chicago: University of Chicago Press, 2010.

Dower, John. *Cultures of War: Pearl Harbor/Hiroshima/9-11/Iraq.* New York: W. W. Norton, 2010.

Dudziak, Mary L. *War Time: An Idea, Its History, and Its Consequences.* New York: Oxford University Press, 2012.

——. "You Didn't See Him Lying . . . beside the Gravel Road in France: Death, Distance and American War Politics. *Diplomatic History* 42 (2018): 1–16.

Durbin, Jeffrey, "Expressions of Mass Grief and Mourning: The Material Culture of Makeshift Memorials." *Material Culture* 35 (Fall 2003): 22–47.

Eagle, Jonna. "Virtuous Victims, Visceral Violence: War and Melodrama in American Culture." In *The Martial Imagination: Cultural Aspects of American Warfare,* edited by Jimmy L. Bryan Jr., 147–62. College Station: Texas A&M University Press, 2013.

Edkins, Jenny. "Politics and Personhood: Reflections on the Portrait Photography." *Alternatives: Global, Local, and Political* 38 (2) (2013): 139–54.

——. *Trauma and the Memory of Politics.* Cambridge: Cambridge University Press, 2003.

Edmonds, Bill. *God Is Not Here: A Soldier's Struggle with the Moral Injuries of War.* New York: Pegasus Books, 2015.

Edy, Jill A., and Patrick C. Meirick. "Wanted Dead or Alive: Media Frames, Frame Adoption and Support for the War in Afghanistan." *Journal of Communications* 57 (2007): 119–41.

Eisenman, Stephen F. *The Abu Ghraib Effect.* London: Reaktion Books, 2007.

Eisman, April. "The Media Manipulation: Patriotism and Propaganda— Mainstream News in the United States in the Weeks Following 9/11." *Critical Quarterly* 57 (July 2003): 55–72.

Faludi, Susan. *The Terror Dream: Fear and Fantasy in Post 9/11 America.* New York: Metropolitan Books, 2007.

Farber, David. "Fighting (against) the Wars in Iraq and Afghanistan." In *Understanding the U.S. Wars in Iraq and Afghanistan,* edited by Beth Bailey and Richard H. Immerman, 194–219. New York: New York University Press, 2015.

Faust, Drew Gilpin. *The Republic of Suffering: Death and the American Civil War.* New York: Knopf, 2008.

Finkel, David. *Thank You for Your Service.* New York: Farrar, Straus and Giroux, 2013.

Fischer, Hannah. "Iraqi Civilian Casualties Estimates." Congressional Research Service, January 12, 2009.

Foote, Kenneth E. *Shadowed Ground: America's Landscape of Violence and Tragedy.* Austin: University of Texas Press, 2003.

Forsythe, David P. *The Politics of Prisoner Abuse: The United States and Enemy Prisoners after 9/11.* Cambridge: Cambridge University Press, 2011.

Foster, Gaines. *Ghosts of the Confederacy: Defeat, the Lost Cause, and the Emergence of the New South.* New York: Oxford University Press, 1987.

Franklin, Cynthia G., and Laura E. Lyons. "From Grief to Grievance: Ethics and Politics in the Testimony of Anti-War Mothers." *Journal of Life Writing* (October 2008): 237–45.

Fried, Richard M. *The Russians Are Coming! The Russians Are Coming!: Pageantry and Patriotism in Cold War America.* New York: Oxford University Press, 1998.

Gabriel, Brigitte. *Because They Hate: A Survivor of Islamic Terror Warns America.* New York: St. Martin's Griffin, 2006.

Gaines, Jane. "The Production of Outrage: The Iraq War and the Radical Documentary Tradition." *Framework* 48 (Fall 2007): 36–55.

Gantz, Aaron. *Winter Soldiers: Iraq and Afghanistan.* Chicago: Haymarket Books, 2008.

Gardella, Peter. *American Angels: Useful Spirits in the Material World.* Lawrence: University Press of Kansas, 2007.

Gerstle, Gary. *American Crucible: Race and Nation in the Twentieth Century.* Princeton, NJ: Princeton University Press, 2001.

Giridharadas, Anand. *The True American: Murder and Mercy in Texas.* New York: W. W. Norton, 2014.

Giroux, Henry. *Against the New Authoritarianism: Politics after Abu Ghraib.* Winnipeg: Arbeiter Ring, 2005.

Gold, Elliot Michael. *A Mother's Tears: Mothers Remember Their Sons Lost in Iraq.* Altaneda, CA: Telespan, 2004.

Goldberger, Paul. *Up from Zero: Politics, Architecture, and the Rebuilding of New York.* New York: Random House, 2005.

Goldstone, Dwonna. "An African-American Professor Reflects on What 9/11 Meant for African-Americans and Herself." *Journal of American Culture* 29 (March 2005): 29–34.

Gonzales, Roberto, and Steven Raphael. "Illegality: A Contemporary Portrait of Immigration." *RSF: The Russell Sage Foundation Journal of the Social Sciences* (July 2017): 1–17.

Greenspan, Elizabeth. *Battle for Ground Zero: Inside the Political Struggle to Rebuild the World Trade Center.* New York: Palgrave Macmillan, 2013.

———. "Spontaneous Memorials, Museums, and Public History: Memorialization of September 11, 2001 at the Pentagon." *Public Historian* 25 (Spring 2003): 129–32.

Gross, Andrew S., and Mary Ann Snyder-Korber. "Introduction: Trauma's Continuum—September 11 Reconsidered." *Amerikastudien/American Studies* 55 (2010): 369–84.

Gutmann, Matthew, and Catherine Lutz. *Breaking Ranks: Iraq Veterans Speak Out against the War.* Berkeley: University of California Press, 2010.

Haberski, Ray. *God and War: American Civil Religion since 1945.* New Brunswick, NJ: Rutgers University Press, 2012.

Hagopian, Patrick. *The Vietnam War in American Memory: Veterans, Memorials, and the Politics of Healing.* Amherst: University of Massachusetts Press, 2009.

Hammond, Jane, and Amanda Porter. "Collecting Leaves: Assembling Memory: Jane Hammond's 'Fallen' and the Function of War." *Archives of American Art Journal* 47 (2006): 66–77.

Hansen, Jonathan M. *The Lost Promise of Patriotism: Debating American Identity.* Chicago: University of Chicago Press, 2003.

Haraj, Yuval Noah. "Martial Illusions: War and Disillusionment in the Twentieth Century and Renaissance Military Memoirs." *Journal of Military History* 69 (January 2005): 43–72.

Hariman, Robert, and John Lucaites. *No Caption Needed: Iconic Photographs, Public Culture, and Liberal Democracy.* Chicago: University of Chicago Press, 2007.

Hass, Kristin Ann. *Carried to the Wall: American Memory and the Vietnam Veterans Memorial.* Berkeley: University of California Press, 1998.

Hawley, George. *The Alt-Right: What Everyone Needs to Know.* New York: Oxford University Press, 2019.

Hersh, Seymour M. "Torture at Abu Ghraib." *New Yorker,* May 10, 2004, 43–46.

Herzog, Toby C. *Vietnam War Stories: Innocence Lost.* London: Routledge, 1992.

Hibish, Hussein, ed. *Report on Hate Crimes and Discrimination against Arab Americans: The Post September 9/11 Backlash.* Washington, DC: American-Arab Anti-Discrimination Committee, 2003.

Higham, John. *Strangers in the Land: Patterns of American Nativism, 1860–1925.* New York: Atheneum, 1967.

Hing, Bill Ong. "Misusing Immigration Policies in the Name of Homeland Security." *CR: The New Centennial Review* 6 (Spring 2006): 195–224.

Holloway, David. *Cultures of the War on Terror: Empire, Ideology, and the Remaking of 9/11.* Montreal: McGill-Queen's University Press, 2008.

Huebner, Andrew J. *Love and Death in the Great War.* New York: Oxford University Press, 2018.

Hyman, Jonathan. "The Public Face of 9/11: Memory and Portraiture in the Landscape." *Journal of American History* 154 (June 2007): 183–88.

Iraq Body Count (IBC). "IBC Response to the Lancet Study Estimating '100,000' Iraq War Deaths." November 7, 2004. http://www.iraqbodycount.org/analysis /beyond/lancet10000 (June 7, 2018).

———. "Total Violent Deaths Including Combatants, 2003–2013." December 13, 2013. http://www.iraqbodycount.org/analysis/reference/announcements (June 7, 2018).

Ivie, Robert L., and Oscar Giner. *Hunt the Devil: A Demonology of US War Culture.* Tuscaloosa: University of Alabama Press, 2015.

Jacobson, Robin Dale. *The New Nativism: Proposition 187 and the Debate over Immigration.* Minneapolis: University of Minnesota Press, 2008.

Janney, Caroline. *Remembering the Civil War: Reunion and the Limits of Reconciliation.* Chapel Hill: University of North Carolina Press, 2013.

Jensen, Robert. "The Problem with Patriotism: Steps toward the Redemption of American Journalism and Democracy. In *Bring 'Em On: Media and Politics in the Iraq War*, edited by Lee Artz and Yahya R. Kamalipour, 67–83. Lanham, MD: Rowman & Littlefield, 2005.

Johnston, Steven. *American Dionysia: Violence, Tragedy, and the Democratic Politics*. Cambridge: Cambridge University Press, 2015.

——. "This Patriotism Which Is Not One." *Polity* 34 (Spring 2002): 285–312.

——. *The Truth about Patriotism*. Durham, NC: Duke University Press, 2007.

Kaplan, Amy. *The Anarchy of Empire in the Making of U.S. Culture*. Cambridge, MA: Harvard University Press, 2002.

——. "Violent Belongings and the Question of Empire Today." *American Quarterly* 56 (March 2004): 1–18.

Kaplan, Jeffrey. "Islamophobia in America?: September 11 and Islamophobia Hate Crimes." *Terrorism and Political Violence* 18 (2006): 1–33.

Karam, Nicoletta. *The 9/11 Backlash: A Decade of U.S. Hate Crimes Targeting the Innocent*. Berkeley, CA: Beatitude, 2012.

Karpinski, Janis. *One Woman's Army: The Commanding General of Abu Ghraib Tells Her Story*. New York: Hyperion, 2005.

Keen, David. *Endless War: Hidden Functions of the War on Terror*. London: Pluto, 2006.

Kellner, David. *Cinema Wars: Hollywood Films and the Politics of the Bush-Cheney Era*. West Sussex, UK: Wiley-Blackwell, 2010.

Kemper, Bob. *Rubble: How 9/11 Families Rebuilt Their Lives and Inspired America*. Dulles, VA: Potomac Books, 2011.

Kennedy, Liam. "Soldier Photography: Visualizing the War in Iraq." *Review of International Studies* 35 (2009): 817–33.

Kilde, Jeanne Halgren. "The Park 51/Ground Zero Controversy and Sacred Sites as Contested Space." *Religions* 2 (2011): 297–311.

King, Erika G., and Robert A. Wells. *Framing the Iraq War Endgame: War Denouement in an Age of Terror*. New York: Palgrave Macmillan, 2009.

Kline, Joe. *Charlie Mike: True Stories Who Brought Their Mission Home*. New York: Simon & Schuster, 2015.

Kopecek, Michael. "Human Rights: Facing a National Past, Dissidents, and Civic Patriotism and the Return of History in Central Europe." *Geschichte und Gesellschaft* 38 (December 2010): 570–62.

Kovic, Ron. *Born on the Fourth of July*. New York: McGraw-Hill, 1976.

Kozol, Wendy. *Distant Wars Visible: The Ambivalence of Witnessing*. Minneapolis: University of Minnesota Press, 2014.

Kucinich, Dennis. *A Prayer for America*. New York: Thunder's Mouth, 2003.

Kuntzel, Matthias. *Jihad and Jew-Hatred, Islamism, Nazism, and the Roots of 9/11*. New York: Telos, 2017.

LaCapra, Dominick. "Revisiting the Historians' Debate." *History and Memory* 9 (Fall 1997): 81–82.

LaPierre, Wayne. *Guns, Freedom, and Terrorism*. Nashville, TN: Thomas Nelson, 2003.

Lawson, Melinda. *Patriot Fires: Forging a New American Nationalism in the Civil War North.* Lawrence: University Press of Kansas, 2002.

Leitz, Lisa. *Fighting for Peace: Veterans and Military Families in the Anti-Iraq War Movement.* Minneapolis: University of Minnesota Press, 2014.

Levinson, Nan. *War Is Not a Game: The New Antiwar Soldier and the Environment They Built.* New Brunswick, NJ: Rutgers University Press, 2014.

Levitt, Linda. "Speaking Memory, Building History: The Influence of Victims' Families at the World Trade Center Site." *Radical History Review* 11 (Fall 2011): 65–78.

Linenthal, Edward T., Jonathan Hyman, and Christine Gruber, eds. *The Landscapes of 9/11: A Photographer's Journey; Photographs of Jonathan Hyman.* Austin: University of Texas Press, 2013.

Lofy, Bill. *Paul Wellstone: The Life of a Progressive.* Ann Arbor: University of Michigan Press, 2005.

Long, Michael, and Tracey Wegner Sadd, eds. *God and Country?: Diverse Perspectives on Christianity and Patriotism.* New York: Palgrave Macmillan, 2007.

Louis, Nancy. *United We Stand.* Edina, MN: ABDO and Daughter, 2002.

Low, Seth. "The Memorialization of September 11th: Dominant and Local Discourses on the Rebuilding of the World Trade Center Site." *American Ethnologist* 31 (August 2004): 326–39.

Lyons, Matthew N. "Fragmented Nationalism: Right-Wing Responses to September 11 in Historical Context." *Pennsylvania Magazine of History and Biography* 127 (October 2003): 377–418.

Maira, Sunaina Marr. *Missing: Youth, Citizenship, and Empire after 9/11.* Durham, NC: Duke University Press, 2009.

———. *The 9/11 Generation: Youth, Rights, and Solidarity in the War on Terror.* New York: New York University Press, 2016.

Malkin, Michelle. *In Defense of Internment: The Case for Racial Profiling in World War II and the War on Terror.* Washington, DC: Regnery, 2004.

Malveaux, Julianne, and Regina Green, eds. *The Paradox of Loyalty: An African-American Response to the War on Terrorism.* Chicago: Third World Press, 2002.

Maney, Gregory M., Woehrle, Lynne M., and Patrick G. Coy. "Harnessing and Challenging Hegemony: The U.S. Peace Movement after 9/11." *Sociological Review* 48, no. 3 (Fall 2005): 357–81.

Margalit, Avishai. *The Ethics of Memory.* Cambridge, MA: Harvard University Press, 2002.

Mathy, Jean-Phillipe. *Melancholy Politics: Loss, Mourning and Memory in Late-Modern France.* University Park, PA: Penn State University Press, 2011.

Mayer, Jane. *The Dark Side: The Inside Story of How the War on Terror Turned into a War on American Ideals.* New York: Random House, 2009.

McConnell, Stuart. *Glorious Contentment: The Grand Army of the Republic, 1865–1900.* Chapel Hill: University of North Carolina Press, 1992.

McElya, Micki. *The Politics of Mourning: Death and Honor in Arlington National Cemetery.* Cambridge, MA: Harvard University Press, 2016.

——. "Remembering 9/11's Pentagon Victims and Reframing History in Arlington National Cemetery." *Radical History Review* 111 (Fall 2011): 51–63.

Mejia, Camilo. *Road from AR Ramadi: The Private Rebellion of Staff Sgt. Camilo Mejia.* New York: New Press, 2007.

Mitchell, Greg. *So Wrong for Losing: How the Press, Pundits, and the President Failed in Iraq.* New York: Sinclair Books, 2013.

Moore, Michael. *The Official Fahrenheit 9/11 Reader.* New York: Simon & Schuster, 2004.

Moy, Catherine, and Melanie Morgan. *American Mourning: The Intimate Story of Two Families Joined by War-Torn by Belief.* Nashville, TN: Cumberland House, 2006.

Murdock, Maureen. *Unreliable Truth: On Memoir and Memory.* New York: Seal, 2003.

Nandy, Lisa. "Patriotism and the Left." *New Statesman.* March, 25, 2015. http://newstatesman.com/politics/2015/03/patriotism-and-left.

Ngai, Mae. "The Architecture of Race in American Immigration Law: A Reexamination of the Immigration Law of 1924." *Journal of American History* 86 (June 1999): 67–92.

Nguyen, Tram. *We Are All Suspects Now: Untold Stories from Immigrant Communities after 9/11.* Boston: Beacon, 2005.

Nobel, Philip. *Sixteen Acres: Architecture and the Outrageous Struggle for the Future of Ground Zero.* New York: Henry Holt, 2005.

Noon, David Hoagland. "Cold War Revival: Neoconservatives and Historical Memory in the War on Terror." *American Studies* 48 (Fall 2007): 75–99.

Nussbaum, Martha. *For the Love of Country?.* Boston: Beacon, 2002.

O'Leary, Cecilia. *To Die For: The Paradox of American Patriotism.* Princeton, NJ: Princeton University Press, 1999.

Peek, Lori. *Behind the Backlash: Muslim Americans after 9/11.* Philadelphia, PA: Temple University Press, 2010.

Pershing, Linda, and Nacelle Y. Bellinger. "From Sorrow to Activism: A Father's Memorial to His Son Alexander Arredondo, Killed in U.S. Occupation of Iraq." *Journal of American Folklore* 123 (2010): 179–217.

"Portraits 9/11/01: The Collected 'Portraits of Grief' from the New York Times. New York: Henry Holt, 2002.

Potorti, David. *September 11 Families for Peaceful Tomorrows: Turning our Grief into Action of Peace.* New York: DVD Books, 2003.

Powers, Gerald. "The U.S. Bishops and War since the Peace Pastoral." *U.S. Catholic Historian* 27 (September 2009): 73–96.

Randell, Karen. "It Was Like a Movie: The Impossibility of Representation in Oliver Stone's *World Trade Center.*" In *Reframing 9/11: Film, Popular Culture, and the War on Terror,* edited by Jeff Birkenstein, Anna Froula and Karen Randell, 141–52. New York: Continuum, 2010.

Riegler, Thomas. "9/11 on the Screen: Giving Memory and Meaning to All that 'Howling Space' at Ground Zero." *Radical History Review* 11 (2011): 155–56.

Riley, Alexander T. *Angel Patriots: The Crash of United Flight 93 and the Myth of America*. New York: New York University Press, 2015.

Roberts, Les, Riyadh Lafta, Richard Garfield, Jamal Khudhairi, and Gilbert Burnham. "Mortality Before and After the 2003 Invasion of Iraq." *The Lancet* 364 (2004): 1857–68.

Rosenfeld, Gavril D. *After Auschwitz: Jewish Architecture and the Memory of the Holocaust*. New Haven, CT: Yale University Press, 2010.

Rothschild, Matthew. *You Have No Rights: Stories of America in an Age of Repression*. New York: New Press, 2007, 9–20.

Rubin, Derek, and Jaap Verheul, eds. *American Multiculturalism after 9/11: Transatlantic Perspectives*. Amsterdam: University of Amsterdam Press, 2009.

Ruppert, Mark. "Globalizing Common Sense: A Marxian-Gramcian (Re-)vision of the Politics of Governance/Resistance." *Review of International Studies* 29 (2003): 181–98.

Salita, Stephen. "Beyond Orientalism and Islamophobia: 9/11 Anti-Arab Racism and the Mythos of National Pride." *CR: The New Centennial Review* 6 (Fall 2006): 245–66.

Santino, Jack, ed. *Spontaneous Shrines and the Public Memorialization of Death*. New York: Palgrave Macmillan, 2006.

Savage, Kirk. *Monument Wars: Washington, D.C., the National Mall, and the Transformation of the Memorial Landscape*. Berkeley: University of California Press, 2011.

Schuster, M. A. "A National Survey of Stress Reactions after 9/11 Terrorists Attacks." *New England Journal of Medicine* 345 (November 15, 2001): 1507–21.

Scott, Catherine. *Neoliberalism and Foreign Policy*. New York: Palgrave Macmillan, 2018.

Seidler-Ramirez, Jan. "Collecting the National Conversation." In *The Landscapes of 9/11: A Phtographer's Journey*, edited by Edward Linenthal, Jonathan Hyman, and Christine Gruber, 79–111. Austin: University of Texas Press, 2013.

Sen, Amartya. *Identity and Violence: The Illusion of Destiny*. New York: W. W. Norton, 2007.

Sharpton, Al. *Al on America*. New York: Kensington, 2002.

Shaw, Todd C. "'Two Warring Ideals': Double Consciousness, Dialogue, and African American Patriotism Post-9/11." *Journal of African-American Studies* 8 (June 2004): 20–37.

Sheehy, Gail. *Middletown, America: One Town's Passage from Trauma to Hope*. New York: Random House, 2005.

Sheeler, Jim. *Final Salute: A Story of Unfinished Lives*. London: Penguin, 2008.

Shelton, John. "Rituals of Mourning and National Innocence." *Journal of American Culture* 28 (2005): 35–48.

Sherman, Daniel, and Daniel Nardin, eds. *Terror, Culture, Politics: Rethinking 9/11*. Bloomington: Indiana University Press, 2006.

Sherman, Nancy. *Afterwar: The Moral Wounds of Our Soldiers*. New York: Oxford University Press, 2015.

———. *The Untold War: Inside the Hearts, Minds, and Souls of Our Soldiers.* New York: W. W. Norton, 2010.

Shiekh, Irum. *Detained without Cause: Muslims' Stories of Detention and Deportation in America after 9/11.* New York: Palgrave Macmillan, 2011.

Sileo, Tom, and Tom Manion. *Brothers Forever: The Enduring Bond between a Marine and a Navy SEAL that Transcended the Ultimate Sacrifice.* New York: Da Capo, 2014.

Simko, Christina. *The Politics of Consolation: Memory and Meaning of September 11.* New York: Oxford University Press, 2015.

Simmons, Martha, and Frank A. Thomas, eds. *9.11.01: African-American Leaders Respond to an American Tragedy.* Valley Forge, PA: Judson, 2001.

Simon, Roger I., Sharon Rosenberg, and Claudia Eppert, eds. *Between Hope and Despair: Pedagogy and the Remembrance of Historical Trauma.* Lanham, MD: Rowman & Littlefield, 2000.

Simpson, David. "After 9/11: The Fate of Strangers." *Amerikastudien/American Studies* 57, no. 2 (2012): 193–206.

Skita, Linda J. "Patriotism or National Understanding Post-September 11, 2001, Flag-Display Behavior." *Journal of Applied Social Psychology* 35 (2005): 1995–2005.

Slattery, Karen, and Ann C. Garner. "Mothers of Soldiers in Wartime: A National News Narrative." *Critical Studies in Media Communications* 24 (2007): 429–45.

Sloboda, John. "Iraq Body Count: A Case Study in the Uses of Incident-Based Conflict Casualty Data," Oxford Scholarship Online (2013), http://www.OxfordScholarship.com (May 31, 2018).

Slotkin, Richard. *Gunfighter Nation: The Myth of the Frontier in Twentieth-Century America.* Norman: University of Oklahoma Press, 1992.

Smith, Christina M., and Kelly M. McDonald. "The Arizona 9/11 Memorial: A Case Study in Public Dissent and Argumentation through Blogs." *Augmentation and Advocacy* 47 (Fall 2010): 123–39.

Smith, W. Leon. *The Vigil: 26 Days in Crawford, Texas.* New York: Disinformation Company, 2005.

Snyder-Korber, Mary Ann. "Introduction: Trauma's Continuum—September 11th Reconsidered." *Amerikastudien/American Studies* 55 (2010): 369–84.

———. "'Portraits of Grief' and the Work of September 11 Mourning." *Amerikastudien/American Studies* 55 (2010): 451–78.

Sodaro, Amy. *Exhibiting Atrocity: Memorial Museums and the Politics of Past Violence.* New Brunswick, NJ: Rutgers University Press, 2018.

Spencer, Hawes. *Summer of Hate: Charlottesville, USA.* Charlottesville: University of Virginia Press, 2018.

Spencer, Robert, and David Horowitz. *Obama and Islam.* Sherman Oaks, CA: David Horowitz Freedom Center, 2013.

Stahl, Roger. *Militainment: War, Media, and Pop Culture.* New York: Routledge, 2010.

Stier, Oren Baruch, and J. Shawn Landres, eds. *Religion, Violence, Memory, and Place*. Bloomington: Indiana University Press, 2006.

Stowe, Simon. "Agonistic Homecoming: Frederick Douglass, Joseph Lowery and the Democratic Value of African-American Public Mourning." *American Political Science Review* 104 (November 2010): 681–97.

———. "Pericles at Gettysburg and Ground Zero: Tragedy, Patriotism, and Public Mourning." *American Political Science Review* 101 (May 2007): 195–208.

Sturken, Marita. "The Aesthetics of Absence: Rebuilding Ground Zero." *American Ethnologist* 32 (2004): 311–25.

———. "The 9/11 Memorial Museum and the Remaking of Ground Zero." *American Quarterly* 67 (June 2015): 471–90.

———. *Tourists of History: Memory, Kitsch and Consumption from Oklahoma City to Ground Zero*. Durham, NC: Duke University Press, 2007.

Svendsen, Erika S., and Lindsay K. Campbell. "Living Memorials: Understanding the Social Meaning of Community-Based Memorials to September, 11, 2001." *Environment and Behavior* 42 (2008): 318–34.

Thomas, Janet. *The Battle in Seattle: The Story behind and beyond the WTO Demonstrations*. Golden, CO: Fulcrum, 2000.

Thompson, J. William. *From Memory to Memorial: Shanksville, America, and Flight 93*. University Park, PA: Penn State University Press, 2017.

Thorpe, Helen. *Soldier Girls: The Battles of Three Women at Home and at War*. New York: Scribner, 2004.

Tirman, John. *The Death of Others: The Fate of Civilians in American Wars*. New York: Oxford University Press, 2011.

Toplin, Robert Brent. *Michael Moore's Fahrenheit 9/11: How One Film Divided a Nation*. Lawrence: University Press of Kansas, 2006.

Trout, Stephen. *On the Battlefield of Memory: The First World War and American Remembrance, 1919–1941*. Tuscaloosa: University of Alabama Press, 2010.

Updegraff, John, Roxane Cohen Silver, and E. Alison Holman. "Searching for and Finding Meaning in Collective Trauma: Results from a Longitudinal Study of the 9/11 Terrorist Attacks." *Journal of Personality and Social Psychology* 95 (October 2008): 709–22.

Vasi, Bogdan Ion, and David Strang. "Civil Liberty in America: The Diffusion of Municipal Bill of Rights Resolutions after the Passage of the USA Patriot Act." *American Journal of Sociology* 114 (May 2009): 1716–64.

Volpp, Leti. "The Citizen and the Terrorist." *UCLA Law Review* 49 (February 2002): 1575–1600.

Walgrave, Steffan, and Dieter Rucht. *The World Says No to War: Demonstrations against the War on Iraq*. Minneapolis: University of Minnesota Press, 2010.

Weber, Cynthia. "Fahrenheit 9/11: The Temperature at Which Morality Burns." *Journal of American Studies* 40 (2006): 113–31.

———. *Imagining America at War: Morality, Politics and Film*. New York: Routledge, 2006.

Welch, Michael. *Scapegoats of September 11th: Hate Crimes and State Crimes in the War on Terror*. New Brunswick, NJ: Rutgers University Press, 2006.

Wesley, Marilyn C. "The Hero of the Hour: Ideology and Violence in the Works of Richard Harding Davis." *American Literary Realism* 32 (Winter 2000): 109–24.

West, Bing. *No True Glory: A Frontline Account of the Battle of Fallujah.* New York: Bantam, 2005.

West, Mark, and Chris Carey. "(Re)Enacting Frontier Justice: The Bush Administration's Tactical Narrative of the Old West Fantasy after September 11." *Quarterly Journal of Speech* 92 (November 2006): 379–412.

Westwell, Guy. "Regarding the Pain of Others: Scenarios of Obligation in Post 9/11 U.S. Cinema." *Journal of American Studies* 45 (2011): 811–34.

White, G. M. "National Subjects: September 11 and Pearl Harbor." *American Ethnologist* 31, 293–310.

Woodward, Bob. *Bush at War.* New York: Simon & Schuster, 2002.

———. *Fear: Trump in the White House.* New York: Simon & Schuster, 2018.

———. *Plan of Attack: The Definitive Account of the Decision to Invade Iraq.* New York: Simon and Schuster, 2004.

Wool, Zoe. *After War: The Weight of Life at Walter Reed.* Durham, NC: Duke University Press, 2015.

Wright, Evan. *Generation Kill: Devil Dogs, Iceman, Captain America, and the New Face of American War.* New York: G. P. Putnam's Sons, 2004.

Young, James. *The Stages of Memory: Reflections on Memorial Art, Loss, and the Spaces Between.* Amherst: University of Massachusetts Press, 2016.

Zelizer, Barbie, and Stuart Allan, eds. *Journalism after September 11.* London: Routledge, 2013.

Websites

American-Arab Anti-Discrimination Committee Research Institute. *Report on Hate Crimes and Discrimination against Arab Americans: The Post September 9/11 Backlash.* Washington, DC, 2003. http://www.mbda.gov/Sites /mdba.gov/files/Migrated/files-attachments/September_11_Backlash.pdf (September 17, 2017).

American-Arab Anti-Discrimination Committee Research Institute. *Report on Hate Crimes and Discrimination against Arab Americans, 2003–2007.* Washington, DC, 2008. http://www.issuelab.org/resources/8080/8080.pdf (September 15, 2017).

American Civil Liberties Union. *The Human Cost—Civilian Casualties in Iraq and Afghanistan. Oct. 31, 2003.* https://www.aclu.org/human-cost-civilian -casualties-iraq-afghanistan (October 13, 2020).

———. *Worlds Apart: How Deporting Immigrants after 9/11 Tore Families Apart and Shattered Communities.* New York, December 2004. http://www.aclu.org /report/worlds-how-deporting-immigrants-after-911-tore-families-apart-and -shattered-communities (September 19, 2018).

Amnesty International. *United States of America: Amnesty International's Concerns Regarding Post September 11 Detentions in the USA.* London, 2002. http://www .Amnesty.org/en/documents/AmR51/044/2002/en (September 20, 2018).

Cole, Juan. "Kucinich-Paul Congressional Hearings." December 3, 2006. http://ww.juancole.com/2006/12/kucinich-paul-congressional-hearings (January 20, 2018).

Human Rights Watch. "The Road to Abu Ghraib." June 2004. http://www.hrw.org /reports/2004/USA0604.pdf (August 7, 2017).

Pew Research Center. *Trends in Public Opinion about the War in Iraq, 2003–2007.* http://www.pewresearch.org/2007/03/15/trends-in-public-opinion-about-the -war-in-Iraq-20032007 (August 5, 2016).

Sikh American Legal Defense and Education Fund. *The First 9/11 Backlash Fatality: The Murder of Balbir Singh Sodhi.* 2011. Saledf.org/wp-content /Uploads/2011/08/Balbir_Sodhi_Backlash_Murder.pdf (August 16, 2017).

———. *Federal Civil Rights Engagement with Arab And Muslim American Communities Post 9/11.* www.usgov/pkubs/ARAB_Muslim-9-30-14.pdf (August 8, 2017).

Index

Leitz, Lisa, 143
Libeskind, Daniel, 54–55, 58
Library of Congress, 45; collection of popular responses to 9/11 attacks, 19–20, 28–31
Limbaugh, Rush, 117, 131
Lincoln, Abraham, 7–8, 10–11, 35, 62
Lower Manhattan Development Corporation (LMDC), 54, 56–57, 60, 64
Luttrell, Marcus, 153–56
Lynch, Jessica, 174–77

MacMichael, Lynn, 145
makeshift memorials, 22, 48, 50–51, 63, 66, 73, 78, 114, 230, 246
Manion, Travis, 157–59
Manning, Lauren, 62–63
McCain, John, 193, 250
McCoy, Michael, 135–36
McGrath, Mike, 133–34
Mehmood, Anser and Uzma, 241–43
memorials, 1, 14–16, 47–49, 51, 55–59, 141–48, 246, 249; Arizona Memorial to 9/11, 231–32; "Arlington West," 143–44; "Dog Tag Memorial," 141–43; Empty Sky, 69–70; Flight 93, 70–77; iraqimemorial.org, 132–33; in Lafayette, CA, 145–48; living memorials, 83–86; National September 11 Memorial and Museum, 52, 55–57, 59–61; National World War II Memorial, 13–14; Pentagon Memorial, 81–83; state and local, 66–71, 74–77, 84–86, 231–32, 246; Vietnam Veterans Memorial, 14, 47–48, 59, 77, 99; white crosses, 143–46. *See also* makeshift memorials
Mestrovic, S. G., 131
Meyer, Dakota, 162–65
Mfume, Kweisi, 25
A Mighty Heart, 196–97
militarism, 3, 6, 12, 124, 251
Moore, Michael, 117, 193. See also *Fahrenheit 9/11*
mourning, 5, 8, 13–14, 38–40, 47, 50, 63–70, 77–81, 112–15, 201–3; in film,

189–91; images of, 137–47; in soldiers' memoirs, 169–71
Moussaoui, Zacarias, 39, 84
Murtha, John, 108–12
Muslims, 103, 151, 154, 195–97, 199, 232–33; demonization of and hate crimes against, 93, 102, 215–30, 232–37, 250–51; resisting mistreatment, 193, 221, 223; state repression of, 5, 238–44

nationalism, 3, 6–7, 14, 151–53, 244, 248
National Park Service, 71, 73–74
National Rifle Association (NRA), 27–28, 155
nativism, 216–17, 244
Navy SEALs, 150, 152–59, 166, 180, 193, 249
neo-liberalism, 8, 91
Nussbaum, Martha, 6

Obama, Barack, 2, 4, 141, 156, 164, 250–51; backlash against the presidency of, 237, 249; and Muslims, 233–36
Off to War: From Rural Arkansas to Iraq, 200–201
Operation Enduring Freedom, 36, 124
Opton, Suzanne, 136–38
Osman, Abdullah and Sukra, 240–41
Owen, Mark, 150, 156

Pataki, George, 54, 58, 60, 64
Patel, Vasudev, 225–27
Patriot Act of 2001, 5, 101, 215, 238–39, 246
patriotism, 11–12, 23, 54, 80, 132, 215–16, 233, 245, 248, 250–52; and commemorative efforts, 60, 73, 84–85, 231; displays of after 9/11 attacks, 18, 23, 26–29, 53, 59, 62; in film, 181, 192, 199, 213; and hate crimes, 225–26; post-9/11 debates over, 1–9, 14–16, 36–37, 42, 98, 100, 111–17, 123; in soldiers' memoirs, 150–51, 157, 164, 177, 180

Printed in the USA
CPSIA information can be obtained
at www.ICGtesting.com
CBHW031430080424
6581CB00002B/60

9 781469 679303